HISTORY

OF THE

CONQUEST OF MEXICO.

HISTORY

OF THE

CONQUEST OF MEXICO

By WILLIAM H. PRESCOTT

"Victrices aquilas alium laturus in orbem."
Lucan, Pharsalia, lib. v., v. 238.

EDITED BY JOHN FOSTER KIRK

VOLUME III.

PHILADELPHIA:
J. B. LIPPINCOTT COMPANY.

Mexico—Vol. III.

Lippincott's Press, Philadelphia.

CONTENTS OF VOL. III.

BOOK VI.

SIEGE AND SURRENDER OF MEXICO.

CHAPTER I.

A*

CHAPTER II.

CHAPTER III.

CHAPTER IV.

CONSPIRACY IN THE ARMY.—BRIGANTINES LAUNCHED.—
MUSTER OF FORCES.—EXECUTION OF XICOTENCATL.—
MARCH OF THE ARMY.—BEGINNING OF THE SIEGE . 73

CHAPTER V.

INDIAN FLOTILLA DEFEATED.—OCCUPATION OF THE CAUSE-
WAYS.—DESPERATE ASSAULTS.—FIRING OF THE PAL-
ACES.—SPIRIT OF THE BESIEGED.—BARRACKS FOR THE
TROOPS

CHAPTER VI.

1*

CHAPTER VII.

CHAPTER VIII.

BOOK VII.

CONCLUSION.—SUBSEQUENT CAREER OF CORTÉS.

CHAPTER I.

CHAPTER II.

MODERN MEXICO.—SETTLEMENT OF THE COUNTRY.—CON-
DITION OF THE NATIVES.—CHRISTIAN MISSIONARIES.—
CULTIVATION OF THE SOIL.—VOYAGES AND EXPEDI-
TIONS 239

CHAPTER III.

DEFECTION OF OLID.—DREADFUL MARCH TO HONDURAS.
—EXECUTION OF GUATEMOZIN.—DOÑA MARINA.—AR-
RIVAL AT HONDURAS 263

CHAPTER IV.

CHAPTER V.

APPENDIX, PART I.

ORIGIN OF THE MEXICAN CIVILIZATION.—ANALOGIES
WITH THE OLD WORLD.

APPENDIX, PART II.

ORIGINAL DOCUMENTS.

BOOK SIXTH.

SIEGE AND SURRENDER OF MEXICO.

CONQUEST OF MEXICO.

BOOK VI.

SIEGE AND SURRENDER OF MEXICO.

CHAPTER I.

ARRANGEMENTS AT TEZCUCO.—SACK OF IZTAPALAPAN.
—ADVANTAGES OF THE SPANIARDS.—WISE POLICY OF
CORTÉS.—TRANSPORTATION OF THE BRIGANTINES.

1521.

THE city of Tezcuco was the best position, probably, which Cortés could have chosen for the headquarters of the army. It supplied all the accommodations for lodging a numerous body of troops, and all
the facilities for subsistence, incident to a large and
populous town.[1] It furnished, moreover, a multitude
of artisans and laborers for the uses of the army. Its
territories, bordering on the Tlascalan, afforded a
ready means of intercourse with the country of his

[1] "Así mismo hizo juntar todos los bastimentos que fuéron necesarios para sustentar el Exército y Guarniciones de Gente que andaban
en favor de Cortés, y así hizo traer á la Ciudad de Tezcuco el Maiz
que habia en las Troxes y Graneros de las Provincias sugetas al **Reyno**
de Tezcuco." Ixtlilxochitl, Hist. Chich., MS., cap. 91.

(3)

allies; while its vicinity to Mexico enabled the general, without much difficulty, to ascertain the movements in that capital. Its central situation, in short, opened facilities for communication with all parts of the Valley, and made it an excellent *point d'appui* for his future operations.

The first care of Cortés was to strengthen himself in the palace assigned to him, and to place his quarters in a state of defence which might secure them against surprise not only from the Mexicans, but from the Tezcucans themselves. Since the election of their new ruler, a large part of the population had returned to their homes, assured of protection in person and property. But the Spanish general, notwithstanding their show of submission, very much distrusted its sincerity; for he knew that many of them were united too intimately with the Aztecs, by marriage and other social relations, not to have their sympathies engaged in their behalf.[2] The young monarch, however, seemed wholly in his interests; and, to secure him more effectually, Cortés placed several Spaniards near his person, whose ostensible province it was to instruct him in their language and religion, but who were in reality to watch over his conduct and prevent his correspondence with those who might be unfriendly to the Spanish interests.[3]

Tezcuco stood about half a league from the lake. It would be necessary to open a communication with

[2] "No era de espantar que tuviese este recelo, porque sus Enemigos, y los de esta Ciudad eran todos Deudos y Parientes mas cercanos, mas despues el tiempo lo desengañó, y vido la gran lealtad de Ixtlilxochitl, y de todos." Ixtlilxochitl, Hist. Chich., MS., cap. 92.

[3] Bernal Diaz, Hist. de la Conquista, cap. 137.

it, so that the brigantines, when put together in the capital, might be launched upon its waters. It was proposed, therefore, to dig a canal, reaching from the gardens of Nezahualcoyotl, as they were called, from the old monarch who planned them, to the edge of the basin. A little stream, or rivulet, which flowed in that direction, was to be deepened sufficiently for the purpose ; and eight thousand Indian laborers were forthwith employed on this great work, under the direction of the young Ixtlilxochitl.[4]

Meanwhile, Cortés received messages from several places in the neighborhood, intimating their desire to become the vassals of his sovereign and to be taken under his protection. The Spanish commander required, in return, that they should deliver up every Mexican who should set foot in their territories. Some noble Aztecs, who had been sent on a mission to these towns, were consequently delivered into his hands. He availed himself of it to employ them as bearers of a message to their master the emperor. In it he deprecated the necessity of the present hostilities. Those who had most injured him, he said, were no longer among the living. He was willing to forget the past, and invited the Mexicans, by a timely submission, to save their capital from the horrors of a siege.[5] Cortés had no expectation of producing any immediate result by this appeal. But he thought it might lie in the

[4] Bernal Diaz, Hist. de la Conquista, ubi supra.—Ixtlilxochitl, Hist. Chich., MS., cap. 91.

[5] " Los principales, que habian sido en hacerme la Guerra pasada, eran ya muertos ; y que lo pasado fuesse pasado, y que no quisiessen dar causa á que destruyesse sus Tierras, y Ciudades, porque me pesaba mucho de ello." Rel. Terc. de Cortés, ap. Lorenzana, p. 193.

minds of the Mexicans, and that, if there was a party among them disposed to treat with him, it might afford them encouragement, as showing his own willingness to co-operate with their views. At this time, however, there was no division of opinion in the capital. The whole population seemed animated by a spirit of resistance, as one man.

In a former page I have mentioned that it was the plan of Cortés, on entering the Valley, to commence operations by reducing the subordinate cities before striking at the capital itself, which, like some goodly tree whose roots had been severed one after another, would be thus left without support against the fury of the tempest. The first point of attack which he selected was the ancient city of Iztapalapan; a place containing fifty thousand inhabitants, according to his own account, and situated about six leagues distant, on the narrow tongue of land which divides the waters of the great salt lake from those of the fresh. It was the private domain of the last sovereign of Mexico; where, as the reader may remember, he entertained the white men the night before their entrance into the capital, and astonished them by the display of his princely gardens. To this monarch they owed no good will, for he had conducted the operations on the *noche triste*. He was, indeed, no more; but the people of his city entered heartily into his hatred of the strangers, and were now the most loyal vassals of the Mexican crown.

In a week after his arrival at his new quarters, Cortés, leaving the command of the garrison to Sandoval, marched against this Indian city, at the head of two hundred Spanish foot, eighteen horse, and between three and four thousand Tlascalans. Their route lay along the eastern border of the lake, gemmed with many a bright town and hamlet, or, unlike its condition at the present day, darkened with overhanging groves of cypress and cedar, and occasionally opening a broad expanse to their view, with the Queen of the Valley rising gloriously from the waters, as if proudly conscious of her supremacy over the fair cities around her. Farther on, the eye ranged along the dark line of causeway connecting Mexico with the main land, and suggesting many a bitter recollection to the Spaniards.

They quickened their step, and had advanced within two leagues of their point of destination, when they were encountered by a strong Aztec force drawn up to dispute their progress. Cortés instantly gave them battle. The barbarians showed their usual courage, but, after some hard fighting, were compelled to give way before the steady valor of the Spanish infantry, backed by the desperate fury of the Tlascalans, whom the sight of an Aztec seemed to inflame almost to madness. The enemy retreated in disorder, closely followed by the Spaniards. When they had arrived within half a league of Iztapalapan, they observed a number of canoes filled with Indians, who appeared to be laboring on the mole which hemmed in the waters of the salt lake. Swept along in the tide of pursuit, they gave little heed to it, but, following up the chase, entered pell-mell with the fugitives into the city.

The houses stood some of them on dry ground, some on piles in the water. The former were deserted by the inhabitants, most of whom had escaped in canoes across the lake, leaving, in their haste, their effects behind them. The Tlascalans poured at once into the vacant dwellings and loaded themselves with booty; while the enemy, making the best of their way through this part of the town, sought shelter in the buildings erected over the water, or among the reeds which sprung from its shallow bottom. In the houses were many of the citizens also, who still lingered with their wives and children, unable to find the means of transporting themselves from the scene of danger.

Cortés, supported by his own men, and by such of the allies as could be brought to obey his orders, attacked the enemy in this last place of their retreat. Both parties fought up to their girdles in the water. A desperate struggle ensued; as the Aztec fought with the fury of a tiger driven to bay by the huntsmen. It was all in vain. The enemy was overpowered in every quarter. The citizen shared the fate of the soldier, and a pitiless massacre succeeded, without regard to sex or age. Cortés endeavored to stop it. But it would have been as easy to call away the starving wolf from the carcass he was devouring, as the Tlascalan who had once tasted the blood of an enemy. More than six thousand, including women and children, according to the Conqueror's own statement, perished in the conflict.[6]

Darkness meanwhile had set in; but it was dispelled in some measure by the light of the burning houses,

6 " Muriéron de ellos mas de seis mil ánimas, entre Hombres, y Mugeres, y Niños; porque los Indios nuestros Amigos, vista la Victoria, que Dios nos daba, no entendian en otra cosa, sino en matar á diestro y á siniestro." Rel. Terc. de Cortés, ap. Lorenzana, p. 195.

which the troops had set on fire in different parts of
the town. Their insulated position, it is true, prevented
the flames from spreading from one building to another,
but the solitary masses threw a strong and lurid glare
over their own neighborhood, which gave additional
horror to the scene. As resistance was now at an end,
the soldiers abandoned themselves to pillage, and soon
stripped the dwellings of every portable article of any
value.

While engaged in this work of devastation, a mur-
muring sound was heard as of the hoarse rippling of
waters, and a cry soon arose among the Indians that
the dikes were broken ! Cortés now comprehended
the business of the men whom he had seen in the
canoes at work on the mole which fenced in the great
basin of Lake Tezcuco.[7] It had been pierced by the
desperate Indians, who thus laid the country under an
inundation, by suffering the waters of the salt lake to
spread themselves over the lower level, through the
opening. Greatly alarmed, the general called his men
together, and made all haste to evacuate the city.
Had they remained three hours longer, he says, not a
soul could have escaped.[8] They came staggering under
the weight of booty, wading with difficulty through
the water, which was fast gaining upon them. For

[7] " Estándolas quemando, pareció que Nuestro Señor me inspiró, y
trujo á la memoria la Calzada, ó Presa, que habia visto rota en el
Camino, y representóseme el gran daño, que era." Rel. Terc. de
Cortés, loc. cit.

[8] " Y certifico á Vuestra Magestad, que si aquella noche no pasara-
mos el Agua, ó aguardaramos tres horas mas, que ninguno de nosotros
escapara, porque quedabamos cercados de Agua, sin tener paso por
parte ninguna." Ibid., ubi supra.

A*

some distance their path was illumined by the glare of the burning buildings. But, as the light faded away in the distance, they wandered with uncertain steps, sometimes up to their knees, at others up to their waists, in the water, through which they floundered on with the greatest difficulty. As they reached the opening in the dike, the stream became deeper, and flowed out with such a current that the men were unable to maintain their footing. The Spaniards, breasting the flood, forced their way through; but many of the Indians, unable to swim, were borne down by the waters. All the plunder was lost. The powder was spoiled; the arms and clothes of the soldiers were saturated with the brine, and the cold night-wind, as it blew over them, benumbed their weary limbs till they could scarcely drag them along. At dawn they beheld the lake swarming with canoes, full of Indians, who had anticipated their disaster, and who now saluted them with showers of stones, arrows, and other deadly missiles. Bodies of light troops, hovering in the distance, disquieted the flanks of the army in like manner. The Spaniards had no desire to close with the enemy. They only wished to regain their comfortable quarters in Tezcuco, where they arrived on the same day, more disconsolate and fatigued than after many a long march and hard-fought battle.[9]

The close of the expedition, so different from its brilliant commencement, greatly disappointed Cortés.

[9] The general's own Letter to the emperor is so full and precise that it is the very best authority for this event. The story is told also by Bernal Diaz, Hist. de la Conquista, cap. 138,—Oviedo, Hist. de las Ind , MS., lib. 33, cap. 18,—Ixtlilxochitl, Hist. Chich., MS., cap. 92, —Herrera, Hist. general, dec. 3, lib. 1, cap. 2, et auct. aliis.

His numerical loss had, indeed, not been great ; but this affair convinced him how much he had to apprehend from the resolution of a people who, with a spirit worthy of the ancient Hollanders, were prepared to bury their country under water rather than to submit. Still, the enemy had little cause for congratulation ; since, independently of the number of slain, they had seen one of their most flourishing cities sacked, and in part, at least, laid in ruins,—one of those, too, which in its public works displayed the nearest approach to civilization. Such are the triumphs of war !

The expedition of Cortés, notwithstanding the disasters which checkered it, was favorable to the Spanish cause. The fate of Iztapalapan struck a terror throughout the Valley. The consequences were soon apparent in the deputations sent by the different places eager to offer their submission. Its influence was visible, indeed, beyond the mountains. Among others, the people of Otumba, the town near which the Spaniards had gained their famous victory, sent to tender their allegiance and to request the protection of the powerful strangers. They excused themselves, as usual, for the part they had taken in the late hostilities, by throwing the blame on the Aztecs.

But the place of most importance which thus claimed their protection was Chalco, situated on the eastern extremity of the lake of that name. It was an ancient city, peopled by a kindred tribe of the Aztecs, and once their formidable rival. The Mexican emperor, distrusting their loyalty, had placed a garrison within their walls to hold them in check. The rulers of the city now sent a message secretly to Cortés, proposing to put themselves under his protection, if he would enable them to expel the garrison.

The Spanish commander did not hesitate, but instantly detached a considerable force under Sandoval for this object. On the march, his rear-guard, composed of Tlascalans, was roughly handled by some light troops of the Mexicans. But he took his revenge in a pitched battle which took place with the main body of the enemy at no great distance from Chalco. They were drawn up on a level ground, covered with green crops of maize and maguey. The field is traversed by the road which at this day leads from the last-mentioned city to Tezcuco.[10] Sandoval, charging the enemy at the head of his cavalry, threw them into disorder. But they quickly rallied, formed again, and renewed the battle with greater spirit than ever. In a second attempt he was more fortunate ; and, breaking through their lines by a desperate onset, the brave cavalier succeeded, after a warm but ineffectual struggle on their part, in completely routing and driving them from the field. The conquering army continued its march to Chalco, which the Mexican garrison had already evacuated, and was received in triumph by the assembled citizens, who seemed eager to testify their gratitude for their deliverance from the Aztec yoke. After taking such measures as he could for the permanent security of the place, Sandoval returned to Tezcuco, accompanied by the two young lords of the city, sons of the late cacique.

They were courteously received by Cortés ; and they informed him that their father had died, full of years,

[10] Lorenzana, p. 199, nota.

a short time before. With his last breath he had expressed his regret that he should not have lived to see Malinche. He believed that the white men were the beings predicted by the oracles as one day to come from the East and take possession of the land;[11] and he enjoined it on his children, should the strangers return to the Valley, to render them their homage and allegiance. The young caciques expressed their readiness to do so; but, as this must bring on them the vengeance of the Aztecs, they implored the general to furnish a sufficient force for their protection.[12]

Cortés received a similar application from various other towns, which were disposed, could they do so with safety, to throw off the Mexican yoke. But he was in no situation to comply with their request. He now felt more sensibly than ever the incompetency of his means to his undertaking. "I assure your Majesty," he writes in his letter to the emperor, "the greatest uneasiness which I feel, after all my labors and fatigues, is from my inability to succor and support our Indian friends, your Majesty's loyal vassals."[13] Far from having a force competent to this, he had scarcely enough for his own protection. His vigilant

[11] " Porque ciertamente sus antepassados les auian dicho, que auian de señorear aquellas tierras hombres que vernian con barbas de hazia donde sale el Sol, y que por las cosas que han visto, eramos nosotros." Bernal Diaz, Hist. de la Conquista, cap. 139.

[12] Ibid., ubi supra.—Rel. Terc. de Cortés, ap. Lorenzana, p. 200.—Gomara, Crónica, cap. 122.—Venida de los Españoles, p. 15.

[13] " Y certifico á Vuestra Magestad, allende de nuestro trabajo y necesidad, la mayor fatiga, que tenia, era no poder ayudar, y socorrer á los Indios nuestros Amigos, que por ser Vasallos de Vuestra Magestad, eran molestados y trabajados de los de Culúa." Rel. Terc., ap. Lorenzana, p. 204.

enemy had an eye on all his movements, and, should he cripple his strength by sending away too many detachments or by employing them at too great a distance, would be prompt to take advantage of it. His only expeditions, hitherto, had been in the neighborhood, where the troops, after striking some sudden and decisive blow, might speedily regain their quarters. The utmost watchfulness was maintained there, and the Spaniards lived in as constant preparation for an assault as if their camp was pitched under the walls of Mexico.

On two occasions the general had sallied forth and engaged the enemy in the environs of Tezcuco. At one time a thousand canoes, filled with Aztecs, crossed the lake to gather in a large crop of Indian corn, nearly ripe, on its borders. Cortés thought it important to secure this for himself. He accordingly marched out and gave battle to the enemy, drove them from the field, and swept away the rich harvest to the granaries of Tezcuco. Another time a strong body of Mexicans had established themselves in some neighboring towns friendly to their interests. Cortés, again sallying, dislodged them from their quarters, beat them in several skirmishes, and reduced the places to obedience. But these enterprises demanded all his resources, and left him nothing to spare for his allies. In this exigency, his fruitful genius suggested an expedient for supplying the deficiency of his means.

Some of the friendly cities without the Valley, observing the numerous beacon-fires on the mountains, inferred that the Mexicans were mustering in great strength, and that the Spaniards must be hard pressed in their new quarters. They sent messengers to Γez-

cuco, expressing their apprehension, and offering reinforcements, which the general, when he set out on
his march, had declined. He returned many thanks
for the proffered aid; but, while he declined it for
himself, as unnecessary, he indicated in what manner
their services might be effectual for the defence of
Chalco and the other places which had invoked his
protection. But his Indian allies were in deadly feud
with these places, whose inhabitants had too often
fought under the Aztec banner not to have been engaged in repeated wars with the people beyond the
mountains.

Cortés set himself earnestly to reconcile these differences. He told the hostile parties that they should be
willing to forget their mutual wrongs, since they had
entered into new relations. They were now vassals of
the same sovereign, engaged in a common enterprise
against the formidable foe who had so long trodden
them in the dust. Singly they could do little, but
united they might protect each other's weakness and
hold their enemy at bay till the Spaniards could come
to their assistance. These arguments finally prevailed;
and the politic general had the satisfaction to see the
high-spirited and hostile tribes forego their long-
cherished rivalry, and, resigning the pleasures of revenge, so dear to the barbarian, embrace one another
as friends and champions in a common cause. To this
wise policy the Spanish commander owed quite as much
of his subsequent successes as to his arms.[14]

Thus the foundations of the Mexican empire were

[14] Rel. Terc. de Cortés, ap. Lorenzana, pp. 204, 205.—Oviedo, Hist.
de las Ind., MS., lib. 33, cap. 19.

hourly loosening, as the great vassals around the capital, on whom it most relied, fell off one after another from their allegiance. The Aztecs, properly so called, formed but a small part of the population of the Valley. This was principally composed of cognate tribes, members of the same great family of the Nahuatlacs who had come upon the plateau at nearly the same time. They were mutual rivals, and were reduced one after another by the more warlike Mexican, who held them in subjection, often by open force, always by fear. Fear was the great principle of cohesion which bound together the discordant members of the monarchy ; and this was now fast dissolving before the influence of a power more mighty than that of the Aztec. This, it is true, was not the first time that the conquered races had attempted to recover their independence. But all such attempts had failed for want of concert. It was reserved for the commanding genius of Cortés to extinguish their old hereditary feuds, and, combining their scattered energies, to animate them with a common principle of action.[15]

[15] Oviedo, in his admiration of his hero, breaks out into the following panegyric on his policy, prudence, and military science, which, as he truly predicts, must make his name immortal. It is a fair specimen of the manner of the sagacious old chronicler. "Sin dubda alguna la habilidad y esfuerzo, é prudencia de Hernando Cortés mui dignas son que entre los cavalleros, é gente militar en nuestros tiempos se tengan en mucha estimacion, y en los venideros nunca se desacuerden. Por causa suya me acuerdo muchas veces de aquellas cosas que se escriven del capitan Viriato nuestro Español y Estremeño ; y por Hernando Cortés me ocurren al sentido las muchas fatigas de aquel espejo de caballería Julio César dictador, como parece por sus comentarios, é por Suetonio é Plutarco é otros autores que en conformidad escriviéron los grandes hechos suyos. Pero los de Her-

Encouraged by this state of things, the Spanish general thought it a favorable moment to press his negotiations with the capital. He availed himself of the presence of some noble Mexicans, taken in the late action with Sandoval, to send another message to their master. It was in substance a repetition of the first, with a renewed assurance that, if the city would return to its allegiance to the Spanish crown, the authority of Guatemozin should be confirmed and the persons and property of his subjects be respected. To this communication no reply was made. The young Indian emperor had a spirit as dauntless as that of Cortés himself. On his head descended the full effects of that vicious system of government bequeathed to him by his ancestors. But, as he saw his empire crumbling beneath him, he sought to uphold it by his own energy and resources. He anticipated the defection of some vassals by establishing garrisons within their walls. Others he conciliated by exempting them from tributes or greatly lightening their burdens, or by advancing them to posts of honor and authority in the state. He showed, at the same time, his implacable animosity towards the Christians by commanding that every one taken within his dominions should be straightway sent to the capital, where he was sacrificed, with

nando Cortés en un Mundo nuevo, é tan apartadas provincias de Europa, é con tantos trabajos é necesidades é pocas fuerzas, é con gente tan innumerable, é tan bárbara é bellicosa, é apacentada en carne humana, é aun habida por excelente é sabroso manjar entre sus adversarios; é faltándole á él ó á sus mílites el pan é vino é los otros mantenimientos todos de España, y en tan diferenciadas regiones é aires é tan desviado é léjos de socorro é de su príncipe, cosas son de admiracion." Hist. de las Ind., MS., lib. 33, cap. 20.

all the barbarous ceremonies prescribed by the Aztec ritual.[16]

While these occurrences were passing, Cortés re-

[16] Among other chiefs, to whom Guatemozin applied for assistance in the perilous state of his affairs, was Tangapan, lord of Michoacán, an independent and powerful state in the West, which had never been subdued by the Mexican army. The accounts which the Aztec emperor gave him, through his ambassadors, of the white men, were so alarming, according to Ixtlilxochitl, who tells the story, that the king's sister voluntarily starved herself to death, from her apprehensions of the coming of the terrible strangers. Her body was deposited, as usual, in the vaults reserved for the royal household, until preparations could be made for its being burnt. On the fourth day, the attendants who had charge of it were astounded by seeing the corpse exhibit signs of returning life. The restored princess, recovering her speech, requested her brother's presence. On his coming, she implored him not to think of hurting a hair of the heads of the mysterious visitors. She had been permitted, she said, to see the fate of the departed in the next world. The souls of all her ancestors she had beheld tossing about in unquenchable fire ; while those who embraced the faith of the strangers were in glory. As a proof of the truth of her assertion, she added that her brother would see, on a great festival near at hand, a young warrior, armed with a torch brighter than the sun, in one hand, and a flaming sword, like that worn by the white men, in the other, passing from east to west over the city. Whether the monarch waited for the vision, or ever beheld it, is not told us by the historian. But, relying perhaps on the miracle of her resurrection as quite a sufficient voucher, he disbanded a very powerful force which he had assembled on the plains of Avalos for the support of his brother of Mexico. This narrative, with abundance of supernumerary incidents, not necessary to repeat, was commemorated in the Michoacán picture-records, and reported to the historian of Tezcuco himself by the grandson of Tangapan. (See Ixtlilxochitl, Hist. Chich., MS., cap. 91.) Whoever reported it to him, it is not difficult to trace the same pious fingers in it which made so many wholesome legends for the good of the Church on the Old Continent, and which now found, in the credulity of the New, a rich harvest for the same godly work.

ceived the welcome intelligence that the brigantines were completed and waiting to be transported to Tezcuco. He detached a body for the service, consisting of two hundred Spanish foot and fifteen horse, which he placed under the command of Sandoval. This cavalier had been rising daily in the estimation both of the general and of the army. Though one of the youngest officers in the service, he possessed a cool head and a ripe judgment, which fitted him for the most delicate and difficult undertakings. There were others, indeed, as Alvarado and Olid, for example, whose intrepidity made them equally competent to achieve a brilliant *coup-de-main*. But the courage of Alvarado was too often carried to temerity or perverted by passion; while Olid, dark and doubtful in his character, was not entirely to be trusted. Sandoval was a native of Medellin, the birthplace of Cortés himself. He was warmly attached to his commander, and had on all occasions proved himself worthy of his confidence. He was a man of few words, showing his worth rather by what he did than what he said. His honest, soldier-like deportment made him a favorite with the troops, and had its influence even on his enemies. He unfortunately died in the flower of his age. But he discovered talents and military skill which, had he lived to later life, would undoubtedly have placed his name on the roll with those of the greatest captains of his nation.

Sandoval's route was to lead him by Zoltepec, a small city where the massacre of the forty-five Spaniards, already noticed, had been perpetrated. The cavalier received orders to find out the guilty parties, if possible, and to punish them for their share in the transaction.

When the Spaniards arrived at the spot, they found that the inhabitants, who had previous notice of their approach, had all fled. In the deserted temples they discovered abundant traces of the fate of their countrymen; for, besides their arms and clothing, and the hides of their horses, the heads of several soldiers, prepared in such a way that they could be well preserved, were found suspended as trophies of the victory. In a neighboring building, traced with charcoal on the walls, they found the following inscription in Castilian: "In this place the unfortunate Juan Juste, with many others of his company, was imprisoned."[17] This hidalgo was one of the followers of Narvaez, and had come with him into the country in quest of gold, but had found, instead, an obscure and inglorious death. The eyes of the soldiers were suffused with tears as they gazed on the gloomy record, and their bosoms swelled with indignation as they thought of the horrible fate of the captives. Fortunately, the inhabitants were not then before them. Some few, who subsequently fell into their hands, were branded as slaves. But the greater part of the population, who threw themselves, in the most abject manner, on the mercy of the Conquerors, imputing the blame of the affair to the Aztecs, the Spanish commander spared, from pity, or contempt.[18]

[17] "Aquí estuvo preso el sin ventura de Juã Iuste cõ otros muchos que traia en mi compañía." Bernal Diaz, Hist. de la Conquista, cap. 140.

[18] Ibid., ubi supra.—Oviedo, Hist. de las Ind., MS., lib. 33, cap. 19.—Rel. Terc. de Cortés, ap. Lorenzana, p. 206

He now resumed his march on Tlascala; but scarcely had he crossed the borders of the republic, when he descried the flaunting banners of the convoy which transported the brigantines, as it was threading its way through the defiles of the mountains. Great was his satisfaction at the spectacle, for he had feared a detention of some days at Tlascala before the preparations for the march could be completed.

There were thirteen vessels in all, of different sizes. They had been constructed under the direction of the experienced ship-builder, Martin Lopez, aided by three or four Spanish carpenters and the friendly natives, some of whom showed no mean degree of imitative skill. The brigantines, when completed, had been fairly tried on the waters of the Zahuapan. They were then taken to pieces, and, as Lopez was impatient of delay, the several parts, the timbers, anchors, iron-work, sails, and cordage, were placed on the shoulders of the *tamanes*, and, under a numerous military escort, were thus far advanced on the way to Tezcuco.[19] Sandoval dismissed a part of the Indian convoy, as superfluous.

Twenty thousand warriors he retained, dividing them into two equal bodies for the protection of the *tamanes* in the centre.[20] His own little body of Spaniards he

[19] " Y despues de hechos por orden de Cortés, y probados en el rio que llaman de Tlaxcalla Zahuapan, que se atajó para probarlos los bergantines, y los tornáron á desbaratar por llevarlos á cuestas sobre hombros de los de Tlaxcalla á la ciudad de Tetzcuco, donde se echáron en la laguna, y se armáron de artillería y municion." Camargo, Hist. de Tlascala, MS.

[20] Rel. Terc. de Cortés, ap. Lorenzana, p. 207.—Bernal Diaz says sixteen thousand. (Hist. de la Conquista, ubi supra.) There is a won-

distributed in like manner.   The Tlascalans in the van
marched under the command of a chief who gloried
in the name of Chichemecatl.   For some reason Sandoval afterwards changed the order of march, and
placed this division in the rear,—an arrangement which
gave great umbrage to the doughty warrior that led it,
who asserted his right to the front, the place which he
and his ancestors had always occupied, as the post of
danger.   He was somewhat appeased by Sandoval's
assurance that it was for that very reason he had been
transferred to the rear, the quarter most likely to be
assailed by the enemy.   But even then he was greatly
dissatisfied on finding that the Spanish commander was
to march by his side, grudging, it would seem, that
any other should share the laurel with himself.

Slowly and painfully, encumbered with their heavy
burden, the troops worked their way over steep emi-
nences and rough mountain-passes, presenting, one
might suppose, in their long line of march, many a
vulnerable point to an enemy.   But, although small
parties of warriors were seen hovering at times on their
flanks and rear, they kept at a respectful distance, not
caring to encounter so formidable a foe.   On the fourth
day the warlike caravan arrived in safety before Tezcuco.

Their approach was beheld with joy by Cortés and
the soldiers, who hailed it as the signal of a speedy
termination of the war.   The general, attended by his
officers, all dressed in their richest attire, came out to
welcome the convoy.   It extended over a space of two
leagues ; and so slow was its progress that six hours
derful agreement between the several Castilian writers as to the number of forces, the order of march, and the events that occurred on it.

elapsed before the closing files had entered the city.[21]
The Tlascalan chiefs displayed all their wonted bravery
of apparel, and the whole array, composed of the
flower of their warriors, made a brilliant appearance.
They marched by the sound of atabal and cornet, and,
as they traversed the streets of the capital amidst the
acclamations of the soldiery, they made the city ring
with the shouts of "Castile and Tlascala, long live
our sovereign, the emperor!"[22]

"It was a marvellous thing," exclaims the Conqueror, in his Letters, "that few have seen, or even
heard of, — this transportation of thirteen vessels of
war on the shoulders of men for nearly twenty leagues
across the mountains!"[23] It was, indeed, a stupendous achievement, and not easily matched in ancient
or modern story; one which only a genius like that of
Cortés could have devised, or a daring spirit like his
have so successfully executed. Little did he foresee,
when he ordered the destruction of the fleet which first

[21] "Estendíase tanto la Gente, que dende que los primeros comenzáron á entrar, hasta que los postreros hobiéron acabado, se pasáron
mas de seis horas; sin quebrar el hilo de la Gente." Rel. Terc. de
Cortés, ap. Lorenzana, p. 208.

[22] "Dando vozes y silvos y diziendo: Viua, viua el Emperador,
nuestro Señor, y Castilla, Castilla, y Tlascala, Tlascala." (Bernal
Diaz, Hist. de la Conquista, cap. 140.) For the particulars of Sandoval's expedition, see, also, Oviedo, Hist. de las Ind., MS., lib. 33,
cap. 19,—Gomara, Crónica, cap. 124,—Torquemada, Monarch. Ind.,
lib. 4, cap. 84,—Ixtlilxochitl, Hist. Chich., MS., cap. 92,—Herrera,
Hist. general, dec. 3, lib. 1, cap. 2.

[23] "Que era cosa maravillosa de ver, y assí me parece que es de
oir, llevar trece Fustas diez y ocho leguas por Tierra." (Rel. Terc.
de Cortés, ap. Lorenzana, p. 207.) "En rem Romano populo," exclaims Martyr, "quando illustrius res illorum vigebant, non facilem!"
De Orbe Novo, dec. 5, cap. 8.

brought him to the country, and with his usual forecast commanded the preservation of the iron-work and rigging,—little did he foresee the important uses for which they were to be reserved ; so important, that on their preservation may be said to have depended the successful issue of his great enterprise.[24]

He greeted his Indian allies with the greatest cordiality, testifying his sense of their services by those honors and attentions which he knew would be most grateful to their ambitious spirits. " We come," exclaimed the hardy warriors, " to fight under your banner ; to avenge our common quarrel, or to fall by your side;" and, with their usual impatience, they urged him to lead them at once against the enemy. " Wait," replied the general, bluntly, " till you are rested, and you shall have your hands full."[25]

[24] Two memorable examples of a similar transportation of vessels across the land are recorded, the one in ancient, the other in modern history ; and both, singularly enough, at the same place, Tarentum. in Italy. The first occurred at the siege of that city by Hannibal (see Polybius, lib. 8) ; the latter some seventeen centuries later, by the Great Captain, Gonsalvo de Cordova. But the distance they were transported was inconsiderable. A more analogous example is that of Balboa, the bold discoverer of the Pacific. He made arrangements to have four brigantines transported a distance of twenty-two leagues across the Isthmus of Darien, a stupendous labor, and not entirely successful, as only two reached their point of destination. (See Herrera, Hist. general, dec. 2, lib. 2, cap. 11.) This took place in 1516, in the neighborhood, as it were, of Cortés, and may have suggested to his enterprising spirit the first idea of his own more successful, as well as more extensive, undertaking.

[25] " Y ellos me dijéron, que trahian deseo de se ver con los de Culúa, y que viesse lo que mandaba, que ellos, y aquella Gente venian con deseos, y voluntad de se vengar, ó morir con nosotros ; y yo les di las gracias, y les dije, que reposassen, y que presto les daria las manos llenas." Rel. Terc. de Cortés, ap. Lorenzana, p. 208.

CHAPTER II.

1521.

IN the course of three or four days, the Spanish
general furnished the Tlascalans with the opportunity
so much coveted, and allowed their boiling spirits to
effervesce in active operations. He had for some time
meditated an expedition to reconnoitre the capital and
its environs, and to chastise, on the way, certain places
which had sent him insulting messages of defiance and
which were particularly active in their hostilities. He
disclosed his design to a few only of his principal
officers, from his distrust of the Tezcucans, whom he
suspected to be in correspondence with the enemy.

Early in the spring, he left Tezcuco, at the head of
three hundred and fifty Spaniards and the whole strength
of his allies. He took with him Alvarado and Olid,
and intrusted the charge of the garrison to Sandoval.
Cortés had had practical acquaintance with the incom-
petence of the first of these cavaliers for so delicate a
post, during his short but disastrous rule in Mexico.

But all his precautions had not availed to shroud his
designs from the vigilant foe, whose eye was on all his
movements; who seemed even to divine his thoughts

and to be prepared to thwart their execution.   He had advanced but a few leagues, when he was met by a considerable body of Mexicans, drawn up to dispute his progress.   A sharp skirmish took place, in which the enemy were driven from the ground, and the way was left open to the Christians.   They held a circuitous route to the north, and their first point of attack was the insular town of Xaltocan, situated on the northern extremity of the lake of that name, now called San Christóbal.   The town was entirely surrounded by water, and communicated with the main land by means of causeways, in the same manner as the Mexican capital.   Cortés, riding at the head of his cavalry, advanced along the dike till he was brought to a stand by finding a wide opening in it, through which the waters poured, so as to be altogether impracticable, not only for horse, but for infantry.   The lake was covered with canoes filled with Aztec warriors, who, anticipating the movement of the Spaniards, had come to the aid of the city.   They now began a furious discharge of stones and arrows on the assailants, while they were themselves tolerably well protected from the musketry of their enemy by the light bulwarks with which, for that purpose, they had fortified their canoes.

The severe volleys of the Mexicans did some injury to the Spaniards and their allies, and began to throw them into disorder, crowded as they were on the narrow causeway, without the means of advancing, when Cortés ordered a retreat.   This was followed by renewed tempests of missiles, accompanied by taunts and fierce yells of defiance.   The battle-cry of the Aztec, like the war-whoop of the North American Indian, was an appalling note, according to the Conqueror's own acknowledgment, in the ears of the Spaniards.[1] At this juncture, the general fortunately obtained informa-tion from a deserter, one of the Mexican allies, of a ford, by which the army might traverse the shallow lake and penetrate into the place. He instantly de-spatched the greater part of the infantry on the ser-vice, posting himself with the remainder and with the horse at the entrance of the passage, to cover the attack and prevent any interruption in the rear.

The soldiers, under the direction of the Indian guide, forded the lake without much difficulty, though in some places the water came above their girdles. During the passage, they were annoyed by the enemy's missiles; but when they had gained the dry level they took ample revenge, and speedily put all who resisted to the sword. The greater part, together with the townsmen, made their escape in the boats. The place was now abandoned to pillage. The troops found in it many women, who had been left to their fate; and these, together with a considerable quantity of cotton stuffs, gold, and articles of food, fell into the hands of the victors, who, setting fire to the deserted city, returned in triumph to their comrades.[2]

Continuing his circuitous route, Cortés presented himself successively before three other places, each of

---

[1] " De lejos comenzáron á gritar, como lo suelen hacer en la Guerra, que cierto es cosa espantosa oillos." Rel. Terc., ap. Lorenzana, p. 209.

[2] Ibid., loc. cit.—Bernal Diaz, Hist. de la Conquista, cap. 141.— Oviedo, Hist. de las Ind., MS., lib. 33, cap. 20.—Ixtlilxochitl, Venida de los Españoles, pp. 13, 14.—Idem, Hist. Chich., MS., cap. 92.— Gomara, Crónica, cap. 125.

which had been deserted by the inhabitants in anticipation of his arrival.[3] The principal of these, Azcapozalco, had once been the capital of an independent
state. It was now the great slave-market of the Aztecs,
where their unfortunate captives were brought and
disposed of at public sale. It was also the quarter
occupied by the jewellers, and the place whence the
Spaniards obtained the goldsmiths who melted down
the rich treasures received from Montezuma. But they
found there only a small supply of the precious metals,
or, indeed, of anything else of value, as the people had
been careful to remove their effects. They spared the
buildings, however, in consideration of their having
met with no resistance.

During the nights, the troops bivouacked in the open
fields, maintaining the strictest watch, for the country
was all in arms, and beacons were flaming on every
hill-top, while dark masses of the enemy were occasionally descried in the distance. The Spaniards were
now traversing the most opulent region of Anahuac.
Cities and villages were scattered over hill and valley,
with cultivated environs blooming around them, all
giving token of a dense and industrious population.
In the centre of this brilliant circumference stood the

[3] These towns rejoiced in the melodious names of Tenajocoan,
Quauhtitlan, and Azcapozalco. I have constantly endeavored to
spare the reader, in the text, any unnecessary accumulation of Mexican names, which, as he is aware by this time, have not even brevity
to recommend them. [Alaman, with some justice, remarks that these
names appear unmelodious to an English writer who does not know
how to pronounce them, for the same reason as English names would
appear unmelodious tc a Mexican. Conquista de Méjico (trad. de
Vega), tom. ii. p. 115.]

Indian metropolis, with its gorgeous tiara of pyramids and temples, attracting the eye of the soldier from every other object, as he wound round the borders of the lake. Every inch of ground which the army trod was familiar to them,—familiar as the scenes of childhood, though with very different associations, for it had been written on their memories in characters of blood. On the right rose the Hill of Montezuma,[4] crowned by the *teocalli* under the roof of which the shattered relics of the army had been gathered on the day following the flight from the capital. In front lay the city of Tacuba, through whose inhospitable streets they had hurried in fear and consternation ; and away to the east of it stretched the melancholy causeway.

It was the general's purpose to march at once on Tacuba and establish his quarters in that ancient capital for the present. He found a strong force encamped under its walls, prepared to dispute his entrance. Without waiting for their advance, he rode at full gallop against them with his little body of horse. The arquebuses and cross-bows opened a lively volley on their extended wings, and the infantry, armed with their swords and copper-headed lances and supported by the Indian battalions, followed up the attack of the horse with an alacrity which soon put the enemy to flight. The Spaniards usually opened the combat with a charge of cavalry. But, had the science of the Aztecs been equal to their courage, they might with their long spears have turned the scale of battle, sometimes at least, in their own favor ; for it was with the

4 [The Hill of Los Remedios. Conquista de Méjico (trad. de Vega), tom. ii. p. 116.]

3*

same formidable weapon that the Swiss mountaineers, but a few years before this period of our history, broke and completely foiled the famous *ordonnance* of Charles the Bold, the best-appointed cavalry of their day. But the barbarians were ignorant of the value of this weapon when opposed to cavalry. And, indeed, the appalling apparition of the war-horse and his rider still held a mysterious power over their imaginations, which contributed, perhaps, quite as much as the effective force of the cavalry itself, to their discomfiture. Cortés led his troops without further opposition into the suburbs of Tacuba, the ancient Tlacopan, where he established himself for the night.

On the following morning he found the indefatigable Aztecs again under arms, and, on the open ground before the city, prepared to give him battle. He marched out against them, and, after an action hotly contested, though of no long duration, again routed them. They fled towards the town, but were driven through the streets at the point of the lance, and were compelled, together with the inhabitants, to evacuate the place. The city was then delivered over to pillage; and the Indian allies, not content with plundering the houses of every thing portable within them, set them on fire, and in a short time a quarter of the town —the poorer dwellings, probably, built of light, combustible materials—was in flames. Cortés and his troops did all in their power to stop the conflagration, but the Tlascalans were a fierce race, not easily guided at any time, and when their passions were once kindled it was impossible even for the general himself to control them. They were a terrible auxiliary, and, from their insubordination, as terrible sometimes to friend as to foe.[5]

Cortés proposed to remain in his present quarters for some days, during which time he established his own residence in the ancient palace of the lords of Tlacopan. It was a long range of low buildings, like most of the royal residences in the country, and offered good accommodations for the Spanish forces. During his halt here, there was not a day on which the army was not engaged in one or more rencontres with the enemy. They terminated almost uniformly in favor of the Spaniards, though with more or less injury to them and to their allies. One encounter, indeed, had nearly been attended with more fatal consequences.

The Spanish general, in the heat of pursuit, had allowed himself to be decoyed upon the great causeway,—the same which had once been so fatal to his army. He followed the flying foe until he had gained the farther side of the nearest bridge, which had been repaired since the disastrous action of the *noche triste.* When thus far advanced, the Aztecs, with the rapidity of lightning, turned on him, and he beheld a large reinforcement in their rear, all fresh on the field, prepared to support their countrymen. At the same time,

[5] They burned this place, according to Cortés, in retaliation of the injuries inflicted by the inhabitants on their countrymen in the retreat: "Y en amaneciendo los Indios nuestros Amigos comenzáron á saquear, y quemar toda la Ciudad, salvo el Aposento donde estabamos, y pusiéron tanta diligencia, que aun de él se quemó un Quarto; y esto se hizo, porque quando salímos la otra vez desbaratados de Temixtitan, pasando por esta Ciudad, los Naturales de ella juntamente con los de Temixtitan nos hiciéron muy cruel Guerra, y nos matáron muchos Españoles." Rel. Terc., ap. Lorenzana, p. 210.

swarms of boats, unobserved in the eagerness of the chase, seemed to start up as if by magic, covering the waters around. The Spaniards were now exposed to a perfect hail-storm of missiles, both from the causeway and the lake; but they stood unmoved amidst the tempest, when Cortés, too late perceiving his error, gave orders for the retreat. Slowly, and with admirable coolness, his men receded, step by step, offering a resolute front to the enemy.[6] The Mexicans came on with their usual vociferation, making the shores echo to their war-cries, and striking at the Spaniards with their long pikes, and with poles, to which the swords taken from the Christians had been fastened. A cavalier, named Volante, bearing the standard of Cortés, was felled by one of their weapons, and, tumbling into the lake, was picked up by the Mexican boats. He was a man of a muscular frame, and, as the enemy were dragging him off, he succeeded in extricating himself from their grasp, and, clenching his colors in his hand, with a desperate effort sprang back upon the causeway. At length, after some hard fighting, in which many of the Spaniards were wounded and many of their allies slain, the troops regained the land, where Cortés, with a full heart, returned thanks to Heaven for what he might well regard as a providential deliverance.[7] It was a salutary lesson; though he should scarcely have

[6] " Luego mandó, que todos se retraxessen; y con el mejor concierto que pudo, y no bueltas las espaldas, sino los rostros á los contrarios, pie contra pie, como quien haze represas." Bernal Diaz, Hist. de la Conquista, cap. 141.

[7] " Desta manera se escapó Cortés aquella vez del poder de México, y quando se vió en tierra firme, dió muchas gracias á Dios." Ibid., ubi supra.

needed one, so soon after the affair of Iztapalapan, to warn him of the wily tactics of his enemy.

It had been one of Cortés' principal objects in this expedition to obtain an interview, if possible, with the Aztec emperor, or with some of the great lords at his court, and to try if some means for an accommodation could not be found, by which he might avoid the appeal to arms. An occasion for such a parley presented itself when his forces were one day confronted with those of the enemy, with a broken bridge interposed between them. Cortés, riding in advance of his people, intimated by signs his peaceful intent, and that he wished to confer with the Aztecs. They respected the signal, and, with the aid of his interpreter, he requested that if there were any great chief among them he would come forward and hold a parley with him. The Mexicans replied, in derision, they were all chiefs, and bade him speak openly whatever he had to tell them. As the general returned no answer, they asked why he did not make another visit to the capital, and tauntingly added, " Perhaps Malinche does not expect to find there another Montezuma, as obedient to his commands as the former."[8] Some of them complimented the Tlascalans with the epithet of *women*, who, they said, would never have ventured so near the capital but for the protection of the white men.

The animosity of the two nations was not confined to these harmless though bitter jests, but showed itself in regular cartels of defiance, which daily passed between the principal chieftains. These were followed

---

[8] " Pensais, que hay agora otro Muteczuma, para que haga todo, lo que quisieredes?" Rel. Terc. de Cortés, ap. Lorenzana, p. 211.

B*

by combats, in which one or more champions fought on a side, to vindicate the honor of their respective countries. A fair field of fight was given to the warriors, who conducted these combats *à l'outrance* with the punctilio of a European tourney; displaying a valor worthy of the two boldest of the races of Anahuac, and a skill in the management of their weapons, which drew forth the admiration of the Spaniards.[9]

Cortés had now been six days in Tacuba. There was nothing further to detain him, as he had accomplished the chief objects of his expedition. He had humbled several of the places which had been most active in their hostility; and he had revived the credit of the Castilian arms, which had been much tarnished by their former reverses in this quarter of the Valley. He had also made himself acquainted with the condition of the capital, which he found in a better posture of defence than he had imagined. All the ravages of the preceding year seemed to be repaired, and there was no evidence, even to his experienced eye, that the wasting hand of war had so lately swept over the land. The Aztec troops, which swarmed through the Valley, seemed to be well appointed, and showed an invincible spirit, as if prepared to resist to the last. It is true, they had been beaten in every encounter. In the open field they were no match for the Spaniards, whose cavalry they could never comprehend, and whose fire-arms easily penetrated the cotton mail which formed the stoutest defence of the Indian warrior. But, entangled in the long streets and narrow lanes of the

[9] "Y peleaban los unos con los otros muy hermosamente." Rel. Terc. de Cortés, ubi supra.— Oviedo, Hist. de las Ind., MS., lib. 33, cap. 20.

metropolis, where every house was a citadel, the Spaniards, as experience had shown, would lose much of
their superiority. With the Mexican emperor, con-
fident in the strength of his preparations, the general
saw there was no probability of effecting an accommodation. He saw, too, the necessity of the most careful
preparations on his own part—indeed, that he must
strain his resources to the utmost—before he could
safely venture to rouse the lion in his lair.

The Spaniards returned by the same route by which
they had come. Their retreat was interpreted into a
flight by the natives, who hung on the rear of the army,
uttering vainglorious vaunts, and saluting the troops
with showers of arrows, which did some mischief.
Cortés resorted to one of their own stratagems to rid
himself of this annoyance. He divided his cavalry
into two or three small parties, and concealed them
among some thick shrubbery which fringed both sides
of the road. The rest of the army continued its march.
The Mexicans followed, unsuspicious of the ambuscade,
when the horse, suddenly darting from their place of
concealment, threw the enemy's flanks into confusion,
and the retreating columns of infantry, facing about
suddenly, commenced a brisk attack, which completed
their consternation. It was a broad and level plain,
over which the panic-struck Mexicans made the best
of their way, without attempting resistance; while the
cavalry, riding them down and piercing the fugitives
with their lances, followed up the chase for several
miles, in what Cortés calls a truly beautiful style.[10]

[10] " Y comenzámos á lanzear en ellos, y duró el alcanze cerca de
dos leguas todas llanas, como la palma, que fué muy hermosa cosa."
Rel. Terc., ap. Lorenzana, p. 212.

The army experienced no further annoyance from the enemy.

On their arrival at Tezcuco they were greeted with joy by their comrades, who had received no tidings of them during the fortnight which had elapsed since their departure. The Tlascalans, immediately on their return, requested the general's permission to carry back to their own country the valuable booty which they had gathered in their foray,—a request which, however unpalatable, he could not refuse.[11]

The troops had not been in quarters more than two or three days, when an embassy arrived from Chalco, again soliciting the protection of the Spaniards against the Mexicans, who menaced them from several points in their neighborhood. But the soldiers were so much exhausted by unintermitted vigils, forced marches, battles, and wounds, that Cortés wished to give them a breathing-time to recruit, before engaging in a new expedition. He answered the application of the Chalcans by sending his missives to the allied cities, calling on them to march to the assistance of their confederate. It is not to be supposed that they could comprehend the import of his despatches. But the paper, with its mysterious characters, served for a warrant to the officer who bore it, as the interpreter of the general's commands.

But, although these were implicitly obeyed, the

[11] For the particulars of this expedition of Cortés, see, besides his own Commentaries so often quoted, Oviedo, Hist. de las Ind., MS., lib. 33, cap. 20,—Torquemada, Monarch. Ind., lib. 4, cap. 85,—Gomara, Crónica, cap. 125,—Ixtlilxochitl, Venida de los Españoles, pp. 13, 14,—Bernal Diaz, Hist. de la Conquista, cap. 141.

Chalcans felt the danger so pressing that they soon repeated their petition for the Spaniards to come in person to their relief. Cortés no longer hesitated; for he was well aware of the importance of Chalco, not merely on its own account, but from its position, which commanded one of the great avenues to Tlascala, and to Vera Cruz, the intercourse with which should run no risk of interruption. Without further loss of time, therefore, he detached a body of three hundred Spanish foot and twenty horse, under the command of Sandoval, for the protection of the city.

That active officer soon presented himself before Chalco, and, strengthened by the reinforcement of its own troops and those of the confederate towns, directed his first operations against Huaxtepec, a place of some importance, lying five leagues or more to the south among the mountains. It was held by a strong Mexican force, watching their opportunity to make a descent upon Chalco. The Spaniards found the enemy drawn up at a distance from the town, prepared to receive them. The ground was broken and tangled with bushes, unfavorable to the cavalry, which, in consequence, soon fell into disorder; and Sandoval, finding himself embarrassed by their movements, ordered them, after sustaining some loss, from the field. In their place he brought up his musketeers and crossbowmen, who poured a rapid fire into the thick columns of the Indians. The rest of the infantry, with sword and pike, charged the flanks of the enemy, who, bewildered by the shock, after sustaining considerable slaughter, fell back in an irregular manner, leaving the field of battle to the Spaniards.

The victors proposed to bivouac there for the night. But, while engaged in preparations for their evening meal, they were aroused by the cry of "To arms, to arms! the enemy is upon us!" In an instant the trooper was in his saddle, the soldier grasped his musket or his good Toledo, and the action was renewed with greater fury than before. The Mexicans had received a reinforcement from the city. But their second attempt was not more fortunate than their first; and the victorious Spaniards, driving their antagonists before them, entered and took possession of the town itself, which had already been evacuated by the inhabitants.[12]

Sandoval took up his quarters in the dwelling of the lord of the place, surrounded by gardens which rivalled those of Iztapalapan in magnificence and surpassed them in extent. They are said to have been two leagues in circumference, having pleasure-houses, and numerous tanks stocked with various kinds of fish; and they were embellished with trees, shrubs, and plants, native and exotic, some selected for their beauty and fragrance, others for their medicinal properties. They were scientifically arranged; and the whole establishment displayed a degree of horticultural taste and knowledge of which it would not have been easy to find a counterpart, at that day, in the more civilized communities of Europe.[13] Such is the testimony not

[12] Rel. Terc. de Cortés, ap. Lorenzana, pp. 214, 215.—Gomara, Crónica, cap. 146.—Bernal Diaz, Hist. de la Conquista, cap. 142.—Oviedo, Hist. de las Ind., MS., lib. 33, cap. 21.

[13] "Which gardens," says Cortés, who afterwards passed a day there, "are the largest, freshest, and most beautiful that were ever seen. They have a circuit of two leagues, and through the middle

only of the rude Conquerors, but of men of science, who visited these beautiful repositories in the day of their glory.[14]

After halting two days to refresh his forces in this agreeable spot, Sandoval marched on Jacapichtla, about twelve miles to the eastward. It was a town, or rather fortress, perched on a rocky eminence almost inaccessible from its steepness. It was garrisoned by a Mexican force, who rolled down on the assailants, as they attempted to scale the heights, huge fragments of rock, which, thundering over the sides of the precipice, carried ruin and desolation in their path. The Indian confederates fell back in dismay from the attempt. But Sandoval, indignant that any achievement should be too difficult for a Spaniard, commanded his cavaliers to dismount, and, declaring that he "would carry the place or die in the attempt," led on his men with the cheering cry of "St. Jago."[15] With renewed courage, they now followed their gallant leader up the

flows a very pleasant stream of water. At distances of two bow-shots are buildings surrounded by grounds planted with fruit-trees of various kinds, with many shrubs and odorous flowers. Truly the whole place is wonderful for its pleasantness and its extent." (Rel. Terc., ap. Lorenzana, pp. 221, 222.) Bernal Diaz is not less emphatic in his admiration. Hist. de la Conquista, cap. 142.

[14] The distinguished naturalist Hernandez has frequent occasion to notice this garden, which furnished him with many specimens for his great work. It had the good fortune to be preserved after the Conquest, when particular attention was given to its medicinal plants, for the use of a great hospital established in the neighborhood. See Clavigero, Stor. del Messico, tom. ii. p. 153.

[15] " É como esto vió el dicho Alguacil Mayor, y los Españoles, determináron de morir, ó subilles por fuerza á lo alto del Pueblo, y con el apellido de *Señor Santiago*, comenzáron á subir." Rel. Terc., ap. Lorenzana, p. 214.—Oviedo, Hist. de las Ind., MS., lib. 33, cap. 21.

ascent, under a storm of lighter missiles, mingled with huge masses of stone, which, breaking into splinters, overturned the assailants and made fearful havoc in their ranks. Sandoval, who had been wounded on the preceding day, received a severe contusion on the head, while more than one of his brave comrades were struck down by his side. Still they clambered up, sustaining themselves by the bushes or projecting pieces of rock, and seemed to force themselves onward as much by the energy of their wills as by the strength of their bodies.

After incredible toil, they stood on the summit, face to face with the astonished garrison. For a moment they paused to recover breath, then sprang furiously on their foes. The struggle was short, but desperate. Most of the Aztecs were put to the sword. Some were thrown headlong over the battlements, and others, letting themselves down the precipice, were killed on the borders of a little stream that wound round its base, the waters of which were so polluted with blood that the victors were unable to slake their thirst with them for a full hour ! [16]

Sandoval, having now accomplished the object of his expedition, by reducing the strongholds which had so long held the Chalcans in awe, returned in triumph to Tezcuco. Meanwhile, the Aztec emperor, whose vigilant eye had been attentive to all that had passed, thought that the absence of so·many of its warriors

[16] So says the *Conquistador.* (Rel. Terc., ap. Lorenzana, p. 215.) Diaz, who will allow no one to hyperbolize but himself, says, " For as long as one might take to say an Ave Maria!" (Hist. de la Conquista, cap. 142.) Neither was present.

afforded a favorable opportunity for recovering Chalco. He sent a fleet of boats, for this purpose, across the lake, with a numerous force under the command of some of his most valiant chiefs.[17] Fortunately, the absent Chalcans reached their city before the arrival of the enemy; but, though supported by their Indian allies, they were so much alarmed by the magnitude of the hostile array that they sent again to the Spaniards, invoking their aid.

The messengers arrived at the same time with Sandoval and his army. Cortés was much puzzled by the contradictory accounts. He suspected some negligence in his lieutenant, and, displeased with his precipitate return in this unsettled state of the affair, ordered him back at once, with such of his forces as were in fighting condition. Sandoval felt deeply injured by this proceeding, but he made no attempt at exculpation, and, obeying his commander in silence, put himself at the head of his troops and made a rapid countermarch on the Indian city.[18]

Before he reached it, a battle had been fought between the Mexicans and the confederates, in which the latter, who had acquired unwonted confidence from their recent successes, were victorious. A number of Aztec nobles fell into their hands in the engagement,

[17] The gallant Captain Diaz, who affects a sobriety in his own estimates, which often leads him to disparage those of the chaplain Gomara, says that the force consisted of 20,000 warriors in 2000 canoes. Hist. de la Conquista, loc. cit.

[18] "El Cortés no le quiso escuchar á Sandoual de enojo, creyendo que por su culpa, ó descuido, recibiã mala obra nuestros amigos los de Chalco; y luego sin mas dilacion, ni le oyr, le mandó bolver." Ibid., ubi supra.

4*

whom they delivered to Sandoval to be carried off as
prisoners to Tezcuco.   On his arrival there, the cavalier, wounded by the unworthy treatment he had received, retired to his own quarters without presenting
himself before his chief.

During his absence, the inquiries of Cortés had satisfied him of his own precipitate conduct, and of the
great injustice he had done his lieutenant.   There was
no man in the army on whose services he set so high a
value, as the responsible situations in which he had
placed him plainly showed ; and there was none for
whom he seems to have entertained a greater personal
regard.   On Sandoval's return, therefore, Cortés instantly sent to request his attendance ; when, with a
soldier's frankness, he made such an explanation as
soothed the irritated spirit of the cavalier,—a matter
of no great difficulty, as the latter had too generous a
nature, and too earnest a devotion to his commander
and the cause in which they were embarked, to harbor
a petty feeling of resentment in his bosom. [19]

During the occurrence of these events the work was
going forward actively on the canal, and the brigantines were within a fortnight of their completion.   The
greatest vigilance was required, in the mean time, to
prevent their destruction by the enemy, who had already
made three ineffectual attempts to burn them on the
stocks.   The precautions which Cortés thought it
necessary to take against the Tezcucans themselves
added not a little to his embarrassment.

[19] Besides the authorities already quoted for Sandoval's expedition,
see Gomara, Crónica, cap. 126,—Ixtlilxochitl, Hist. Chich., MS., cap.
92,—Torquemada, Monarch. Ind., lib. 4, cap. 86.

At this time he received embassies from different Indian states, some of them on the remote shores of the Mexican Gulf, tendering their allegiance and soliciting his protection. For this he was partly indebted to the good offices of Ixtlilxochitl, who, in consequence of his brother's death, was now advanced to the sovereignty of Tezcuco. This important position greatly increased his consideration and authority through the country, of which he freely availed himself to bring the natives under the dominion of the Spaniards.[20]

The general received also at this time the welcome intelligence of the arrival of three vessels at Villa Rica, with two hundred men on board, well provided with arms and ammunition, and with seventy or eighty horses. It was a most seasonable reinforcement. From what quarter it came is uncertain; most probably from Hispaniola. Cortés, it may be remembered, had sent for supplies to that place; and the authorities of the island, who had general jurisdiction over the affairs of the colonies, had shown themselves, on more than one occasion, well inclined towards him, probably considering him, under all circumstances, as better fitted than any other man to achieve the conquest of the country.[21]

[20] " Ixtlilxochitl procuraba siempre traer á la devocion y amistad de los Cristianos no tan solamente á los de el Reyno de Tezcuco sino aun los de las Provincias remotas, rogándoles que todos se procurasen dar de paz al Capitan Cortés, y que aunque de las guerras pasadas algunos tuviesen culpa, era tan afable y deseaba tanto la paz que luego al punto los reciviria en su amistad." Ixtlilxochitl, Hist. Chich., MS., cap. 92.

[21] Cortés speaks of these vessels as coming at the same time, but does not intimate from what quarter. (Rel. Terc., ap. Lorenzana, p. 216.) Bernal Diaz, who notices only one, says it came from Castile.

The new recruits soon found their way to Tezcuco ; as the communications with the port were now open and unobstructed. Among them were several cavaliers of consideration, one of whom, Julian de Alderete, the royal treasurer, came over to superintend the interests of the crown.

There was also in the number a Dominican friar, who brought a quantity of pontifical bulls, offering indulgences to those engaged in war against the infidel. The soldiers were not slow to fortify themselves with the good graces of the Church ; and the worthy father, after driving a prosperous traffic with his spiritual wares, had the satisfaction to return home, at the end of a few months, well freighted, in exchange, with the more substantial treasures of the Indies.[22]

(Hist. de la Conquista, cap. 143.) But the old soldier wrote long after the events he commemorates, and may have confused the true order of things. It seems hardly probable that so important a reinforcement should have arrived from Castile, considering that Cortés had yet received none of the royal patronage, or even sanction, which would stimulate adventurers in the mother country to enlist under his standard.

[22] Bernal Diaz, Hist. de la Conquista, cap. 143.—Oviedo, Hist. de las Ind., MS., lib. 33, cap. 21.—Herrera, Hist. general, dec. 3, lib. 1, cap. 6.

CHAPTER III.

1521.

NOTWITHSTANDING the relief which had been afforded to the people of Chalco, it was so ineffectual that envoys from that city again arrived at Tezcuco, bearing a hieroglyphical chart, on which were depicted several strong places in their neighborhood, garrisoned by the Aztecs, from which they expected annoyance. Cortés determined, this time, to take the affair into his own hands, and to scour the country so effectually as to place Chalco, if possible, in a state of security. He did not confine himself to this object, but proposed, before his return, to pass quite round the great lakes, and reconnoitre the country to the south of them, in the same manner as he had before done to the west. In the course of his march he would direct his arms against some of the strong places from which the Mexicans might expect support in the siege. Two or three weeks must elapse before the completion of the brigantines; and, if no other good resulted from the expedition, it would give active occupation to his troops, whose turbulent spirits might fester into discontent in the monotonous existence of a camp.

He selected for the expedition thirty horse and three hundred Spanish infantry, with a considerable body of Tlascalan and Tezcucan warriors. The remaining garrison he left in charge of the trusty Sandoval, who, with the friendly lord of the capital, would watch over the construction of the brigantines and protect them from the assaults of the Aztecs.

On the fifth of April he began his march, and on the following day arrived at Chalco, where he was met by a number of the confederate chiefs. With the aid ot his faithful interpreters, Doña Marina and Aguilar, he explained to them the objects of his present expedition, stated his purpose soon to enforce the blockade of Mexico, and required their co-operation with the whole strength of their levies. To this they readily assented; and he soon received a sufficient proof of their friendly disposition in the forces which joined him on the march, amounting, according to one of the army, to more than had ever before followed his banner.[1]

Taking a southerly direction, the troops, after leaving Chalco, struck into the recesses of the wild sierra, which, with its bristling peaks, serves as a formidable palisade to fence round the beautiful Valley; while within its rugged arms it shuts up many a green and fruitful pasture of its own. As the Spaniards passed through its deep gorges, they occasionally wound round the base of some huge cliff or rocky eminence, on

[1] "Viniéron tantos, que en todas las entradas que yo auia ido, despues que en la Nueua España entré, nunca ví tanta gente de guerra de nuestros amigos, como aora fuéron en nuestra compañía." Bernal Diaz, Hist. de la Conquista, cap. 144.

which the inhabitants had built their towns, in the same manner as was done by the people of Europe in the feudal ages; a position which, however favorable to the picturesque, intimates a sense of insecurity as the cause of it, which may reconcile us to the absence of this striking appendage of the landscape in our own more fortunate country.

The occupants of these airy pinnacles took advantage of their situation to shower down stones and arrows on the troops as they defiled through the narrow passes of the sierra. Though greatly annoyed by their incessant hostilities, Cortés held on his way, till, winding round the base of a castellated cliff occupied by a strong garrison of Indians, he was so severely pressed that he felt to pass on without chastising the aggressors would imply a want of strength which must disparage him in the eyes of his allies. Halting in the valley, therefore, he detached a small body of light troops to scale the heights, while he remained with the main body of the army below, to guard against surprise from the enemy.

The lower region of the rocky eminence was so steep that the soldiers found it no easy matter to ascend, scrambling, as well as they could, with hand and knee. But, as they came into the more exposed view of the garrison, the latter rolled down huge masses of rock, which, bounding along the declivity and breaking into fragments, crushed the foremost assailants and mangled their limbs in a frightful manner. Still they strove to work their way upward, now taking advantage of some gulley worn by the winter torrent, now sheltering themselves behind a projecting cliff, or some straggling tree anchored among the crevices of the mountain. It was all in vain. For no sooner did they emerge again into open view than the rocky avalanche thundered on their heads with a fury against which steel helm and cuirass were as little defence as gossamer. All the party were more or less wounded. Eight of the number were killed on the spot,—a loss the little band could ill afford,—and the gallant ensign, Corral, who led the advance, saw the banner in his hand torn into shreds.[2] Cortés, at length, convinced of the impracticability of the attempt, at least without a more severe loss than he was disposed to incur, commanded a retreat. It was high time; for a large body of the enemy were on full march across the valley to attack him.

He did not wait for their approach, but, gathering his broken files together, headed his cavalry and spurred boldly against them. On the level plain the Spaniards were on their own ground. The Indians, unable to sustain the furious onset, broke, and fell back before it. The flight soon became a rout, and the fiery cavaliers, dashing over them at full gallop, or running them through with their lances, took some revenge for their late discomfiture. The pursuit continued for some miles, till the nimble foe made their escape into the rugged fastnesses of the sierra, where the Spaniards did not care to follow. The weather was sultry, and, as the country was nearly destitute of water, the men and horses suffered extremely. Before evening they reached a spot overshadowed by a grove of wild mulberry-trees,

[2] " Todos descalabrados, y corriendo sangre, y las vanderas rotas, y ocho muertos." Bernal Diaz, Hist. de la Conquista, ubi supra.

in which some scanty springs afforded a miserable supply to the army.

Near the place rose another rocky summit of the sierra, garrisoned by a stronger force than the one which they had encountered in the former part of the day; and at no great distance stood a second fortress at a still greater height, though considerably smaller than its neighbor. This was also tenanted by a body of warriors, who, as well as those of the adjoining cliff, soon made active demonstration of their hostility by pouring down missiles on the troops below. Cortés, anxious to retrieve the disgrace of the morning, ordered an assault on the larger and, as it seemed, more practicable eminence. But, though two attempts were made with great resolution, they were repulsed with loss to the assailants. The rocky sides of the hill had been artificially cut and smoothed, so as greatly to increase the natural difficulties of the ascent. The shades of evening now closed around; and Cortés drew off his men to the mulberry-grove, where he took up his bivouac for the night, deeply chagrined at having been twice foiled by the enemy on the same day.

During the night, the Indian force which occupied the adjoining height passed over to their brethren, to aid them in the encounter which they foresaw would be renewed on the following morning. No sooner did the Spanish general, at the break of day, become aware of this manœuvre, than, with his usual quickness, he took advantage of it. He detached a body of musketeers and crossbowmen to occupy the deserted eminence, purposing, as soon as this was done, to lead the assault in person against the other. It was not long before the Castilian banner was seen streaming from the rocky pinnacle, when the general instantly led up his men to the attack.   And, while the garrison were meeting them resolutely on that quarter, the detachment on the neighboring heights poured into the place a well-directed fire, which so much distressed the enemy that in a very short time they signified their willingness to capitulate.[3]

On entering the place, the Spaniards found that a plain of some extent ran along the crest of the sierra, and that it was tenanted not only by men, but by women and their families, with their effects.   No violence was offered by the victors to the property or persons of the vanquished ; and the knowledge of this lenity induced the Indian garrison, who had made so stout a resistance on the morning of the preceding day, to tender their submission.[4]

After a halt of two days in this sequestered region, the army resumed its march in a southwesterly direction on Huaxtepec, the same city which had surrendered to

[3] For the assault on the rocks,—the topography of which it is impossible to verify from the narratives of the Conquerors,—see Bernal Diaz, Hist. de la Conquista, cap. 144,—Rel. Terc. de Cortés, ap. Lorenzana, pp. 218–221,—Gomara, Crónica, cap. 127,—Ixtlilxochitl, Venida de los Españolés, pp. 16, 17,—Oviedo, Hist. de las Ind., MS., lib. 33, cap. 21.

[4] Cortés, according to Bernal Diaz, ordered the troops who took possession of the second fortress "not to meddle with a grain of maize belonging to the besieged."   Diaz, giving this a very liberal interpretation, proceeded forthwith to load his Indian *tamanes* with everything but maize, as fair booty.   He was interrupted in his labors, however, by the captain of the detachment, who gave a more narrow construction to his general's orders, much to the dissatisfaction of the latter, if we may trust the doughty chronicler.   Ibid., ubi supra.

Sandoval. Here they were kindly received by the cacique, and entertained in his magnificent gardens, which Cortés and his officers, who had not before seen them, compared with the best in Castile.[5] Still thread-ing the wild mountain mazes, the army passed through Jauhtepec and several other places, which were aban-doned at their approach. As the inhabitants, however, hung in armed bodies on their flanks and rear, doing them occasionally some mischief, the Spaniards took their revenge by burning the deserted towns.

Thus holding on their fiery track, they descended the bold slope of the Cordilleras, which on the south are far more precipitous than on the Atlantic side. Indeed, a single day's journey is sufficient to place the traveller on a level several thousand feet lower than that occupied by him in the morning; thus conveying him, in a few hours, through the climates of many degrees of latitude. The route of the army led them across many an acre covered with lava and blackened scoriæ, attesting the volcanic character of the region; though this was frequently relieved by patches of verdure, and even tracts of prodigal fertility, as if Nature were desirous to compensate by these extraor-dinary efforts for the curse of barrenness which else-where had fallen on the land. On the ninth day of their march the troops arrived before the strong city of Quauhnahuac, or Cuernavaca, as since called by the

<hr>

5 "Adonde estaua la huerta que he dicho, que es la mejor que auia visto en toda mi vida, y ansí lo torno á dezir, que Cortés, y el Teso-rero Alderete, desque entonces la viéron, y passeáron algo de ella, se admiráron, y dixéron, que mejor cosa de huerta no auian visto en Castilla." Bernal Diaz, Hist. de la Conquista, cap. 144.

Spaniards.[6] It was the ancient capital of the Tlahuicas, and the most considerable place for wealth and population in this part of the country. It was tributary to the Aztecs, and a garrison of this nation was quartered within its walls. The town was singularly situated, on a projecting piece of land, encompassed by *barrancas*, or formidable ravines, except on one side, which opened on a rich and well-cultivated country. For, though the place stood at an elevation of between five and six thousand feet above the level of the sea, it had a southern exposure so sheltered by the mountain barrier on the north that its climate was as soft and genial as that of a much lower region.

The Spaniards, on arriving before this city, the limit of their southerly progress, found themselves separated from it by one of the vast barrancas before noticed, which resembled one of those frightful rents not unfrequent in the Mexican Andes, the result, no doubt, of some terrible convulsion in earlier ages. The rocky sides of the ravine sank perpendicularly down, so bare as scarcely to exhibit even a vestige of the cactus, or of the other hardy plants with which Nature in these fruitful regions so gracefully covers up her deformities. The bottom of the chasm, however, showed a striking contrast to this, being literally choked up with a rich and spontaneous vegetation; for the huge walls of rock which shut in these barrancas,

[6] This barbarous Indian name is tortured into all possible variations by the old chroniclers. The town soon received from the Spaniards the name which it now bears, of Cuernavaca, and by which it is indicated on modern maps. "Prevalse poi quello di *Cuernabaca*, col quale è presentemente conosciuta dagli Spagnuoli." Clavigero, Stor. del Messico, tom. iii. p. 185, nota.

while they screen them from the cold winds of the Cordilleras, reflect the rays of a vertical sun, so as to produce an almost suffocating heat in the enclosure, stimulating the soil to the rank fertility of the *tierra caliente.* Under the action of this forcing apparatus, —so to speak,—the inhabitants of the towns on their margin above may with ease obtain the vegetable products which are to be found on the sultry level of the lowlands.*

At the bottom of the ravine was seen a little stream, which, oozing from the stony bowels of the sierra, tumbled along its narrow channel and contributed by its perpetual moisture to the exuberant fertility of the valley. This rivulet, which at certain seasons of the year was swollen to a torrent, was traversed at some distance below the town, where the sloping sides of the barranca afforded a more practicable passage, by two rude bridges, both of which had been broken, in anticipation of the coming of the Spaniards. The latter had now arrived on the brink of the chasm which intervened between them and the city. It was, as has been remarked, of no great width, and the army drawn up on its borders was directly exposed to the archery of the garrison, on whom its own fire made little impression, protected as they were by their defences.

The general, annoyed by his position, sent a detachment to seek a passage lower down, by which the troops might be landed on the other side. But, although the banks of the ravine became less formidable as they

---

* [" The whole of this description," remarks Alaman, " agrees perfectly with the present aspect of Cuernavaca and the *barrancas* surrounding it."—ED.]

descended, they found no means of crossing the river, till a path unexpectedly presented itself, on which, probably, no one before had ever been daring enough to venture.

From the cliffs on the opposite sides of the barranca, two huge trees shot up to an enormous height, and, inclining towards each other, interlaced their boughs so as to form a sort of natural bridge. Across this avenue, in mid-air, a Tlascalan conceived it would not be difficult to pass to the opposite bank. The bold mountaineer succeeded in the attempt, and was soon followed by several others of his countrymen, trained to feats of agility and strength among their native hills. The Spaniards imitated their example. It was a perilous effort for an armed man to make his way over this aerial causeway, swayed to and fro by the wind, where the brain might become giddy, and where a single false movement of hand or foot would plunge him in the abyss below. Three of the soldiers lost their hold and fell. The rest, consisting of some twenty or thirty Spaniards and a considerable number of Tlascalans, alighted in safety on the other bank.[7] There hastily forming, they marched with all speed on the city. The enemy, engaged in their contest with the Castilians on the opposite brink of the ravine, were taken by surprise,—which, indeed, could scarcely have been exceeded if they had seen their foe drop from the clouds on the field of battle.

[7] The stout-hearted Diaz was one of those who performed this dangerous feat, though his head swam so, as he tells us, that he scarcely knew how he got on. " Porque de mí digo, que verdaderaměte quando passaua, q̃ lo ví mui peligroso, é malo de passar, y se me desvanecia la cabeça, y todavía passé yo, y otros veinte, ó treinta soldados, y muchos Tlascaltecas." Hist. de la Conquista, ubi supra.

They made a brave resistance, however, when fortunately the Spaniards succeeded in repairing one of the dilapidated bridges in such a manner as to enable both cavalry and foot to cross the river, though with much delay. The horse, under Olid and Andres de Tapia, instantly rode up to the succor of their countrymen. They were soon followed by Cortés at the head of the remaining battalions, and the enemy, driven from one point to another, were compelled to evacuate the city and to take refuge among the mountains. The buildings in one quarter of the town were speedily wrapt in flames. The place was abandoned to pillage, and, as it was one of the most opulent marts in the country, it amply compensated the victors for the toil and danger they had encountered. The trembling caciques, returning soon after to the city, appeared before Cortés, and, deprecating his resentment by charging the blame, as usual, on the Mexicans, threw themselves on his mercy. Satisfied with their submission, he allowed no further violence to the inhabitants.[8]

Having thus accomplished the great object of his expedition across the mountains, the Spanish commander turned his face northwards, to recross the formidable barrier which divided him from the Valley. The ascent, steep and laborious, was rendered still more difficult by fragments of rock and loose stones, which encumbered the passes. The mountain sides and summits were

[8] For the preceding account of the capture of Cuernavaca, see Bernal Diaz, ubi supra,—Oviedo, Hist. de las Ind., MS., lib. 33, cap. 21,—Ixtlilxochitl, Hist. Chich., MS., cap. 93,—Herrera, Hist. general, dec. 3, lib. 1, cap. 8,—Torquemada, Monarch. Ind., lib. 4, cap. 87,— Rel. Terc. de Cortés, ap. Lorenzana, pp. 223, 224.

shaggy with thick forests of pine and stunted oak, which threw a melancholy gloom over the region, still further heightened at the present day by its being a favorite haunt of banditti.

The weather was sultry, and, as the stony soil was nearly destitute of water, the troops suffered severely from thirst. Several of them, indeed, fainted on the road, and a few of the Indian allies perished from exhaustion.[9] The line of march must have taken the army across the eastern shoulder of the mountain, called the *Cruz del Marques*, or Cross of the Marquess, from a huge stone cross erected there to indicate the boundary of the territories granted by the Crown to Cortés, as Marquis of the Valley. Much, indeed, of the route lately traversed by the troops lay across the princely domain subsequently assigned to the Conqueror.[10]

The Spaniards were greeted from these heights with a different view from any which they had before had of the Mexican Valley, made more attractive in their eyes, doubtless, by contrast with the savage scenery in which they had lately been involved. It was its most pleasant and populous quarter; for nowhere did its cities and

[9] "Una Tierra de Pinales, despoblada, y sin ninguna agua, la qual y un Puerto pasámos con grandíssimo trabajo, y sin beber: tanto, que muchos de los Indios que iban con nosotros pereciéron de sed." Rel. Terc. de Cortés, ap. Lorenzana, p. 224.

[10] The city of Cuernavaca was comprehended in the patrimony of the dukes of Monteleone, descendants and heirs of the *Conquistador*. —The Spaniards, in their line of march towards the north, did not deviate far, probably, from the great road which now leads from Mexico to Acapulco, still exhibiting in this upper portion of it the same characteristic features as at the period of the Conquest.

villages cluster together in such numbers as round the lake of sweet water. From whatever quarter seen, however, the enchanting region presented the same aspect of natural beauty and cultivation, with its flourishing villas, and its fair lake in the centre, whose dark and polished surface glistened like a mirror, deep set in the huge frame-work of porphyry in which nature had enclosed it.

The point of attack selected by the general was Xochimilco, or "the field of flowers," as its name implies, from the floating gardens which rode at anchor, as it were, on the neighboring waters.[11] It was one of the most potent and wealthy cities in the Valley, and a stanch vassal of the Aztec crown. It stood, like the capital itself, partly in the water, and was approached in that quarter by causeways of no great length. The town was composed of houses like those of most other places of like magnitude in the country, mostly of cottages or huts made of clay and the light bamboo, mingled with aspiring *teocallis*, and edifices of stone, belonging to the more opulent classes.

As the Spaniards advanced, they were met by skir-mishing parties of the enemy, who, after dismissing a light volley of arrows, rapidly retreated before them. As they took the direction of Xochimilco, Cortés inferred that they were prepared to resist him in considerable force. It exceeded his expectations.

On traversing the principal causeway, he found it occupied at the farther extremity by a numerous body of warriors, who, stationed on the opposite side of a bridge, which had been broken, were prepared to dis-

[11] Clavigero, Stor. del Messico, tom. iii. p. 187, nota.

C*

pute his passage   They had constructed a temporary
barrier of palisades, which screened them from the fire
of the musketry.   But the water in its neighborhood
was very shallow, and the cavaliers and infantry,
plunging into it, soon made their way, swimming or
wading, as they could, in face of a storm of missiles,
to the landing near the town.   Here they closed with
the enemy, and hand to hand, after a sharp struggle,
drove them back on the city ; a few, however, taking
the direction of the open country, were followed up
by the cavalry.   The great mass, hotly pursued by the
infantry, were driven through street and lane, without
much further resistance.   Cortés, with a few followers,
disengaging himself from the tumult, remained near
the entrance of the city.   He had not been there long
when he was assailed by a fresh body of Indians, who
suddenly poured into the place from a neighboring
dike.   The general, with his usual fearlessness, threw
himself into the midst, in hopes to check their advance.
But his own followers were too few to support him, and
he was overwhelmed by the crowd of combatants.   His
horse lost his footing and fell ; and Cortés, who received a severe blow on the head before he could rise,
was seized and dragged off in triumph by the Indians.
At this critical moment, a Tlascalan, who perceived
the general's extremity, sprang, like one of the wild
ocelots of his own forests, into the midst of the assailants, and endeavored to tear him from their grasp.
Two of the general's servants also speedily came to
the rescue, and Cortés, with their aid and that of the
brave Tlascalan, succeeded in regaining his feet and
shaking off his enemies.   To vault into the saddle and

brandish his good lance was but the work of a moment. Others of his men quickly came up, and the clash of arms reaching the ears of the Spaniards, who had gone in pursuit, they returned, and, after a desperate conflict, forced the enemy from the city. Their retreat, however, was intercepted by the cavalry, returning from the country, and, thus hemmed in between the opposite columns, they were cut to pieces, or saved themselves only by plunging into the lake.[12]

This was the greatest personal danger which Cortés had yet encountered. His life was in the power of the barbarians, and, had it not been for their eagerness to take him prisoner, he must undoubtedly have lost it. To the same cause may be frequently attributed the preservation of the Spaniards in these engagements. The next day he sought, it is said, for the Tlascalan who came so boldly to his rescue, and, as he could learn nothing of him, he gave the credit of his preservation to his patron, St. Peter.[13] He may well be excused for presuming the interposition of his good Genius to shield him from the awful doom of the cap-

---

[12] Rel. Terc. de Cortés, ap. Lorenzana, p. 226.—Herrera, Hist. general, dec. 3, lib. 1, cap. 8.—Oviedo, Hist. de las Ind., MS., lib. 33, cap. 21.—This is the general's own account of the matter. Diaz, however, says that he was indebted for his rescue to a Castilian, named Olea, supported by some Tlascalans, and that his preserver received ·hree severe wounds himself on the occasion. (Hist. de la Conquista, cap. 145.) This was an affair, however, in which Cortés ought to be better informed than any one else, and one, moreover, not likely to slip his memory. The old soldier has probably confounded it with another and similar adventure of his commander.

[13] " Otro Dia buscó Cortés al Indio, que le socorrió, i muerto, ni vivo no pareció ; i Cortés, por la devocion de San Pedro, juzgo que él le avia aiudado." Herrera, Hist. general, dec. 3, lib. 1, cap. 8.

tive,—a doom not likely to be mitigated in his case. That heart must have been a bold one, indeed, which, from any motive, could voluntarily encounter such a peril! Yet his followers did as much, and that, too, for a much inferior reward.

The period which we are reviewing was still the age of chivalry, — that stirring and adventurous age, of which we can form little conception in the present day of sober, practical reality. The Spaniard, with his nice point of honor, high romance, and proud, vainglorious vaunt, was the true representative of that age. The Europeans generally had not yet learned to accommodate themselves to a life of literary toil, or to the drudgery of trade or the patient tillage of the soil. They left these to the hooded inmate of the cloister, the humble burgher, and the miserable serf. Arms was the only profession worthy of gentle blood,—the only career which the high-mettled cavalier could tread with honor. The New World, with its strange and mysterious perils, afforded a noble theatre for the exercise of his calling; and the Spaniard entered on it with all the enthusiasm of a paladin of romance.

Other nations entered on it also, but with different motives. The French sent forth their missionaries to take up their dwelling among the heathen, who, in the good work of winning souls to Paradise, were content to wear—nay, sometimes seemed to court—the crown of martyrdom. The Dutch, too, had their mission, but it was one of worldly lucre, and they found a recompense for toil and suffering in their gainful traffic with the natives. While our own Puritan fathers, with the true Anglo-Saxon spirit, left their pleasant homes across the waters, and pitched their tents in the howling wilderness, that they might enjoy the sweets of civil and religious freedom. But the Spaniard came over to the New World in the true spirit of a knight-errant, courting adventure however perilous, wooing danger, as it would seem, for its own sake. With sword and lance, he was ever ready to do battle for the Faith; and, as he raised his old war-cry of "St. Jago," he fancied himself fighting under the banner of the military apostle, and felt his single arm a match for more than a hundred infidels! It was the expiring age of chivalry; and Spain, romantic Spain, was the land where its light lingered longest above the horizon.

It was not yet dusk when Cortés and his followers re-entered the city; and the general's first act was to ascend a neighboring *teocalli* and reconnoitre the surrounding country. He there beheld a sight which might have troubled a bolder spirit than his. The surface of the salt lake was darkened with canoes, and the causeway, for many a mile, with Indian squadrons, apparently on their march towards the Christian camp. In fact, no sooner had Guatemozin been apprised of the arrival of the white men at Xochimilco than he mustered his levies in great force to relieve the city. They were now on their march, and, as the capital was but four leagues distant, would arrive soon after night-fall.[14]

Cortés made active preparations for the defence of

[14] " Por el Agua á una muy grande flota de Canoas, que creo, que pasaban de dos mil; y en ellas venian mas de doce mil Hombres de Guerra; é por la Tierra llegó tanta multitud de Gente, que todos los Campos cubrian.' Rel. Terc. de Cortés, ap. Lorenzana, p. 227.

his quarters.   He stationed a corps of pikemen along
the landing where the Aztecs would be likely to dis-
embark.   He doubled the sentinels, and, with his principal officers, made the rounds repeatedly in the course
of the night.   In addition to other causes for watchfulness, the bolts of the crossbowmen were nearly exhausted, and the archers were busily employed in
preparing and adjusting shafts to the copper heads,
of which great store had been provided for the army.
There was little sleep in the camp that night.[15]

It passed away, however, without molestation from
the enemy.   Though not stormy, it was exceedingly
dark.   But, although the Spaniards on duty could see
nothing, they distinctly heard the sound of many oars
in the water, at no great distance from the shore.   Yet
those on board the canoes made no attempt to land,
distrusting, or advised, it may be, of the preparations
made for their reception.   With early dawn they were
under arms, and, without waiting for the movement of
the Spaniards, poured into the city and attacked them
in their own quarters.

The Spaniards, who were gathered in the area round
one of the *teocallis*, were taken at disadvantage in the
town, where the narrow lanes and streets, many of them
covered with a smooth and slippery cement, offered
obvious impediments to the manœuvres of cavalry.
But Cortés hastily formed his musketeers and cross-

[15] " Y acordóse que huviesse mui buena vela en todo nuestro Real,
repartida á los puertos, é azequias por donde auian de venir á desem-
barcar, y los de acauallo mui á punto toda la noche ensillados y
enfrenados, aguardando en la calçada, y tierra firme, y todos los
Capitanes, y Cortés con ellos, haziendo vela y ronda toda la noche."
Bernal Diaz, Hist. de la Conquista, cap. 145.

bowmen, and poured such a lively, well-directed fire into the enemy's ranks as threw him into disorder and compelled him to recoil. The infantry, with their long pikes, followed up the blow; and the horse, charging at full speed as the retreating Aztecs emerged from the city, drove them several miles along the main land.

At some distance, however, they were met by a strong reinforcement of their countrymen, and, rallying, the tide of battle turned, and the cavaliers, swept along by it, gave the rein to their steeds and rode back at full gallop towards the town. They had not proceeded very far, when they came upon the main body of the army, advancing rapidly to their support. Thus strengthened, they once more returned to the charge, and the rival hosts met together in full career, with the shock of an earthquake. For a time, victory seemed to hang in the balance, as the mighty press reeled to and fro under the opposite impulse, and a confused shout rose up towards heaven, in which the war-whoop of the savage was mingled with the battle-cry of the Christian,—a still stranger sound on these sequestered shores. But, in the end, Castilian valor, or rather Castilian arms and discipline, proved triumphant. The enemy faltered, gave way, and, recoiling step by step, the retreat soon terminated in a rout, and the Spaniards, following up the flying foe, drove them from the field with such dreadful slaughter that they made no further attempt to renew the battle.

The victors were now undisputed masters of the city. It was a wealthy place, well stored with Indian fabrics, cotton, gold, feather-work, and other articles of luxury and use, affording a rich booty to the soldiers. While engaged in the work of plunder, a party of the enemy, landing from their canoes, fell on some of the stragglers, laden with merchandise, and made four of them prisoners. It created a greater sensation among the troops than if ten times that number had fallen on the field. Indeed, it was rare that a Spaniard allowed himself to be taken alive. In the present instance the unfortunate men were taken by surprise. They were hurried to the capital, and soon after sacrificed; when their arms and legs were cut off, by the command of the ferocious young chief of the Aztecs, and sent round to the different cities, with the assurance that this should be the fate of the enemies of Mexico! [16]

From the prisoners taken in the late engagement, Cortés learned that the forces already sent by Guatemozin formed but a small part of his levies; that his policy was to send detachment after detachment, until the Spaniards, however victorious they might come off from the contest with each individually, would, in the end, succumb from mere exhaustion, and thus be vanquished, as it were, by their own victories.

The soldiers having now sacked the city, Cortés did

[16] Diaz, who had an easy faith, states, as a fact, that the limbs of the unfortunate men were cut off *before* their sacrifice: "Manda cortar pies y braços á los tristes nuestros compañeros, y las embia por muchos pueblos nuestros amigos de los q̃ nos auian venido de paz, y les embia á dezir, que antes que bolvamos á Tezcuco, piensa no quedará ninguno de nosotros á vida, y con los coraçones y sangre hizo sacrificio á sus ídolos." (Hist. de la Conquista, cap. 145.)—This is not very probable. The Aztecs did not, like our North American Indians, torture their enemies from mere cruelty, but in conformity to the prescribed regulations of their ritual. The captive was a religious victim.

not care to await further assaults from the enemy in his present quarters. On the fourth morning after his arrival, he mustered his forces on a neighboring plain. They came, many of them reeling under the weight of their plunder. The general saw this with uneasiness. They were to march, he said, through a populous country, all in arms to dispute their passage. To secure their safety, they should move as light and unencumbered as possible. The sight of so much spoil would sharpen the appetite of their enemies, and draw them on, like a flock of famished eagles after their prey. But his eloquence was lost on his men, who plainly told him they had a right to the fruit of their victories, and that what they had won with their swords they knew well enough how to defend with them.

Seeing them thus bent on their purpose, the general did not care to balk their inclinations. He ordered the baggage to the centre, and placed a few of the cavalry over it; dividing the remainder between the front and rear, in which latter post, as that most exposed to attack, he also stationed his arquebusiers and crossbowmen. Thus prepared, he resumed his march, but first set fire to the combustible buildings of Xochimilco, in retaliation for the resistance he had met there.[17] The light of the burning city streamed high into the air, sending its ominous glare far and wide across the waters, and telling the inhabitants on their margin that the fatal strangers so long predicted by

---

[17] "Y al cabo dejándola toda quemada y asolada nos partímos; y cierto era mucho para ver, porque tenia muchas Casas, y Torres de sus Ídolos de cal y canto." Rel. Terc. de Cortés, ap. Lorenzana, p. 228.

their oracles had descended like a consuming flame upon their borders.[18]

Small bodies of the enemy were seen occasionally at a distance, but they did not venture to attack the army on its march, which, before noon, brought them to Cojohuacan, a large town about two leagues distant from Xochimilco. One could scarcely travel that distance in this populous quarter of the Valley without meeting with a place of considerable size, oftentimes the capital of what had formerly been an independent state. The inhabitants, members of different tribes, and speaking dialects somewhat different, belonged to the same great family of nations, who had come from the real or imaginary region of Aztlan, in the far Northwest. Gathered round the shores of their Alpine sea, these petty communities continued, after their incorporation with the Aztec monarchy, to maintain a spirit of rivalry in their intercourse with one another, which—as with the cities on the Mediterranean in the

[18] For other particulars of the actions at Xochimilco, see Oviedo, Hist. de las Ind., MS., lib. 23, cap. 21,—Herrera, Hist. general, dec. 3, lib. 1, cap. 8, 11,—Ixtlilxochitl, Venida de los Españoles, p. 18,—Torquemada, Monarch. Ind., lib. 4, cap. 87, 88,—Bernal Diaz, Hist. de la Conquista, cap. 145.—The Conqueror's own account of these engagements has not his usual perspicuity, perhaps from its brevity. A more than ordinary confusion, indeed, prevails in the different reports of them, even those proceeding from contemporaries, making it extremely difficult to collect a probable narrative from authorities not only contradicting one another, but themselves. It is rare, at any time, that two accounts of a battle coincide in all respects; the range of observation for each individual is necessarily so limited and different, and it is so difficult to make a cool observation at all, in the hurry and heat of conflict. Any one who has conversed with the survivors will readily comprehend this, and be apt to conclude that, wherever he may look for truth, it will hardly be on the battle-ground.

feudal ages—quickened their mental energies, and
raised the Mexican Valley higher in the scale of civilization than most other quarters of Anahuac.

The town at which the army had now arrived was
deserted by its inhabitants; and Cortés halted two days
there to restore his troops and give the needful attention to the wounded.[19] He made use of the time to
reconnoitre the neighboring ground, and, taking with
him a strong detachment, descended on the causeway
which led from Cojohuacan to the great avenue of
Iztapalapan.[20] At the point of intersection, called
Xoloc, he found a strong barrier, or fortification, behind which a Mexican force was intrenched. Their
archery did some mischief to the Spaniards as they

[19] This place, recommended by the exceeding beauty of its situation,
became, after the Conquest, a favorite residence of Cortés, who founded
a nunnery in it, and commanded in his will that his bones should be
removed thither from any part of the world in which he might die:
" Que mis huesos—los lleven á la mi Villa de Coyoacan, y allí les den
tierra en el Monesterio de Monjas, que mando hacer y edificar en la
dicha mi Villa." Testamento de Hernan Cortés, MS.

[20] This, says Archbishop Lorenzana, was the modern *calzada de la
Piedad.* (Rel. Terc. de Cortés, p. 229, nota.) But it is not easy to
reconcile this with the elaborate chart which M. de Humboldt has
given of the Valley. A short arm, which reached from this city in the
days of the Aztecs, touched obliquely the great southern avenue by
which the Spaniards first entered the capital. As the waters which
once entirely surrounded Mexico have shrunk into their narrow basin,
the face of the country has undergone a great change, and, though
the foundations of the principal causeways are still maintained, it is
not always easy to discern vestiges of the ancient avenues.*

---

* [" La calzada de Iztapalapan," says Alaman, who has made a
minute study of the topography, " es la de San Antonio Abad, que
conduce á San Augustin de las Cuevas ó Tlalpam."—ED.]

came within bowshot. But the latter, marching intrepidly forward in face of the arrowy shower, stormed the works, and, after an obstinate struggle, drove the enemy from their position.[21] Cortés then advanced some way on the great causeway of Iztapalapan ; but he beheld the farther extremity darkened by a numerous array of warriors, and, as he did not care to engage in unnecessary hostilities, especially as his ammunition was nearly exhausted, he fell back and retreated to his own quarters.

The following day, the army continued its march, taking the road to Tacuba, but a few miles distant. On the way it experienced much annoyance from straggling parties of the enemy, who, furious at the sight of the booty which the invaders were bearing away, made repeated attacks on their flanks and rear. Cortés retaliated, as on the former expedition, by one of their own stratagems, but with less success than before ; for, pursuing the retreating enemy too hotly, he fell with his cavalry into an ambuscade which they had prepared for him in their turn. He was not yet a match for their wily tactics. The Spanish cavaliers were enveloped in a moment by their subtle foe, and separated from the rest of the army. But, spurring on their good steeds, and charging in a solid column together, they succeeded in breaking through the Indian array, and in making their escape, except two individuals,

[21] "We came to a wall which they had built across the causeway and the foot-soldiers began to attack it ; and though it was very thick and stoutly defended, and ten Spaniards were wounded, at length they gained it, killing many of the enemy, although the musketeers were without powder and the bowmen without arrows." Rel. Terc., ubi supra.

who fell into the enemy's hands. They were the general's own servants, who had followed him faithfully through the whole campaign, and he was deeply affected by their loss,—rendered the more distressing by the consideration of the dismal fate that awaited them. When the little band rejoined the army, which had halted, in some anxiety at their absence, under the walls of Tacuba, the soldiers were astonished at the dejected mien of their commander, which too visibly betrayed his emotion.[22]

The sun was still high in the heavens when they entered the ancient capital of the Tepanecs. The first care of Cortés was to ascend the principal *teocalli* and survey the surrounding country. It was an admirable point of view, commanding the capital, which lay but little more than a league distant, and its immediate environs. Cortés was accompanied by Alderete, the treasurer, and some other cavaliers, who had lately joined his banner. The spectacle was still new to them; and, as they gazed on the stately city, with its broad lake covered with boats and barges hurrying to and fro, some laden with merchandise, or fruits and vegetables, for the markets of Tenochtitlan, others crowded with warriors, they could not withhold their admiration at the life and activity of the scene, declaring that nothing but the hand of Providence could have led their countrymen safe through the heart of this powerful empire.[23]

[22] "Y estando en esto viene Cortés, con el qual nos alegrámos, puesto que él venia muy triste y como lloroso." Bernal Diaz, Hist. de la Conquista, cap. 145.

[23] "Pues quando viéron la gran ciudad de México, y la laguna, y tanta multitud de canoas, que vnas ivan cargadas con bastimentos, y

In the midst of the admiring circle, the brow of Cortés alone was observed to be overcast, and a sigh, which now and then stole audibly from his bosom, showed the gloomy working of his thoughts.[24] "Take comfort," said one of the cavaliers, approaching his commander, and wishing to console him, in his rough way, for his recent loss; "you must not lay these things so much to heart; it is, after all, but the fortune of war." The general's answer showed the nature of his meditations. "You are my witness," said he, "how often I have endeavored to persuade yonder capital peacefully to submit. It fills me with grief when I think of the toil and the dangers my brave followers have yet to encounter before we can call it ours. But the time is come when we must put our hands to the work."[25]

There can be no doubt that Cortés, with every other man in his army, felt he was engaged on a holy crusade, and that, independently of personal considerations, he could not serve Heaven better than by planting the Cross on the blood-stained towers of the heathen metropolis. But it was natural that he should feel

otras ivan á pescar, y otras valdías, mucho mas se espantáron, porque no las auian visto, hasta en aquella saçon: y dixéron, que nuestra venida en esta Nueua España, que no eran cosas de hombres humanos, sino que la gran misericordia de Dios era quiē nos sostenia." Bernal Diaz, Hist. de la Conquista, cap. 145.

[24] "En este instante suspiró Cortés cõ vna muy grā tristeza, mui mayor q̃ la q̃ de antes traia." Ibid., loc. cit.

[25] "Y Cortés le dixo, que ya veia quantas vezes auia embiado á México á rogalles con la paz, y que la tristeza no la tenia por sola vna cosa, sino en pensar en los grandes trabajos en que nos auiamos de ver, hasta tornar á señorear; y que con la ayuda de Dios presto lo porniamos por la obra." Ibid., ubi supra.

some compunction as he gazed on the goodly scene, and thought of the coming tempest, and how soon the opening blossoms of civilization which there met his eye must wither under the rude breath of War. It was a striking spectacle, that of the great Conqueror thus brooding in silence over the desolation he was about to bring on the land! It seems to have made a deep impression on his soldiers, little accustomed to such proofs of his sensibility; and it forms the burden of some of those *romances*, or national ballads, with which the Castilian minstrel, in the olden time, delighted to commemorate the favorite heroes of his country, and which, coming mid-way between oral tradition and chronicle, have been found as imperishable a record as chronicle itself.[26]

Tacuba was the point which Cortés had reached on his former expedition round the northern side of the Valley. He had now, therefore, made the entire circuit of the great lake; had reconnoitred the several approaches to the capital, and inspected with his own

[26] Diaz gives the opening *redondillas* of the *romance*, which I have not been able to find in any of the printed collections:

> " En Tacuba está Cortés,
> cō su esquadron esforçado,
> triste estaua, y muy penoso,
> triste, y con gran cuidado,
> la vna mano en la mexilla,
> y la otra en el costado," etc.

It may be thus done into pretty literal doggerel:

> In Tacuba stood Cortés,
> With many a care opprest,
> Thoughts of the past came o'er him,
> And he bowed his haughty crest.
> One hand upon his cheek he laid,
> The other on his breast,
> While his valiant squadrons round him, etc.

eyes the dispositions made on the opposite quarters for its defence. He had no occasion to prolong his stay in Tacuba, the vicinity of which to Mexico must soon bring on him its whole warlike population.

Early on the following morning he resumed his march, taking the route pursued in the former expedition north of the small lakes. He met with less annoyance from the enemy than on the preceding days ; a circumstance owing in some degree, perhaps, to the state of the weather, which was exceedingly tempestuous. The soldiers, with their garments heavy with moisture, ploughed their way with difficulty through miry roads flooded by the torrents. On one occasion, as their military chronicler informs us, the officers neglected to go the rounds of the camp at night, and the sentinels to mount guard, trusting to the violence of the storm for their protection. Yet the fate of Narvaez might have taught them not to put their faith in the elements.

At Acolman, in the Acolhuan territory, they were met by Sandoval, with the friendly cacique of Tezcuco, and several cavaliers, among whom were some recently arrived from the Islands. They cordially greeted their countrymen, and communicated the tidings that the canal was completed, and that the brigantines, rigged and equipped, were ready to be launched on the bosom of the lake. There seemed to be no reason, therefore, for longer postponing operations against Mexico.— With this welcome intelligence, Cortés and his victorious legions made their entry for the last time into the Acolhuan capital, having consumed just three weeks in completing the circuit of the Valley.

CHAPTER IV.

CONSPIRACY IN THE ARMY.—BRIGANTINES LAUNCHED.—
MUSTER OF FORCES.—EXECUTION OF XICOTENCATL.—
MARCH OF THE ARMY.—BEGINNING OF THE SIEGE.

1521.

AT the very time when Cortés was occupied with reconnoitring the Valley, preparatory to his siege of the capital, a busy faction in Castile was laboring to subvert his authority and defeat his plans of conquest altogether. The fame of his brilliant exploits had spread not only through the Isles, but to Spain and many parts of Europe, where a general admiration was felt for the invincible energy of the man who with his single arm, as it were, could so long maintain a contest with the powerful Indian empire. The absence of the Spanish monarch from his dominions, and the troubles of the country, can alone explain the supine indifference shown by the government to the prosecution of this great enterprise. To the same causes it may be ascribed that no action was had in regard to the suits of Velasquez and Narvaez, backed as they were by so potent an advocate as Bishop Fonseca, president of the Council of the Indies. The reins of government had fallen into the hands of Adrian of Utrecht, Charles's preceptor, and afterwards Pope,—a man of learning, and not without sagacity, but slow and timid in his policy, and altogether incapable of that decisive action which suited the bold genius of his predecessor, Cardinal Ximenes.

In the spring of 1521, however, a number of ordinances passed the Council of the Indies, which threatened an important innovation in the affairs of New Spain. It was decreed that the Royal Audience of Hispaniola should abandon the proceedings already instituted against Narvaez for his treatment of the commissioner Ayllon; that that unfortunate commander should be released from his confinement at Vera Cruz; and that an arbitrator should be sent to Mexico with authority to investigate the affairs and conduct of Cortés and to render ample justice to the governor of Cuba. There were not wanting persons at court who looked with dissatisfaction on these proceedings, as an unworthy requital of the services of Cortés, and who thought the present moment, at any rate, not the most suitable for taking measures which might discourage the general and perhaps render him desperate. But the arrogant temper of the bishop of Burgos overruled all objections; and the ordinances, having been approved by the Regency, were signed by that body, April 11, 1521. A person named Tápia, one of the functionaries of the Audience at St. Domingo, was selected as the new commissioner to be despatched to Vera Cruz. Fortunately, circumstances occurred which postponed the execution of the design for the present, and permitted Cortés to go forward unmolested in his career of conquest.[1]

But, while thus allowed to remain, for the present at

[1] Herrera, Hist. general, dec. 3, lib. 1, cap. 15.—Relacion de Alonso de Verzara, Escrivano Público de Vera Cruz, MS., dec. 21.

least, in possession of authority, he was assailed by a danger nearer home, which menaced not only his authority, but his life. This was a conspiracy in the army, of a more dark and dangerous character than any hitherto formed there. It was set on foot by a common soldier, named Antonio Villafaña, a native of Old Castile, of whom nothing is known but his share in this transaction. He was one of the troop of Narvaez,—that leaven of disaffection, which had remained with the army, swelling with discontent on every light occasion, and ready at all times to rise into mutiny. They had voluntarily continued in the service after the secession of their comrades at Tlascala; but it was from the same mercenary hopes with which they had originally embarked in the expedition,—and in these they were destined still to be disappointed. They had little of the true spirit of adventure which distinguished the old companions of Cortés; and they found the barren laurels of victory but a sorry recompense for all their toils and sufferings.

With these men were joined others, who had causes of personal disgust with the general; and others, again, who looked with distrust on the result of the war. The gloomy fate of their countrymen who had fallen into the enemy's hands filled them with dismay. They felt themselves the victims of a chimerical spirit in their leader, who, with such inadequate means, was urging to extremity so ferocious and formidable a foe; and they shrank with something like apprehension from thus pursuing the enemy into his own haunts, where he would gather tenfold energy from despair.

These men would have willingly abandoned the

enterprise and returned to Cuba; but how could they do it? Cortés had control over the whole route from the city to the sea-coast; and not a vessel could leave its ports without his warrant. Even if he were put out of the way, there were others, his principal officers, ready to step into his place and avenge the death of their commander. It was necessary to embrace these, also, in the scheme of destruction; and it was proposed, therefore, together with Cortés, to assassinate Sandoval, Olid, Alvarado, and two or three others most devoted to his interests. The conspirators would then raise the cry of liberty, and doubted not that they should be joined by the greater part of the army, or enough, at least, to enable them to work their own pleasure. They proposed to offer the command, on Cortés' death, to Francisco Verdugo, a brother-in-law of Velasquez. He was an honorable cavalier, and not privy to their design. But they had little doubt that he would acquiesce in the command thus in a manner forced upon him, and this would secure them the protection of the governor of Cuba, who, indeed, from his own hatred of Cortés, would be disposed to look with a lenient eye on their proceedings.

The conspirators even went so far as to appoint the subordinate officers, an *alguacil mayor* in place of Sandoval, a quartermaster-general to succeed Olid, and some others.[2] The time fixed for the execution of the plot was soon after the return of Cortés from his ex-

[2] "Haziã Alguazil mayor é Alférez, y Alcaldes, y Regidores, y Contador, y Tesorero, y Ueedor, y otras cosas deste arte, y aun repartido entre ellos nuestros bienes, y cauallos." Bernal Diaz, Hist. de la Conquista, cap. 146.

pedition. A parcel, pretended to have come by a fresh arrival from Castile, was to be presented to him while at table, and, when he was engaged in breaking open the letters, the conspirators were to fall on him and his officers and despatch them with their poniards. Such was the iniquitous scheme devised for the destruction of Cortés and the expedition. But a conspiracy, to be successful, especially when numbers are concerned, should allow but little time to elapse between its conception and its execution.

On the day previous to that appointed for the perpetration of the deed, one of the party, feeling a natural compunction at the commission of the crime, went to the general's quarters and solicited a private interview with him. He threw himself at his commander's feet, and revealed all the particulars relating to the conspiracy, adding that in Villafaña's possession a paper would be found, containing the names of his accomplices. Cortés, thunderstruck at the disclosure, lost not a moment in profiting by it. He sent for Alvarado, Sandoval, and one or two other officers marked out by the conspirator, and, after communicating the affair to them, went at once with them to Villafaña's quarters, attended by four alguacils.

They found him in conference with three or four friends, who were instantly taken from the apartment and placed in custody. Villafaña, confounded at this sudden apparition of his commander, had barely time to snatch a paper, containing the signatures of the confederates, from his bosom, and attempt to swallow it. But Cortés arrested his arm, and seized the paper. As he glanced his eye rapidly over the fatal list, he was

much moved at finding there the names of more than
one who had some claim to consideration in the army.
He tore the scroll in pieces, and ordered Villafaña to
be taken into custody. He was immediately tried by
a military court hastily got together, at which the general himself presided. There seems to have been no
doubt of the man's guilt. He was condemned to death,
and, after allowing him time for confession and absolution, the sentence was executed by hanging him from
the window of his own quarters.[3]

Those ignorant of the affair were astonished at the
spectacle ; and the remaining conspirators were filled
with consternation when they saw that their plot was
detected, and anticipated a similar fate for themselves.
But they were mistaken. Cortés pursued the matter
no further. A little reflection convinced him that to
do so would involve him in the most disagreeable, and
even dangerous, perplexities. And, however much the
parties implicated in so foul a deed might deserve
death, he could ill afford the loss even of the guilty,
with his present limited numbers. He resolved, therefore, to content himself with the punishment of the
ringleader.

He called his troops together, and briefly explained
to them the nature of the crime for which Villafaña
had suffered. He had made no confession, he said,
and the guilty secret had perished with him. He then
expressed his sorrow that any should have been found
in their ranks capable of so base an act, and stated
his own unconsciousness of having wronged any indi-

[3] Bernal Diaz, Hist. de la Conquista, cap. 146.—Oviedo, Hist. de las
Ind., MS., lib. 33, cap. 48.—Herrera, Hist. general, dec. 3, lib. 1, cap. 1.

vidual among them; but, if he had done so, he invited them frankly to declare it, as he was most anxious to afford them all the redress in his power.[4] But there was no one of his audience, whatever might be his grievances, who cared to enter his complaint at such a moment; least of all were the conspirators willing to do so, for they were too happy at having, as they fancied, escaped detection, to stand forward now in the ranks of the malecontents. The affair passed off, therefore, without further consequences.

The conduct of Cortés in this delicate conjuncture shows great coolness, and knowledge of human nature. Had he suffered his detection, or even his suspicion, of the guilty parties to take air, it would have placed him in hostile relations with them for the rest of his life. It was a disclosure of this kind, in the early part of Louis the Eleventh's reign, to which many of the troubles of his later years were attributed.[5] The mask once torn away, there is no longer occasion to consult even appearances. The door seems to be closed against reform. The alienation, which might have been changed by circumstances or conciliated by kindness, settles into a deep and deadly rancor. And Cortés would have been surrounded by enemies in his own camp more implacable than those in the camp of the Aztecs.

As it was, the guilty soldiers had suffered too serious

[4] Herrera, Hist. general, ubi supra.

[5] So says M. de Barante in his picturesque *rifacimento* of the ancien chronicles: " Les procès du connétable et de monsieur de Némours, bien d'autres révélations, avaient fait éclater leur mauvais vouloir, ou du moins leur peu de fidélité pour le roi; ils ne pouvaient donc douter qu'il désirât ou complotât leur ruine." Histoire des Ducs de Bourgogne (Paris, 1838), tom. xi. p. 169.

apprehensions to place their lives hastily in a similar jeopardy. They strove, on the contrary, by demonstrations of loyalty, and the assiduous discharge of their duties, to turn away suspicion from themselves. Cortés, on his part, was careful to preserve his natural demeanor, equally removed from distrust and—what was perhaps more difficult—that studied courtesy which intimates, quite as plainly, suspicion of the party who is the object of it. To do this required no little address. Yet he did not forget the past. He had, it is true, destroyed the scroll containing the list of the conspirators. But the man that has once learned the names of those who have conspired against his life has no need of a written record to keep them fresh in his memory. Cortés kept his eye on all their movements, and took care to place them in no situation, afterwards, where they could do him injury.[6]

This attempt on the life of their commander excited a strong sensation in the army, with whom his many dazzling qualities and brilliant military talents had made him a general favorite. They were anxious to testify their reprobation of so foul a deed, coming from their own body, and they felt the necessity of taking some effectual measures for watching over the safety of one with whom their own destinies, as well as the fate of the enterprise, were so intimately connected. It was arranged, therefore, that he should be provided with a guard of soldiers, who were placed under the direction of a trusty cavalier named Antonio de Qui-

[6] " Y desde allí adelante, aunque mostraua gran voluntad á las personas que eran en la cōjuraciō, siempre se rezelaua dellos." Bernal Diaz, Hist. de la Conquista, cap. 146.

ñones. They constituted the general's body-guard during the rest of the campaign, watching over him day and night, and protecting him from domestic treason no less than from the sword of the enemy.

As was stated at the close of the last chapter, the Spaniards, on their return to quarters, found the construction of the brigantines completed, and that they were fully rigged, equipped, and ready for service. The canal, also, after having occupied eight thousand men for nearly two months, was finished.

It was a work of great labor; for it extended half a league in length, was twelve feet wide, and as many deep. The sides were strengthened by palisades of wood, or solid masonry. At intervals, dams and locks were constructed, and part of the opening was through the hard rock. By this avenue the brigantines might now be safely introduced on the lake.[7]

Cortés was resolved that so auspicious an event should be celebrated with due solemnity. On the 28th of April, the troops were drawn up under arms, and the whole population of Tezcuco assembled to witness the ceremony. Mass was performed, and every man in the army, together with the general, confessed and received the sacrament. Prayers were offered up by Father Olmedo, and a benediction invoked on the little navy, the first—worthy of the name—ever launched on

[7] Ixtlilxochitl, Venida de los Españoles, p. 19.—Rel. Terc. de Cortés, ap. Lorenzana, p. 234.—"Obra grandíssima," exclaims the Conqueror, "y mucho para ver."—"Fuéron en guarde de estos bergantines," adds Camargo, "mas de diez mil hombres de guerra con los maestros dellas, hasta que los armáron y echáron en el agua y laguna de Méjico, que fué obra de mucho efecto para tomarse Méjico." Hist. de Tlascala, MS.

D*

American waters.[8]   The signal was given by the firing
of a cannon, when the vessels, dropping down the
canal, one after another, reached the lake in good
order ; and, as they emerged on its ample bosom, with
music sounding, and the royal ensign of Castile proudly
floating from their masts, a shout of admiration arose
from the countless multitudes of spectators, which
mingled with the roar of artillery and musketry from
the vessels and the shore ![9]   It was a novel spectacle
to the simple natives ; and they gazed with wonder on
the gallant ships, which, fluttering like sea-birds on
their snowy pinions, bounded lightly over the waters,
as if rejoicing in their element.   It touched the stern
hearts of the Conquerors with a glow of rapture, and,
as they felt that Heaven had blessed their undertaking,
they broke forth, by general accord, into the noble
anthem of the *Te Deum*.   But there was no one of
that vast multitude for whom the sight had deeper interest than their commander.   For he looked on it as
the work, in a manner, of his own hands ; and his
bosom swelled with exultation, as he felt he was now
possessed of a power strong enough to command the
lake, and to shake the haughty towers of Tenochtitlan.[10]

[8] The brigantines were still to be seen, preserved, as precious
memorials, long after the conquest, in the dock-yards of Mexico.
Toribio, Hist. de los Indios, MS., Parte 1, cap. 1.

[9] " Dada la señal, soltó la Presa, fuéron saliendo los Vergantines,
sin tocar vno á otro, i apartándose por la Laguna, desplegáron las
Vanderas, tocó la Música, disparáron su Artillería, respondió la del
Exército, así de Castellanos, como de Indios." Herrera, Hist. general, dec. 3, lib. 1, cap. 6..

[10] Ibid., ubi supra.—Rel. Terc. de Cortés, ap. Lorenzana, p. 234.—
Ixtlilxochitl, Venida de los Españoles, p. 19.—Oviedo, Hist. de las
Ind., MS., lib. 33, cap. 48.—The last-mentioned chronicler indulges

The general's next step was to muster his forces in the great square of the capital. He found they amounted to eighty-seven horse, and eight hundred and eighteen foot, of which one hundred and eighteen were arquebusiers and crossbowmen. He had three large field-pieces of iron, and fifteen lighter guns or falconets of brass.[11] The heavier cannon had been transported from Ver Cruz to Tezcuco, a little while before, by the faithful Tlascalans. He was well supplied with shot and balls, with about ten hundred-weight of powder, and fifty thousand copper-headed arrows, made after a pattern furnished by him to the natives.[12] The number and appointments of the army much exceeded what they had been at any time since the flight from Mexico, and showed the good effects of the late arrivals from the Islands. Indeed, taking the fleet into the account, Cortés had never before been in so good a condition for carrying on his operations. Three hundred of the men were sent to man the vessels, thirteen, or rather twelve, in number, one of the smallest having been found, on trial, too dull a sailer to be of service. Half of the crews were required to navigate the ships. There was some difficulty in finding hands for this,

in no slight swell of exultation at this achievement of his hero, which in his opinion throws into shade the boasted exploits of the great Sesostris. "Otras muchas é notables cosas, cuenta este actor que he dicho de aqueste Rey Sesori, en que no me quiero detener, ni las tengo en tanto como esta tranchea, ó canja que es dicho, y los Vergantines de que tratamos, los quáles diéron ocasion á que se oviesen mayores Thesoros é Provincias, é Reynos, que no tuvo Sesori, para la corona Real de Castilla por la industria de Hernando Cortés." Ibid., lib. 33, cap. 22.

[11] Rel. Terc. de Cortés, ap. Lorenzana, p. 234.

[12] Bernal Diaz, Hist. de la Conquista, cap. 147.

as the men were averse to the employment. Cortés selected those who came from Palos, Moguer, and other maritime towns, and, notwithstanding their frequent claims of exemption, as hidalgos, from this menial occupation, he pressed them into the service.[13] Each vessel mounted a piece of heavy ordnance, and was placed under an officer of respectability, to whom Cortés gave a general code of instructions for the government of the little navy, of which he proposed to take the command in person.

He had already sent to his Indian confederates, announcing his purpose of immediately laying siege to Mexico, and called on them to furnish their promised levies within the space of ten days at furthest. The Tlascalans he ordered to join him in Tezcuco; the others were to assemble at Chalco, a more convenient place of rendezvous for the operations in the southern quarter of the Valley. The Tlascalans arrived within the time prescribed, led by the younger Xicotencatl, supported by Chichemecatl, the same doughty warrior who had convoyed the brigantines to Tezcuco. They came fifty thousand strong, according to Cortés,[14]

---

[13] Bernal Diaz, Hist. de la Conquista, ubi supra.—*Hidalguía*, besides its legal privileges, brought with it some fanciful ones to its possessor; if, indeed, it be considered a privilege to have excluded him from many a humble, but honest, calling, by which the poor man might have gained his bread. (For an amusing account of these, see Doblado's Letters from Spain, let. 2.) In no country has the *poor gentleman* afforded so rich a theme for the satirist, as the writings of Le Sage, Cervantes, and Lope de Vega abundantly show.

[14] "Y los Capitanes de Tascaltecal con toda su gente, muy lúcida, y bien armada, . . . y segun la cuenta, que los Capitanes nos diéron, pasaban de cinquenta mil Hombres de Guerra." (Rel. Terc. de Cortés, ap. Lorenzana, p. 236.) "I toda la Gente," adds Herrera,

making a brilliant show with their military finery, and marching proudly forward under the great national banner, emblazoned with a spread eagle, the arms of the republic.[15]   With as blithe and manly a step as if they were going to the battle-ground, they defiled through the gates of the capital, making its walls ring with the friendly shouts of "Castile and Tlascala."

The observations which Cortés had made in his late tour of reconnoissance had determined him to begin the siege by distributing his forces into three separate camps, which he proposed to establish at the extremities of the principal causeways.   By this arrangement the troops would be enabled to move in concert on the capital, and be in the best position to intercept its supplies from the surrounding country.   The first of these points was Tacuba, commanding the fatal causeway of the *noche triste*.   This was assigned to Pedro de Alvarado, with a force consisting, according to Cortés' own statement, of thirty horse, one hundred and sixty-eight Spanish infantry, and five-and-twenty thousand Tlascalans.   Cristóval de Olid had command of the second army, of much the same magnitude, which was to take up its position at Cojohuacan, the city, it will be remembered, overlooking the short

"tardó tres Dias en entrar, segun en sus Memoriales dice Alonso de Ojeda, ni con ser Tezcuco tan gran Ciudad, cabian en ella." Hist. general, dec. 3, lib. 1, cap. 13.

15 " Y sus vāderas tēdidas, y el aue blāca q̄ tienen por armas, q̄ parece águila, con sus alas tendidas." (Bernal Diaz, Hist. de la Conquista, cap. 149.)   A spread eagle of gold, Clavigero considers as the arms of the republic. (Clavigero, Stor. del Messico, tom. ii. p. 145.)   But, as Bernal Diaz speaks of it as "white," it may have been the white heron, which belonged to the house of Xicotencatl.

causeway connected with that of Iztapalapan. Gonzalo de Sandoval had charge of the third division, of equal strength with each of the two preceding, but which was to draw its Indian levies from the forces assembled at Chalco. This officer was to march on Iztapalapan and complete the destruction of that city, begun by Cortés soon after his entrance into the Valley. It was too formidable a post to remain in the rear of the army. The general intended to support the attack with his brigantines, after which the subsequent movements of Sandoval would be determined by circumstances.[16]

Having announced his intended dispositions to his officers, the Spanish commander called his troops together, and made one of those brief and stirring harangues with which he was wont on great occasions to kindle the hearts of his soldiery. "I have taken the last step," he said; "I have brought you to the goal for which you have so long panted. A few days will place you before the gates of Mexico,—the capital from which you were driven with so much ignominy. But we now go forward under the smiles of Providence. Does any one doubt it? Let him but compare our present condition with that in which we found ourselves not twelve months since, when, broken and dispirited, we sought shelter within the walls of Tlascala; nay, with that in which we were but a few months

[16] The precise amount of each division, as given by Cortés, was,—in that of Alvarado, 30 horse, 168 Castilian infantry, and 25,000 Tlascalans; in that of Olid, 33 horse, 178 infantry, 20,000 Tlascalans; and in Sandoval's, 24 horse, 167 infantry, 30,000 Indians. (Rel. Terc., ap. Lorenzana, p. 236.) Diaz reduces the number of native troops to one-third. Hist. de la Conquista, cap. 150.

since, when we took up our quarters in Tezcuco.[17]
Since that time our strength has been nearly doubled.
We are fighting the battles of the Faith, fighting for
our honor, for riches, for revenge. I have brought
you face to face with your foe. It is for you to do
the rest.''[18]

The address of the bold chief was answered by the
thundering acclamations of his followers, who declared
that every man would do his duty under such a leader;
and they only asked to be led against the enemy.[19]
Cortés then caused the regulations for the army, published at Tlascala, to be read again to the troops, with
the assurance that they should be enforced to the letter.

It was arranged that the Indian forces should pre-
cede the Spanish by a day's march, and should halt
for their confederates on the borders of the Tezcucan
territory. A circumstance occurred soon after their
departure which gave bad augury for the future. A

[17] " Que se alegrassen, y esforzassen mucho, pues que veian, que
nuestro Señor nos encaminaba para haber victoria de nuestros Enemigos: porque bien sabian, que quando habiamos entrado en Tesaico,
no habiamos trahido mas de quarenta de Caballo, y que Dios nos
habia socorrido mejor, que lo habiamos pensado." Rel. Terc. de
Cortés, ap. Lorenzana, p. 235.

[18] Oviedo expands what he nevertheless calls the "brebe é sub-
stancial·oracion" of Cortés into treble the length of it as found in
the general's own pages; in which he is imitated by most of the other
chroniclers. Hist. de las Ind., MS., lib. 33, cap. 22.

[19] " Y con estas últimas palabras cesó; y todos respondiéron sin
discrepancia, é á una voce dicentes; Sirvanse Dios y el Emperador
nuestro Señor de tan buen capitan, y de nosotros, que así lo harémos
todos como quien somos, y como se debe esperar de buenos Españoles,
y con tanta voluntad, y deseo, dicho que parecia que cada hora les
era perder vn año de tiempo por estar ya á las manos con los Enemigos." Oviedo, Hist. de las Ind., MS., ubi supra.

quarrel had arisen in the camp at Tezcuco between a Spanish soldier and a Tlascalan chief, in which the latter was badly hurt. He was sent back to Tlascala, and the matter was hushed up, that it might not reach the ears of the general, who, it was known, would not pass it over lightly. Xicotencatl was a near relative of the injured party, and on the first day's halt he took the opportunity to leave the army, with a number of his followers, and set off for Tlascala. Other causes are assigned for his desertion.[20] It is certain that from the first he had looked on the expedition with an evil eye, and had predicted that no good would come of it. He came into it with reluctance, as, indeed, he detested the Spaniards in his heart.

His partner in the command instantly sent information of the affair to the Spanish general, still encamped at Tezcuco. Cortés, who saw at once the mischievous consequences of this defection at such a time, detached a party of Tlascalan and Tezcucan Indians after the fugitive, with instructions to prevail on him, if possible, to return to his duty. They overtook him on the road, and remonstrated with him on his conduct, contrasting it with that of his countrymen generally, and of his own father in particular, the steady friend of the white men. "So much the worse," replied the chieftain : "if they had taken my counsel, they would never have become the dupes of the perfidious strangers."[21]

[20] According to Diaz, the desire to possess himself of the lands of his comrade Chichemecatl, who remained with the army (Hist. de la Conquista, cap. 150); according to Herrera, it was an amour that carried him home. (Hist. general, dec. 3, lib. 1, cap. 17.) Both and all agree on the chief's aversion to the Spaniards and to the war.

[21] "Y la respuesta que le embió á dezir fué, que si el viejo de su

Finding their remonstrances received only with anger or contemptuous taunts, the emissaries returned without accomplishing their object.

Cortés did not hesitate on the course he was to pursue. "Xicotencatl," he said, "had always been the enemy of the Spaniards, first in the field, and since in the council-chamber; openly, or in secret, still the same,—their implacable enemy. There was no use in parleying with the false-hearted Indian." He instantly despatched a small body of horse with an alguacil to arrest the chief wherever he might be found, even though it were in the streets of Tlascala, and to bring him back to Tezcuco. At the same time, he sent information of Xicotencatl's proceedings to the Tlascalan senate, adding that desertion among the Spaniards was punished with death.

The emissaries of Cortés punctually fulfilled his orders. They arrested the fugitive chief,—whether in Tlascala or in its neighborhood is uncertain, — and brought him a prisoner to Tezcuco, where a high gallows, erected in the great square, was prepared for his reception. He was instantly led to the place of execution; his sentence and the cause for which he suffered were publicly proclaimed, and the unfortunate cacique expiated his offence by the vile death of a malefactor. His ample property, consisting of lands, slaves, and some gold, was all confiscated to the Castilian crown.[22]

padre, y Masse Escaci le huvieran creido, que no se huvieran señoreado tanto dellos, que les haze hazer todo lo que quiere : *y por no gastar mas palabras, dixo, que no queria venir.*" Bernal Diaz, Hist. de la Conquista, cap. 150.

[22] So says Herrera, who had in his possession the memorial of

Thus perished Xicotencatl, in the flower of his age, —as dauntless a warrior as ever led an Indian army to battle. He was the first chief who successfully resisted the arms of the invaders; and, had the natives of Anahuac, generally, been animated with a spirit like his, Cortés would probably never have set foot in the capital of Montezuma. He was gifted with a clearer insight into the future than his countrymen; for he saw that the European was an enemy far more to be dreaded than the Aztec. Yet, when he consented to fight under the banner of the white men, he had no right to desert it, and he incurred the penalty prescribed by the code of savage as well as of civilized nations. It is said, indeed, that the Tlascalan senate aided in apprehending him, having previously answered Cortés that his crime was punishable with death by their own laws.[23] It was a bold act, however, thus to execute him in the midst of his people. For he

Ojeda, one of the Spaniards employed to apprehend the chieftain. (Hist. general, dec. 3, lib. 1, cap. 17, and Torquemada, Monarch. Ind., lib. 4, cap. 90.) Bernal Diaz, on the other hand, says that the Tlascalan chief was taken and executed on the road. (Hist. de la Conquista, cap. 150.) But the latter chronicler was probably absent at the time with Alvarado's division, in which he served. Solís, however, prefers his testimony, on the ground that Cortés would not have hazarded the execution of Xicotencatl before the eyes of his own troops. (Conquista, lib. 5, cap. 19.) But the Tlascalans were already well on their way towards Tacuba. A very few only could have remained in Tezcuco, which was occupied by the citizens and the Castilian army,—neither of them very likely to interfere in the prisoner's behalf. His execution there would be an easier matter than in the territory of Tlascala, which he had probably reached before his apprehension.

[23] Herrera, Hist. general, dec. 3, lib. 1, cap. 17.—Torquemada, Monarch. Ind., lib. 4, cap. 90.

was a powerful chief, heir to one of the four seigniories of the republic. His chivalrous qualities made him popular, especially with the younger part of his countrymen; and his garments were torn into shreds at his death and distributed as sacred relics among them. Still, no resistance was offered to the execution of the sentence, and no commotion followed it. He was the only Tlascalan who ever swerved from his loyalty to the Spaniards.

According to the plan of operations settled by Cortés, Sandoval, with his division, was to take a southern direction, while Alvarado and Olid would make the northern circuit of the lakes. These two cavaliers, after getting possession of Tacuba, were to advance to Chapoltepec and demolish the great aqueduct there, which supplied Mexico with water. On the tenth of May they commenced their march; but at Acolman, where they halted for the night, a dispute arose between the soldiers of the two divisions, respecting their quarters. From words they came to blows, and a defiance was even exchanged between the leaders, who entered into the angry feelings of their followers.[24] Intelligence of this was soon communicated to Cortés, who sent at once to the fiery chiefs, imploring them, by their regard for him and the common cause, to lay aside their differences, which must end in their own ruin and that of the expedition. His remonstrance prevailed, at least, so far as to establish a show of reconciliation between the parties. But Olid was not

[24] "Y sobre ello ya auiamos echado mano á las armas los de nuestra Capitanía contra los de Christóual de Oli, y aun los Capitanes desafiados." Bernal Diaz, Hist. de la Conquista, cap. 150.

a man to forget, or easily to forgive; and Alvarado, though frank and liberal, had an impatient temper much more easily excited than appeased. They were never afterwards friends.[25]

The Spaniards met with no opposition on their march. The principal towns were all abandoned by the inhabitants, who had gone to strengthen the garrison of Mexico, or taken refuge with their families among the mountains. Tacuba was in like manner deserted, and the troops once more established themselves in their old quarters in the lordly city of the Tepanecs.[26]

Their first undertaking was to cut off the pipes that conducted the water from the royal streams of Chapoltepec to feed the numerous tanks and fountains which sparkled in the court-yards of the capital. The aqueduct, partly constructed of brick-work and partly of stone and mortar, was raised on a strong though narrow dike, which transported it across an arm of the lake; and the whole work was one of the most pleasing monuments of Mexican civilization. The Indians,

[25] Bernal Diaz, Hist. de la Conquista, cap. 150.—Rel. Terc. de Cortés, ap. Lorenzana, p. 237.—Gomara, Crónica, cap. 130.—Oviedo, Hist. de las Ind., MS., lib. 33, cap. 22.

[26] The Tepanec capital, shorn of its ancient splendors, is now only interesting from its historic associations. "These plains of Tacuba," says the spirited author of "Life in Mexico," "once the theatre of fierce and bloody conflicts, and where, during the siege of Mexico, Alvarado 'of the leap' fixed his camp, now present a very tranquil scene. Tacuba itself is now a small village of mud huts, with some fine old trees, a few very old ruined houses, a ruined church, and some traces of a building, which ——— assured us had been the palace of their last monarch; whilst others declare it to have been the site of the Spanish encampment." Vol. i. let. 13.

well aware of its importance, had stationed a large body of troops for its protection. A battle followed, in which both sides suffered considerably, but the Spaniards were victorious. A part of the aqueduct was demolished, and during the siege no water found its way again to the capital through this channel.

On the following day the combined forces descended on the fatal causeway, to make themselves masters, if possible, of the nearest bridge. They found the dike covered with a swarm of warriors, as numerous as on the night of their disaster, while the surface of the lake was dark with the multitude of canoes. The intrepid Christians strove to advance under a perfect hurricane of missiles from the water and the land, but they made slow progress. Barricades thrown across the causeway embarrassed the cavalry and rendered it nearly useless. The sides of the Indian boats were fortified with bulwarks, which shielded the crews from the arquebuses and cross-bows; and, when the warriors on the dike were hard pushed by the pikemen, they threw themselves fearlessly into the water, as if it were their native element, and, reappearing along the sides of the dike, shot off their arrows and javelins with fatal execution. After a long and obstinate struggle, the Christians were compelled to fall back on their own quarters with disgrace, and—including the allies—with nearly as much damage as they had inflicted on the enemy. Olid, disgusted with the result of the engagement, inveighed against his companion as having involved them in it by his wanton temerity, and drew off his forces the next morning to his own station at Cojohuacan.

The camps, separated by only two leagues, maintained an easy communication with each other. They found abundant employment in foraging the neighboring country for provisions, and in repelling the active sallies of the enemy; on whom they took their revenge by cutting off his supplies. But their own position was precarious, and they looked with impatience for the arrival of the brigantines under Cortés. It was in the latter part of May that Olid took up his quarters at Cojohuacan; and from that time may be dated the commencement of the siege of Mexico.[27]

[27] Rel. Terc. de Cortés, ap. Lorenzana, pp. 237–239.—Ixtlilxochitl, Hist. Chich., MS., cap. 94.—Oviedo, Hist. de las Ind., MS., lib. 33, cap. 22.—Bernal Diaz, Hist. de la Conquista, cap. 50.—Gomara, Crónica, cap. 130.—Clavigero settles this date at the day of Corpus Christi, May 30th. (Clavigero, Stor. del Messico, tom. iii. p. 196.) But the Spaniards left Tezcuco May 10th, according to Cortés; and three weeks could not have intervened between their departure and their occupation of Cojohuacan. Clavigero disposes of this difficulty, it is true, by dating the beginning of their march on the 20th instead of the 10th of May; following the chronology of Herrera, instead of that of Cortés. Surely the general is the better authority of the two.

CHAPTER V.

1521.

No sooner had Cortés received intelligence that his two officers had established themselves in their respective posts, than he ordered Sandoval to march on Iztapalapan. The cavalier's route led him through a country for the most part friendly ; and at Chalco his little body of Spaniards was swelled by the formidable muster of Indian levies who awaited there his approach. After this junction, he continued his march without opposition till he arrived before the hostile city, under whose walls he found a large force drawn up to receive him. A battle followed, and the natives, after maintaining their ground sturdily for some time, were compelled to give way, and to seek refuge either on the water, or in that part of the town which hung over it. The remainder was speedily occupied by the Spaniards.

Meanwhile, Cortés had set sail with his flotilla, intending to support his lieutenant's attack by water. On drawing near the southern shore of the lake, he passed under the shadow of an insulated peak, since named from him the "Rock of the Marquis." It was held by a body of Indians, who saluted the fleet, as it passed, with showers of stones and arrows. Cortés, resolving to punish their audacity, and to clear the lake of his troublesome enemy, instantly landed with a hundred and fifty of his followers. He placed himself at their head, scaled the steep ascent, in the face of a driving storm of missiles, and, reaching the summit, put the garrison to the sword. There was a number of women and children, also, gathered in the place, whom he spared.[1]

On the top of the eminence was a blazing beacon, serving to notify to the inhabitants of the capital when the Spanish fleet weighed anchor. Before Cortés had regained his brigantine, the canoes and *piraguas* of the enemy had left the harbors of Mexico, and were seen darkening the lake for many a rood. There were several hundred of them, all crowded with warriors, and advancing rapidly by means of their oars over the calm bosom of the waters.[2]

Cortés, who regarded his fleet, to use his own language, as "the key of the war," felt the importance of striking a decisive blow in the first encounter with the enemy.[3] It was with chagrin, therefore, that he

---

[1] "It was a beautiful victory," exclaims the Conqueror. "É entrámoslos de tal manera, que ninguno de ellos se escapó, excepto las Mugeres, y Niños ; y en este combate me hiriéron veinte y cinco Españoles, pero fué muy hermosa Victoria." Rel. Terc., ap. Lorenzana, p. 241.

[2] About five hundred boats, according to the general's own estimate (Ibid., loc. cit.) ; but more than four thousand, according to Bernal Diaz (Hist. de la Conquista, cap. 150) ; who, however, was not present.

[3] "Y como yo deseaba mucho, que el primer reencuentro, que con

found his sails rendered useless by the want of wind.
He calmly awaited the approach of the Indian squadron,
which, however, lay on their oars at something more
than musket-shot distance, as if hesitating to encounter
these leviathans of their waters. At this moment, a
light air from land rippled the surface of the lake; it
gradually freshened into a breeze, and Cortés, taking
advantage of the friendly succor, which he may be
excused, under all the circumstances, for regarding as
especially sent him by Heaven, extended his line of
battle, and bore down, under full press of canvas, on
the enemy.[4]

The latter no sooner encountered the bows of their
formidable opponents than they were overturned and
sent to the bottom by the shock, or so much damaged
that they speedily filled and sank. The water was
covered with the wreck of broken canoes, and with
the bodies of men struggling for life in the waves and
vainly imploring their companions to take them on
board their over-crowded vessels. The Spanish fleet,
as it dashed through the mob of boats, sent off its
volleys to the right and left with a terrible effect,
completing the discomfiture of the Aztecs. The latter
made no attempt at resistance, scarcely venturing a
single flight of arrows, but strove with all their strength
to regain the port from which they had so lately issued.

ellos obiessemos, fuesse de mucha victoria; y se hiciesse de manera,
que ellos cobrassen mucho temor de los bergantines, porque la llave
de toda la Guerra estaba en ellos." Rel. Terc., ap. Lorenzana, pp.
241, 242.

[4] "Plugo á nuestro Señor, que estándonos mirando los unos á los
otros, vino un viento de la Tierra muy favorable para embestir con
ellos." Ibid., p. 242.

They were no match in the chase, any more than in the fight, for their terrible antagonist, who, borne on the wings of the wind, careered to and fro at his pleasure, dealing death widely around him, and making the shores ring with the thunders of his ordnance. A few only of the Indian flotilla succeeded in recovering the port, and, gliding up the canals, found a shelter in the bosom of the city, where the heavier burden of the brigantines made it impossible for them to follow. This victory, more complete than even the sanguine temper of Cortés had prognosticated, proved the superiority of the Spaniards, and left them, henceforth, undisputed masters of the Aztec sea.[5]

It was nearly dusk when the squadron, coasting along the great southern causeway, anchored off the point of junction, called Xoloc, where the branch from Cojohuacan meets the principal dike. The avenue widened at this point, so as to afford room for two towers, or turreted temples, built of stone, and surrounded by walls of the same material, which presented altogether a position of some strength, and, at the

5 Rel. Terc., ap. Lorenzana, loc. cit.—Oviedo, Hist. de las Ind., MS., lib. 33, cap. 48.—Sahagun, Hist. de Nueva-España, MS., lib. 12, cap. 32.—I may be excused for again quoting a few verses from a beautiful description in " Madoc," and one as pertinent as it is beautiful:

> " Their thousand boats, and the ten thousand oars,
> From whose broad bowls the waters fall and flash,
> And twice ten thousand feathered helms, and shields,
> Glittering with gold and scarlet plumery.
> Onward they come with song and swelling horn;
> . . . . . On the other side
> Advance the *British* barks ; the freshening breeze
> Fills the broad sail ; around the rushing keel
> The waters sing, while proudly they sail on,
> Lords of the water."
>
>   MADOC, Part 2, canto 25.

present moment, was garrisoned by a body of Aztecs. They were not numerous, and Cortés, landing with his soldiers, succeeded without much difficulty in dislodging the enemy and in getting possession of the works.

It seems to have been originally the general's design to take up his own quarters with Olid at Cojohuacan. But, if so, he now changed his purpose, and wisely fixed on this spot as the best position for his encampment. It was but half a league distant from the capital, and, while it commanded its great southern avenue, had a direct communication with the garrison at Cojohuacan, through which he might receive supplies from the surrounding country. Here, then, he determined to establish his headquarters. He at once caused his heavy iron cannon to be transferred from the brigantines to the causeway, and sent orders to Olid to join him with half his force, while Sandoval was instructed to abandon his present quarters and advance to Cojohuacan, whence he was to detach fifty picked men of his infantry to the camp of Cortés. Having made these arrangements, the general busily occupied himself with strengthening the works at Xoloc and putting them in the best posture of defence.

During the first five or six days after their encampment the Spaniards experienced much annoyance from the enemy, who too late endeavored to prevent their taking up a position so near the capital, and which, had they known much of the science of war, they would have taken better care themselves to secure. Contrary to their usual practice, the Indians made their attacks by night as well as by day. The water swarmed with canoes, which hovered at a distance in terror of the brigantines, but still approached near enough, especially under cover of the darkness, to send showers of arrows into the Christian camp, that fell so thick as to hide the surface of the ground and impede the movements of the soldiers. Others ran along the western side of the causeway, unprotected as it was by the Spanish fleet, and plied their archery with such galling effect that the Spaniards were forced to make a temporary breach in the dike, wide enough to admit two of their own smaller vessels, which, passing through, soon obtained as entire command of the interior basin as they before had of the outer. Still, the bold barbarians, advancing along the causeway, marched up within bow-shot of the Christian ramparts, sending forth such yells and discordant battle-cries that it seemed, in the words of Cortés, "as if heaven and earth were coming together." But they were severely punished for their temerity, as the batteries, which commanded the approaches to the camp, opened a desolating fire, that scattered the assailants and drove them back in confusion to their own quarters.[6]

The two principal avenues to Mexico, those on the south and the west, were now occupied by the Christians. There still remained a third, the great dike of Tepejacac, on the north, which, indeed, taking up the principal street, that passed in a direct line through the

[6] "Y era tanta la multitud," says Cortés, "que por el Agua, y por la Tierra no viamos sino Gente, y daban tantas gritas, y alaridos, que parecia que se hundia el Mundo." Rel. Terc., p. 245.—Oviedo, Hist. de las Ind., MS., lib. 33, cap. 23.—Ixtlilxochitl, Hist. Chich., MS. cap. 95.—Sahagun, Hist. de Nueva-España, MS., lib. 12, cap. 32.

heart of the city, might be regarded as a continuation of the dike of Iztapalapan. By this northern route a means of escape was still left open to the besieged, and they availed themselves of it, at present, to maintain their communications with the country and to supply themselves with provisions. Alvarado, who observed this from his station at Tacuba, advised his commander of it, and the latter instructed Sandoval to take up his position on the causeway. That officer, though suffering at the time from a severe wound received from a lance in one of the late skirmishes, hastened to obey, and thus, by shutting up its only communication with the surrounding country, completed the blockade of the capital.[7]

But Cortés was not content to wait patiently the effects of a dilatory blockade, which might exhaust the patience of his allies and his own resources. He determined to support it by such active assaults on the city as should still further distress the besieged and hasten the hour of surrender. For this purpose he ordered a simultaneous attack, by the two commanders at the other stations, on the quarters nearest their encampments.

On the day appointed, his forces were under arms with the dawn. Mass, as usual, was performed; and the Indian confederates, as they listened with grave attention to the stately and imposing service, regarded with undisguised admiration the devotional reverence shown by the Christians, whom, in their simplicity,

7 Rel. Terc. de Cortés, ap. Lorenzana, pp. 246, 247.—Bernal Diaz, Hist. de la Conquista, cap. 150.—Herrera, Hist. de las Ind., dec. 3, lib. 1, cap. 17.—Defensa, MS., cap. 28.

they looked upon as little less than divinities them-selves.[8]   The Spanish infantry marched in the van, led on by Cortés, attended by a number of cavaliers, dis-mounted like himself.   They had not moved far upon the causeway, when they were brought to a stand by one of the open breaches, that had formerly been trav-ersed by a bridge.   On the farther side a solid rampart of stone and lime had been erected, and behind this a strong body of Aztecs were posted, who discharged on the Spaniards, as they advanced, a thick volley of arrows.   The latter vainly endeavored to dislodge them with their fire-arms and cross-bows ; they were too well secured behind their defences.

Cortés then ordered two of the brigantines, which had kept along, one on each side of the causeway, in order to co-operate with the army, to station them-selves so as to enfilade the position occupied by the enemy.   Thus placed between two well-directed fires, the Indians were compelled to recede.   The soldiers on board the vessels, springing to land, bounded like deer up the sides of the dike.   They were soon fol-lowed by their countrymen under Cortés, who, throw-ing themselves into the water, swam the undefended chasm and joined in pursuit of the enemy.   The Mex-icans fell back, however, in something like order, till they reached another opening in the dike, like the former, dismantled of its bridge, and fortified in the

[8] "Así como fué de dia se dixo vna misa de Espíritu Santo, que todos los Christianos oyéron con mucha devocion ; é aun los Indios, como simples, é no entendientes de tan alto misterio, con admiracion estaban atentos notando el silencio de los cathólicos y el acatamiento que al altar, y al sacerdote los Christianos toviéron hasta recevir la benedicion."   Oviedo, Hist. de las Ind., MS., lib. 33, cap. 24.

same manner by a bulwark of stone, behind which the retreating Aztecs, swimming across the chasm, and reinforced by fresh bodies of their countrymen, again took shelter.

They made good their post, till, again assailed by the cannonade from the brigantines, they were compelled to give way. In this manner breach after breach was carried; and at every fresh instance of success a shout went up from the crews of the vessels, which, answered by the long files of the Spaniards and their confederates on the causeway, made the Valley echo to its borders.

Cortés had now reached the end of the great avenue, where it entered the suburbs. There he halted to give time for the rear-guard to come up with him. It was detained by the labor of filling up the breaches in such a manner as to make a practicable passage for the artillery and horse and to secure one for the rest of the army on its retreat. This important duty was intrusted to the allies, who executed it by tearing down the ramparts on the margins and throwing them into the chasms, and, when this was not sufficient,—for the water was deep around the southern causeway,—by dislodging the great stones and rubbish from the dike itself, which was broad enough to admit of it, and adding them to the pile, until it was raised above the level of the water.

The street on which the Spaniards now entered was the great avenue that intersected the town from north to south, and the same by which they had first visited the capital.[9] It was broad and perfectly straight, and,

9 [This street, which is now called the Calle del Rastro, and traverses

in the distance, dark masses of warriors might be seen
gathering to the support of their countrymen, who
were prepared to dispute the further progress of the
Spaniards. The sides were lined with buildings, the
terraced roofs of which were also crowded with combatants, who, as the army advanced, poured down a
pitiless storm of missiles on their heads, which glanced
harmless, indeed, from the coat of mail, but too often
found their way through the more common *escaupil* of
the soldier, already gaping with many a ghastly rent.
Cortés, to rid himself of this annoyance for the future,
ordered his Indian pioneers to level the principal buildings as they advanced ; in which work of demolition,
no less than in the repair of the breaches, they proved
of inestimable service.[10]

The Spaniards, meanwhile, were steadily, but slowly,
advancing, as the enemy recoiled before the rolling
fire of musketry, though turning, at intervals, to discharge their javelins and arrows against their pursuers.
In this way they kept along the great street until their
course was interrupted by a wide ditch or canal, once
traversed by a bridge, of which only a few planks now
remained. These were broken by the Indians the

the whole city from north to south, leading from the Calle del Relox
to the causeway of Guadalupe or Tepeyacac, was known at the period
immediately following the Conquest as the Calle de Iztapalapa, which
name was given to it through its whole extent. In the time of the
ancient Mexicans its course was intercepted by the great temple, the
principal door of which fronted upon it. After this edifice had been
demolished, the street was opened from one end to the other. Conquista de Méjico (trad. de Vega), tom. ii. p. 157.]

[10] Sahagun, Hist. de Nueva-España, MS., lib. 12, cap. 32.—Ixtlilxochitl, Hist. Chich., MS., cap. 95.—Oviedo, Hist. de las Ind., MS.,
lib. 33, cap. 23.—Rel. Terc. de Cortés, ap. Lorenzana, pp. 247, 248.

moment they had crossed, and a formidable array of spears was instantly seen bristling over the summit of a solid rampart of stone, which protected the opposite side of the canal. Cortés was no longer supported by his brigantines, which the shallowness of the canals prevented from penetrating into the suburbs. He brought forward his arquebusiers, who, protected by the targets of their comrades, opened a fire on the enemy. But the balls fell harmless from the bulwarks of stone ; while the assailants presented but too easy a mark to their opponents.

The general then caused the heavy guns to be brought up, and opened a lively cannonade, which soon cleared a breach in the works, through which the musketeers and crossbowmen poured in their volleys thick as hail. The Indians now gave way in disorder, after having held their antagonists at bay for two hours.[11] The latter, jumping into the shallow water, scaled the oppo-

---

[11] Rel. Terc. de Cortés, ubi supra.—Ixtlilxochitl, Hist. Chich., MS., cap. 95.—Here terminates the work last cited of the Tezcucan chronicler ; who has accompanied us from the earliest period of our narrative down to this point in the final siege of the capital. Whether the concluding pages of the manuscript have been lost, or whether he was interrupted by death, it is impossible to say. But the deficiency is supplied by a brief sketch of the principal events of the siege, which he has left in another of his writings. He had, undoubtedly, uncommon sources of information in his knowledge of the Indian languages and picture-writing, and in the oral testimony which he was at pains to collect from the actors in the scenes he describes. All these advantages are too often counterbalanced by a singular incapacity for discriminating —I will not say, between historic truth and falsehood (for what is truth ?)—but between the probable, or rather the possible, and the impossible. One of the generation of primitive converts to the Romish faith, he lived in a state of twilight civilization, when, if miracles were not easily wrought, it was at least easy to believe them.

E*

site bank without further resistance, and drove the enemy along the street towards the square, where the sacred pyramid reared its colossal bulk high over the other edifices of the city.

It was a spot too familiar to the Spaniards. On one side stood the palace of Axayacatl, their old quarters, the scene to many of them of so much suffering.[12] Opposite was the pile of low, irregular buildings once the residence of the unfortunate Montezuma;[13] while a third side of the square was flanked by the *Coatepantli*, or Wall of Serpents, which encompassed the great *teocalli* with its little city of holy edifices.[14] The Spaniards halted at the entrance of the square, as if oppressed, and for the moment overpowered, by the bitter recollections that crowded on their minds. But their intrepid leader, impatient at their hesitation, loudly called on them to advance before the Aztecs had time to rally; and, grasping his target in one hand, and waving his sword high above his head with the other, he cried his war-cry of "St. Jago," and led them at once against the enemy.[15]

[12] [In the street of Santa Teresa. Conquista de Méjico (trad. de Vega), tom. ii. p. 158.]

[13] [Which forms now what is called " El Empedradillo." Ibid.]

[14] [This wall, adorned with serpents, and crowned with the heads, strung together on stakes, of the human victims sacrificed in the temple, formed the front of the Plaza on the south side, extending from the corner of the Calle de Plateros east, towards the chains that enclose the cemetery of the cathedral. Ibid.]

[15] " I con todo eso no se determinaban los Christianos de entrar en la Plaça; por lo qual diciendo Hernando Cortés, que no era tiempo de mostrar cansancio, ni cobardía, con vna Rodela en la mano, apellidando Santiago, arremetió el primero." Herrera, Hist. general, dec. 3, lib. 1, cap. 18.

The Mexicans, intimidated by the presence of their detested foe, who, in spite of all their efforts, had again forced his way into the heart of their city, made no further resistance, but retreated, or rather fled, for refuge into the sacred enclosure of the *teocalli*, where the numerous buildings scattered over its ample area afforded many good points of defence. A few priests, clad in their usual wild and blood-stained vestments, were to be seen lingering on the terraces which wound round the stately sides of the pyramid, chanting hymns in honor of their god, and encouraging the warriors below to battle bravely for his altars.[16]

The Spaniards poured through the open gates into the area, and a small party rushed up the winding corridors to its summit. No vestige now remained there of the Cross, or of any other symbol of the pure faith to which it had been dedicated. A new effigy of the Aztec war-god had taken the place of the one demolished by the Christians, and raised its fantastic and hideous form in the same niche which had been occupied by its predecessor. The Spaniards soon tore away its golden mask and the rich jewels with which it was bedizened, and, hurling the struggling priests down the sides of the pyramid, made the best of their way to their comrades in the area. It was full time.[17]

[16] Sahagun, Hist. de Nueva-España, MS., lib. 12, cap. 32.

[17] Ixtlilxochitl, in his Thirteenth Relacion, embracing among other things a brief notice of the capture of Mexico, of which an edition has been given to the world by the industrious Bustamante, bestows the credit of this exploit on Cortés himself. "En la capilla mayor donde estaba Huitzilopoxctli, que llegáron Cortés é Ixtlilxuchitl á un tiempo, y ambos embistiéron con el ídolo. *Cortés cogió la máscara de oro que tenia puesta este ídolo* con ciertas piedras preciosas que estaban engastadas en ella." Venida de los Españoles, p. 29.

The Aztecs, indignant at the sacrilegious outrage perpetrated before their eyes, and gathering courage from the inspiration of the place, under the very presence of their deities, raised a yell of horror and vindictive fury, as, throwing themselves into something like order, they sprang, by a common impulse, on the Spaniards. The latter, who had halted near the entrance, though taken by surprise, made an effort to maintain their position at the gateway. But in vain; for the headlong rush of the assailants drove them at once into the square, where they were attacked by other bodies of Indians, pouring in from the neighboring streets. Broken, and losing their presence of mind, the troops made no attempt to rally, but, crossing the square, and abandoning the cannon, planted there, to the enemy, they hurried down the great street of Iztapalapan. Here they were soon mingled with the allies, who choked up the way, and who, catching the panic of the Spaniards, increased the confusion, while the eyes of the fugitives, blinded by the missiles that rained on them from the *azoteas*, were scarcely capable of distinguishing friend from foe. In vain Cortés endeavored to stay the torrent, and to restore order. His voice was drowned in the wild uproar, as he was swept away, like drift-wood, by the fury of the current.

All seemed to be lost;—when suddenly sounds were heard in an adjoining street, like the distant tramp of horses galloping rapidly over the pavement. They drew nearer and nearer, and a body of cavalry soon emerged on the great square. Though but a handful in number, they plunged boldly into the thick of the

enemy. We have often had occasion to notice the
superstitious dread entertained by the Indians of the
horse and his rider. And, although the long residence
of the cavalry in the capital had familiarized the natives in some measure with their presence, so long a
time had now elapsed since they had beheld them
that all their former mysterious terrors revived in full
force; and, when thus suddenly assailed in flank by
the formidable apparition, they were seized with a
panic and fell into confusion. It soon spread to the
leading files, and Cortés, perceiving his advantage,
turned with the rapidity of lightning, and, at this
time supported by his followers, succeeded in driving
the enemy with some loss back into the enclosure.

It was now the hour of vespers, and, as night must
soon overtake them, he made no further attempt to
pursue his advantage. Ordering the trumpets, therefore, to sound a retreat, he drew off his forces in good
order, taking with him the artillery which had been
abandoned in the square. The allies first went off the
ground, followed by the Spanish infantry, while the
rear was protected by the horse, thus reversing the
order of march on their entrance. The Aztecs hung
on the closing files, and, though driven back by frequent charges of the cavalry, still followed in the distance, shooting off their ineffectual missiles, and filling
the air with wild cries and howlings, like a herd of
ravenous wolves disappointed of their prey. It was
late before the army reached its quarters at Xoloc.[18]

[18] "Los de Caballo revolvian sobre ellos, que siempre alanceaban,
ó mataban algunos; é como la Calle era muy larga, hubo lugar de
hacerse esto quatro, ó cinco veces. É aunque los Enemigos vian

Cortés had been well supported by Alvarado and Sandoval in this assault on the city; though neither of these commanders had penetrated the suburbs, deterred, perhaps, by the difficulties of the passage, which in Alvarado's case were greater than those presented to Cortés, from the greater number of breaches with which the dike in his quarter was intersected. Something was owing, too, to the want of brigantines, until Cortés supplied the deficiency by detaching half of his little navy to the support of his officers. Without their co-operation, however, the general himself could not have advanced so far, nor, perhaps, have succeeded at all in setting foot within the city. The success of this assault spread consternation not only among the Mexicans, but their vassals, as they saw that the formidable preparations for defence were to avail little against the white man, who had so soon, in spite of them, forced his way into the very heart of the capital. Several of the neighboring places, in consequence, now showed a willingness to shake off their allegiance, and claimed the protection of the Spaniards. Among these were the territory of Xochimilco, so roughly treated by the invaders, and some tribes of Otomies, a rude but valiant people, who dwelt on the western confines of the Valley.[19] Their support was

que recibian daño, venian los Perros tan rabiosos, que en ninguna manera los podiamos detener, ni que nos dejassen de seguir." Rel. Terc. de Cortés, ap. Lorenzana, p. 250.—Herrera, Hist. general, dec. 3, lib. 1, cap. 18.—Sahagun, Hist. de Nueva-España, MS., lib. 12, cap. 32.—Oviedo, Hist. de las Ind., MS., lib. 33, cap. 23.

[19] The great mass of the Otomies were an untamed race, who roamed over the broad tracks of the plateau, far away to the north. But many of them, who found their way into the Valley, became blended

valuable, not so much from the additional reinforcements which it brought, as from the greater security
it gave to the army, whose outposts were perpetually
menaced by these warlike barbarians.[20]

The most important aid which the Spaniards received
at this time was from Tezcuco, whose prince, Ixtlilxochitl, gathered the whole strength of his levies, to the
number of fifty thousand, if we are to credit Cortés,
and led them in person to the Christian camp. By the
general's orders, they were distributed among the three
divisions of the besiegers.[21]

Thus strengthened, Cortés prepared to make another
attack upon the capital, and that before it should have
time to recover from the former. Orders were given
to his lieutenants on the other causeways to march at
the same time, and co-operate with him, as before, in
the assault. It was conducted in precisely the same

with the Tezcucan, and even with the Tlascalan nation, making some
of the best soldiers in their armies.

[20] [The Otomies inhabited all the country of Tula on the west,
where their language is well preserved. Conquista de Méjico (trad.
de Vega), tom. ii. p. 161.]

[21] " Istrisuchil [Ixtlilxochitl], que es de edad de veinte y tres, ó
veinte y quatro años, muy esforzado, amado, y temido de todos."
(Rel. Terc. de Cortés, ap. Lorenzana, p. 251.) The greatest obscurity
prevails among historians in respect to this prince, whom they seem
to have confounded very often with his brother and predecessor on
the throne of Tezcuco. It is rare that either of them is mentioned
by any other than his baptismal name of Hernando ; and, if Herrera
is correct in the assertion that this name was assumed by both, it may
explain in some degree the confusion. (Hist. general, dec. 3, lib. 1,
cap. 18.) I have conformed in the main to the old Tezcucan chronicler, who gathered his account of his kinsman, as he tells us, from the
records of his nation, and from the oral testimony of the contemporaries of the prince himself. Venida de los Españoles, pp. 30, 31.

manner as on the previous entry, the infantry taking the van, and the allies and cavalry following. But, to the great dismay of the Spaniards, they found two-thirds of the breaches restored to their former state, and the stones and other materials, with which they had been stopped, removed by the indefatigable enemy. They were again obliged to bring up the cannon, the brigantines ran alongside, and the enemy was dislodged, and driven from post to post, in the same manner as on the preceding attack. In short, the whole work was to be done over again. It was not till an hour after noon, that the army had won a footing in the suburbs.

Here their progress was not so difficult as before; for the buildings, from the terraces of which they had experienced the most annoyance, had been swept away. Still, it was only step by step that they forced a passage in face of the Mexican militia, who disputed their advance with the same spirit as before. Cortés, who would willingly have spared the inhabitants, if he could have brought them to terms, saw them with regret, as he says, thus desperately bent on a war of extermination. He conceived that there would be no way more likely to affect their minds than by destroying at once some of the principal edifices, which they were accustomed to venerate as the pride and ornament of the city.[22]

[22] "Daban ocasion, y nos forzaban á que totalmente les destruyessemos. É de esta postrera tenia mas sentimiento, y me pesaba en el alma, y pensaba que forma ternia para los atemorizar, de manera, que viniessen en conocimiento de su yerro, y de el daño, que podian recibir de nosotros, y no hacia sino quemalles, y derrocalles las Torres de sus Ídolos, y sus Casas." Rel. Terc. de Cortés, ap. Lorenzana, p. 254.

Marching into the great square, he selected, as the first to be destroyed, the old palace of Axayacatl, his former barracks. The ample range of low buildings was, it is true, constructed of stone ; but the interior, as well as the outworks, the turrets, and roofs, was of wood. The Spaniards, whose associations with the pile were of so gloomy a character, sprang to the work of destruction with a satisfaction like that which the French mob may have felt in the demolition of the Bastile. Torches and firebrands were thrown about in all directions; the lower parts of the building were speedily on fire, which, running along the inflammable hangings and wood-work of the interior, rapidly spread to the second floor. There the element took freer range, and, before it was visible from without, sent up from every aperture and crevice a dense column of vapor, that hung like a funereal pall over the city. This was dissipated by a bright sheet of flame, which enveloped all the upper regions of the vast pile, till, the supporters giving way, the wide range of turreted chambers fell, amidst clouds of dust and ashes, with an appalling crash, that for a moment stayed the Spaniards in the work of devastation.[23]

It was but for a moment. On the other side of the square, adjoining Montezuma's residence, were several buildings, as the reader is aware, appropriated to animals. One of these was now marked for destruction,

[23] [The ruins of this building were brought to light in the process of laying the foundations of the houses recently constructed on the southern side of the street of Santa Teresa, adjoining the convent of the Conception. Conquista de Méjico (trad. de Vega), tom. ii. p. 162.]

—the House of Birds, filled with specimens of all the painted varieties which swarmed over the wide forests of Mexico. It was an airy and elegant building, after the Indian fashion, and, viewed in connection with its object, was undoubtedly a remarkable proof of refinement and intellectual taste in a barbarous monarch. Its light, combustible materials, of wood and bamboo, formed a striking contrast to the heavy stone edifices around it, and made it obviously convenient for the present purpose of the invaders. The torches were applied, and the fanciful structure was soon wrapped in flames, that sent their baleful splendors far and wide over city and lake. Its feathered inhabitants either perished in the fire, or those of stronger wing, bursting the burning lattice-work of the aviary, soared high into the air, and, fluttering for a while over the devoted city, fled with loud screams to their native forests beyond the mountains.

The Aztecs gazed with inexpressible horror on this destruction of the venerable abode of their monarchs and of the monuments of their luxury and splendor. Their rage was exasperated almost to madness as they beheld their hated foes the Tlascalans busy in the work of desolation, and aided by the Tezcucans, their own allies, and not unfrequently their kinsmen. They vented their fury in bitter execrations, especially on the young prince Ixtlilxochitl, who, marching side by side with Cortés, took his full share in the dangers of the day. The warriors from the house-tops poured the most opprobrious epithets on him as he passed, denouncing him as a false-hearted traitor; false to his country and his blood,—reproaches not altogether

unmerited, as his kinsman, who chronicles the circumstance, candidly confesses.[24] He gave little heed to
their taunts, however, holding on his way with the
dogged resolution of one true to the cause in which he
was embarked; and, when he entered the great square,
he grappled with the leader of the Aztec forces,
wrenched a lance from his grasp, won by the latter
from the Christians, and dealt him a blow with his
mace, or *maquahuitl*, which brought him lifeless to the
ground.[25]

The Spanish commander, having accomplished the
work of destruction, sounded a retreat, sending on the
Indian allies, who blocked up the way before him. The
Mexicans, maddened by their losses, in wild transports
of fury hung close on his rear, and, though driven back
by the cavalry, still returned, throwing themselves desperately under the horses, striving to tear the riders
from their saddles, and content to throw away their
own lives for one blow at their enemy. Fortunately,
the greater part of their militia was engaged with the
assailants on the opposite quarters of the city, but, thus
crippled, they pushed the Spaniards under Cortés so
vigorously that few reached the camp that night without bearing on their bodies some token of the desperate
conflict.[26]

[24] " Y desde las azoteas deshonrarle llamándole de traidor contra su
patria y deudos, y otras razones pesadas, que á la verdad *á ellos les
sobraba la razon;* mas Ixtlilxuchitl callaba y peleaba, que mas esti-
maba la amistad y salud de los Cristianos que todo esto." Venida de
los Españoles, p. 32.

[25] Ibid., p. 29.

[26] For the preceding pages relating to this second assault, see Rel.
Terc. de Cortés, ap. Lorenzana, pp. 254-256,—Sahagun, Hist. de

On the following day, and, indeed, on several days following, the general repeated his assaults with as little care for repose as if he and his men had been made of iron. On one occasion he advanced some way down the street of Tacuba, in which he carried three of the bridges, desirous, if possible, to open a communication with Alvarado, posted on the contiguous causeway. But the Spaniards in that quarter had not penetrated beyond the suburbs, still impeded by the severe character of the ground, and wanting, it may be, somewhat of that fiery impetuosity which the soldier feels who fights under the eye of his chief.

In each of these assaults the breaches were found more or less restored to their original state by the pertinacious Mexicans, and the materials, which had been deposited in them with so much labor, again removed. It may seem strange that Cortés did not take measures to guard against the repetition of an act which caused so much delay and embarrassment to his operations. He notices this in his Letter to the Emperor, in which he says that to do so would have required either that he should have established his quarters in the city itself, which would have surrounded him with enemies and cut off his communications with the country, or that he should have posted a sufficient guard of Spaniards—for the natives were out of the question—to protect the breaches by night, a duty altogether beyond the strength of men engaged in so arduous service through the day.[27]

Nueva-España, MS., lib. 12, cap. 33,—Oviedo, Hist. de las Ind., MS., lib. 33, cap. 24,—Defensa, MS., cap. 28.

[27] Rel. Terc., ap. Lorenzana, p. 259.

Yet this was the course adopted by Alvarado; who stationed at night a guard of forty soldiers for the defence of the opening nearest to the enemy. This was relieved by a similar detachment, in a few hours, and this again by a third, the two former still lying on their post; so that on an alarm a body of one hundred and twenty soldiers was ready on the spot to repel an attack. Sometimes, indeed, the whole division took up their bivouac in the neighborhood of the breach, resting on their arms, and ready for instant action.[28]

But a life of such incessant toil and vigilance was almost too severe even for the stubborn constitutions of the Spaniards. "Through the long night," exclaims Diaz, who served in Alvarado's division, "we kept our dreary watch; neither wind, nor wet, nor cold availing anything. There we stood, smarting as we were from the wounds we had received in the fight of the preceding day." [29] It was the rainy season, which continues in that country from July to September;[30] and the surface of the causeways, flooded by the storms,

---

[28] Bernal Diaz, Hist. de la Conquista, cap. 151.—According to Herrera, Alvarado and Sandoval did not conceal their disapprobation of the course pursued by their commander in respect to the breaches: "I Alvarado, i Sandoval, por su parte, tambien lo hiciéron mui bien, culpando á Hernando Cortes por estas retiradas, queriendo muchos que se quedara en lo ganado, por no bolver tantas veces á ello." Hist. general, dec. 3, lib. 1, cap. 19.

[29] "Porque como era de noche, no aguardauan mucho, y desta manera que he dicho velauamos, que ni porque llouiesse, ni vientos, ni frios, y aunque estauamos metidos en medio de grandes lodos, y heridos, alli auiamos de estar." Hist. de la Conquista, cap. 151.

[30] [That is to say, the more violent part of the rainy season, which lasts, in fact, from May or June to October. Conquista de Méjico (trad. de Vega), tom. ii. p. 165.]

and broken up by the constant movement of such large bodies of men, was converted into a marsh, or rather quagmire, which added inconceivably to the distresses of the army.

The troops under Cortés were scarcely in a better situation. But few of them could find shelter in the rude towers that garnished the works of Xoloc. The greater part were compelled to bivouac in the open air, exposed to all the inclemency of the weather. Every man, unless his wounds prevented it, was required by the camp regulations to sleep on his arms; and they were often roused from their hasty slumbers by the midnight call to battle. For Guatemozin, contrary to the usual practice of his countrymen, frequently selected the hours of darkness to aim a blow at the enemy. "In short," exclaims the veteran soldier above quoted, "so unintermitting were our engagements, by day and by night, during the three months in which we lay before the capital, that to recount them all would but exhaust the reader's patience, and make him fancy he was perusing the incredible feats of a knight-errant of romance."[31]

The Aztec emperor conducted his operations on a systematic plan, which showed some approach to military science. He not unfrequently made simultaneous attacks on the three several divisions of the Spaniards established on the causeways, and on the garrisons at

[31] "Porque nouenta y tres dias estuuímos sobre esta tan fuerte ciudad, cada dia é de noche teniamos guerras, y combates; é no lo pongo aquí por capítulos lo que cada dia haziamos, porque me parece que seria gran proligidad, é seria cosa para nunca acabar, y pareceria a los libros de Amadis, é de otros corros de caualleros." Hist. de la Conquista, ubi supra.

their extremities. To accomplish this, he enforced the service not merely of his own militia of the capital, but of the great towns in the neighborhood, who all moved in concert, at the well-known signal of the beacon-fire, or of the huge drum struck by the priests on the summit of the temple. One of these general attacks, it was observed, whether from accident or design, took place on the eve of St. John the Baptist, the anniversary of the day on which the Spaniards made their second entry into the Mexican capital.[32]

Notwithstanding the severe drain on his forces by this incessant warfare, the young monarch contrived to relieve them in some degree by different detachments, which took the place of one another. This was apparent from the different uniforms and military badges of the Indian battalions that successively came and disappeared from the field. At night a strict guard was maintained in the Aztec quarters, a thing not common with the nations of the plateau. The outposts of the hostile armies were stationed within sight of each other. That of the Mexicans was usually placed in the neighborhood of some wide breach, and its position was marked by a large fire in front. The hours for relieving guard were intimated by the shrill Aztec whistle, while bodies of men might be seen moving behind the flame, which threw a still ruddier glow over the cinnamon-colored skins of the warriors.

While thus active on land, Guatemozin was not idle on the water. He was too wise, indeed, to cope with

[32] Bernal Diaz, Hist. de la Conquista, ubi supra.—Sahagun, Hist. de Nueva-España, MS., lib. 12, cap. 33.

the Spanish navy again in open battle; but he resorted to stratagem, so much more congenial to Indian warfare. He placed a large number of canoes in ambuscade among the tall reeds which fringed the southern shores of the lake, and caused piles, at the same time, to be driven into the neighboring shallows. Several *piraguas*, or boats of a larger size, then issued forth, and rowed near the spot where the Spanish brigantines were moored. Two of the smallest vessels, supposing the Indian barks were conveying provisions to the besieged, instantly stood after them, as had been foreseen. The Aztec boats fled for shelter to the reedy thicket where their companions lay in ambush. The Spaniards, following, were soon entangled among the palisades under the water. They were instantly surrounded by the whole swarm of Indian canoes, most of the men were wounded, several, including the two commanders, slain, and one of the brigantines fell—a useless prize—into the hands of the victors. Among the slain was Pedro Barba, captain of the crossbowmen, a gallant officer, who had highly distinguished himself in the Conquest. This disaster occasioned much mortification to Cortés. It was a salutary lesson, that stood him in good stead during the remainder of the war.[33]

Thus the contest was waged by land and by water,— on the causeway, the city, and the lake. Whatever else might fail, the capital of the Aztec empire was true to itself, and, mindful of its ancient renown, opposed a bold front to its enemies in every direction.

[33] Bernal Diaz, Hist. de la Conquista, cap. 151.—Sahagun, Hist. de Nueva-España, MS., lib. 12, cap. 34.

As in a body whose extremities have been struck with death, life still rallied in the heart, and seemed to beat there, for the time, with even a more vigorous pulsation than ever.

It may appear extraordinary that Guatemozin should have been able to provide for the maintenance of the crowded population now gathered in the metropolis, especially as the avenues were all in the possession of the besieging army.[34]   But, independently of the preparations made with this view before the siege, and of the loathsome sustenance daily furnished by the victims for sacrifice, supplies were constantly obtained from the surrounding country across the lake.   This was so conducted, for a time, as in a great measure to escape observation; and even when the brigantines were commanded to cruise day and night, and sweep the waters of the boats employed in this service, many still contrived, under cover of the darkness, to elude the vigilance of the cruisers, and brought their cargoes into port.   It was not till the great towns in the neighborhood cast off their allegiance that the supply began to fail, from the failure of its sources.   This defection was more frequent, as the inhabitants became convinced that the government, incompetent to its own defence, must be still more so to theirs; and the Aztec metropolis saw its great vassals fall off one after another, as the tree over which decay is stealing parts with its leaves at the first blast of the tempest.[35]

[34] I recollect meeting with no estimate of their numbers; nor, in the loose arithmetic of the Conquerors, would it be worth much.   They must, however, have been very great, to enable them to meet the assailants so promptly and efficiently on every point.

[35] Defensa, MS., cap. 28.—Sahagun, Hist. de Nueva-España, MS.,

The cities which now claimed the Spanish general's protection supplied the camp with an incredible number of warriors; a number which, if we admit Cortés' own estimate, one hundred and fifty thousand,[36] could have only served to embarrass his operations on the long extended causeways. Yet it is true that the Valley, teeming with towns and villages, swarmed with a population—and one, too, in which every man was a warrior—greatly exceeding that of the present day. These levies were distributed among the three garrisons at the terminations of the causeways; and many found active employment in foraging the country for provisions, and yet more in carrying on hostilities against the places still unfriendly to the Spaniards.

Cortés found further occupation for them in the construction of barracks for his troops, who suffered greatly from exposure to the incessant rains of the season, which were observed to fall more heavily by night than by day. Quantities of stone and timber were obtained from the buildings that had been demolished in the city. They were transported in the brigantines to the causeway, and from these materials a row of huts or barracks was constructed, extending on either side of the works of Xoloc. It may give some idea of the great breadth of the causeway at this place, one of the deepest parts of the lake, to add that, although the barracks were erected in parallel lines on the opposite

lib. 12, cap. 34.—The principal cities were Mexicaltzinco, Cuitlahuac, Iztapalapan, Mizquiz, Huitzilopochco, Colhuacan.

[36] "Y como aquel dia llevabamos mas de ciento y cincuenta mil Hombres de Guerra." Rel. Terc., ap. Lorenzana, p. 280.

sides of it, there still remained space enough for the army to defile between.[37]

By this arrangement, ample accommodations were furnished for the Spanish troops and their Indian attendants, amounting in all to about two thousand. The great body of the allies, with a small detachment of horse and infantry, were quartered at the neighboring post of Cojohuacan, which served to protect the rear of the encampment and to maintain its communications with the country. A similar disposition of forces took place in the other divisions of the army, under Alvarado and Sandoval, though the accommodations provided for the shelter of the troops on their causeways were not so substantial as those for the division of Cortés.

The Spanish camp was supplied with provisions from the friendly towns in the neighborhood, and especially from Tezcuco.[38] They consisted of fish, the fruits of the country, particularly a sort of fig borne by the *tuna (cactus opuntia)*, and a species of cherry, or something much resembling it, which grew abundantly at this

[37] "Y vea Vuestra Magestad," says Cortés to the emperor, "que tan ancha puede ser la Calzada, que va por lo mas hondo de la Laguna, que de la una parte, y de la otra iban estas Casas, y quedaba en medio hecha Calle, que muy á placer á pie, y á caballo ibamos, y veniamos por ella." Rel. Terc., ap. Lorenzana, p. 260.

[38] The greatest difficulty under which the troops labored, according to Diaz, was that of obtaining the requisite medicaments for their wounds. But this was in a great degree obviated by a Catalan soldier, who by virtue of his prayers and incantations wrought wonderful cures both on the Spaniards and their allies. The latter, as the more ignorant, flocked in crowds to the tent of this military Æsculapius, whose success was doubtless in a direct ratio to the faith of his patients. Hist. de la Conquista, ubi supra.

season. But their principal food was the *tortillas*, cakes of Indian meal, still common in Mexico, for which bake-houses were established, under the care of the natives, in the garrison towns commanding the causeways.[39] The allies, as appears too probable, reinforced their frugal fare with an occasional banquet on human flesh, for which the battle-field unhappily afforded them too much facility, and which, however shocking to the feelings of Cortés, he did not consider himself in a situation, at that moment, to prevent.[40]

Thus the tempest, which had been so long mustering,

[39] Diaz mourns over this unsavory diet. (Hist. de la Conquista, loc. cit.) Yet the Indian fig is an agreeable, nutritious fruit; and the *tortilla*, made of maize flour, with a slight infusion of lime, though not precisely a *morceau friand*, might pass for very tolerable camp fare. According to the lively Author of "Life in Mexico," it is made now precisely as it was in the days of the Aztecs. If so, a cooking receipt is almost the only thing that has not changed in this country of revolutions.

[40] " Quo strages," says Martyr, "erat crudelior, eo magis copiose ac opipare cœnabant Guazuzingui & Tascaltecani, cæterique prouinciales auxiliarii, qui soliti sunt hostes in prœlio cadentes intra suos ventres sepelire; nec vetare ausus fuisset Cortesius." (De Orbe Novo, dec. 5, cap. 8.) "Y los otros les mostraban los de su Ciudad hechos pedazos, diciéndoles, que los habian de cenar aquella noche, y almorzar otro dia, como de hecho lo hacian." (Rel. Terc. de Cortés, ap. Lorenzana, p. 256.) Yet one may well be startled by the assertion of Oviedo, that the carnivorous monsters fished up the bloated bodies of those drowned in the lake to swell their repast! "Ni podian ver los ojos de los Christianos, é Cathólicos, mas espantable é aborrecida cosa, que ver en el Real de los Amigos confederados el continuo exercicio de comer carne asada, ó cocida de los Indios enemigos, é aun de los que mataban en las canoas, ó se ahogaban, é despues el agua los echaba en la superficie de la laguna, ó en la costa, no los dexaban de pescar, é aposentar en sus vientres." Hist. de las Ind., MS., lib. 33, cap. 24.

broke at length, in all its fury, on the Aztec capital. Its unhappy inmates beheld the hostile regions encompassing them about, with their glittering files stretching as far as the eye could reach. They saw themselves deserted by their allies and vassals in their utmost need; the fierce stranger penetrating into their secret places, violating their temples, plundering their palaces, wasting the fair city by day, firing its suburbs by night, and intrenching himself in solid edifices under their walls, as if determined never to withdraw his foot while one stone remained upon another. All this they saw; yet their spirits were unbroken; and, though famine and pestilence were beginning to creep over them, they still showed the same determined front to their enemies. Cortés, who would gladly have spared the town and its inhabitants, beheld this resolution with astonishment. He intimated more than once, by means of the prisoners whom he released, his willingness to grant them fair terms of capitulation. Day after day he fully expected his proffers would be accepted. But day after day he was disappointed.[41] He had yet to learn how tenacious was the memory of the Aztecs, and that, whatever might be the horrors of their present situation, and their fears for the future, they were all forgotten in their hatred of the white man.

[41] " I confidently expected both on that and the preceding day that they would come with proposals of peace, as I had myself, whether victorious or otherwise, constantly made overtures to that end. But on their part we never perceived a sign of such intention." Rel. Terc. de Cortés, ap. Lorenzana, p. 261.

CHAPTER VI.

1521.

FAMINE was now gradually working its way into the
heart of the beleaguered city. It seemed certain that,
with this strict blockade, the crowded population must
in the end be driven to capitulate, though no arm
should be raised against them. But it required time;
and the Spaniards, though constant and enduring by
nature, began to be impatient of hardships scarcely
inferior to those experienced by the besieged. In some
respects their condition was even worse, exposed as
they were to the cold, drenching rains, which fell with
little intermission, rendering their situation dreary and
disastrous in the extreme.

In this state of things, there were many who would
willingly have shortened their sufferings and taken the
chance of carrying the place by a *coup de main*. Others
thought it would be best to get possession of the great
market of Tlatelolco, which, from its situation in the
northwestern part of the city, might afford the means
of communication with the camps of both Alvarado
and Sandoval. This place, encompassed by spacious
porticoes, would furnish accommodations for a numer-

(126)

ous host ; and, once established in the capital, the Spaniards would be in a position to follow up the blow with far more effect than at a distance.

These arguments were pressed by several of the officers, particularly by Alderete, the royal treasurer, a person of much consideration, not only from his rank, but from the capacity and zeal he had shown in the service. In deference to their wishes, Cortés summoned a council of war, and laid the matter before it. The treasurer's views were espoused by most of the high-mettled cavaliers, who looked with eagerness to any change of their present forlorn and wearisome life ; and Cortés, thinking it, probably, more prudent to adopt the less expedient course than to enforce a cold and reluctant obedience to his own opinion, suffered himself to be overruled.[1]

A day was fixed for the assault, which was to be made simultaneously by the two divisions under Alvarado and the commander-in-chief. Sandoval was instructed to draw off the greater part of his forces from the northern causeway and to unite himself with Alvarado, while seventy picked soldiers were to be detached to the support of Cortés.

On the appointed morning, the two armies, after the usual celebration of mass, advanced along their respective causeways against the city.[2] They were sup-

[1] Such is the account explicitly given by Cortés to the emperor. (Rel. Terc., ap. Lorenzana, p. 264.) Bernal Diaz, on the contrary, speaks of the assault as first conceived by the general himself. (Hist. de la Conquista, cap. 151.) Yet Diaz had not the best means of knowing ; and Cortés would hardly have sent home a palpable misstatement that could have been so easily exposed.

[2] This punctual performance of mass by the army, in storm and in

ported, in addition to the brigantines, by a numerous fleet of Indian boats, which were to force a passage up the canals, and by a countless multitude of allies, whose very numbers served in the end to embarrass their operations. After clearing the suburbs, three avenues presented themselves, which all terminated in the square of Tlatelolco. The principal one, being of much greater width than the other two, might rather be called a causeway than a street, since it was flanked by deep canals on either side. Cortés divided his force into three bodies. One of them he placed under Alderete, with orders to occupy the principal street. A second he gave in charge to Andres de Tápia and Jorge de Alvarado; the former a cavalier of courage and capacity, the latter a younger brother of Don Pedro, and possessed of the intrepid spirit which belonged to that chivalrous family. These were to penetrate by one of the parallel streets, while the general himself, at the head of the third division, was to occupy the other. A small body of cavalry, with two or three field-pieces, was stationed as a reserve in front of the great street of Tacuba, which was designated as the rallying-point for the different divisions.[3]

sunshine, by day and by night, among friends and enemies, draws forth a warm eulogium from the archiepiscopal editor of Cortés: " En el Campo, en una Calzada, entre Enemigos, trabajando dia, y noche, nunca se omitia la Missa, páraque toda la obra se atribuyesse á Dios, y mas en unos Meses, en que incomodan las Aguas de el Cielo; y encima del Agua las Habitaciones, ó malas Tiendas." Lorenzana, p. 266, nota.

[3] In the treasurer's division, according to the general's Letter, there were 70 Spanish foot, 7 or 8 horse, and 15,000 or 20,000 Indians; in Tápia's, 80 foot, and 10,000 allies; and in his own, 8 horse, 100 infantry, and " an infinite number of allies." (Ibid., ubi supra.) The

Cortés gave the most positive instructions to his captains not to advance a step without securing the means of retreat by carefully filling up the ditches and the openings in the causeway. The neglect of this precaution by Alvarado, in an assault which he had made on the city but a few days before, had been attended with such serious consequences to his army that Cortés rode over, himself, to his officer's quarters, for the purpose of publicly reprimanding him for his disobedience of orders. On his arrival at the camp, however, he found that his offending captain had conducted the affair with so much gallantry, that the intended reprimand — though well deserved — subsided into a mild rebuke.[4]

The arrangements being completed, the three divisions marched at once up the several streets. Cortés, dismounting, took the van of his own squadron, at the head of his infantry. The Mexicans fell back as he advanced, making less resistance than usual. The Spaniards pushed on, carrying one barricade after another, and carefully filling up the gaps with rubbish, so as to secure themselves a footing. The canoes supported the attack, by moving along the canals and grappling with those of the enemy; while numbers of the nimble-footed Tlascalans, scaling the terraces, passed on from one house to another, where they were connected, hurling the defenders into the streets below.

looseness of the language shows that a few thousands more or less were of no great moment in the estimate of the Indian forces.

4 " Otro dia de mañana acordé de ir á su Real para le reprehender lo pasado. . . . Y visto, no les imputé tanta culpa, como antes parecia tener, y platicado cerca de lo que habia de hacer, yo me bolví á nuestro Real aquel dia." Rel. Terc. de Cortés, ap. Lorenzana, pp. 263, 264.

F*

The enemy, taken apparently by surprise, seemed incapable of withstanding for a moment the fury of the assault; and the victorious Christians, cheered on by the shouts of triumph which arose from their companions in the adjoining streets, were only the more eager to be first at the destined goal.

Indeed, the facility of his success led the general to suspect that he might be advancing too fast; that it might be a device of the enemy to draw them into the heart of the city and then surround or attack them in the rear. He had some misgivings, moreover, lest his too ardent officers, in the heat of the chase, should, notwithstanding his commands, have overlooked the necessary precaution of filling up the breaches. He accordingly brought his squadron to a halt, prepared to baffle any insidious movement of his adversary. Meanwhile he received more than one message from Alderete, informing him that he had nearly gained the market. This only increased the general's apprehension that, in the rapidity of his advance, he might have neglected to secure the ground. He determined to trust no eyes but his own, and, taking a small body of troops, proceeded at once to reconnoitre the route followed by the treasurer.

He had not proceeded far along the great street, or causeway, when his progress was arrested by an opening ten or twelve paces wide, and filled with water, at least two fathoms deep, by which a communication was formed between the canals on the opposite sides. A feeble attempt had been made to stop the gap with the rubbish of the causeway, but in too careless a manner to be of the least service; and a few straggling stones and pieces of timber only showed that the work had been abandoned almost as soon as begun.[5] To add to his consternation, the general observed that the sides of the causeway in this neighborhood had been pared off, and, as was evident, very recently.   He saw in all this the artifice of the cunning enemy, and had little doubt that his hot-headed officer had rushed into a snare deliberately laid for him.   Deeply alarmed, he set about repairing the mischief as fast as possible, by ordering his men to fill up the yawning chasm.

But they had scarcely begun their labors, when the hoarse echoes of conflict in the distance were succeeded by a hideous sound of mingled yells and war-whoops, that seemed to rend the very heavens.   This was followed by a rushing noise, as of the tread of thronging multitudes, showing that the tide of battle was turned back from its former course, and was rolling on towards the spot where Cortés and his little band of cavaliers were planted.

His conjecture proved too true.   Alderete had followed the retreating Aztecs with an eagerness which increased with every step of his advance.   He had carried the barricades which had defended the breach, without much difficulty, and, as he swept on, gave orders that the opening should be stopped.   But the blood of the high-spirited cavaliers was warmed by the

5 " Y hallé, que habian pasado una quebrada de la Calle, que era de diez, ó doce pasos de ancho; y el Agua, que por ella pasaba, era de hondura de mas de dos estados, y al tiempo que la pasáron habian echado en ella madera, y cañas de carrizo, y como pasaban pocos á pocos, y con tiento, no se habia hundido la madera y cañas." Rel. Terc. de Cortés, ap. Lorenzana, p. 268.—See also Oviedo, Hist. de las Ind., MS., lib. 33, cap. 48.

chase, and no one cared to be detained by the ignoble occupation of filling up the ditches, while he could gather laurels so easily in the fight ; and they all pressed on, exhorting and cheering one another with the assurance of being the first to reach the square of Tlatelolco.   In this way they suffered themselves to be decoyed into the heart of the city; when suddenly the horn of Guatemozin—the sacred symbol, heard only in seasons of extraordinary peril—sent forth a long and piercing note from the summit of a neighboring *teocalli*. In an instant, the flying Aztecs, as if maddened by the blast, wheeled about, and turned on their pursuers. At the same time, countless swarms of warriors from the adjoining streets and lanes poured in upon the flanks of the assailants, filling the air with the fierce, unearthly cries which had reached the ears of Cortés, and drowning, for a moment, the wild dissonance which reigned in the other quarters of the capital.[6]

The army, taken by surprise, and shaken by the fury of the assault, was thrown into the utmost disorder.   Friends and foes, white men and Indians, were mingled together in one promiscuous mass.   Spears, swords, and war-clubs were brandished together in the air.   Blows fell at random.   In their eagerness to

[6] Gomara, Crónica, cap. 138.—Ixtlilxochitl, Venida de los Españoles, p. 37.—Oviedo, Hist. de las Ind., MS., lib. 33, cap. 26.—Guatemozin's horn rang in the ears of Bernal Diaz for many a day after the battle. "Guatemuz, y manda tocar su corneta, q̃ era vna señal q̃ quando aquella se tocasse, era q̃ auian de pelear sus Capitanes de manera, q̃ hiziessen presa, ó morir sobre ello ; y retumbaua el sonido, q̃ se metia en los oidos, y de q̃ lo oyéro aquellos sus esquadrones, y Capitanes: saber yo aquí dezir aora, con q̃ rabia, y esfuerço se metian entre nosotros á nos echar mano, es cosa de espanto." Hist. de la Conquista, cap. 152.

escape, they trod down one another. Blinded by the
missiles which now rained on them from the *azoteas,*
they staggered on, scarcely knowing in what direction,
or fell, struck down by hands which they could not
see. On they came, like a rushing torrent sweeping
along some steep declivity, and rolling in one confused
tide towards the open breach, on the farther side of
which stood Cortés and his companions, horror-struck
at the sight of the approaching ruin. The foremost
files soon plunged into the gulf, treading one another
under the flood, some striving ineffectually to swim,
others, with more success, to clamber over the heaps
of their suffocated comrades. Many, as they attempted
to scale the opposite sides of the slippery dike, fell
into the water, or were hurried off by the warriors in
the canoes, who added to the horrors of the rout by
the fresh storm of darts and javelins which they poured
on the fugitives.

Cortés, meanwhile, with his brave followers, kept
his station undaunted on the other side of the breach.
" I had made up my mind," he says, " to die, rather
than desert my poor followers in their extremity!" [7]
With outstretched hands he endeavored to rescue as
many as he could from the watery grave, and from the
more appalling fate of captivity. He as vainly tried
to restore something like presence of mind and order
among the distracted fugitives. His person was too
well known to the Aztecs, and his position now made
him a conspicuous mark for their weapons. Darts,

[7] " É como el negocio fué tan de súpito, y ví que mataban la Gente,
determiné de me quedar allí, y morir peleando." Rel. Terc., ap.
Lorenzana, p. 268.

stones, and arrows fell around him thick as hail, but glanced harmless from his steel helmet and armor of proof. At length a cry of "Malinche," "Malinche," arose among the enemy; and six of their number, strong and athletic warriors, rushing on him at once, made a violent effort to drag him on board their boat. In the struggle he received a severe wound in the leg, which, for the time, disabled it. There seemed to be no hope for him; when a faithful follower, Cristóval de Olea, perceiving his general's extremity, threw himself on the Aztecs, and with a blow cut off the arm of one savage, and then plunged his sword in the body of another. He was quickly supported by a comrade named Lerma, and by a Tlascalan chief, who, fighting over the prostrate body of Cortés, despatched three more of the assailants; though the heroic Olea paid dearly for his self-devotion, as he fell mortally wounded by the side of his general.[8]

[8] Ixtlilxochitl, who would fain make his royal kinsman a sort of residuary legatee for all unappropriated, or even doubtful, acts of heroism, puts in a sturdy claim for him on this occasion. A painting, he says, on one of the gates of a monastery of Tlatelolco, long recorded the fact that it was the Tezcucan chief who saved the life of Cortés. (Venida de los Españoles, p. 38.) But Camargo gives the full credit of it to Olea, on the testimony of "a famous Tlascalan warrior," present in the action, who reported it to him. (Hist. de Tlascala, MS.) The same is stoutly maintained by Bernal Diaz, the townsman of Olea, to whose memory he pays a hearty tribute, as one of the best men and bravest soldiers in the army. (Hist. de la Conquista, cap. 152, 204.) Saavedra, the poetic chronicler,—something more of chronicler than poet,—who came on the stage before all that had borne arms in the Conquest had left it, gives the laurel also to Olea, whose fate he commemorates in verses that at least aspire to historic fidelity:

> "Túvole con las manos abraçado,
> Y Francisco de Olea el valeroso,

The report soon spread among the soldiers that their commander was taken ; and Quiñones, the captain of his guard, with several others, pouring in to the rescue, succeeded in disentangling Cortés from the grasp of his enemies, who were struggling with him in the water, and, raising him in their arms, placed him again on the causeway. One of his pages, meanwhile, had advanced some way through the press, leading a horse for his master to mount. But the youth received a wound in the throat from a javelin, which prevented him from effecting his object. Another of his attend-ants was more successful. It was Guzman, his cham-berlain ; but, as he held the bridle while Cortés was assisted into the saddle, he was snatched away by the Aztecs, and, with the swiftness of thought, hurried off by their canoes. The general still lingered, unwilling to leave the spot while his presence could be of the least service. But the faithful Quiñones, taking his horse by the bridle, turned his head from the breach, exclaiming, at the same time, that "his master's life was too important to the army to be thrown away there."[9]

> Vn valiente Español, y su criado,
> Le tiró vn tajo brauo y riguroso :
> Las dos manos á cercen le ha cortado,
> Y él le libró del trance trabajoso.
> Huuo muy gran rumor, porque dezian,
> Que ya en prision amarga le tenian.

> "Llegáron otros Indios arriscados,
> Y á Olea matáron en vn punto,
> Cercáron á Cortés por todos lados,
> Y al miserable cuerpo ya difunto :
> Y viendo sus sentidos recobrados,
> Puso mano á la espada y daga junto.
> Antonio de Quiñones llegó luego,
> Capitan de la guarda ardiendo en fuego."

EL PEREGRINO INDIANO, Canto 20.

9 " É aquel Capitan que estaba con el General, que se decia Antonio

Yet it was no easy matter to force a passage through the press. The surface of the causeway, cut up by the feet of men and horses, was knee-deep in mud, and in some parts was so much broken that the water from the canals flowed over it. The crowded mass, in their efforts to extricate themselves from their perilous position, staggered to and fro like a drunken man. Those on the flanks were often forced by the lateral pressure of their comrades down the slippery sides of the dike, where they were picked up by the canoes of the enemy, whose shouts of triumph proclaimed the savage joy with which they gathered in every new victim for the sacrifice. Two cavaliers, riding by the general's side, lost their footing, and rolled down the declivity into the water. One was taken and his horse killed. The other was happy enough to escape. The valiant ensign, Corral, had a similar piece of good fortune. He slipped into the canal, and the enemy felt sure of their prize, when he again succeeded in recovering the causeway, with the tattered banner of Castile still flying above his head. The barbarians set up a cry of disappointed rage as they lost possession of a trophy to which the people of Anahuac attached, as we have seen, the highest importance, hardly inferior in their eyes to the capture of the commander-in-chief himself.[10]

Cortés at length succeeded in regaining the firm

de Quiñones, díxole: Vamos, Señor, de aquí, y salvemos vuestra Persona, pues que ya esto está de manera, que es morir desesperado atender; é sin vos, ninguno de nosotros puede escapar, que no es esfuerzo, sino poquedad, porfiar aquí otra cosa." Oviedo, Hist. de las Ind., MS., lib. 33, cap. 26.

[10] It may have been the same banner which is noticed by Mr.

ground, and reaching the open place before the great
street of Tacuba. Here, under a sharp fire of the
artillery, he rallied his broken squadrons, and, charging
at the head of the little body of horse, which, not
having been brought into action, were still fresh, he
beat off the enemy. He then commanded the retreat
of the two other divisions. The scattered forces again
united; and the general, sending forward his Indian
confederates, took the rear with a chosen body of cavalry to cover the retreat of the army, which was effected
with but little additional loss.[11]

Andres de Tápia was despatched to the western
causeway to acquaint Alvarado and Sandoval with the
failure of the enterprise. Meanwhile the two captains
had penetrated far into the city. Cheered by the
triumphant shouts of their countrymen in the adjacent
streets, they had pushed on with extraordinary vigor,
that they might not be outstripped in the race of glory.
They had almost reached the market-place, which lay
nearer to their quarters than to the general's, when
they heard the blast from the dread horn of Guatemozin,[12] followed by the overpowering yell of the bar-

Bullock as treasured up in the Hospital of Jesus, "where," says he,
"we beheld the identical embroidered standard under which the great
captain wrested this immense empire from the unfortunate Montezuma." Six Months in Mexico, vol. i. chap. 10.

[11] For this disastrous affair, besides the Letter of Cortés, and the
Chronicle of Diaz, so often quoted, see Sahagun, Hist. de Nueva-
España, MS., lib. 12, cap. 33,—Camargo, Hist. de Tlascala, MS.,—
Gomara, Crónica, cap. 138,—Torquemada, Monarch. Ind., lib. 4, cap.
94,—Oviedo, Hist. de las Ind., MS., lib. 33, cap. 26, 48.

[12] "El resonido de la corneta de Guatemuz."—Astolfo's magic horn
was not more terrible:

barians, which had so startled the ears of Cortés; till at length the sounds of the receding conflict died away in the distance. The two captains now understood that the day must have gone hard with their countrymen. They soon had further proof of it, when the victorious Aztecs, returning from the pursuit of Cortés, joined their forces to those engaged with Sandoval and Alvarado, and fell on them with redoubled fury. At the same time they rolled on the ground two or three of the bloody heads of the Spaniards, shouting the name of "Malinche." The captains, struck with horror at the spectacle,—though they gave little credit to the words of the enemy,—instantly ordered a retreat. Indeed, it was not in their power to maintain their ground against the furious assaults of the besieged, who poured on them, swarm after swarm, with a desperation of which, says one who was there, "although it seems as if it were now present to my eyes, I can give but a faint idea to the reader. God alone could have brought us off safe from the perils of that day."[13] The fierce barbarians followed up the Spaniards to their very intrenchments. But here they were met,

> " Dico che 'l corno è di sì orribil suono,
> Ch' ovunque s' oda, fa fuggir la gente.
> Non può trovarsi al mondo un cor sì buono,
> Che possa non fuggir come lo sente.
> Rumor di vento e di tremuoto, e 'l tuono,
> A par del suon di questo, era niente."
>
> ORLANDO FURIOSO, Canto 15, st. 15.

[13] " Por q̃ yo no lo sé aquí escriuir q̃ aora q̃ me pongo á pensar en ello, es como si visiblemente lo viesse, mas bueluo á dezir, y ansí es verdad, q̃ si Dios no nos diera esfuerço, segun estauamos todos heridos : él nos saluo, q̃ de otra manera no nos podiamos llegar á nuestros ranchos." Bernal Diaz, Hist. de la Conquista, cap. 152.

first by the cross-fire of the brigantines, which, dashing through the palisades planted to obstruct their movements, completely enfiladed the causeway, and next by that of the small battery erected in front of the camp, which, under the management of a skilful engineer, named Medrano, swept the whole length of the defile. Thus galled in front and on flank, the shattered columns of the Aztecs were compelled to give way and take shelter under the defences of the city.

The greatest anxiety now prevailed in the camp regarding the fate of Cortés; for Tápia had been detained on the road by scattered parties of the enemy, whom Guatemozin had stationed there to interrupt the communication between the camps. He arrived at length, however, though bleeding from several wounds. His intelligence, while it reassured the Spaniards as to the general's personal safety, was not calculated to allay their uneasiness in other respects.

Sandoval, in particular, was desirous to acquaint himself with the actual state of things and the further intentions of Cortés. Suffering as he was from three wounds, which he had received in that day's fight, he resolved to visit in person the quarters of the commander-in-chief. It was mid-day—for the busy scenes of the morning had occupied but a few hours—when Sandoval remounted the good steed on whose strength and speed he knew he could rely. It was a noble animal, well known throughout the army, and worthy of its gallant rider, whom it had carried safe through all the long marches and bloody battles of the Conquest.[14]

[14] This renowned steed, who might rival the Babieca of the Cid, was named Motilla, and, when one would pass unqualified praise on a

On the way he fell in with Guatemozin's scouts, who gave him chase, and showered around him volleys of missiles, which, fortunately, found no vulnerable point in his own harness or that of his well-barbed charger.

On arriving at the camp, he found the troops there much worn and dispirited by the disaster of the morning. They had good reason to be so. Besides the killed, and a long file of wounded, sixty-two Spaniards, with a multitude of allies, had fallen alive into the hands of the enemy,—an enemy who was never known to spare a captive. The loss of two field-pieces and seven horses crowned their own disgrace and the triumph of the Aztecs. This loss, so insignificant in European warfare, was a great one here, where both horses and artillery, the most powerful arms of war against the barbarians, were not to be procured without the greatest cost and difficulty.[15]

Cortés, it was observed, had borne himself throughout this trying day with his usual intrepidity and coolness. The only time he was seen to falter was when the Mexicans threw down before him the heads of several Spaniards, shouting, at the same time, "Sando-

horse, he would say, "He is as good as Motilla." So says that prince of chroniclers, Diaz, who takes care that neither beast nor man shall be defrauded of his fair guerdon in these campaigns against the infidel. He was of a chestnut color, it seems, with a star in his forehead, and, luckily for his credit, with only one foot white. See Hist. de la Conquista, cap. 152, 205.

[15] The cavaliers might be excused for not wantonly venturing their horses, if, as Diaz asserts, they could only be replaced at an expense of eight hundred or a thousand dollars apiece : "Porque costaua en aquella sazon vn cauallo ochocientos pesos, y aun algunos costauan á mas de mil." Hist. de la Conquista, cap. 151. See, also, *ante*, Book II. chap. 3, note 14.

val," "Tonatiuh," the well-known epithet of Alvarado. At the sight of the gory trophies he grew deadly pale; but, in a moment recovering his usual confidence, he endeavored to cheer up the drooping spirits of his followers. It was with a cheerful countenance that he now received his lieutenant; but a shade of sadness was visible through this outward composure, showing how the catastrophe of the *puente cuidada*, "the sorrowful bridge," as he mournfully called it, lay heavy at his heart.

To the cavalier's anxious inquiries as to the cause of the disaster, he replied, "It is for my sins that it has befallen me, son Sandoval;" for such was the affectionate epithet with which Cortés often addressed his best-beloved and trusty officer. He then explained to him the immediate cause, in the negligence of the treasurer. Further conversation followed, in which the general declared his purpose to forego active hostilities for a few days. "You must take my place," he continued, "for I am too much crippled at present to discharge my duties. You must watch over the safety of the camps. Give especial heed to Alvarado's. He is a gallant soldier, I know it well; but I doubt the Mexican hounds may, some hour, take him at disadvantage." [16] These few words showed the general's own estimation of his two lieutenants; both equally brave and chivalrous, but the one uniting with these

[16] "Mira pues veis que yo no puedo ir á todas partes, á vos os encomiendo estos trabajos, pues veis q̃ estoy herido y coxo; ruego os pongais cobro en estos tres reales; bien sé q̃ Pedro de Alvarado, y sus Capitanes, y soldados aurán batallado, y hecho como caualleros, mas temo el gran poder destos perros no les ayan desbaratado." Bernal Diaz, Hist. de la Conquista, cap. 152.

qualities the circumspection so essential to success in perilous enterprises, in which the other was signally deficient. The future conqueror of Guatemala had to gather wisdom, as usual, from the bitter fruits of his own errors. It was under the training of Cortés that he learned to be a soldier. The general, having concluded his instructions, affectionately embraced his lieutenant, and dismissed him to his quarters.

It was late in the afternoon when he reached them; but the sun was still lingering above the western hills, and poured his beams wide over the Valley, lighting up the old towers and temples of Tenochtitlan with a mellow radiance, that little harmonized with the dark scenes of strife in which the city had so lately been involved. The tranquillity of the hour, however, was on a sudden broken by the strange sounds of the great drum in the temple of the war-god,—sounds which recalled the *noche triste*, with all its terrible images, to the minds of the Spaniards, for that was the only occasion on which they had ever heard them.[17] They intimated some solemn act of religion within the unhallowed precincts of the *teocalli;* and the soldiers, startled by the mournful vibrations, which might be heard for leagues across the Valley, turned their eyes to the quarter whence they proceeded. They there beheld a long procession winding up the huge sides of the pyramid; for the camp of Alvarado was pitched scarcely a mile from the city, and objects are distinctly visible at a great distance in the transparent atmosphere of the table-land.

[17] "Vn atambor de muy triste sonido, enfin como instrumento de demonios, y retumbaua tanto, que se oia dos, ó tres leguas." Bernal Diaz, Hist. de la Conquista, loc. cit.

As the long file of priests and warriors reached the flat summit of the *teocalli,* the Spaniards saw the figures of several men stripped to their waists, some of whom, by the whiteness of their skins, they recognized as their own countrymen. They were the victims for sacrifice. Their heads were gaudily decorated with coronals of plumes, and they carried fans in their hands. They were urged along by blows, and compelled to take part in the dances in honor of the Aztec war-god. The unfortunate captives, then stripped of their sad finery, were stretched, one after another, on the great stone of sacrifice. On its convex surface their breasts were heaved up conveniently for the diabolical purpose of the priestly executioner, who cut asunder the ribs by a strong blow with his sharp razor of *itztli,* and, thrusting his hand into the wound, tore away the heart, which, hot and reeking, was deposited on the golden censer before the idol. The body of the slaughtered victim was then hurled down the steep stairs of the pyramid, which, it may be remembered, were placed at the same angle of the pile, one flight below another; and the mutilated remains were gathered up by the savages beneath, who soon prepared with them the cannibal repast which completed the work of abomination ! [18]

[18] Bernal Diaz, Hist. de la Conquista, ubi supra.—Oviedo, Hist. de las Ind., MS., lib. 33, cap. 48.—" Sacándoles los corazones, sobre una piedra que era como un pilar cortado, tan grueso como un hombre y algo mas, y tan alto como medio estadio; allí á cada uno echado de espaldas sobre aquella piedra, que se llama Techcatl, uno le tiraba por un brazo, y otro por el otro, y tambien por las piernas otros dos, y venia uno de aquellos Sátrapas, con un pedernal, como un hierro de lanza enhastado, en un palo de dos palmos de largo, le daba un golpe

We may imagine with what sensations the stupefied Spaniards must have gazed on this horrid spectacle, so near that they could almost recognize the persons of their unfortunate friends, see the struggles and writhing of their bodies, hear—or fancy that they heard—their screams of agony! yet so far removed that they could render them no assistance. Their limbs trembled beneath them, as they thought what might one day be their own fate; and the bravest among them, who had hitherto gone to battle as careless and light-hearted as to the banquet or the ball-room, were unable, from this time forward, to encounter their ferocious enemy without a sickening feeling, much akin to fear, coming over them.[19]

Such was not the effect produced by this spectacle

con ambas manos en el pecho; y sacando aquel pedernal, por la misma llaga metia la mano, y arrancábale el corazon, y luego fregaba con él la boca del Ídolo; y echaba á rodar el cuerpo por las gradas abajo, que serian como cinquenta ó sesenta gradas, por allí abajo iba quebrando las piernas y los brazos, y dando cabezasos con la cabeza, *hasta que llegaba abajo aun vivo.*" Sahagun, Hist. de Nueva-España, MS., lib. 12, cap. 35.

[19] At least, such is the honest confession of Captain Diaz, as stout-hearted a soldier as any in the army. He consoles himself, however, with the reflection that the tremor of his limbs intimated rather an excess of courage than a want of it, since it arose from a lively sense of the great dangers into which his daring spirit was about to hurry him! The passage in the original affords a good specimen of the inimitable *naïveté* of the old chronicler: " Digan agora todos aquellos caualleros, que desto del militar entienden, y se han hallado en trances peligrosos de muerte, á que fin echarán mi temor, si es á mucha flaqueza de animo, ó á mucho esfuerço, porque como he dicho, sentia yo en mi pensamiento, que auia de poner por mi persona, batallando en parte que por fuerça auia de temer la muerte mas que otras vezes, y por esto me temblaua el coraçon, y temia la muerte." Hist. de la Conquista, cap. 156.

on the Mexican forces, gathered at the end of the causeway. Like vultures maddened by the smell of distant carrion, they set up a piercing cry, and, as they shouted that "such should be the fate of all their enemies," swept along in one fierce torrent over the dike. But the Spaniards were not to be taken by surprise; and, before the barbarian horde had come within their lines, they opened such a deadly fire from their battery of heavy guns, supported by the musketry and cross-bows, that the assailants were compelled to fall back slowly, but fearfully mangled, to their former position.

The five following days passed away in a state of inaction, except, indeed, so far as was necessary to repel the sorties made from time to time by the militia of the capital. The Mexicans, elated with their success, meanwhile, abandoned themselves to jubilee; singing, dancing, and feasting on the mangled relics of their wretched victims. Guatemozin sent several heads of the Spaniards, as well as of the horses, round the country, calling on his old vassals to forsake the banners of the white men, unless they would share the doom of the enemies of Mexico. The priests now cheered the young monarch and the people with the declaration that the dread Huitzilopochtli, their offended deity, appeased by the sacrifices offered up on his altars, would again take the Aztecs under his protection, and deliver their enemies, before the expiration of eight days, into their hands.[20]

[20] Herrera, Hist. general, dec. 3, lib. 2, cap. 20.—Ixtlilxochitl, Venida de los Españoles, pp. 41, 42.—"Y nos dezian, que de aí á ocho dias no auia de quedar ninguno de nosotros á vida, porque assí se lo auian

This comfortable prediction, confidently believed by the Mexicans, was thundered in the ears of the besieging army in tones of exultation and defiance. However it may have been contemned by the Spaniards, it had a very different effect on their allies. The latter had begun to be disgusted with a service so full of peril and suffering and already protracted far beyond the usual term of Indian hostilities. They had less confidence than before in the Spaniards. Experience had shown that they were neither invincible nor immortal, and their recent reverses made them even distrust the ability of the Christians to reduce the Aztec metropolis. They recalled to mind the ominous words of Xicotencatl, that "so sacrilegious a war could come to no good for the people of Anahuac." They felt that their arm was raised against the gods of their country. The prediction of the oracle fell heavy on their hearts. They had little doubt of its fulfilment, and were only eager to turn away the bolt from their own heads by a timely secession from the cause.

They took advantage, therefore, of the friendly cover of night to steal away from their quarters. Company after company deserted in this manner, taking the direction of their respective homes. Those belonging to the great towns of the Valley, whose allegiance was the most recent, were the first to cast it off. Their example was followed by the older confederates, the militia of Cholula, Tepeaca, Tezcuco, and even the faithful Tlascala. There were, it is true, some exceptions to these, and among them Ixtlilxochitl, the young

prometido la noche antes sus Dioses." Bernal Diaz, Hist. de la Conquista, cap. 153.

lord of Tezcuco, and Chichemecatl, the valiant Tlascalan chieftain, who, with a few of their immediate
followers, still remained true to the banner under which
they had enlisted. But their number was insignificant.
The Spaniards beheld with dismay the mighty array,
on which they relied for support, thus silently melting
away before the breath of superstition. Cortés alone
maintained a cheerful countenance. He treated the
prediction with contempt, as an invention of the
priests, and sent his messengers after the retreating
squadrons, beseeching them to postpone their departure, or at least to halt on the road, till the time, which
would soon elapse, should show the falsehood of the
prophecy.

The affairs of the Spaniards at this crisis must be
confessed to have worn a gloomy aspect. Deserted by
their allies, with their ammunition nearly exhausted,
cut off from the customary supplies from the neighborhood, harassed by unintermitting vigils and fatigues,
smarting under wounds, of which every man in the
army had his share, with an unfriendly country in their
rear and a mortal foe in front, they might well be
excused for faltering in their enterprise. They found
abundant occupation by day in foraging the country,
and in maintaining their position on the causeways
against the enemy, now made doubly daring by success and by the promises of their priests ; while at
night their slumbers were disturbed by the beat of the
melancholy drum, the sounds of which, booming far
over the waters, tolled the knell of their murdered comrades. Night after night fresh victims were led up to
the great altar of sacrifice ; and, while the city blazed

with the illumination of a thousand bonfires on the terraced roofs of the dwellings and in the areas of the temples, the dismal pageant, showing through the fiery glare like the work of the ministers of hell, was distinctly visible from the camp below. One of the last of the sufferers was Guzman, the unfortunate chamberlain of Cortés, who lingered in captivity eighteen days before he met his doom.[21]

Yet in this hour of trial the Spaniards did not falter. Had they faltered, they might have learned a lesson of fortitude from some of their own wives, who continued with them in the camp, and who displayed a heroism, on this occasion, of which history has preserved several examples. One of these, protected by her husband's armor, would frequently mount guard in his place when he was wearied. Another, hastily putting on a soldier's *escaupil* and seizing a sword and lance, was seen, on one occasion, to rally their retreating countrymen and lead them back against the enemy. Cortés would have persuaded these Amazonian dames to remain at

[21] Sahagun, Hist. de Nueva-España, MS., lib. 12, cap. 36.—Ixtlil-xochitl, Venida de los Españoles, pp. 41, 42.—The Castilian scholar will see that I have not drawn on my imagination for the picture of these horrors: "Digamos aora lo que los Mexicanos hazian de noche en sus grandes, y altos Cues; y es, q̃ tañian su maldito atambor, que dixe otra vez que era el de mas maldito sonido, y mas triste q̃ se podia inuẽtar, y sonaua muy lexos; y tañian otros peores instrumentos. En fin, cosas diabólicas, y teniã graudes lumbres, y dauã grãdíssimos gritos, y siluos, y en aquel instãte estauan sacrificando de nuestros cõpañeros, de los q̃ tomárõ á Cortés, que supímos q̃ sacrificáron diez dias arreo, hasta que los acabáron, y el postrero dexárõ á Christoual de Guzman, q̃ viuo lo tuuiéron diez y ocho dias, segun dixérõ tres Capitanes Mexicanos q̃ prẽdímos." Bernal Diaz, Hist. de la Conquista, cap. 153.

Tlascala; but they proudly replied, "It was the duty of Castilian wives not to abandon their husbands in danger, but to share it with them,—and die with them, if necessary." And well did they do their duty.[22]

Amidst all the distresses and multiplied embarrassments of their situation, the Spaniards still remained true to their purpose. They relaxed in no degree the severity of the blockade. Their camps still occupied the only avenues to the city; and their batteries, sweeping the long defiles at every fresh assault of the Aztecs, mowed down hundreds of the assailants. Their brigantines still rode on the waters, cutting off the communication with the shore. It is true, indeed, the loss of the auxiliary canoes left a passage open for the occasional introduction of supplies to the capital.[23] But the whole amount of these supplies was small; and its crowded population, while exulting in their temporary advantage and the delusive assurances of their priests, were beginning to sink under the withering grasp of an enemy within, more terrible than the one which lay before their gates.

[22] " Que no era bien, que Mugeres Castellanas dexasen á sus Maridos, iendo á la Guerra, i que adonde ellos muriesen, moririan ellas." (Herrera, Hist. general, dec. 3, lib. 1, cap. 22.) The historian has embalmed the names of several of these heroines in his pages, who are, doubtless, well entitled to share the honors of the Conquest: Beatriz de Palacios, María de Estrada, Juana Martin, Isabel Rodriguez, and Beatriz Bermudez.

[23] Ibid., ubi supra

CHAPTER VII.

1521.

THUS passed away the eight days prescribed by the
oracle ; and the sun which rose upon the ninth beheld
the fair city still beset on every side by the inexora-
ble foe. It was a great mistake of the Aztec priests
—one not uncommon with false prophets, anxious to
produce a startling impression on their followers—to
assign so short a term for the fulfilment of their prediction.[1]

The Tezcucan and Tlascalan chiefs now sent to
acquaint their troops with the failure of the prophecy,
and to recall them to the Christian camp. The Tlascalans, who had halted on the way, returned, ashamed
of their credulity, and with ancient feelings of animosity heightened by the artifice of which they had
been the dupes. Their example was followed by many
of the other confederates, with the levity natural to a
people whose convictions are the result not of reason,

[1] And yet the priests were not so much to blame, if, as Solís assures
us, "the Devil went about very industriously in those days, insinuating
into the ears of his flock what he could not into their hearts." Conquista, lib. 5, cap 22.

but of superstition. In a short time the Spanish general found himself at the head of an auxiliary force which, if not so numerous as before, was more than adequate to all his purposes. He received them with politic benignity; and, while he reminded them that they had been guilty of a great crime in thus abandoning their commander, he was willing to overlook it in consideration of their past services. They must be aware that these services were not necessary to the Spaniards, who had carried on the siege with the same vigor during their absence as when they were present. But he was unwilling that those who had shared the dangers of the war with him should not also partake its triumphs, and be present at the fall of their enemy, which he promised, with a confidence better founded than that of the priests in their prediction, should not be long delayed.

Yet the menaces and machinations of Guatemozin were still not without effect in the distant provinces. Before the full return of the confederates, Cortés received an embassy from Cuernavaca, ten or twelve leagues distant, and another from some friendly towns of the Otomies, still farther off, imploring his protection against their formidable neighbors, who menaced them with hostilities as allies of the Spaniards. As the latter were then situated, they were in a condition to receive succor much more than to give it.[2] Most of the officers were, accordingly, opposed to granting a request compliance with which must still further impair their diminished strength. But Cortés knew the impor-

[2] "Y teniamos necesidad antes de ser socorridos, que de dar socorro." Rel. Terc. de Cortes, ap. Lorenzana, p. 272.

tance, above all, of not betraying his own inability to grant it. "The greater our weakness," he said, "the greater need have we to cover it under a show of strength."[3]

He immediately detached Tápia with a body of about a hundred men in one direction, and Sandoval with a somewhat larger force in the other, with orders that their absence should not in any event be prolonged beyond ten days.[4] The two captains executed their commissions promptly and effectually. They each met and defeated his adversary in a pitched battle, laid waste the hostile territories, and returned within the time prescribed. They were soon followed by ambassadors from the conquered places, soliciting the alliance of the Spaniards; and the affair terminated by an accession of new confederates, and, what was more important, a conviction in the old that the Spaniards were both willing and competent to protect them.

Fortune, who seldom dispenses her frowns or her favors single-handed, further showed her good will to the Spaniards, at this time, by sending a vessel into Vera Cruz laden with ammunition and military stores. It was part of the fleet destined for the Florida coast by the romantic old knight, Ponce de Leon. The cargo was immediately taken by the authorities of the

[3] "God knows," says the general, "the peril in which we all stood; pero como nos convenia mostrar mas esfuerzo y ánimo, que nunca, y morir peleando, disimulabamos nuestro flaqueza assí con los Amigos como con los Enemigos." Rel. Terc. de Cortés, ap. Lorenzana, p. 275.

[4] Tápia's force consisted of 10 horse and 80 foot; the chief alguacil, as Sandoval was styled, had 18 horse and 100 infantry. Ibid., loc. cit. —Also Oviedo, Hist. de las Ind., MS., lib. 33, cap. 26.

port, and forwarded, without delay, to the camp, where it arrived most seasonably, as the want of powder, in particular, had begun to be seriously felt.[5] With strength thus renovated, Cortés determined to resume active operations, but on a plan widely differing from that pursued before.

In the former deliberations on the subject, two courses, as we have seen, presented themselves to the general. One was to intrench himself in the heart of the capital and from this point carry on hostilities; the other was the mode of proceeding hitherto followed. Both were open to serious objections, which he hoped would be obviated by the one now adopted. This was to advance no step without securing the entire safety of the army, not only on its immediate retreat, but in its future inroads. Every breach in the causeway, every canal in the streets, was to be filled up in so solid a manner that the work should not be again disturbed. The materials for this were to be furnished by the buildings, every one of which, as the army advanced, whether public or private, hut, temple, or palace, was to be demolished! Not a building in their path was to be spared. They were all indiscriminately to be levelled, until, in the Conqueror's own language, "the water should be converted into dry land," and a

---

[5] "Pólvora y Ballestas, de que teníamos muy estrema necesidad." (Rel. Terc. de Cortés, ap. Lorenzana, p. 278.) It was probably the expedition in which Ponce de Leon lost his life; an expedition to the very land which the chivalrous cavalier had himself first visited in quest of the Fountain of Health. The story is pleasantly told by Irving, as the reader may remember, in his " Companions of Columbus."

G*

smooth and open ground be afforded for the manœuvres of the cavalry and artillery![6]

Cortés came to this terrible determination with great
difficulty. He sincerely desired to spare the city, "the
most beautiful thing in the world,"[7] as he enthusias-
tically styles it, and which would have formed the most
glorious trophy of his conquest. But in a place where
every house was a fortress and every street was cut up
by canals so embarrassing to his movements, experience proved it was vain to think of doing so and becoming master of it. There was as little hope of a
peaceful accommodation with the Aztecs, who, so far
from being broken by all they had hitherto endured,
and the long perspective of future woes, showed a
spirit as haughty and implacable as ever.[8]

The general's intentions were learned by the Indian
allies with unbounded satisfaction; and they answered
his call for aid by thousands of pioneers, armed with
their *coas*, or hoes of the country, all testifying the
greatest alacrity in helping on the work of destruction.[9]

[6] The calm and simple manner in which the *Conquistador*, as usual,
states this in his *Commentaries*, has something appalling in it from its
very simplicity : "Acordé de tomar un medio para nuestra seguridad,
y para poder mas estrechar á los Enemigos; y fué, que como fuessemos ganando por las Calles de la Ciudad, que fuessen derrocando
todas las Casas de ellas, del un lado, y del otro; por manera, que no
fuessemos un paso adelante, sin lo dejar todo asolado, y lo que era
Agua, hacerlo Tierra-firme, aunque hobiesse toda la dilacion, que se
pudiesse seguir." Rel. Terc., ap. Lorenzana, p. 279.

[7] "Porque era la mas hermosa cosa del Mundo." Ibid., p. 278.

[8] "Mas antes en el pelear, y en todos sus ardides, los hallabamos
con mas ánimo, que nunca." Ibid., p. 279.

[9] Yet we shall hardly credit the Tezcucan historian's assertion that
a hundred thousand Indians flocked to the camp for this purpose!

In a short time the breaches in the great causeways were filled up so effectually that they were never again molested. Cortés himself set the example by carrying stones and timber with his own hands.[10] The buildings in the suburbs were then thoroughly levelled, the canals were filled up with the rubbish, and a wide space around the city was thrown open to the manœuvres of the cavalry, who swept over it free and unresisted. The Mexicans did not look with indifference on these preparations to lay waste their town and leave them bare and unprotected against the enemy. They made incessant efforts to impede the labors of the besiegers; but the latter, under cover of their guns, which kept up an unintermitting fire, still advanced in the work of desolation.[11]

The gleam of fortune which had so lately broken out on the Mexicans again disappeared; and the dark mist, after having been raised for a moment, settled on the doomed capital more heavily than before. Famine,

" Viniesen todos los labradores con sus coas para este efecto con toda brevedad: . . . llegáron *mas de cien mil de ellos.*" Ixtlilxochitl, Venida de los Españoles, p. 42.

[10] Bernal Diaz, Hist. de la Conquista, cap. 153.

[11] Sahagun, who gathered the story from the actors, and from the aspect of the scene before the devastation had been wholly repaired, writes with the animation of an eye-witness: " La guerra por agua y por tierra fué tan porfiada y tan sangrienta, que era espanto de verla, y no hay posibilidad, para decir las particularidades que pasaban; eran tan espesas las saetas, y dardos, y piedras, y palos, que se arrojavan los unos á los otros, que quitavan la claridad del sol; era tan grande la vocería, y grita, de hombres y mugeres, y niños que voceaban y lloraban, que era cosa de grima; era tan grande la polvareda, y ruido, en derrocar y quemar casas, y robar lo que en ellas habia, y cautivar niños y mugeres, *que parecia un juicio.*" Hist. de Nueva-España, MS., lib. 12, cap. 38.

with all her hideous train of woes, was making rapid strides among its accumulated population. The stores provided for the siege were exhausted. The casual supply of human victims, or that obtained by some straggling pirogue from the neighboring shores, was too inconsiderable to be widely felt.[12] Some forced a scanty sustenance from a mucilaginous substance gathered in small quantities on the surface of the lake and canals.[13] Others appeased the cravings of appetite by devouring rats, lizards, and the like loathsome reptiles, which had not yet deserted the starving city. Its days seemed to be already numbered. But the page of history has many an example to show that there are no limits to the endurance of which humanity is capable, when animated by hatred and despair.

With the sword thus suspended over it, the Spanish commander, desirous to make one more effort to save the capital, persuaded three Aztec nobles, taken in one of the late actions, to bear a message from him to Guatemozin ; though they undertook it with reluctance, for fear of the consequences to themselves. Cortés told the emperor that all had now been done that brave men could do in defence of their country.

[12] The flesh of the Christians failed to afford them even the customary nourishment, since the Mexicans said it was intolerably bitter ; a miracle considered by Captain Diaz as expressly wrought for this occasion. Hist. de la Conquista, cap. 153.

[13] Ibid., ubi supra.—When dried in the sun, this slimy deposit had a flavor not unlike that of cheese, and formed part of the food of the poorer classes at all times, according to Clavigero. Stor. del Messico, tom. ii. p. 222.*

* [This was the *ahuahutle* before described. See *ante*, vol. ii. p. 109 ; note.—ED.]

There remained no hope, no chance of escape, for the Mexicans. Their provisions were exhausted; their communications were cut off; their vassals had deserted them; even their gods had betrayed them. They stood alone, with the nations of Anahuac banded against them. There was no hope but in immediate surrender. He besought the young monarch to take compassion on his brave subjects, who were daily perishing before his eyes; and on the fair city, whose stately buildings were fast crumbling into ruins. "Return to the allegiance," he concludes, "which you once proffered to the sovereign of Castile. The past shall be forgotten. The persons and property, in short, all the rights, of the Aztecs shall be respected. You shall be confirmed in your authority, and Spain will once more take your city under her protection." [14]

The eye of the young monarch kindled, and his dark cheek flushed with sudden anger, as he listened to proposals so humiliating. But, though his bosom glowed with the fiery temper of the Indian, he had the qualities of a "gentle cavalier," says one of his enemies, who knew him well. [15] He did no harm to the envoys; but, after the heat of the moment had passed off, he gave the matter a calm consideration, and called a council of his wise men and warriors to deliberate upon it. Some were for accepting the proposals, as offering the only chance of preservation. But the priests took a different view of the matter. They knew that the ruin of their own order must follow the triumph of

[14] Bernal Diaz, Hist. de la Conquista, cap. 154.

[15] "Mas como el Guatemuz era mancebo, *y muy gentil-hombre* y de buena disposicion." Ibid., ubi supra.

Christianity. "Peace was good," they said, "but not with the white men." They reminded Guatemozin of the fate of his uncle Montezuma, and the requital he had met with for all his hospitality; of the seizure and imprisonment of Cacama, the cacique of Tezcuco; of the massacre of the nobles by Alvarado; of the insatiable avarice of the invaders, which had stripped the country of its treasures; of their profanation of the temples; of the injuries and insults which they had heaped without measure on the people and their religion. "Better," they said, "to trust in the promises of their own gods, who had so long watched over the nation. Better, if need be, give up our lives at once for our country, than drag them out in slavery and suffering among the false strangers." [16]

The eloquence of the priests, artfully touching the various wrongs of his people, roused the hot blood of Guatemozin. "Since it is so," he abruptly exclaimed, "let us think only of supplying the wants of the people. Let no man, henceforth, who values his life, talk of surrender. We can at least die like warriors." [17]

The Spaniards waited two days for the answer to

[16] "Mira primero lo que nuestros Dioses te han prometido, toma buen consejo sobre ello y no te fies de Malinche, ni de sus palabras, que mas vale que todos muramos en esta ciudad peleando, que no vernos en poder de quiē nos harán esclauos, y nos atormentarán." Bernal Diaz, Hist. de la Conquista, cap. 154.

[17] "Y entonces el Guatemuz medio enojado les dixo: Pues assi quereis que sea, guardad mucho el maiz, y bastimentos que tenemos, y muramos todos peleando: y desde aquí adelante ninguno sea osado á me demandar pazes, si no yo le mataré: y allí todos prometiéron de pelear noches, y dias, y morir en la defensa de su ciudad." Ibid., ubi supra.

their embassy. At length it came, in a general sortie
of the Mexicans, who, pouring through every gate
of the capital, like a river that has burst its banks,
swept on, wave upon wave, to the very intrenchments
of the besiegers, threatening to overwhelm them by
their numbers. Fortunately, the position of the latter
on the dikes secured their flanks, and the narrowness
of the defile gave their small battery of guns all the
advantages of a larger one. The fire of artillery and
musketry blazed without intermission along the several
causeways, belching forth volumes of sulphurous smoke,
that, rolling heavily over the waters, settled dark
around the Indian city and hid it from the surrounding country. The brigantines thundered, at the same
time, on the flanks of the columns, which, after some
ineffectual efforts to maintain themselves, rolled back
in wild confusion, till their impotent fury died away in
sullen murmurs within the capital.

Cortés now steadily pursued the plan he had laid
down for the devastation of the city. Day after day
the several armies entered by their respective quarters,
Sandoval probably directing his operations against the
northeastern district. The buildings, made of the
porous *tetzontli*, though generally low, were so massy
and extensive, and the canals were so numerous, that
their progress was necessarily slow. They, however,
gathered fresh accessions of strength every day from
the numbers who flocked to the camp from the surrounding country, and who joined in the work of destruction with a hearty good will which showed their
eagerness to break the detested yoke of the Aztecs.
The latter raged with impotent anger as they beheld

their lordly edifices, their temples, all they had been accustomed to venerate, thus ruthlessly swept away; their canals, constructed with so much labor and what to them seemed science, filled up with rubbish; their flourishing city, in short, turned into a desert, over which the insulting foe now rode triumphant. They heaped many a taunt on the Indian allies. "Go on," they said, bitterly: "the more you destroy, the more you will have to build up again hereafter. If we conquer, you shall build for us; and if your white friends conquer, they will make you do as much for them." [18] The event justified the prediction.

In their rage they rushed blindly on the corps which covered the Indian pioneers. But they were as often driven back by the impetuous charge of the cavalry, or received on the long pikes of Chinantla, which did good service to the besiegers in their operations. At the close of day, however, when the Spaniards drew off their forces, taking care to send the multitudinous host of confederates first from the ground, the Mexicans usually rallied for a more formidable attack. Then they poured out from every lane and by-way, like so many mountain streams, sweeping over the broad level cleared by the enemy, and falling impetuously on their flanks and rear. At such times they inflicted considerable loss in their turn, till an ambush, which Cortés laid for them among the buildings adjoining the great

---

[18] "Los de la Ciudad como veian tanto estrago, por esforzarse, decian á nuestros Amigos, que no ficiessen sino quemar, y destruir, que ellos se las harian tornar á hacer de nuevo, porque si ellos eran vencedores, ya ellos sabian, que habia de ser assí, y si no que las habian de hacer para nosotros." Rel. Terc. de Cortés ap. Lorenzana, p. 286.

temple, did them so much mischief that they were compelled to act with more reserve.

At times the war displayed something of a chivalrous character, in the personal rencontres of the combatants. Challenges passed between them, and especially between the native warriors. These combats were usually conducted on the *azoteas*, whose broad and level surface afforded a good field of fight. On one occasion, a Mexican of powerful frame, brandishing a sword and buckler which he had won from the Christians, defied his enemies to meet him in single fight. A young page of Cortés', named Nuñez, obtained his master's permission to accept the vaunting challenge of the Aztec, and, springing on the *azotea*, succeeded, after a hard struggle, in discomfiting his antagonist, who fought at a disadvantage with weapons in which he was unpractised, and, running him through the body, brought off his spoils in triumph and laid them at the general's feet.[19]

The division of Cortés had now worked its way as far north as the great street of Tacuba, which opened a communication with Alvarado's camp, and near which stood the palace of Guatemozin. It was a spacious stone pile, that might well be called a fortress. Though deserted by its royal master, it was held by a strong body of Aztecs, who made a temporary defence, but of little avail against the battering enginery of the besiegers. It was soon set on fire, and its crumbling

[19] Rel. Terc. de Cortés, ap. Lorenzana, pp. 282-284.—Herrera, Hist. general, dec. 3, lib. 1, cap. 22, lib. 2, cap. 2.—Gomara, Crónica, cap. 140.—Oviedo, Hist. de las Ind., MS., lib. 33, cap. 28.—Ixtlilxochitl, Venida de los Españoles, p. 43.

walls were levelled in the dust, like those other stately edifices of the capital, the boast and admiration of the Aztecs, and some of the fairest fruits of their civilization. "It was a sad thing to witness their destruction," exclaims Cortés; "but it was part of our plan of operations, and we had no alternative." [20]

These operations had consumed several weeks, so that it was now drawing towards the latter part of July. During this time the blockade had been maintained with the utmost rigor, and the wretched inhabitants were suffering all the extremities of famine. Some few stragglers were taken, from time to time, in the neighborhood of the Christian camp, whither they had wandered in search of food. They were kindly treated, by command of Cortés, who was in hopes to induce others to follow their example, and thus to afford a means of conciliating the inhabitants, which might open the way to their submission. But few were found willing to leave the shelter of the capital, and they preferred to take their chance with their suffering countrymen rather than trust themselves to the mercies of the besiegers.

From these few stragglers, however, the Spaniards heard a dismal tale of woe respecting the crowded population in the interior of the city. All the ordinary means of sustenance had long since failed, and they now supported life as they could, by means of such roots as they could dig from the earth, by gnawing the bark of trees, by feeding on the grass,—on anything,

[20] "No se entendió sino en quemar, y hallanar Casas, que era lástima cierto de lo ver; pero como no nos convenia hacer otra cosa, eramos forzado seguir aquella órden." Rel. Terc. de Cortés, p. 286.

in short, however loathsome, that could allay the craving of appetite.   Their only drink was the brackish water of the soil saturated with the salt lake.[21]   Under this unwholesome diet, and the diseases engendered by it, the population was gradually wasting away.   Men sickened and died every day, in all the excruciating torments produced by hunger, and the wan and ema- ciated survivors seemed only to be waiting for their time.

The Spaniards had visible confirmation of all this as they penetrated deeper into the city and approached the district of Tlatelolco, now occupied by the be- sieged.   They found the ground turned up in quest of roots and weeds, the trees stripped of their green stems, their foliage, and their bark.   Troops of famished In- dians flitted in the distance, gliding like ghosts among the scenes of their former residence.   Dead bodies lay unburied in the streets and court-yards, or filled up the canals.   It was a sure sign of the extremity of the Aztecs; for they held the burial of the dead as a solemn and im- perative duty.   In the early part of the siege they had religiously attended to it.   In its later stages they were still careful to withdraw the dead from the public eye, by bringing their remains within the houses.   But the number of these, and their own sufferings, had now so fearfully increased that they had grown indifferent to this, and they suffered their friends and their kinsmen

[21] " No tenian agua dulce para beber, ni para de ninguna manera de comer; bebian del agua salada y hedionda, comian ratones y lagar- tijas, y cortezas de árboles, y otras cosas no comestibles; y de esta causa enfermáron muchos, y muriéron muchos." Sahagun, Hist. de Nueva-España, MS., lib. 12, cap. 39.—Also Rel. Terc. de Cortés, ap. Lorenzana, p. 289.

to lie and moulder on the spot where they drew their last breath![22]

As the invaders entered the dwellings, a more appalling spectacle presented itself;—the floors covered with the prostrate forms of the miserable inmates, some in the agonies of death, others festering in their corruption; men, women, and children inhaling the poisonous atmosphere, and mingled promiscuously together; mothers with their infants in their arms perishing of hunger before their eyes, while they were unable to afford them the nourishment of nature; men crippled by their wounds, with their bodies frightfully mangled, vainly attempting to crawl away, as the enemy entered. Yet even in this state they scorned to ask for mercy, and glared on the invaders with the sullen ferocity of the wounded tiger that the huntsmen have tracked to his forest cave. The Spanish commander issued strict orders that mercy should be shown to these poor and disabled victims. But the Indian allies made no distinction. An Aztec, under whatever circumstances, was an enemy; and, with hideous shouts of triumph, they pulled down the burning buildings on their heads,

[22] " Y es verdad y juro amen, que toda la laguna, y casas, y barbacoas estauan llenas de ouerpos, y cabeças de hombres muertos, que yo no sé de que manera lo escriua." (Bernal Diaz, Hist. de la Conquista, cap. 156.) Clavigero considers that it was a scheme of the Mexicans to leave the dead unburied, in order that the stench might annoy and drive off the Spaniards. (Stor. del Messico, tom. iii. p. 231, nota.) But this policy would have operated much more to the detriment of the besieged than of the besiegers, whose presence in the capital was but transitory. It is much more natural to refer it to the same cause which has led to a similar conduct under similar circumstances elsewhere, whether occasioned by pestilence or famine.

consuming the living and the dead in one common funeral pile !

Yet the sufferings of the Aztecs, terrible as they were, did not incline them to submission. There were many, indeed, who, from greater strength of constitution, or from the more favorable circumstances in which they were placed, still showed all their wonted energy of body and mind, and maintained the same undaunted and resolute demeanor as before. They fiercely rejected all the overtures of Cortés, declaring they would rather die than surrender, and adding, with a bitter tone of exultation, that the invaders would be at least disappointed in their expectations of treasure, for it was buried where they could never find it ! [23]

The women, it is said, shared in this desperate—it should rather be called heroic—spirit. They were indefatigable in nursing the sick and dressing their wounds; they aided the warriors in battle, by supplying them with the Indian ammunition of stones and arrows, prepared their slings, strung their bows, and displayed, in short, all the constancy and courage shown by the noble maidens of Saragossa in our day, and by those of Carthage in the days of antiquity. [24]

[23] Gonzalo de las Casas, Defensa, MS., cap. 28.—Martyr, De Orbe Novo, dec. 5, cap. 8.—Ixtlilxochitl, Venida de los Españoles, p. 45.—Rel. Terc. de Cortés, ap. Lorenzana, p. 289.—Oviedo, Hist. de las Ind., MS., lib. 33, cap. 29.

[24] " Muchas cosas acaeciéron en este cerco, que entre otras generaciones estobieran discantadas é tenidas en mucho, en especial de las Mugeres de Temixtitan, de quien ninguna mencion se ha fecho. Y soy certificado, que fué cosa maravillosa y para espantar, ver la prontitud y constancia que tobiéron en servir á sus maridos, y en curar los heridos, é en el labrar de las piedras para los que tiraban con

Cortés had now entered one of the great avenues leading to the market-place of Tlatelolco, the quarter towards which the movements of Alvarado were also directed. A single canal only lay in his way; but this was of great width and stoutly defended by the Mexican archery. At this crisis, the army one evening, while in their intrenchments on the causeway, were surprised by an uncommon light that arose from the huge *teocalli* in that part of the city which, being at the north, was the most distant from their own position. This temple, dedicated to the dread war-god, was inferior only to the pyramid in the great square; and on it the Spaniards had more than once seen their unhappy countrymen led to slaughter. They now supposed that the enemy were employed in some of their diabolical ceremonies,—when the flame, mounting higher and higher, showed that the sanctuaries themselves were on fire. A shout of exultation at the sight broke forth from the assembled soldiers, as they assured one another that their countrymen under Alvarado had got possession of the building.

It was indeed true. That gallant officer, whose position on the western causeway placed him near the district of Tlatelolco, had obeyed his commander's instructions to the letter, razing every building to the ground in his progress, and filling up the ditches with their ruins. He at length found himself before the great *teocalli* in the neighborhood of the market. He ordered a company, under a cavalier named Gutierre de Badajoz, to storm the place, which was defended by

hondas, é en otros oficios para mas que mugeres." Oviedo, Hist. de las Ind., MS., lib. 33, cap. 48.

a body of warriors, mingled with priests, still more
wild and ferocious than the soldiery. The garrison,
rushing down the winding terraces, fell on the assailants with such fury as compelled them to retreat in confusion and with some loss. Alvarado ordered another
detachment to their support. This last was engaged,
at the moment, with a body of Aztecs, who hung on
its rear as it wound up the galleries of the *teocalli*.
Thus hemmed in between two enemies, above and
below, the position of the Spaniards was critical. With
sword and buckler, they plunged desperately on the
ascending Mexicans, and drove them into the court-
yard below, where Alvarado plied them with such
lively volleys of musketry as soon threw them into
disorder and compelled them to abandon the ground.
Being thus rid of annoyance in the rear, the Spaniards
returned to the charge. They drove the enemy up
the heights of the pyramid, and, reaching the broad
summit, a fierce encounter followed in mid-air,—such
an encounter as takes place where death is the certain
consequence of defeat. It ended, as usual, in the discomfiture of the Aztecs, who were either slaughtered
on the spot still wet with the blood of their own
victims, or pitched headlong down the sides of the
pyramid.

The area was covered with the various symbols of
the barbarous worship of the country, and with two
lofty sanctuaries, before whose grinning idols were displayed the heads of several Christian captives who had
been immolated on their altars. Although overgrown
by their long, matted hair and bushy beards, the Spaniards could recognize, in the livid countenances, their

comrades who had fallen into the hands of the enemy. Tears fell from their eyes as they gazed on the melancholy spectacle and thought of the hideous death which their countrymen had suffered. They removed the sad relics with decent care, and after the Conquest deposited them in consecrated ground, on a spot since covered by the Church of the Martyrs.[25]

They completed their work by firing the sanctuaries, that the place might be no more polluted by these abominable rites. The flame crept slowly up the lofty pinnacles, in which stone was mingled with wood, till at length, bursting into one bright blaze, it shot up its spiral volume to such a height that it was seen from the most distant quarters of the Valley. It was this which had been hailed by the soldiery of Cortés, and it served as the beacon-light to both friend and foe, intimating the progress of the Christian arms.

The commander-in-chief and his division, animated by the spectacle, made, in their entrance on the following day, more determined efforts to place themselves alongside of their companions under Alvarado. The broad canal, above noticed as the only impediment now lying in his way, was to be traversed ; and on the farther side the emaciated figures of the Aztec warriors were gathered in numbers to dispute the passage, like the gloomy shades that wander—as ancient poets tell us—on the banks of the infernal river. They poured down, however, a storm of missiles, which were no shades, on the heads of the Indian laborers while

[25] Oviedo, Hist. de las Ind., MS., lib. 33, cap. 29.—Bernal Diaz, Hist. de la Conquista, cap. 155.—Rel. Terc. de Cortés, ap. Lorenzana, pp. 287-289.

occupied with filling up the wide gap with the ruins of the surrounding buildings. Still they toiled on in defiance of the arrowy shower, fresh numbers taking the place of those who fell. And when at length the work was completed, the cavalry rode over the rough plain at full charge against the enemy, followed by the deep array of spearmen, who bore down all opposition with their invincible phalanx.

The Spaniards now found themselves on the same ground with Alvarado's division. Soon afterwards, that chief, attended by several of his staff, rode into their lines, and cordially embraced his countrymen and companions in arms, for the first time since the beginning of the siege. They were now in the neighborhood of the market. Cortés, taking with him a few of his cavaliers, galloped into it. It was a vast enclosure, as the reader has already seen, covering many an acre.[26] Its dimensions were suited to the immense multitudes who gathered there from all parts of the Valley in the flourishing days of the Aztec monarchy. It was surrounded by porticoes and pavilions for the accommodation of the artisans and traders who

[26] *Ante*, vol. ii. p. 130.—The *tianguez* still continued of great dimensions, though with faded magnificence, after the Conquest, when it is thus noticed by Father Sahagun: " Entráron en la plaza ó Tianguez de esta Tlaltilulco (lugar muy espacioso mucho mas de lo que ahora es), el cual se podia llamar emporio de toda esta nueva España : al cual venian á tratar gentes de toda esta nueva España, y aun de los Reinos á ella contiguos, y donde se vendian y compraban todas cuantas cosas hay en toda esta tierra, y en los Reinos de Quahtimalla y Xalisco (cosa cierto mucho de ver), yo lo ví por muchos años morando en esta Casa del Señor Santiago aunque ya no era tanto como antes de la Conquista." Hist. de Nueva-España, MS., lib. 12, cap. 37.

there displayed their various fabrics and articles of merchandise. The flat roofs of the piazzas were now covered with crowds of men and women, who gazed in silent dismay on the steel-clad horsemen, that profaned these precincts with their presence for the first time since their expulsion from the capital. The multitude, composed for the most part, probably, of unarmed citizens, seemed taken by surprise; at least, they made no show of resistance; and the general, after leisurely viewing the ground, was permitted to ride back unmolested to the army.

On arriving there, he ascended the *teocalli*, from which the standard of Castile, supplanting the memorials of Aztec superstition, was now triumphantly floating. The Conqueror, as he strode among the smoking embers on the summit, calmly surveyed the scene of desolation below. The palaces, the temples, the busy marts of industry and trade, the glittering canals, covered with their rich freights from the surrounding country, the royal pomp of groves and gardens, all the splendors of the imperial city, the capital of the Western World, forever gone,—and in their place a barren wilderness! How different the spectacle which the year before had met his eye, as it wandered over the same scenes from the heights of the neighboring *teocalli*, with Montezuma at his side! Seven-eighths of the city were laid in ruins, with the occasional exception, perhaps, of some colossal temple which it would have required too much time to demolish.[27] The

---

[27] "É yo miré dende aquella Torre, lo que teniamos ganado de la Ciudad, que sin duda de ocho partes teniamos ganado las siete." Rel. Terc. de Cortés, ap. Lorenzana, p. 289.

remaining eighth, comprehending the district of Tlatelolco, was all that now remained to the Aztecs, whose
population—still large after all its losses—was crowded
into a compass that would hardly have afforded accommodations for a third of their numbers. It was the
quarter lying between the great northern and western
causeways, and is recognized in the modern capital as
the *Barrio de San Jago* and its vicinity. It was the
favorite residence of the Indians after the Conquest,[28]
though at the present day thinly covered with humble
dwellings, forming the straggling suburbs, as it were,
of the metropolis. Yet it still affords some faint vestiges of what it was in its prouder days; and the
curious antiquary, and occasionally the laborer, as he
turns up the soil, encounters a glittering fragment of
obsidian, or the mouldering head of a lance or arrow,
or some other warlike relic, attesting that on this spot
the retreating Aztecs made their last stand for the
independence of their country.[29]

On the day following, Cortés, at the head of his
battalions, made a second entry into the great *tianguez*.
But this time the Mexicans were better prepared for
his coming. They were assembled in considerable

[28] Toribio, Hist. de los Ind., MS., Parte 3, cap. 7.—The remains
of the ancient foundations may still be discerned in this quarter, while
in every other *etiam periêre ruinæ !*

[29] Bustamante, the Mexican editor of Sahagun, mentions that he
has now in his possession several of these military spoils. "Toda la
llanura del Santuario de nuestra Señora de los Ángeles y de Santiago
Tlaltilolco se ve sembrada de fragmentos de lanzas cortantes, de macanas, y flechas de piedra obsidiana, de que usaban los Mexicanos ó
sea Chinapos, y yo he recogido no pocos que conservo en mi poder."
Hist. de Nueva-España, lib. 12, nota 21.

force in the spacious square. A sharp encounter followed; but it was short. Their strength was not equal to their spirit, and they melted away before the rolling fire of musketry, and left the Spaniards masters of the enclosure.

The first act was to set fire to some temples, of no great size, within the market-place, or more probably on its borders. As the flames ascended, the Aztecs, horror-struck, broke forth into piteous lamentations at the destruction of the deities on whom they relied for protection.[30]

The general's next step was at the suggestion of a soldier named Sotelo, a man who had served under the Great Captain in the Italian wars, where he professed to have gathered knowledge of the science of engineering, as it was then practised. He offered his services to construct a sort of catapult, a machine for discharging stones of great size, which might take the place of the regular battering-train in demolishing the buildings. As the ammunition, notwithstanding the liberal supplies which from time to time had found their way into the camp, now began to fail, Cortés eagerly acceded to a proposal so well suited to his exigences. Timber and stone were furnished, and a number of hands were employed, under the direction of the self-styled engineer, in constructing the ponderous

[30] " Y como comenzó á arder, levantóse una llama tan alta que parecia llegar al cielo, al espectáculo de esta quema, todos los hombres y mugeres que se habian acogido á las tiendas que cercaban todo el Tianguez comenzáron á llorar á voz en grito, que fué cosa de espanto oirlos ; porque quemado aquel delubro satánico luego entendiéron que habian de ser del todo destruidos y robados." Sahagun, Hist. de Nueva-España, MS., lib. 12, cap. 37.

apparatus, which was erected on a solid platform of masonry, thirty paces square and seven or eight feet high, that covered the centre of the market-place. This was a work of the Aztec princes, and was used as a scaffolding on which mountebanks and jugglers might exhibit their marvelous feats for the amusement of the populace, who took great delight in these performances.[31]

The erection of the machine consumed several days, during which hostilities were suspended, while the artisans were protected from interruption by a strong corps of infantry. At length the work was completed; and the besieged, who with silent awe had beheld from the neighboring *azoteas* the progress of the mysterious engine which was to lay the remainder of their capital in ruins, now looked with terror for its operation. A stone of huge size was deposited on the timber. The machinery was set in motion; and the rocky fragment was discharged with a tremendous force from the catapult. But, instead of taking the direction of the Aztec buildings, it rose high and perpendicularly into the air, and, descending whence it sprung, broke the ill-omened machine into splinters! It was a total failure. The Aztecs were released from their apprehensions, and the soldiery made many a merry jest on the catastrophe, somewhat at the expense of their commander, who testified no little vexation at the disappointment, and still more at his own credulity.[32]

[31] Vestiges of the work are still visible, according to M. de Humboldt, within the limits of the porch of the chapel of St. Jago. Essai politique, tom. ii. p. 44.

[32] Bernal Diaz, Hist. de la Conquista, cap. 155.—Rel. Terc. de Cortés, ap. Lorenzana, p. 290.—Sahagun, Hist. de Nueva-España, MS., lib. 12, cap. 37.

CHAPTER VIII.

DREADFUL SUFFERINGS OF THE BESIEGED. — SPIRIT OF GUATEMOZIN.—MURDEROUS ASSAULTS.—CAPTURE OF GUATEMOZIN. — EVACUATION OF THE CITY. —TERMINATION OF THE SIEGE.—REFLECTIONS.

1521.

THERE was no occasion to resort to artificial means to precipitate the ruin of the Aztecs. It was accelerated every hour by causes more potent than those arising from mere human agency. There they were,—pent up in their close and suffocating quarters, nobles, commoners, and slaves, men, women, and children, some in houses, more frequently in hovels,—for this part of the city was not the best,—others in the open air in canoes, or in the streets, shivering in the cold rains of night, and scorched by the burning heat of day.[1] An old chronicler mentions the fact of two women of rank remaining three days and nights up to their necks in the water among the reeds, with only a handful of maize for their support.[2] The ordinary means of sus-

[1] "Estaban los tristes Mejicanos, hombres y mugeres, niños y niñas, viejos y viejas, heridos y enfermos, en un lugar bien estrecho, y bien apretados los unos con los otros, y con grandísima falta de bastimentos, y al calor del Sol, y al frio de la noche, y cada hora esperando la muerte." Sahagun, Hist. de Nueva-España, MS., lib. 12, cap. 39.

[2] Torquemada had the anecdote from a nephew of one of the Indian matrons, then a very old man himself. Monarch. Ind., lib. 4, cap. 102.

(174)

taining life were long since gone. They wandered about in search of anything, however unwholesome or revolting, that might mitigate the fierce gnawings of hunger. Some hunted for insects and worms on the borders of the lake, or gathered the salt weeds and moss from its bottom, while at times they might be seen casting a wistful look at the green hills beyond, which many of them had left to share the fate of their brethren in the capital.

To their credit, it is said by the Spanish writers that they were not driven, in their extremity, to violate the laws of nature by feeding on one another.[3] But, unhappily, this is contradicted by the Indian authorities, who state that many a mother, in her agony, devoured the offspring which she had no longer the means of supporting. This is recorded of more than one siege in history; and it is the more probable here, where the sensibilities must have been blunted by familiarity with the brutal practices of the national superstition.[4]

But all was not sufficient, and hundreds of famished wretches died every day from extremity of suffering.

3 Torquemada, Monarch. Ind., ubi supra.—Bernal Diaz, Hist. de la Conquista, cap. 156.

4 " De los niños, no quedó nadie, que las mismas madres y padres los comian (que era gran lástima de ver, y mayormente de sufrir)." (Sahagun, Hist. de Nueva-España, MS., lib. 12, cap. 39.) The historian derived his accounts from the Mexicans themselves, soon after the event.—One is reminded of the terrible denunciations of Moses "The tender and delicate woman among you, which would not adventure to set the sole of her foot upon the ground for delicateness and tenderness, her eye shall be evil toward . . . her children which she shall bear; for she shall eat them, for want of all things, secretly, in the siege and straitness wherewith thine enemy shall distress thee in thy gates." Deuteronomy, chap. 28, vs. 56, 57.

Some dragged themselves into the houses, and drew their last breath alone and in silence. Others sank down in the public streets. Wherever they died, there they were left. There was no one to bury or to remove them. Familiarity with the spectacle made men indifferent to it. They looked on in dumb despair, waiting for their own turn. There was no complaint, no lamentation, but deep, unutterable woe.

If in other quarters of the town the corpses might be seen scattered over the streets, here they were gathered in heaps. "They lay so thick," says Bernal Diaz, "that one could not tread except among the bodies."[5] "A man could not set his foot down," says Cortés, yet more strongly, "unless on the corpse of an Indian."[6] They were piled one upon another, the living mingled with the dead. They stretched themselves on the bodies of their friends, and lay down to sleep there. Death was everywhere. The city was a vast charnel-house, in which all was hastening to decay and decomposition. A poisonous steam arose from the mass of putrefaction, under the action of alternate rain and heat, which so tainted the whole atmosphere that the Spaniards, including the general himself, in their brief visits to the quarter, were made ill by it, and it bred a pestilence that swept off even greater numbers than the famine.[7]

[5] "No podiamos andar sino entre cuerpos, y cabeças de Indios muertos." Hist. de la Conquista, cap. 156.

[6] "No tenian donde estar sino sobre los cuerpos muertos de los suyos." Rel. Terc., ap. Lorenzana, p. 291.

[7] Bernal Diaz, Hist. de la Conquista, ubi supra.—Herrera, Hist. general, dec. 3, lib. 2, cap. 8.—Sahagun, Hist. de Nueva-España, MS., lib. 12, cap. 41.—Gonzalo de las Casas, Defensa, MS., cap. 28.

Men's minds were unsettled by these strange and accumulated horrors. They resorted to all the superstitious rites prescribed by their religion, to stay the pestilence. They called on their priests to invoke the gods in their behalf. But the oracles were dumb, or gave only gloomy responses. Their deities had deserted them, and in their place they saw signs of celestial wrath, telling of still greater woes in reserve. Many, after the siege, declared that, among other prodigies, they beheld a stream of light, of a blood-red color, coming from the north in the direction of Tepejacac, with a rushing noise like that of a whirlwind, which swept round the district of Tlatelolco, darting out sparkles and flakes of fire, till it shot far into the centre of the lake![8] In the disordered state of their nerves, a mysterious fear took possession of their senses. Prodigies were of familiar occurrence, and the most familiar phenomena of nature were converted into prodigies.[9] Stunned by their calamities, reason was bewildered, and they became the sport of the wildest and most superstitious fancies.

In the midst of these awful scenes, the young emperor of the Aztecs remained, according to all ac-

---

[8] "Un torbellino de fuego como sangre embuelto en brasas y en centellas, que partia de hacia Tepeacac (que es donde está ahora Santa María de Guadalupe) y fué haciendo gran ruido, hacia donde estaban acorralados los Mejicanos y Tlaltilulcanos ; y dió una vuelta para enrededor de ellos, y no dicen si los empeció algo, sino que habiendo dado aquella vuelta, se entró por la laguna adelante ; y allí desapareció." Sahagun, Hist. de Nueva-España, MS., lib. 12, cap. 40.

[9] "Inclinatis ad credendum animis," says the philosophic Roman historian, "loco ominum etiam fortuita." Tacitus, Hist., lib. 2, sec. 1.

H*

counts, calm and courageous. With his fair capital laid in ruins before his eyes, his nobles and faithful subjects dying around him, his territory rent away, foot by foot, till scarce enough remained for him to stand on, he rejected every invitation to capitulate, and showed the same indomitable spirit as at the commencement of the siege. When Cortés, in the hope that the extremities of the besieged would incline them to listen to an accommodation, persuaded a noble prisoner to bear to Guatemozin his proposals to that effect, the fierce young monarch, according to the general, ordered him at once to be sacrificed.[10] It is a Spaniard, we must remember, who tells the story.

Cortés, who had suspended hostilities for several days, in the vain hope that the distresses of the Mexicans would bend them to submission, now determined to drive them to it by a general assault. Cooped up as they were within a narrow quarter of the city, their position favored such an attempt. He commanded Alvarado to hold himself in readiness, and directed Sandoval—who, besides the causeway, had charge of the fleet, which lay off the Tlatelolcan district—to support the attack by a cannonade on the houses near the water. He then led his forces into the city, or rather across the horrid waste that now encircled it.

On entering the Indian precincts, he was met by several of the chiefs, who, stretching forth their emaciated arms, exclaimed, "You are the children of the Sun. But the Sun is swift in his course. Why are

---

[10] "Y como lo lleváron delante de Guatimucin su Señor, y él le comenzó á hablar sobre la Paz, dizque luego lo mandó matar y sacrificar." Rel. Terc., ap. Lorenzana, p. 293.

you, then, so tardy? Why do you delay so long to put an end to our miseries? Rather kill us at once, that we may go to our god Huitzilopochtli, who waits for us in heaven to give us rest from our sufferings!"[11]

Cortés was moved by their piteous appeal, and answered that he desired not their death, but their submission. "Why does your master refuse to treat with me," he said, "when a single hour will suffice for me to crush him and all his people?" He then urged them to request Guatemozin to confer with him, with the assurance that he might do it in safety, as his person should not be molested.

The nobles, after some persuasion, undertook the mission; and it was received by the young monarch in a manner which showed—if the anecdote before related of him be true—that misfortune had at length asserted some power over his haughty spirit. He consented to the interview, though not to have it take place on that day, but the following, in the great square of Tlatelolco. Cortés, well satisfied, immediately withdrew from the city and resumed his position on the causeway.

The next morning he presented himself at the place appointed, having previously stationed Alvarado there with a strong corps of infantry, to guard against treachery. The stone platform in the centre of the square was covered with mats and carpets, and a

[11] "Que pues ellos me tenian por Hijo del Sol, y el Sol en tanta brevedad como era en un dia y una noche daba vuelta á todo el Mundo, que porque yo assí brevemente no los acababa de matar, y los quitaba de penar tanto, porque ya ellos tenian deseos de morir, y irse al Cielo para su Ochilobus [Huitzilopochtli], que los estaba esperando para descansar." Rel. Terc., ap. Lorenzana, p. 292.

banquet was prepared to refresh the famished monarch and his nobles. Having made these arrangements, he awaited the hour of the interview.

But Guatemozin, instead of appearing himself, sent his nobles, the same who had brought to him the general's invitation, and who now excused their master's absence on the plea of illness. Cortés, though disappointed, gave a courteous reception to the envoys, considering that it might still afford the means of opening a communication with the emperor. He persuaded them, without much entreaty, to partake of the good cheer spread before them, which they did with a voracity that told how severe had been their abstinence. He then dismissed them with a seasonable supply of provisions for their master, pressing him to consent to an interview, without which it was impossible their differences could be adjusted.

The Indian envoys returned in a short time, bearing with them a present of fine cotton fabrics, of no great value, from Guatemozin, who still declined to meet the Spanish general. Cortés, though deeply chagrined, was unwilling to give up the point. "He will surely come," he said to the envoys, "when he sees that I suffer you to go and come unharmed, you who have been my steady enemies, no less than himself, throughout the war. He has nothing to fear from me." [12]   He

[12] "Y yo les torné á repetir, que no sabia la causa, porque él se recelaba venir ante mí, pues veia que á ellos, que yo sabia q̃ habian sido los causadores principales de la Guerra, y que la habian sustentado, les hacia buen tratamiento, que los dejaba ir, y venir seguramente, sin recibir enojo alguno; que les rogaba, que le tornassen á hablar, y mirassen mucho en esto de su venida, pues á él le convenia, y yo lo hacia por su provecho." Rel. Terc., ap. Lorenzana, pp. 294, 295.

again parted with them, promising to receive their answer the following day.

On the next morning the Aztec chiefs, entering the Christian quarters, announced to Cortés that Guatemozin would confer with him at noon in the market-place. The general was punctual at the hour; but without success. Neither monarch nor ministers appeared there. It was plain that the Indian prince did not care to trust the promises of his enemy. A thought of Montezuma may have passed across his mind. After he had waited three hours, the general's patience was exhausted, and, as he learned that the Mexicans were busy in preparations for defence, he made immediate dispositions for the assault.[13]

The confederates had been left without the walls; for he did not care to bring them within sight of the quarry before he was ready to slip the leash. He now ordered them to join him, and, supported by Alvarado's division, marched at once into the enemy's quarters. He found them prepared to receive him. Their most able-bodied warriors were thrown into the van, covering their feeble and crippled comrades. Women were seen occasionally mingling in the ranks, and, as well as children, thronged the *azoteas*, where, with famine-stricken visages and haggard eyes, they scowled defiance and hatred on their invaders.

As the Spaniards advanced, the Mexicans set up a

[13] The testimony is most emphatic and unequivocal to these repeated efforts on the part of Cortés to bring the Aztecs peaceably to terms. Besides his own Letter to the emperor, see Bernal Diaz, cap. 155,—Herrera, Hist. general, lib. 2, cap. 6, 7,—Torquemada, Monarch. Ind., lib. 4, cap. 100,—Ixtlilxochitl, Venida de los Españoles, pp. 44-48,—Oviedo, Hist. de las Ind., MS., lib. 33, cap. 29, 30.

fierce war-cry, and sent off clouds of arrows with their accustomed spirit, while the women and boys rained down darts and stones from their elevated position on the terraces. But the missiles were sent by hands too feeble to do much damage; and, when the squadrons closed, the loss of strength became still more sensible in the Aztecs. Their blows fell feebly and with doubt-ful aim, though some, it is true, of stronger constitu-tion, or gathering strength from despair, maintained to the last a desperate fight.

The arquebusiers now poured in a deadly fire. The brigantines replied by successive volleys, in the oppo-site quarter. The besieged, hemmed in, like deer surrounded by the huntsmen, were brought down on every side. The carnage was horrible. The ground was heaped up with slain, until the maddened combat-ants were obliged to climb over the human mounds to get at one another. The miry soil was saturated with blood, which ran off like water and dyed the canals themselves with crimson.[14] All was uproar and terrible confusion. The hideous yells of the barbarians, the oaths and execrations of the Spaniards, the cries of the wounded, the shrieks of women and children, the heavy blows of the Conquerors, the death-struggle of their victims, the rapid, reverberating echoes of mus-ketry, the hissing of innumerable missiles, the crash and crackling of blazing buildings, crushing hundreds in their ruins, the blinding volumes of dust and sul-phurous smoke shrouding all in their gloomy canopy,

[14] " Corrian Arroios de Sangre por las Calles, como pueden correr de Agua, quando llueve, y con ímpetu, y fuerça." Torquemada, Monarch. Ind., lib. 4, cap. 103.

made a scene appalling even to the soldiers of Cortés,
steeled as they were by many a rough passage of war,
and by long familiarity with blood and violence. "The
piteous cries of the women and children, in particular," says the general, "were enough to break one's
heart."[15] He commanded that they should be spared,
and that all who asked it should receive quarter. He
particularly urged this on the confederates, and placed
Spaniards among them to restrain their violence.[16] But
he had set an engine in motion too terrible to be con-
trolled. It were as easy to curb the hurricane in its
fury, as the passions of an infuriated horde of savages.
"Never did I see so pitiless a race," he exclaims, "or
anything wearing the form of man so destitute of humanity."[17] They made no distinction of sex or age,
and in this hour of vengeance seemed to be requiting
the hoarded wrongs of a century. At length, sated
with slaughter, the Spanish commander sounded a
retreat. It was full time, if, according to his own
statement,—we may hope it is an exaggeration,—forty

[15] " Era tanta la grita, y lloro de los Niños, y Mugeres, que no habia
Persona, á quien no quebrantasse el corazon." (Rel. Terc., ap. Lorenzana, p. 296.) They were a rash and stiff-necked race, exclaims
his reverend editor, the archbishop, with a charitable commentary!
"*Gens duræ cervicis gens absque consilio.*" Nota.

[16] " Como la gente de la Cibdad se salia á los nuestros, habia el
general proveido, que por todas las calles estubiesen Españoles para
estorvar á los amigos, que no matasen aquellos tristes, que eran sin
número. É tambien dixo á todos los amigos capitanes, que no con-
sintiesen á su gente que matasen á ninguno de los que salian."
Oviedo, Hist. de las Ind., MS., lib. 33, cap. 30.

[17] " La qual crueldad nunca en Generacion tan recia se vió, ni tan
fuera de toda órden de naturaleza, como en los Naturales de estas
partes." Rel. Terc. de Cortés, ap. Lorenzana, p. 296.

thousand souls had perished ![18] Yet their fate was to be envied, in comparison with that of those who survived.

Through the long night which followed, no movement was perceptible in the Aztec quarter. No light was seen there, no sound was heard, save the low moaning of some wounded or dying wretch, writhing in his agony. All was dark and silent,—the darkness of the grave. The last blow seemed to have completely stunned them. They had parted with hope, and sat in sullen despair, like men waiting in silence the stroke of the executioner. Yet, for all this, they showed no disposition to submit. Every new injury had sunk deeper into their souls, and filled them with a deeper hatred of their enemy. Fortune, friends, kindred, home,—all were gone. They were content to throw away life itself, now that they had nothing more to live for.

Far different was the scene in the Christian camp, where, elated with their recent successes, all was alive with bustle and preparation for the morrow. Bonfires were seen blazing along the causeways, lights gleamed from tents and barracks, and the sounds of music and merriment, borne over the waters, proclaimed the joy of the soldiers at the prospect of so soon terminating their wearisome campaign.

On the following morning the Spanish commander again mustered his forces, having decided to follow up the blow of the preceding day before the enemy should have time to rally, and at once to put an end to the

[18] Rel. Terc. de Cortés, ap. Lorenzana, ubi supra.—Ixtlilxochitl says, 50,000 were slain and taken in this dreadful onslaught. Venida de los Españoles, p. 48.

war. He had arranged with Alvarado, on the evening previous, to occupy the market-place of Tlatelolco; and the discharge of an arquebuse was to be the signal for a simultaneous assault. Sandoval was to hold the northern causeway, and, with the fleet, to watch the movements of the Indian emperor, and to intercept the flight to the main land, which Cortés knew he meditated. To allow him to effect this would be to leave a formidable enemy in his own neighborhood, who might at any time kindle the flame of insurrection throughout the country. He ordered Sandoval, however, to do no harm to the royal person, and not to fire on the enemy at all, except in self-defence.[19]

It was the memorable thirteenth of August, 1521, the day of St. Hippolytus,—from this circumstance selected as the patron saint of modern Mexico,—that Cortés led his warlike array for the last time across the black and blasted environs which lay around the Indian capital. On entering the Aztec precincts, he paused, willing to afford its wretched inmates one more chance of escape before striking the fatal blow. He obtained an interview with some of the principal chiefs, and expostulated with them on the conduct of their prince. "He surely will not," said the general, "see you all perish, when he can so easily save you." He then urged them to prevail on Guatemozin to hold a conference with him, repeating the assurances of his personal safety.

[19] "Adonde estauan retraidos el Guatemuz con toda la flor de sus Capitanes, y personas mas nobles que en Mexico auia, y le mandó que no matasse ni hiriesse á ningunos Indios, saluo si no le diessen guerra, é que aunque se la diessen, que solamente se defendiesse." Bernal Diaz, Hist. de la Conquista, cap. 156.

The messengers went on their mission, and soon returned with the *cihuacoatl* at their head, a magistrate of high authority among the Mexicans. He said, with a melancholy air, in which his own disappointment was visible, that "Guatemozin was ready to die where he was, but would hold no interview with the Spanish commander;" adding, in a tone of resignation, "it is for you to work your pleasure." "Go, then," replied the stern Conqueror, "and prepare your countrymen for death. Their hour is come."[20]

He still postponed the assault for several hours. But the impatience of his troops at this delay was heightened by the rumor that Guatemozin and his nobles were preparing to escape with their effects in the *piraguas* and canoes which were moored on the margin of the lake. Convinced of the fruitlessness and impolicy of further procrastination, Cortés made his final dispositions for the attack, and took his own station on an *azotea* which commanded the theatre of operations.

When the assailants came into the presence of the enemy, they found them huddled together in the utmost confusion, all ages and sexes, in masses so dense that they nearly forced one another over the brink of the causeways into the water below. Some had climbed on the terraces, others feebly supported themselves against the walls of the buildings. Their squalid and tattered garments gave a wildness to their appearance which

[20] "Y al fin me dijo, que en ninguna manera el Señor vernia ante mí; y antes queria por allá morir, y que á él pesaba mucho de esto, que hiciesse yo lo que quisiesse; y como ví en esto su determinacion, yo le dije ; que se bolviesse á los suyos, y que él, y ellos se aparejassen, porque los queria combatir, y acabar de matar, y assí se fué." Rel. Terc. de Cortés, ap. Lorenzana, p. 298.

still further heightened the ferocity of their expression, as they glared on their enemy with eyes in which hate was mingled with despair. When the Spaniards had approached within bowshot, the Aztecs let off a flight of impotent missiles, showing to the last the resolute spirit, though they had lost the strength, of their better days. The fatal signal was then given by the discharge of an arquebuse,—speedily followed by peals of heavy ordnance, the rattle of fire-arms, and the hellish shouts of the confederates as they sprang upon their victims. It is unnecessary to stain the page with a repetition of the horrors of the preceding day. Some of the wretched Aztecs threw themselves into the water and were picked up by the canoes. Others sank and were suffocated in the canals. The number of these became so great that a bridge was made of their dead bodies, over which the assailants could climb to the opposite banks. Others again, especially the women, begged for mercy, which, as the chroniclers assure us, was everywhere granted by the Spaniards, and, contrary to the instructions and entreaties of Cortés, everywhere refused by the confederates.[21]

While this work of butchery was going on, numbers were observed pushing off in the barks that lined the shore, and making the best of their way across the lake. They were constantly intercepted by the brigantines, which broke through the flimsy array of boats, sending off their volleys to the right and left, as the crews of the latter hotly assailed them. The battle

[21] Oviedo, Hist. de las Ind., MS., lib. 33, cap. 30.—Ixtlilxochitl, Venida de los Españoles, p. 48.—Herrera, Hist. general, dec. 3, lib. 2, cap. 7.—Rel. Terc. de Cortés, ap. Lorenzana, pp. 297, 298.—Gomara, Crónica, cap. 142.

raged as fiercely on the lake as on the land. Many of the Indian vessels were shattered and overturned. Some few, however, under cover of the smoke, which rolled darkly over the waters, succeeded in clearing themselves of the turmoil, and were fast nearing the opposite shore.

Sandoval had particularly charged his captains to keep an eye on the movements of any vessel in which it was at all probable that Guatemozin might be concealed. At this crisis, three or four of the largest *piraguas* were seen skimming over the water and making their way rapidly across the lake. A captain, named Garci Holguin, who had command of one of the best sailers in the fleet, instantly gave them chase. The wind was favorable, and every moment he gained on the fugitives, who pulled their oars with a vigor that despair alone could have given. But it was in vain ; and, after a short race, Holguin, coming alongside of one of the *piraguas*, which, whether from its appearance or from information he had received, he conjectured might bear the Indian emperor, ordered his men to level their cross-bows at the boat. But, before they could discharge them, a cry arose from those in it that their lord was on board. At the same moment a young warrior, armed with buckler and *maquahuitl*, rose up, as if to beat off the assailants. But, as the Spanish captain ordered his men not to shoot, he dropped his weapons, and exclaimed, " I am Guatemoz:n. Lead me to Malinche ; I am his prisoner ; but let no harm come to my wife and my followers." [22]

[22] Ixtlilxochitl, Venida de los Españoles, p. 49.—" No me tiren, que yo soy el Rey de México, y desta tierra, y lo que te ruego es, que no

Holguin assured him that his wishes should be respected, and assisted him to get on board the brigantine, followed by his wife and attendants. These were twenty in number, consisting of Coanaco, the deposed lord of Tezcuco, the lord of Tlacopan, and several other caciques and dignitaries, whose rank, probably, had secured them some exemption from the general calamities of the siege. When the captives were seated on the deck of his vessel, Holguin requested the Aztec prince to put an end to the combat by commanding his people in the other canoes to surrender. But, with a dejected air, he replied, " It is not necessary. They will fight no longer, when they see that their prince is taken." He spoke truth. The news of Guatemozin's capture spread rapidly through the fleet, and on shore, where the Mexicans were still engaged in conflict with their enemies. It ceased, however, at once. They made no further resistance ; and those on the water quickly followed the brigantines, which conveyed their captive monarch to land. It seemed as if the fight had been maintained thus long the better to divert the enemy's attention and cover their master's retreat.[23]

me llegues á mi muger, ni á mis hijos ; ni á ninguna muger, ni á ninguna cosa de lo que aquí traygo, sino que me tomes á mi, y me lleues á Malinche." (Bernal Diaz, Hist. de la Conquista, cap. 156.) M. de Humboldt has taken much pains to identify the place of Guatemozin's capture,—now become dry land,—which he considers to have been somewhere between the Garita de Peralvillo, the square of Santiago, Tlaltelolco, and the bridge of Amaxac. Essai politique, tom. ii. p. 76.*

[23] For the preceding account of the capture of Guatemozin, told

* [According to an old tradition, it was on the Puente del Cabildo, which is within the limits designated by Humboldt. Alaman, Conquista de Méjico (trad. de Vega), tom. ii. p. 209, note.—ED.]

Meanwhile, Sandoval, on receiving tidings of the capture, brought his own brigantine alongside of Holguin's and demanded the royal prisoner to be surrendered to him. But the captain claimed him as his prize. A dispute arose between the parties, each anxious to have the glory of the deed, and perhaps the privilege of commemorating it on his escutcheon. The controversy continued so long that it reached the ears of Cortés, who, in his station on the *azotea*, had learned with no little satisfaction the capture of his enemy. He instantly sent orders to his wrangling officers to bring Guatemozin before him, that he might adjust the difference between them.[24] He charged them, at the same time, to treat their prisoner with respect. He then made preparations for the interview, caused the terrace to be carpeted with crimson cloth and matting, and a table to be spread with provisions, of which the

with little discrepancy, though with more or less minuteness, by the different writers, see Bernal Diaz, Hist. de la Conquista, ubi supra,— Rel. Terc. de Cortés, p. 299,—Gonzalo de las Casas, Defensa, MS.,— Oviedo, Hist. de las Ind., MS., lib. 33, cap. 30,—Torquemada, Monarch. Ind., lib. 4, cap. 101.

[24] The general, according to Diaz, rebuked his officers for their ill-timed contention, reminding them of the direful effects of a similar quarrel between Marius and Sylla respecting Jugurtha. (Hist. de la Conquista, cap. 156.) This piece of pedantry savors much more of the old chronicler than his commander. The result of the whole— not an uncommon one in such cases—was that the emperor granted to neither of the parties, but to Cortés, the exclusive right of commemorating the capture of Guatemozin on his escutcheon. He was permitted to bear three crowns of gold on a sable field, one above the other two, in token of his victory over the three lords of Mexico, Montezuma, his brother Cuitlahua, and Guatemozin. A copy of the instrument containing the grant of the arms of Cortés may be found in the " Disertaciones históricas" of Alaman, tom. ii. apénd. 2.

unhappy Aztecs stood so much in need.[25] His lovely Indian mistress, Doña Marina, was present to act as interpreter. She had stood by his side through all the troubled scenes of the Conquest, and she was there now to witness its triumphant termination.

Guatemozin, on landing, was escorted by a company of infantry to the presence of the Spanish commander. He mounted the *azotea* with a calm and steady step, and was easily to be distinguished from his attendant nobles, though his full, dark eye was no longer lighted up with its accustomed fire, and his features wore an expression of passive resignation, that told little of the fierce and fiery spirit that burned within. His head was large, his limbs well proportioned, his complexion fairer than that of his bronze-colored nation, and his whole deportment singularly mild and engaging.[26]

Cortés came forward with a dignified and studied courtesy to receive him. The Aztec monarch probably knew the person of his conqueror,* for he first broke silence by saying, "I have done all that I could to defend myself and my people. I am now reduced to this state. You will deal with me, Malinche, as you

[25] Sahagun, Hist. de Nueva-España, lib. 12, cap. 40, MS.

[26] For the portrait of Guatemozin I again borrow the faithful pencil of Diaz, who knew him—at least his person—well: "Guatemuz era de muy gentil disposicion, assí de cuerpo, como de fayciones, y la cata algo larga, y alegre, y los ojos mas parecian que quando miraua, que eran con grauedad, y halagüeños, y no auia falta en ellos, y era de edad de veinte y tres, ó veinte y quatro años, y el color tiraua mas á blanco, que al color, y matiz de essotros Indios morenos." Hist. de la Conquista, cap. 156.

[* It was unnecessary to qualify the statement, as they had often seen each other at the court of Montezuma. Alaman, Conquista de Méjico (trad. de Vega), tom. ii. p. 211, note.—ED.]

list." Then, laying his hand on the hilt of a poniard stuck in the general's belt, he added, with vehemence, "Better despatch me with this, and rid me of life at once." [27] Cortés was filled with admiration at the proud bearing of the young barbarian, showing in his reverses a spirit worthy of an ancient Roman. "Fear not," he replied: "you shall be treated with all honor. You have defended your capital like a brave warrior. A Spaniard knows how to respect valor even in an enemy." [28] He then inquired of him where he had left the princess his wife; and, being informed that she still remained under protection of a Spanish guard on board the brigantine, the general sent to have her escorted to his presence.

She was the youngest daughter of Montezuma, and was hardly yet on the verge of womanhood. On the accession of her cousin Guatemozin to the throne, she had been wedded to him as his lawful wife. [29] She is

[27] " Llegóse á mi, y díjome en su lengua : que ya él habia hecho todo, lo que de su parte era obligado para defenderse á sí, y á los suyos, hasta venir en aquel estado ; que ahora ficiesse de él lo que yo quisiesse ; y puso la mano en un puñal, que yo tenia, diciéndome, que le diesse de puñaladas, y le matasse."   (Rel. Terc. de Cortés, ap. Lorenzana, p. 300.)   This remarkable account by the Conqueror himself is confirmed by Diaz, who does not appear to have seen this letter of his commander.   Hist. de la Conquista, cap. 156.

[28] Ibid., cap. 156.—Also Oviedo, Hist. de las Ind., MS., lib. 33, cap. 48,—and Martyr (De Orbe Novo, dec. 5, cap. 8), who, by the epithet of *magnanimo regi*, testifies the admiration which Guatemozin's lofty spirit excited in the court of Castile.

[29] The ceremony of marriage, which distinguished the "lawful wife" from the cóncubine, is described by Don Thoan Cano, in his conversation with Oviedo.   According to this, it appears that the only legitimate offspring which Montezuma left at his death was a son and a daughter, this same princess.—See Appendix, Part 2, No. 11.

celebrated by her contemporaries for her personal charms; and the beautiful princess Tecuichpo is still commemorated by the Spaniards, since from her by a subsequent marriage are descended some of the illustrious families of their own nation.[30] She was kindly received by Cortés, who showed her the respectful attentions suited to her rank. Her birth, no doubt, gave her an additional interest in his eyes, and he may have felt some touch of compunction as he gazed on the daughter of the unfortunate Montezuma. He invited his royal captives to partake of the refreshments which their exhausted condition rendered so necessary. Meanwhile the Spanish commander made his dispositions for the night, ordering Sandoval to escort the prisoners to Cojohuacan, whither he proposed himself immediately to follow. The other captains, Olid and Alvarado, were to draw off their forces to their respective quarters. It was impossible for them to continue in the capital, where the poisonous effluvia from the unburied carcasses loaded the air with infection. A small guard only was stationed to keep order in the wasted suburbs. It was the hour of vespers when Guatemozin surrendered,[31]

[30] For a further account of Montezuma's daughter, see Book VII., chapter iii. of this History.

[31] The event is annually commemorated—or rather was, under the colonial government—by a solemn procession round the walls of the city. It took place on the 13th of August, the anniversary of the surrender, and consisted of the principal cavaliers and citizens on horseback, headed by the viceroy, and displaying the venerable standard of the Conqueror.[*]

———

[* It was the royal standard, not that of Cortés, which was carried on this occasion. The celebration was suppressed by a decree of the córtes of Cadiz in 1812. Alaman, Conquista de Méjico, trad. de Vega, tom. ii. p. 212, note.—ED.]

and the siege might be considered as then concluded. The evening set in dark, and the rain began to fall before the several parties had evacuated the city.[32]

During the night, a tremendous tempest, such as the Spaniards had rarely witnessed, and such as is known only within the tropics, burst over the Mexican Valley. The thunder, reverberating from the rocky amphitheatre of hills, bellowed over the waste of waters, and shook the *teocallis* and crazy tenements of Tenochtitlan —the few that yet survived—to their foundations. The lightning seemed to cleave asunder the vault of heaven, as its vivid flashes wrapped the whole scene in a ghastly glare, for a moment, to be again swallowed up in darkness. The war of elements was in unison with the fortunes of the ruined city. It seemed as if the deities of Anahuac, scared from their ancient abodes, were

[32] Toribio, Hist. de los Ind., MS., Parte 3, cap. 7.—Sahagun, Hist. de Nueva-España, MS., lib. 12, cap. 42.—Bernal Diaz, Hist. de la Conquista, cap. 156.—"The lord of Mexico having surrendered," says Cortés, in his letter to the emperor, " the war, by the blessing of Heaven, was brought to an end, on Wednesday, the 13th day of August, 1521. So that from the day when we first sat down before the city, which was the 30th of May, until its final occupation, seventy-five days elapsed." (Rel. Terc., ap. Lorenzana, p. 300.) It is not easy to tell what event occurred on May 30th to designate the beginning of the siege. Clavigero considers it the occupation of Cojohuacan by Olid. (Stor. del Messico, tom. iii. p. 196.) But I know not on what authority. Neither Bernal Diaz, nor Herrera, nor Cortés, so fixes the date. Indeed, Clavigero says that Alvarado and Olid left Tezcuco May 20th, while Cortés says May 10th. Perhaps Cortés dates from the time when Sandoval established himself on the northern causeway, and when the complete investment of the capital began. Bernal Diaz, more than once, speaks of the siege as lasting three months, computing, probably, from the time when his own division, under Alvarado, took up its position at Tacuba.

borne along shrieking and howling in the blast, as they
abandoned the fallen capital to its fate ! [33]

On the day following the surrender, Guatemozin
requested the Spanish commander to allow the Mexicans to leave the city and to pass unmolested into the
open country. To this Cortés readily assented, as, indeed, without it he could take no steps for purifying
the capital. He gave his orders, accordingly, for the
evacuation of the place, commanding that no one,
Spaniard or confederate, should offer violence to the
Aztecs or in any way obstruct their departure. The
whole number of these is variously estimated at from
thirty to seventy thousand, besides women and children, who had survived the sword, pestilence, and
famine.[34] It is certain they were three days in defiling
along the several causeways,—a mournful train ; [35] husbands and wives, parents and children, the sick and
the wounded, leaning on one another for support, as

[33] It did not, apparently, disturb the slumbers of the troops, who
had been so much deafened by the incessant noises of the siege that,
now these had ceased, "we felt," says Diaz, in his homely way, "like
men suddenly escaped from a belfry, where we had been shut up for
months with a chime of bells ringing in our ears!" Hist. de la Conquista, ubi supra.

[34] Herrera (Hist. general, dec. 3, lib. 2, cap. 7) and Torquemada
(Monarch. Ind., lib. 4, cap. 101) estimate them at 30,000. Ixtlilxochitl says that 60,000 fighting-men laid down their arms (Venida de
los Españoles, p. 49) ; and Oviedo swells the amount still higher, to
70,000. (Hist. de las Ind., MS., lib. 33, cap. 48.)—After the losses of
the siege, these numbers are startling.

[35] " Digo que en tres dias con sus noches iban todas tres calçadas
llenas de Indios, é Indias, y muchachos, llenas de bote en bote, que
nunca dexauan de salir, y tan flacos, y suzios, é amarillos, é hedion-
dos, que era lástima de los ver." Bernal Diaz, Hist. de la Conquista,
cap. 156.

they feebly tottered along, squalid, and but half covered with rags, that disclosed at every step hideous
gashes, some recently received, others festering from
long neglect, and carrying with them an atmosphere
of contagion. Their wasted forms and famine-stricken
faces told the whole history of the siege; and, as the
straggling files gained the opposite shore, they were
observed to pause from time to time, as if to take one
more look at the spot so lately crowned by the imperial city, once their pleasant home, and endeared to
them by many a glorious recollection.

On the departure of the inhabitants, measures were
immediately taken to purify the place, by means of
numerous fires kept burning day and night, especially
in the infected quarter of Tlatelolco, and by collecting the heaps of dead, which lay mouldering in the
streets, and consigning them to the earth. Of the
whole number who perished in the course of the siege
it is impossible to form any probable computation.
The accounts range widely, from one hundred and
twenty thousand, the lowest estimate, to two hundred
and forty thousand.[36] The number of the Spaniards

[36] Cortés estimates the losses of the enemy in the three several
assaults at 67,000, which with 50,000 whom he reckons to have perished from famine and disease would give 117,000. (Rel. Terc., ap.
Lorenzana, p. 298, et alibi.) But this is exclusive of those who fell
previously to the commencement of the vigorous plan of operations
for demolishing the city. Ixtlilxochitl, who seldom allows any one to
beat him in figures, puts the dead, in round numbers, at 240,000, comprehending the flower of the Aztec nobility. (Venida de los Españoles,
p. 51.) Bernal Diaz observes, more generally, " I have read the story
of the destruction of Jerusalem, but I doubt if there was as great
mortality there as in this siege; for there was assembled in the city an
immense number of Indian warriors from all the provinces and towns

who fell was comparatively small, but that of the allies must have been large, if the historian of Tezcuco is correct in asserting that thirty thousand perished of his own countrymen alone.[37]   That the number of those destroyed within the city was immense cannot be doubted, when we consider that, besides its own redundant population, it was thronged with that of the neighboring towns, who, distrusting their strength to resist the enemy, sought protection within its walls.

The booty found there—that is, the treasures of gold and jewels, the only booty of much value in the eyes of the Spaniards—fell far below their expectations.   It did not exceed, according to the general's statement, a hundred and thirty thousand *castellanos* of gold, including the sovereign's share, which, indeed, taking into account many articles of curious and costly workmanship, voluntarily relinquished by the army, greatly exceeded his legitimate fifth.[38]   Yet the Aztecs must have been in possession of a much larger treasure, if it

subject to Mexico, the most of whom perished."   (Hist. de la Conquista, cap. 156.)   "I have conversed," says Oviedo, "with many hidalgos and other persons, and have heard them say that the number of the dead was incalculable,—greater than that at Jerusalem, as described by Josephus."   (Hist. de las Ind., MS., lib. 30, cap. 30.) As the estimate of the Jewish historian amounts to 1,100,000 (Antiquities of the Jews, Eng. trans., book vii. chap. xvii.), the comparison may stagger the most accommodating faith.   It will be safer to dispense with arithmetic where the data are too loose and slippery to afford a foothold for getting at truth.

[37] Ixtlilxochitl, Venida de los Españoles, p. 51.

[38] Rel. Terc., ap. Lorenzana, p. 301.—Oviedo goes into some further particulars respecting the amount of the treasure, and especially of the imperial fifth, to which I shall have occasion to advert hereafter. Hist. de las Ind., MS., lib. 33, cap. 31.

were only the wreck of that recovered from the Spaniards on the night of the memorable flight from Mexico. Some of the spoil may have been sent away from the capital, some spent in preparations for defence, and more of it buried in the earth, or sunk in the water of the lake. Their menaces were not without a meaning. They had, at least, the satisfaction of disappointing the avarice of their enemies.

Cortés had no further occasion for the presence of his Indian allies. He assembled the chiefs of the different squadrons, thanked them for their services, noticed their valor in flattering terms, and, after distributing presents among them, with the assurance that his master the emperor would recompense their fidelity yet more largely, dismissed them to their own homes. They carried off a liberal share of the spoils of which they had plundered the dwellings,—not of a kind to excite the cupidity of the Spaniards,—and returned in triumph, short-sighted triumph! at the success of their expedition and the downfall of the Aztec dynasty.

Great, also, was the satisfaction of the Spaniards at this brilliant termination of their long and laborious campaign. They were, indeed, disappointed at the small amount of treasure found in the conquered city. But the soldier is usually too much absorbed in the present to give much heed to the future ; and, though their discontent showed itself afterwards in a more clamorous form, they now thought only of their triumph, and abandoned themselves to jubilee. Cortés celebrated the event by a banquet, as sumptuous as circumstances would permit, to which all the cavaliers and officers were invited. Loud and long was their revelry, which was carried to such an excess as provoked the animadversion of Father Olmedo, who intimated that this was not the fitting way to testify their sense of the favors shown them by the Almighty. Cortés admitted the justice of the rebuke, but craved some indulgence for a soldier's license in the hour of victory. The following day was appointed for the commemoration of their successes in a more suitable manner.

A procession of the whole army was then formed, with Father Olmedo at its head. The soiled and tattered banners of Castile, which had waved over many a field of battle, now threw their shadows on the peaceful array of the soldiery, as they slowly moved along, rehearsing the litany, and displaying the image of the Virgin and the blessed symbol of man's redemption. The reverend father pronounced a discourse, in which he briefly reminded the troops of their great cause for thankfulness to Providence for conducting them safe through their long and perilous pilgrimage ; and, dwelling on the responsibility incurred by their present position, he besought them not to abuse the rights of conquest, but to treat the unfortunate Indians with humanity. The sacrament was then administered to the commander-in-chief and the principal cavaliers, and the services concluded with a solemn thanksgiving to the God of battles, who had enabled them to carry the banner of the Cross triumphant over this barbaric empire.[39]

[39] Herrera, Hist. general, dec. 3, lib. 2, cap. 8.—Bernal Diaz, Hist. de la Conquista, cap. 156.—Sahagun, Hist. de Nueva-España, MS., lib. 12, cap. 42.—Oviedo, Hist. de las Ind., MS., lib. 33, cap. 30.—Ixtlilxochitl, Venida de los Españoles, pp. 51, 52.

Thus, after a siege of nearly three months' duration, unmatched in history for the constancy and courage of the besieged, seldom surpassed for the severity of its sufferings, fell the renowned capital of the Aztecs. Unmatched, it may be truly said, for constancy and courage, when we recollect that the door of capitulation on the most honorable terms was left open to them throughout the whole blockade, and that, sternly rejecting every proposal of their enemy, they, to a man, preferred to die rather than surrender. More than three centuries had elapsed since the Aztecs, a poor and wandering tribe from the far Northwest, had come on the plateau. There they built their miserable collection of huts on the spot—as tradition tells us—prescribed by the oracle. Their conquests, at first confined to their immediate neighborhood, gradually covered the Valley, then, crossing the mountains, swept over the broad extent of the table-land, descended its precipitous sides, and rolled onwards to the Mexican Gulf and the distant confines of Central America. Their wretched capital, meanwhile, keeping pace with the enlargement of territory, had grown into a flourishing city, filled with buildings, monuments of art, and a numerous population, that gave it the first rank among the capitals of the Western World. At this crisis came over another race from the remote East, strangers like themselves, whose coming had also been predicted by the oracle, and, appearing on the plateau, assailed them in the very zenith of their prosperity, and blotted them out from the map of nations forever! The whole story has the air of fable rather than of history! a legend of romance,—a tale of the genii!

Yet we cannot regret the fall of an empire which did so little to promote the happiness of its subjects or the real interests of humanity. Notwithstanding the lustre thrown over its latter days by the glorious defence of its capital, by the mild munificence of Montezuma, by the dauntless heroism of Guatemozin, the Aztecs were emphatically a fierce and brutal race, little calculated, in their best aspects, to excite our sympathy and regard. Their civilization, such as it was, was not their own, but reflected, perhaps imperfectly, from a race whom they had succeeded in the land. It was, in respect to the Aztecs, a generous graft on a vicious stock, and could have brought no fruit to perfection. They ruled over their wide domains with a sword, instead of a sceptre. They did nothing to ameliorate the condition or in any way promote the progress of their vassals. Their vassals were serfs, used only to minister to their pleasure, held in awe by armed garrisons, ground to the dust by imposts in peace, by military conscriptions in war. They did not, like the Romans, whom they resembled in the nature of their conquests, extend the rights of citizenship to the conquered. They did not amalgamate them into one great nation, with common rights and interests. They held them as aliens,—even those who in the Valley were gathered round the very walls of the capital. The Aztec metropolis, the heart of the monarchy, had not a sympathy, not a pulsation, in common with the rest of the body politic. It was a stranger in its own land.

The Aztecs not only did not advance the condition of their vassals, but, morally speaking, they did much to degrade it. How can a nation where human sacri-

I*

fices prevail, and especially when combined with cannibalism, further the march of civilization? How can the interests of humanity be consulted, where man is levelled to the rank of the brutes that perish? The influence of the Aztecs introduced their gloomy superstition into lands before unacquainted with it, or where, at least, it was not established in any great strength. The example of the capital was contagious. As the latter increased in opulence, the religious celebrations were conducted with still more terrible magnificence; in the same manner as the gladiatorial shows of the Romans increased in pomp with the increasing splendor of the capital. Men became familiar with scenes of horror and the most loathsome abominations. Women and children—the whole nation—became familiar with and assisted at them. The heart was hardened, the manners were made ferocious, the feeble light of civilization, transmitted from a milder race, was growing fainter and fainter, as thousands and thousands of miserable victims, throughout the empire, were yearly fattened in its cages, sacrificed on its altars, dressed and served at its banquets! The whole land was converted into vast human shambles! The empire of the Aztecs did not fall before its time.

Whether these unparalleled outrages furnish a sufficient plea to the Spaniards for their invasion, whether, with the Protestant, we are content to find a warrant for it in the natural rights and demands of civilization, or, with the Roman Catholic, in the good pleasure of the Pope,—on the one or other of which grounds the conquests by most Christian nations in the East and the West have been defended,—it is unnecessary to discuss, as it has already been considered in a former chapter. It is more material to inquire whether, assuming the right, the conquest of Mexico was conducted with a proper regard to the claims of humanity. And here we must admit that, with all allowance for the ferocity of the age and the laxity of its principles, there are passages which every Spaniard who cherishes the fame of his countrymen would be glad to see expunged from their history; passages not to be vindicated on the score of self-defence, or of necessity of any kind, and which must forever leave a dark spot on the annals of the Conquest. And yet, taken as a whole, the invasion, up to the capture of the capital, was conducted on principles less revolting to humanity than most, perhaps than any, of the other conquests of the Castilian crown in the New World.

It may seem slight praise to say that the followers of Cortés used no blood-hounds to hunt down their wretched victims, as in some other parts of the Continent, nor exterminated a peaceful and submissive population in mere wantonness of cruelty, as in the Islands. Yet it is something that they were not so far infected by the spirit of the age, and that their swords were rarely stained with blood unless it was indispensable to the success of their enterprise. Even in the last siege of the capital, the sufferings of the Aztecs, terrible as they were, do not imply any unusual cruelty in the victors; they were not greater than those inflicted on their own countrymen at home, in many a memorable instance, by the most polished nations, not merely of ancient times, but of our own. They were the inevitable consequences which follow from war when, instead of being confined to its legitimate field, it is brought home to the hearthstone, to the peaceful community of the city,—its burghers untrained to arms, its women and children yet more defenceless. In the present instance, indeed, the sufferings of the besieged were in a great degree to be charged on themselves,—on their patriotic but desperate self-devotion. It was not the desire, as certainly it was not the interest, of the Spaniards to destroy the capital or its inhabitants. When any of these fell into their hands, they were kindly entertained, their wants supplied, and every means taken to infuse into them a spirit of conciliation; and this, too, it should be remembered, in despite of the dreadful doom to which they consigned their Christian captives. The gates of a fair capitulation were kept open, though unavailingly, to the last hour.

The right of conquest necessarily implies that of using whatever force may be necessary for overcoming resistance to the assertion of that right. For the Spaniards to have done otherwise than they did would have been to abandon the siege, and, with it, the conquest of the country. To have suffered the inhabitants, with their high-spirited monarch, to escape, would but have prolonged the miseries of war by transferring it to another and more inaccessible quarter. They literally, so far as the success of the expedition was concerned, had no choice. If our imagination is struck with the amount of suffering in this and in similar scenes of the Conquest, it should be borne in mind that it was a natural result of the great masses of men engaged in the conflict. The amount of suffering does not of itself show the amount of cruelty which caused it ; and it is but justice to the Conquerors of Mexico to say that the very brilliancy and importance of their exploits have given a melancholy celebrity to their misdeeds, and thrown them into somewhat bolder relief than strictly belongs to them. It is proper that thus much should be stated, not to excuse their excesses, but that we may be enabled to make a more impartial estimate of their conduct as compared with that of other nations under similar circumstances, and that we may not visit them with peculiar obloquy for evils which necessarily flow from the condition of war.[40] I have not drawn a veil over these evils ; for the historian should not shrink from depicting in their true colors the atrocities of a condition over which success is apt to throw a false halo of glory, but which, bursting asunder the strong bonds of human fellowship, purchases its triumphs by arming the hand of man against his brother, makes a savage of the civilized, and kindles the fires of hell in the bosom of the savage

[40] By none has this obloquy been poured with such unsparing hand on the heads of the old Conquerors as by their own descendants, the modern Mexicans. Ixtlilxochitl's editor, Bustamante, concludes an animated invective against the invaders with recommending that a monument should be raised on the spot—now dry land—where Guatemozin was taken, which, as the proposed inscription itself intimates, should " devote to eternal execration the detested memory of these banditti !" (Venida de los Españoles, p. 52, nota.) One would suppose that the pure Aztec blood, uncontaminated by a drop of Castilian, flowed in the veins of the indignant editor and his compatriots, or at least that their sympathies for the conquered race would make them anxious to reinstate them in their ancient rights. Notwithstanding these bursts of generous indignation, however, which plentifully season the writings of the Mexicans of our day, we do not find that the Revolution, or any of its numerous brood of *pronunciamientos,* has resulted in restoring to them an acre of their ancient territory.

Whatever may be thought of the Conquest in a moral view, regarded as a military achievement it must fill us with astonishment. That a handful of adventurers, indifferently armed and equipped, should have landed on the shores of a powerful empire inhabited by a fierce and warlike race, and, in defiance of the reiterated prohibitions of its sovereign, have forced their way into the interior ;—that they should have done this without knowledge of the language or of the land, without chart or compass to guide them, without any idea of the difficulties they were to encounter, totally uncertain whether the next step might bring them on a hostile nation or on a desert, feeling their way along in the dark, as it were ;—that, though nearly overwhelmed in their first encounter with the inhabitants, they should have still pressed on to the capital of the empire, and, having reached it, thrown themselves unhesitatingly into the midst of their enemies ;—that, so far from being daunted by the extraordinary spectacle there exhibited of power and civilization, they should have been but the more confirmed in their original design ;—that they should have seized the monarch, have executed his ministers before the eyes of his subjects, and, when driven forth with ruin from the gates, have gathered their scattered wreck together, and, after a system of operations pursued with consummate policy and daring, have succeeded in overturning the capital and establishing their sway over the country ;—that all this should have been so effected by a mere handful of indigent adventurers, is a fact little short of the miraculous,—too startling for the probabilities demanded by fiction, and without a parallel in the pages of history.

Yet this must not be understood too literally; for it would be unjust to the Aztecs themselves, at least to their military prowess, to regard the Conquest as directly achieved by the Spaniards alone. This would indeed be to arm the latter with the charmed shield of Ruggiero, and the magic lance of Astolfo, overturning its hundreds at a touch. The Indian empire was in a manner conquered by Indians. The first terrible encounter of the Spaniards with the Tlascalans, which had nearly proved their ruin, did in fact insure their success. It secured to them a strong native support on which to retreat in the hour of trouble, and round which they could rally the kindred races of the land for one great and overwhelming assault. The Aztec monarchy fell by the hands of its own subjects, under the direction of European sagacity and science. Had it been united, it might have bidden defiance to the invaders. As it was, the capital was dissevered from the rest of the country, and the bolt, which might have passed off comparatively harmless had the empire been cemented by a common principle of loyalty and patriotism, now found its way into every crack and crevice of the ill-compacted fabric and buried it in its own ruins. Its fate may serve as a striking proof that a government which does not rest on the sympathies of its subjects cannot long abide; that human institutions, when not connected with human prosperity and progress, must fall,—if not before the increasing light of civilization, by the hand of violence; by violence from within, if not from without. And who shall lament their fall?

With the events of this Book terminates the history, by Solís, of the *Conquista de Méjico;* a history, in many points of view, the most remarkable in the Castilian language. Don Antonio de Solís was born of a respectable family, in October, 1610, at Alcalá de Henares, the nursery of science, and the name of which is associated in Spain with the brightest ornaments of both church and state. Solís, while very young, exhibited the sparks of future genius, especially in the vivacity of his imagination and a sensibility to the beautiful. He showed a decided turn for dramatic composition, and produced a comedy, at the age of seventeen, which would have reflected credit on a riper age. He afterwards devoted himself with assiduity to the study of ethics, the fruits of which are visible in the moral reflections which give a didactic character to the lightest of his compositions.

At the usual age he entered the University of Salamanca, and went through the regular course of the canon and civil law. But the imaginative spirit of Solís took much more delight in the soft revels of the Muses than in the severe discipline of the schools; and he produced a number of pieces for the theatre, much esteemed for the richness of the diction and for the ingenious and delicate texture of the intrigue. His taste for dramatic composition was, no doubt, nourished by his intimacy with the great Calderon, for whose dramas he prepared several *loas*, or prologues. The amiable manners and brilliant acquisitions of Solís recommended him to the favor of the Conde de Oropesa, Viceroy of Navarre, who made him his secretary. The letters written by him while in the service of this nobleman, and afterwards, have some of them been given to the public, and are much commended for the suavity and elegance of expression characteristic of all the writings of their author.

The increasing reputation of Solís attracted the notice of the Court, and in 1661 he was made secretary of the queen dowager,—an office which he had declined under Philip the Fourth,—and he was also preferred to the still more important post of Historiographer of the Indies, an appointment which stimulated his ambition to a bold career, different from anything he had yet attempted. Five years after this event, at the age of fifty-six, he made a most important change in his way of life, by embracing the religious profession, and was admitted to priest's orders in 1666. From this time he discontinued his addresses to the comic Muse, and, if we may credit his biographers, even refused, from conscientious scruples, to engage in the composition of the religious dramas, styled *autos sacramentales.*

although the field was now opened to him by the death of the poet Calderon. But such tenderness of conscience it seems difficult to reconcile with the publication of his various comedies, which took place in 1681. It is certain, however, that he devoted himself zealously to his new profession, and to the historical studies in which his office of chronicler had engaged him. At length the fruits of these studies were given to the world in his *Conquista de Méjico*, which appeared at Madrid in 1684. He designed, it is said, to continue the work to the times after the Conquest. But, if so, he was unfortunately prevented by his death, which occurred about two years after the publication of his history, on the 13th of April, 1686. He died at the age of seventy-six, much regarded for his virtues and admired for his genius, but in that poverty with which genius and virtue are too often requited.

The miscellaneous poems of Solís were collected and published a few years after his death, in one volume quarto; which has since been reprinted. But his great work, that on which his fame is permanently to rest, is his *Conquista de Méjico*. Notwithstanding the field of history had been occupied by so many eminent Spanish scholars, there was still a new career open to Solís. His predecessors, with all their merits, had shown a strange ignorance of the principles of art. They had regarded historical writing not as a work of art, but as a science. They had approached it on that side only, and thus divorced it from its legitimate connection with *belles-lettres*. They had thought only of the useful, and nothing of the beautiful; had addressed themselves to the business of instruction, not to that of giving pleasure; to the man of letters, studious to hive up knowledge, not to the man of leisure, who turns to books as a solace or a recreation. Such writers are never in the hands of the many,—not even of the cultivated many. They are condemned to the closet of the student, painfully toiling after truth, and little mindful of the coarse covering under which she may be wrapped. Some of the most distinguished of the national historiographers, as, for example, Herrera and Zurita, two of the greatest names in Castile and Aragon, fall under this censure. They display acuteness, strength of argument, judicious criticism, wonderful patience and industry in accumulating details for their varied and voluminous compilations; but in all the graces of composition—in elegance of style, skilful arrangement of the story, and selection of incidents—they are lamentably deficient. With all their high merits, intellectually considered, they are so defective on the score of art that they can neither be popular, nor reverenced as the great classics of the nation.

Solís saw that the field was unappropriated by his predecessors, and had the address to avail himself of it. Instead of spreading himself over a vast range, where he must expend his efforts on cold and barren generalities, he fixed his attention on one great theme,—one that, by its picturesque accompaniments, the romantic incidents of the story, the adventurous character of the actors and their exploits, was associated with many a proud and patriotic feeling in the bosom of the Spaniard,—one, in fine, that, by the brilliant contrast it afforded of European civilization to the barbaric splendors of an Indian dynasty, was remarkably suited to the kindling imagination of the poet. It was accordingly under its poetic aspect that the eye of Solís surveyed it. He distributed the whole subject with admirable skill, keeping down the subordinate parts, bringing the most important into high relief, and by a careful study of its proportions giving an admirable symmetry to the whole. Instead of bewildering the attention by a variety of objects, he presented to it one great and predominant idea, which shed its light, if I may so say, over his whole work. Instead of the numerous episodes, leading, like so many blind galleries, to nothing, he took the student along a great road, conducting straight towards the mark. At every step which we take in the narrative, we feel ourselves on the advance. The story never falters or stands still. That admirable *liaison* of the parts is maintained, by which one part is held to another, and each preceding event prepares the way for that which is to follow. Even those occasional interruptions, the great stumbling-block of the historian, which cannot be avoided, in consequence of the important bearing which the events that cause them have on the story, are managed with such address that, if the interest is suspended, it is never snapped. Such halting-places, indeed, are so contrived as to afford a repose not unwelcome after the stirring scenes in which the reader has been long involved ; as the traveller, exhausted by the fatigues of his journey, finds refreshment at places which in their own character have little to recommend them.

The work, thus conducted, affords the interest of a grand spectacle, —of some well-ordered drama, in which scene succeeds to scene, act to act, each unfolding and preparing the mind for the one that is to follow, until the whole is consummated by the grand and decisive *dénouement*. With this *dénouement*, the fall of Mexico, Solís has closed his history, preferring to leave the full impression unbroken on the reader's mind rather than to weaken it by prolonging the narrative to the Conqueror's death. In this he certainly consulted effect.

Solís used the same care in regard to style that he showed in the arrangement of his story. It is elaborated with the nicest art, and displays that varied beauty and brilliancy which remind us of those finely variegated woods which, under a high polish, display all the rich tints that lie beneath the surface. Yet this style finds little favor with foreign critics, who are apt to condemn it as tumid, artificial, and verbose. But let the foreign critic beware how he meddles with style, that impalpable essence which surrounds thought as with an atmosphere, giving to it its life and peculiar tone of color, differing in different nations, like the atmospheres which envelop the different planets of our system, and which require to be comprehended that we may interpret the character of the objects seen through their medium. . None but a native can pronounce with any confidence upon style, affected as it is by so many casual and local associations that determine its propriety and its elegance. In the judgment of eminent Spanish critics, the style of Solís claims the merits of perspicuity, copiousness, and classic elegance. Even the foreigner will not be insensible to its power of conveying a living picture to the eye. Words are the colors of the writer, and Solís uses them with the skill of a consummate artist; now displaying the dark tumult of battle, and now refreshing the mind by scenes of quiet magnificence or of soft luxury and repose.

Solís formed himself to some extent on the historical models of antiquity. He introduced set speeches into the mouths of his personages, speeches of his own composing. The practice may claim high authority among moderns as well as ancients, especially among the great Italian historians. It has its advantages, in enabling the writer to convey in a dramatic form the sentiments of the actors, and thus to maintain the charm of historic illusion by never introducing the person of the historian. It has also another advantage, that of exhibiting the author's own sentiments under cover of his hero's,—a more effective mode than if they were introduced as his own. But to one trained in the school of the great English historians the practice has something in it unsatisfactory and displeasing. There is something like deception in it. The reader is unable to determine what are the sentiments of the characters and what those of the author. History assumes the air of romance, and the bewildered student wanders about in an uncertain light, doubtful whether he is treading on fact or fiction.

It is open to another objection, when, as it frequently does, it violates the propriety of costume. Nothing is more difficult than to preserve the keeping of the piece when the new is thus laid on the old,—the imitation of the antique on the antique itself. The declamations of Solís are much prized as specimens of eloquence. But they are too often misplaced; and the rude characters in whose mouths they are inserted are as little in keeping with them as were the Roman heroes with the fashionable wig and sword with which they strutted on the French stage in Louis the Fourteenth's time.

As to the value of the researches made by Solís in the compilation of his work it is not easy to speak, for the page is supported by none of the notes and references which enable us to track the modern author to the quarry whence he has drawn his materials. It was not the usage of the age. The people of that day, and, indeed, of preceding times, were content to take the author's word for his facts. They did not require to know why he affirmed this thing or doubted that; whether he built his story on the authority of a friend or of a foe, of a writer of good report or of evil report. In short, they did not demand a reason for their faith. They were content to take it on trust. This was very comfortable to the historian. It saved him a world of trouble in the process, and it prevented the detection of error, or, at least, of negligence. It prevented it with all who did not carefully go over the same ground with himself. They who have occasion to do this with Solís will probably rise from the examination with no very favorable idea of the extent of his researches: they will find that, though his situation gave him access to the most valuable repositories in the kingdom, he rarely ascends to original documents, but contents himself with the most obvious and accessible; that he rarely discriminates between the contemporary testimony and that of later date; in a word, that in all that constitutes the *scientific* value of history he falls far below his learned predecessor Herrera,— rapid as was the composition of this last.

Another objection that may be made to Solís is his bigotry, or rather his fanaticism. This defect, so repugnant to the philosophic spirit which should preside over the labors of the historian, he possessed, it is true, in common with many of his countrymen. But in him it was carried to an uncommon height; and it was peculiarly unfortunate, since his subject, being the contest between the Christian and the Infidel, naturally drew forth the full display of this failing. Instead of regarding the benighted heathen with the usual measure of aversion in which they were held in the Peninsula after the subjugation of Granada, he considered them as part of the grand confederacy of Satan, not merely breathing the spirit and acting under the invisible influence of the Prince of Darkness, but holding personal communication with him. He seems to have regarded them, in short, as his regular and organized militia. In this view, every act of the unfortunate enemy was a crime. Even good acts were misrepresented, or referred to evil motives; for how could goodness originate with the Spirit of Evil? No better evidence of the results of this way of thinking need be given than that afforded by the ill-favored and un-authorized portrait which the historian has left us of Montezuma,— even in his dying hours. The war of the Conquest was, in short, in the historian's eye, a conflict between light and darkness, between the good principle and the evil principle, between the soldiers of Satan and the chivalry of the Cross. It was a Holy War, in which the sanctity of the cause covered up the sins of the Conquerors, and every one—the meanest soldier who fell in it—might aspire to the crown of martyrdom. With sympathies thus preoccupied, what room was there for that impartial criticism which is the life of history?

The historian's overweening partiality to the Conquerors is still further heightened by those feelings of patriotism—a bastard patriot-ism—which, identifying the writer's own glory with that of his coun-trymen, makes him blind to their errors. This partiality is especially shown in regard to Cortés, the hero of the piece. The lights and shadows of the picture are all disposed with reference to this principal character. The good is ostentatiously paraded before us, and the bad is winked out of sight. Solís does not stop here, but, by the artful gloss which makes the worse appear the better cause, he calls on us to admire his hero sometimes for his very transgressions. No one, not even Gomara himself, is such a wholesale encomiast of the great Conqueror; and, when his views are contradicted by the statements of honest Diaz, Solís is sure to find a motive for the discrepancy in some sinister purpose of the veteran. He knows more of Cortés, of his actions and his motives, than his companion in arms or his ad-miring chaplain.

In this way Solís has presented a beautiful image of his hero,—but it is a hero of romance; a character without a blemish. An eminent Castilian critic has commended him for "having conducted his history with so much art that it has become a panegyric." This may be true; but, if history be panegyric, panegyric is not history.

Yet, with all these defects,—the existence of which no candid critic will be disposed to deny,—the History of Solís has found such favor with his own countrymen that it has been printed and reprinted, with all the refinements of editorial luxury. It has been translated into the principal languages of Europe; and such is the charm of its composition, and its exquisite finish as a work of art, that it will doubtless be as imperishable as the language in which it is written, or the memory of the events which it records.

At this place also we are to take leave of Father Sahagun, who has accompanied us through our narrative. As his information was collected from the traditions of the natives, the contemporaries of the Conquest, it has been of considerable importance in corroborating or contradicting the statements of the Conquerors. Yet its value in this respect is much impaired by the wild and random character of many of the Aztec traditions,—so absurd, indeed, as to carry their own refutation with them. Where the passions are enlisted, what is too absurd to find credit?

The Twelfth Book—as it would appear from his Preface, the Ninth Book originally—of his *Historia de la Nueva-España* is devoted to the account of the Conquest. In 1585, thirty years after the first draft, he re-wrote this part of his great work, moved to it, as he tells us, " by the desire to correct the defects of the first account, in which some things had found their way that had better been omitted, and other things omitted which were well deserving of record." * It might be supposed that the obloquy which the missionary had brought on his head by his honest recital of the Aztec traditions would have made him more circumspect in this *rifacimento* of his former narrative. But I have not found it so, or that there has been any effort to mitigate the statements that bore hardest on his countrymen. As this manuscript copy must have been that which the author himself deemed the most correct, since it is his last revision, and as it is more copious than the printed narrative, I have been usually guided by it.

Señor Bustamante is mistaken in supposing that the edition of this Twelfth Book which he published in Mexico in 1829 is from the *reformed* copy of Sahagun. The manuscript cited in these pages is undoubtedly a transcript of that copy. For in the Preface to it, as we have seen, the author himself declares it. In the intrinsic value of the two drafts there is, after all, but little difference.

---

* " En el libro nono, donde se trata esta Conquista, se hiciéron ciertos defectos; y fué, que algunas cosas se pusiéron en la narracion de este Conquista que fuéron mal puestas; y otras se calláron, que fuéron mal calladas. Por esta causa, este año de mil quinientos ochenta y cinco, enmende este Libro." MS.

BOOK SEVENTH.

(CONCLUSION.)

SUBSEQUENT CAREER OF CORTÉS.

(215)

BOOK VII.

(CONCLUSION.)

SUBSEQUENT CAREER OF CORTÉS.

CHAPTER I.

TORTURE OF GUATEMOZIN.—SUBMISSION OF THE COUN-
TRY.—REBUILDING OF THE CAPITAL. — MISSION TO
CASTILE. — COMPLAINTS AGAINST CORTÉS. — HE IS
CONFIRMED IN HIS AUTHORITY.

1521-1522.

THE history of the Conquest of Mexico terminates
with the surrender of the capital. But the history of
the Conquest is so intimately blended with that of the
extraordinary man who achieved it, that there would
seem to be an incompleteness in the narrative if it were
not continued to the close of his personal career. This
part of the subject has been very imperfectly treated by
preceding writers. I shall therefore avail myself of the
authentic materials in my possession to give a brief
sketch of the brilliant but checkered fortunes which
marked the subsequent career of Cortés.

The first ebullition of triumph was succeeded in the
army by very different feelings, as they beheld the

scanty spoil gleaned from the conquered city, and as they brooded over the inadequate compensation they were to receive for all their toils and sufferings. Some of the soldiers of Narvaez, with feelings of bitter disappointment, absolutely declined to accept their shares. Some murmured audibly against the general, and others against Guatemozin, who, they said, could reveal, if he chose, the place where the treasures were secreted. The white walls of the barracks were covered with epigrams and pasquinades levelled at Cortés, whom they accused of taking " one fifth of the booty as commander-in-chief, and another fifth as king." As Guatemozin refused to make any revelation in respect to the treasure, or rather declared there was none to make, the soldiers loudly insisted on his being put to the torture. But for this act of violence, so contrary to the promise of protection recently made to the Indian prince, Cortés was not prepared ; and he resisted the demand, until the men, instigated, it is said, by the royal treasurer, Alderete, accused the general of a secret understanding with Guatemozin, and of a design to defraud the Spanish sovereigns and themselves. These unmerited taunts stung Cortés to the quick, and in an evil hour he delivered the Aztec prince into the hands of his enemies, to work their pleasure on him.

But the hero who had braved death in its most awful forms was not to be intimidated by bodily suffering. When his companion, the cacique of Tacuba, who was put to the torture with him, testified his anguish by his groans, Guatemozin coldly rebuked him by exclaiming, " And do you think I, then, am taking my pleasure in my bath?"[1] At length Cortés, ashamed of the base part he was led to play, rescued the Aztec prince from his tormentors before it was too late,—not, however, before it was too late for his own honor, which has suffered an indelible stain from this treatment of his royal prisoner.

All that could be wrung from Guatemozin by the extremity of his sufferings was the confession that much gold had been thrown into the water. But, although the best divers were employed, under the eye of Cortés himself, to search the oozy bed of the lake, only a few articles of inconsiderable value were drawn from it. They had better fortune in searching a pond in Guatemozin's gardens, where a sun, as it is called, probably one of the Aztec calendar wheels, made of pure gold, of great size and thickness, was discovered. The cacique of Tacuba had confessed that a quantity of treasure was buried in the ground at one of his own villas. But when the Spaniards carried him to the spot he alleged that "his only motive for saying so was the hope of dying on the road!" The soldiers, disappointed in their expectations, now, with the usual caprice of an unlicensed mob, changed their tone, and openly accused their commander of cruelty to his captive. The charge was well deserved,—but not from them.[2]

[1] "¿Estoi yo en algun deleite, ó baño?" (Gomara, Crónica, cap. 145.) The literal version is not so poetical as "the bed of flowers," into which this exclamation of Guatemozin is usually rendered.

[2] The most particular account of this disgraceful transaction is given by Bernal Diaz, one of those selected to accompany the lord of Tacuba to his villa. (Hist. de la Conquista, cap. 157.) He notices the affair with becoming indignation, but excuses Cortés from a voluntary part in it.

The tidings of the fall of Mexico were borne on the wings of the wind over the plateau, and down the broad sides of the Cordilleras. Many envoys made their appearance from the remote Indian tribes, anxious to learn the truth of the astounding intelligence and to gaze with their own eyes on the ruins of the detested city. Among these were ambassadors from the kingdom of Michoacán, a powerful and independent state, inhabited by one of the kindred Nahuatlac races, and lying between the Mexican Valley and the Pacific. The embassy was soon followed by the king of the country in person, who came in great state to the Castilian quarters. Cortés received him with equal parade, astonished him by the brilliant evolutions of his cavalry and by the thunders of his ordnance, and escorted him in one of the brigantines round the fallen city, whose pile of smouldering palaces and temples was all that now remained of the once dread capital of Anahuac. The Indian monarch gazed with silent awe on the scene of desolation, and eagerly craved the protection of the invincible beings who had caused it.[3] His example was followed by ambassadors from the remote regions which had never yet had intercourse

[3] Rel. Terc. de Cortés, ap. Lorenzana, p. 308.—The simple statement of the Conqueror contrasts strongly with the pompous narrative of Herrera (Hist. general, dec. 3, lib. 3, cap. 3), and with that of Father Cavo, who may have drawn a little on his own imagination. "Cortés en una canoa ricamente entapizada, llevó á el Rey Vehichilze, y á los nobles de Michoacan á México. Este es uno de los palacios de Moctheuzoma (les decia); allí está el gran templo de Huitziloplutli; estas ruinas son del grande edificio de Quauhtemoc, aquellos de la gran plaza del mercado. Conmovido Vehichilze de este espectáculo se le saltáron las lágrimas." Los tres Siglos de México (México, 1836), tom. i. p. 13.

with the Spaniards. Cortés, who saw the boundaries
of his empire thus rapidly enlarging, availed himself of
the favorable dispositions of the natives to ascertain
the products and resources of their several countries.

Two small detachments were sent into the friendly
state of Michoacán, through which country they penetrated to the borders of the great Southern ocean. No
European had as yet descended on its shores so far
north of the equator. The Spaniards eagerly advanced
into its waters, erected a cross on the sandy margin,
and took possession of it, with all the usual formalities, in the name of their Catholic Majesties. On
their return, they visited some of the rich districts
towards the north, since celebrated for their mineral
treasures, and brought back samples of gold and Californian pearls, with an account of their discovery of
the ocean. The imagination of Cortés was kindled,
and his soul swelled with exultation, at the splendid
prospects which their discoveries unfolded. " Most
of all," he writes to the emperor, "do I exult in the
tidings brought me of the Great Ocean. For in it, as
cosmographers, and those learned men who know most
about the Indies, inform us, are scattered the rich isles
teeming with gold and spices and precious stones." [4]
He at once sought a favorable spot for a colony on the
shores of the Pacific, and made arrangements for the
construction of four vessels to explore the mysteries

[4] " Que todos los que tienen alguna ciencia, y experiencia en al
Navegacion de las Indias, han tenido por muy cierto, que descubri-
endo por estas Partes la Mar del Sur, se habian de hallar muchas
Islas ricas de Oro, y Perlas, y Piedras preciosas, y Especería, y se
habian de descubrir y hallar otros muchos secretos y cosas admirables." Rel. Terc. de Cortés, ap. Lorenzana, pp. 302, 303.

of these unknown seas. This was the beginning of his noble enterprises for discovery in the Gulf of California.

Although the greater part of Anahuac, overawed by the successes of the Spaniards, had tendered their allegiance, there were some, especially on the southern slopes of the Cordilleras, who showed a less submissive disposition. Cortés instantly sent out strong detachments under Sandoval and Alvarado to reduce the enemy and establish colonies in the conquered provinces. The highly colored reports which Alvarado, who had a quick scent for gold, gave of the mineral wealth of Oaxaca, no doubt operated with Cortés in determining him to select this region for his own particular domain.

The commander-in-chief, with his little band of Spaniards, now daily recruited by reinforcements from the Islands, still occupied the quarters of Cojohuacan, which they had taken up at the termination of the siege. Cortés did not immediately decide in what quarter of the Valley to establish the new capital which was to take the place of the ancient Tenochtitlan. The situation of the latter, surrounded by water and exposed to occasional inundations, had some obvious disadvantages. But there was no doubt that in some part of the elevated and central plateau of the Valley the new metropolis should be built, to which both European and Indian might look up as to the head of the colonial empire of Spain. At length he decided on retaining the site of the ancient city, moved to it, as he says, " by its past renown, and the memory"—not an enviable one, surely—"in which it was held among the nations ;" and he made preparations for the reconstruction of the capital on a scale of magnificence which should, in his own language, "raise her to the rank of Queen of the surrounding provinces, in the same manner as she had been of yore."[5]

The labor was to be performed by the Indian population, drawn from all quarters of the Valley, and including the Mexicans themselves, great numbers of whom still lingered in the neighborhood of their ancient residence. At first they showed reluctance, and even symptoms of hostility, when called to this work of humiliation by their conquerors. But Cortés had the address to secure some of the principal chiefs in his interests, and under their authority and direction the labor of their countrymen was conducted. The deep groves of the Valley and the forests of the neighboring hills supplied cedar, cypress, and other durable woods for the interior of the buildings, and the quarries of *tetzontli* and the ruins of the ancient edifices furnished abundance of stone. As there were no beasts of draught employed by the Aztecs, an immense number of hands was necessarily required for the work. All within the immediate control of Cortés were pressed into the service. The spot so recently deserted now swarmed with multitudes of Indians of various tribes, and with Europeans, the latter directing, while the others labored. The prophecy of the Aztecs was accomplished.[6] And the work of reconstruction went

5 "Y crea Vuestra Magestad, que cada dia se irá ennobleciendo en tal manera, que como antes fué Principal, y Señora de todas estas Provincias, que lo será tambien de aquí adelante." Rel. Terc. de Cortés, ap. Lorenzana, p. 307.

6 *Ante*, p. 160.

forward with a rapidity like that shown by an Asiatic despot, who concentrates the population of an empire on the erection of a favorite capital.[7]

Yet the condition of Cortés, notwithstanding the success of his arms, suggested many causes for anxiety. He had not received a word of encouragement from home,—not a word, indeed, of encouragement or censure. In what light his irregular course was regarded by the government or the nation was still matter of painful uncertainty. He now prepared another Letter to the emperor, the Third in the published series, written in the same simple and energetic style which has entitled his Commentaries, as they may be called, to a comparison with those of Cæsar. It was dated at Cojohuacan, May 15th, 1522, and in it he recapitulated the events of the final siege of the capital, and his subsequent operations, accompanied by many sagacious reflections, as usual, on the character and resources of the country. With this letter he purposed to send the royal fifth of the spoils of Mexico, and a rich collection of fabrics, especially of gold and jewelry wrought into many rare and fanciful forms. One of the jewels was an emerald, cut in a pyramidal shape,

7 Herrera, Hist. general, dec. 3, lib. 4, cap. 8.—Oviedo, Hist. de las Ind., MS., lib. 33, cap. 32.—Camargo, Hist. de Tlascala, MS.— Gomara, Crónica, cap. 162.—" En la cual (la edificacion de la ciudad) los primeros años andaba mas gente que en la edificacion del templo de Jerusalem, porque era tanta la gente que andaba en las obras, que apénas podia hombre romper por algunas calles y calzadas, aunque son muy anchas." (Toribio, Hist. de los Indios, MS., Parte 1, cap. 1.) Ixtlilxochitl supplies any blank which the imagination might leave, by filling it up with 400,000, as the number of natives employed in this work by Cortés! Venida de los Españoles, p. 60.

of so extraordinary a size that the base was as broad as the palm of the hand! [8] The collection was still further augmented by specimens of many of the natural products, as well as of animals peculiar to the country. [9]

"Sirviéron al Emperador con muchas piedras, i entre ellas con na esmeralda fina, como la palma, pero quadrada, i que se remataba n punta como pirámide." (Gomara, Crónica, cap. 146.) Martyr confirms the account of this wonderful emerald, which, he says, "was reported to the king and council to be nearly as broad as the palm of the hand, and which those who had seen it thought could not be procured for any sum." De Orbe Novo, dec. 8, cap. 4.*

9 [Cortés availed himself of the same opportunity by which the royal fifth was despatched, to send costly or curious presents to numerous individuals and churches in Spain. For this fact I am indebted to the kindness of Mr. George Sumner, who, when in Spain, made a visit to the Archives of Simancas, from which he has furnished me with some interesting particulars for the period on which I am

---

* [Alaman, however, denies that this stone was an emerald, or that any true emeralds were found by the Conquerors in Mexico, notwithstanding the frequent mention of them in contemporary relations. "There are no emeralds," he says, "in our republic; and the stones mistaken for them at the time of the Conquest were jade or serpentine." As an evidence of the ignorance on this subject common in Europe at a former period, he cites the famous instance of the *Sacro Catino* at Genoa, regarded for ages as an emerald of priceless value, but now proved to be an imitation. (Disertaciones históricas, tom. i. p. 161.) It is certain that no emeralds are now found in any part of North America. Yet the Conquerors would seem to have been more discriminating than Señor Alaman represents them. They distinguished the *chalchivitl,* supposed to have been jade, from the emerald, and rejected as valueless other green stones prized by the natives. The case of the *Sacro Catino* does not apply, since it is not pretended that the Mexicans possessed the art of imitating precious stones by means of paste. The fact, therefore, that the emeralds sent and taken to Europe by Cortés were there recognized as genuine affords a presumptive proof in their favor, which has been generally accepted as sufficient by modern writers on the subject.—ED.]

K*

The army wrote a letter to accompany that of Cortés, in which they expatiated on his manifold services and besought the emperor to ratify his proceedings and confirm him in his present authority. The important mission was intrusted to two of the general's confidential officers, Quiñones and Avila. It proved to be unfortunate. The agents touched at the Azores, where Quiñones lost his life in a brawl. Avila, resuming his voyage, was captured by a French privateer, and the rich spoils of the Aztecs went into the treasury of his Most Christian Majesty. Francis the First gazed with pardonable envy on the treasures which his Imperial rival drew from his colonial domains; and he intimated his discontent by peevishly expressing a desire "to see the clause in Adam's testament which entitled his brothers of Castile and Portugal to divide the New World between them." Avila found means, through a private hand, of transmitting his letters, the most im-

engaged. In a file endorsed *Papeles de Cortés* he met with a list, without date, but evidently belonging to the year 1522, of the gold, plumage, and ornaments sent by Cortés to the different persons and institutions in Spain. "The policy of Cortés and his clear-sightedness," Mr. Sumner justly remarks, "are well shown by this. Not a church, not a shrine of any fame, throughout Spain, has been forgotten. To Santa María del Antigua in Sevilla, a rich offering of gold and of plumage; to Santa María del Pilar in Zaragoza, the same; another again to San Jago de Compostella; and one to the Cartuja of Seville, in which the bones of Columbus were then lying. There are plumages and gold for every place of importance. Then the bishops and men of power are not forgotten; for to them also are rich presents sent. In a time when there were no gazettes to trumpet one's fame, what surer way to notoriety than this? What surer way, in Spain, for gaining that security which Cortés so much needed?"]

portant part of his charge, to Spain, where they reached the court in safety.[10]

While these events were passing, affairs in Spain had been taking an unfavorable turn for Cortés. It may seem strange that the brilliant exploits of the Conqueror of Mexico should have attracted so little notice from the government at home. But the country was at that time distracted by the dismal feuds of the *comunidades.* The sovereign was in Germany, too much engrossed by the cares of the empire to allow leisure for those of his own kingdom. The reins of government were in the hands of Adrian, Charles's preceptor; a man whose ascetic and studious habits better qualified him to preside over a college of monks than to fill, as he successively did, the most important posts in Christendom,—first as Regent of Castile, afterwards as Head of the Church. Yet the slow and hesitating Adrian could not have so long passed over in silence the important services of Cortés, but for the hostile interference of Velasquez, the governor of Cuba, sustained by Fonseca, bishop of Burgos, the chief person in the Spanish colonial department. This prelate, from his elevated station, possessed paramount authority in all matters relating to the Indies, and he had exerted it from the first, as we have already seen, in a manner most prejudicial to the interests of Cortés. He had now the address to obtain a warrant from the regent, which was designed to ruin the Conqueror at the very moment when his great enterprise had been crowned with success. The instrument, after

[10] Peter Martyr, De Orbe Novo, dec 8, cap. 4.—Bernal Diaz, Hist. de la Conquista, cap. 169.

recapitulating the offences of Cortés in regard to Velasquez, appoints a commissioner with full power to
visit the country, to institute an inquiry into the general's conduct, to suspend him from his functions, and
even to seize his person and sequestrate his property,
until the pleasure of the Castilian court could be
known. The warrant was signed by Adrian, at Burgos, on the 11th of April, 1521, and countersigned by
Fonseca.[11]

The individual selected for the delicate task of apprehending Cortés and bringing him to trial on the
theatre of his own discoveries and in the heart of his
own camp was named Cristóval de Tápia, *veedor*, or
inspector, of the gold founderies in St. Domingo. He
was a feeble, vacillating man, as little competent to
cope with Cortés in civil matters as Narvaez had shown
himself to be in military.

The commissioner, clothed in his brief authority,
landed, in December, at Villa Rica. But he was
coldly received by the magistrates of the city. His
credentials were disputed, on the ground of some tech-
nical informality. It was objected, moreover, that his
commission was founded on obvious misrepresentations
to the government; and, notwithstanding a most
courteous and complimentary epistle which he received
from Cortés, congratulating him, as an old friend, on

[11] The instrument also conferred similar powers in respect to an inquiry into Narvaez's treatment of the licentiate Ayllon. The whole
document is cited in a deposition drawn up by the notary, Alonso de
Vergara, setting forth the proceedings of Tápia and the municipality
of Villa Rica, dated at Cempoalla, December 24, 1521. The MS.
forms part of the collection of Don Vargas Ponçe, in the archives of
the Academy of History at Madri1.

his arrival, the *veedor* soon found that he was neither to be permitted to penetrate far into the country nor to exercise any control there. He loved money; and, as Cortés knew the weak side of his "old friend," he proposed to purchase his horses, slaves, and equipage, at a tempting price. The dreams of disappointed ambition were gradually succeeded by those of avarice; and the discomfited commissioner consented to re-embark for Cuba, well freighted with gold, if not with glory, and provided with fresh matter of accusation against the high-handed measures of Cortés.[12]

Thus left in undisputed possession of authority, the Spanish commander went forward with vigor in his plans for the settlement of his conquests. The Panuchese, a fierce people on the borders of the Panuco, on the Atlantic coast, had taken up arms against the Spaniards. Cortés marched at the head of a considerable force into their country, defeated them in two pitched battles, and, after a severe campaign, reduced the warlike tribe to subjection.

A subsequent insurrection was punished with greater severity. They rose on the Spaniards, massacred five hundred of their oppressors, and menaced with destruction the neighboring settlement of San Estevan. Cortés ordered Sandoval to chastise the insurgents; and that officer, after a campaign of incredible hardship, com-

---

[12] Relacion de Vergara, MS.—Rel. Terc. de Cortés, ap. Lorenzana, pp. 309–314.—Bernal Diaz, Hist. de la Conquista, cap. 158.—The *regidores* of Mexico and other places remonstrated against Cortés' leaving the Valley to meet Tápia, on the ground that his presence was necessary to overawe the natives. (MS., Coyoacan, Dec. 12, 1521.) The general acquiesced in the force of a remonstrance which it is not improbable was made at his own suggestion.

pletely routed the barbarians, captured four hundred of their chiefs, and, after the affected formalities of a trial, sentenced every man of them to the stake or the gibbet. "By which means," says Cortés, "God be praised! the safety of the Spaniards was secured, and the province once more restored to tranquillity and peace."[13] He had omitted to mention in his letter his ungenerous treatment of Guatemozin. But the undisguised and *naïve* manner, so to speak, in which he details these circumstances to the emperor, shows that he attached no discredit to the deed. It was the just recompense of *rebellion;* a word that has been made the apology for more atrocities than any other word,—save *religion.*

During this interval the great question in respect to Cortés and the colony had been brought to a decisive issue. The general must have succumbed under the insidious and implacable attacks of his enemies, but for the sturdy opposition of a few powerful friends zealously devoted to his interests. Among them may be mentioned his own father, Don Martin Cortés, a discreet and efficient person,[14] and the duke de Bejar, a powerful nobleman, who from an early period had warmly espoused the cause of Cortés. By their representations the timid regent was at length convinced that the measures of Fonseca were prejudicial to the interests of the crown, and an order was issued inter-

[13] "Como ya (loado nuestro Señor) estaba toda la Provincia muy pacífica, y segura." Rel. Quarta de Cortés, ap. Lorenzana, p. 367.

[14] The Muñoz collection of MSS. contains a power of attorney given by Cortés to his father, authorizing him to manage all negotiations with the emperor and with private persons, to conduct all lawsuits on his behalf, to pay over and receive money, etc.

dicting him from further interference in any matters in which Cortés was concerned.

While the exasperated prelate was chafing under this affront, both the commissioners Tápia and Narvaez arrived in Castile. The latter had been ordered to Cojohuacan after the surrender of the capital, where his cringing demeanor formed a striking contrast to the swaggering port which he had assumed on first entering the country. When brought into the presence of Cortés, he knelt down, and would have kissed his hand, but the latter raised him from the ground, and, during his residence in his quarters, treated him with every mark of respect. The general soon afterwards permitted his unfortunate rival to return to Spain, where he proved, as might have been anticipated, a most bitter and implacable enemy.[15]

These two personages, reinforced by the discontented prelate, brought forward their several charges against Cortés with all the acrimony which mortified vanity and the thirst of vengeance could inspire. Adrian was no longer in Spain, having been called to the chair of St. Peter; but Charles the Fifth, after his long absence, had returned to his dominions, in July, 1522. The royal ear was instantly assailed with accusations of Cortés on the one hand and his vindication on the other, till the young monarch, perplexed, and unable to decide on the merits of the question, referred the whole subject to the decision of a board selected for the purpose. It was drawn partly from the members of his privy council, and partly from the Indian depart-

[15] Bernal Diaz, Hist. de la Conquista, cap. 158.

ment, with the Grand Chancellor of Naples as its
president, and constituted altogether a tribunal of the
highest respectability for integrity and wisdom.[16]

By this learned body a patient and temperate hear-
ing was given to the parties. The enemies of Cortés
accused him of having seized and finally destroyed the
fleet intrusted to him by Velasquez and fitted out at
the governor's expense; of having afterwards usurped
powers in contempt of the royal prerogative; of the
unjustifiable treatment of Narvaez and Tápia, when
they had been lawfully commissioned to supersede him;
of cruelty to the natives, and especially to Guatemozin;
of embezzling the royal treasures, and remitting but a
small part of its dues to the crown; of squandering the
revenues of the conquered countries in useless and
wasteful schemes, and particularly in rebuilding the
capital on a plan of unprecedented extravagance; of
pursuing, in short, a system of violence and extortion,
without respect to the public interest or any other end
than his own selfish aggrandizement.

In answer to these grave charges, the friends of
Cortés adduced evidence to show that he had defrayed
with his own funds two-thirds of the cost of the expedition. The powers of Velasquez extended only to
traffic, not to establish a colony. Yet the interest of
the crown required the latter. The army had therefore necessarily assumed this power to themselves; but,
having done so, they had sent intelligence of their pro-

[16] Sayas, Annales de Aragon (Zaragoza, 1666), cap. 63, 78.—It is a
sufficient voucher for the respectability of this court that we find in it
the name of Dr. Galindez de Carbajal, an eminent Castilian jurist,
grown gray in the service of Ferdinand and Isabella, whose confidence
he enjoyed to the highest degree.

ceedings to the emperor and solicited his confirmation
of them. The rupture with Narvaez was that commander's own fault; since Cortés would have met him
amicably, had not the violent measures of his rival,
threatening the ruin of the expedition, compelled him
to an opposite course. The treatment of Tápia was
vindicated on the grounds alleged to that officer by the
municipality at Cempoalla. The violence to Guatemozin was laid at the door of Alderete, the royal
treasurer, who had instigated the soldiers to demand it.
The remittances to the crown, it was clearly proved,
so far from falling short of the legitimate fifth, had
considerably exceeded it. If the general had expended
the revenues of the country on costly enterprises and
public works, it was for the interest of the country that
he did so, and he had incurred a heavy debt by strain-
ing his own credit to the utmost for the same great
objects. Neither did they deny that, in the same
spirit, he was now rebuilding Mexico on a scale suited
to the metropolis of a vast and opulent empire.

They enlarged on the opposition he had experienced
throughout his whole career from the governor of Cuba,
and still more from the bishop of Burgos, which latter
functionary, instead of affording him the aid to have
been expected, had discouraged recruits, stopped his
supplies, sequestered such property as from time to
time he had sent to Spain, and falsely represented his
remittances to the crown as coming from the governor
of Cuba. In short, such and so numerous were the
obstacles thrown in his path that Cortés had been
heard to say " he had found it more difficult to contend against his own countrymen than against the

20*

Aztecs." They concluded with expatiating on the brilliant results of his expedition, and asked if the council were prepared to dishonor the man who, in the face of such obstacles and with scarcely other resources than what he found in himself, had won an empire for Castile such as was possessed by no European potentate ![17]

This last appeal was irresistible. However irregular had been the manner of proceeding, no one could deny the grandeur of the results. There was not a Spaniard that could be insensible to such services, or that would not have cried out "Shame!" at an ungenerous requital of them. There were three Flemings in the council ; but there seems to have been no difference of opinion in the body. It was decided that neither Velasquez nor Fonseca should interfere further in the concerns of New Spain. The difficulties of the former with Cortés were regarded in the nature of a private suit ; and, as such, redress must be sought by the regular course of law. The acts of Cortés were confirmed in their full extent. He was constituted Governor, Captain-General, and Chief Justice of New Spain, with power to appoint to all offices, civil and military, and to order any person to leave the country whose residence there he might deem prejudicial to the interests of the crown. This judgment of the council was ratified by Charles the Fifth, and the commission investing Cortés with these ample powers was signed by the emperor at Valladolid, October 15th, 1522. A liberal salary was provided, to enable the governor of

[17] Sayas, Annales de Aragon, cap. 78.—Herrera, Hist. general, dec. 3, lib. 4, cap. 3.—Probanza en la Villa Segura, MS.—Declaraciones de Puertocarrero y de Montejo, MS.

New Spain to maintain his office with suitable dignity. The favor of his sovereign was rendered still more welcome by a letter of the same date, written by him to the general, in which, after expatiating on the services of Cortés, he declares it to be his intention to make him such a requital as they well deserve.[18] The principal officers were recompensed with honors and substantial emoluments ; and the troops, together with some privileges grateful to the vanity of the soldier, received the promise of liberal grants of land. The emperor still further complimented them by a letter written to the army with his own hand, in which he acknowledged its services in the fullest manner.[19]

From this hour the influence of Fonseca in the Indian department was at an end. He did not long survive his chagrin, as he died in the following year. No man was in a situation to do more for the prosperity of his country than the bishop of Burgos. For more than thirty years, ever since the first dawn of discovery under Columbus, he had held supreme control over colonial affairs ; and it lay with him, therefore, in an especial degree, to give ardor to enterprise, and to foster the youthful fortunes of the colonies. But he lay like a

---

[18] [" E porque soy certificado de lo mucho que vos en ese descubrimiento é conquista y en tornar á ganar la dicha ciudad é provincias habeis fecho é trabajado, de que me he tenido é tengo por muy servido, é tengo la voluntad que es razon para vos favorecer y hacer la merced que vuestros servicios y trabajos merecen."—The whole letter is inserted by Alaman in his Disertaciones históricas, tom. i. apénd. 2, p. 144, et seq.]

[19] Nombramiento de Governador y Capitan General y Justicia Mayor de Nueva-España, MS.—Also Bernal Diaz, Hist. de la Conquista, cap. 168.

blight upon them. He looked with an evil eye on the most illustrious of the Spanish discoverers, and sought only to throw impediments in their career. Such had been his conduct towards Columbus, and such to Cortés. By a wise and generous policy, he might have placed his name among the great lights of his age. As it was, he only served to bring these into greater lustre by contrast with his own dark and malignant nature. His career shows the overweening ascendency which the ecclesiastical profession possessed in Castile in the sixteenth century; when it could raise a man to so important a station, for which he was totally unfit, and keep him there after he had proved himself to be so.[20]

The messengers who bore the commission of Cortés to Mexico touched on their way at Cuba, where the tidings were proclaimed by sound of trumpet. It was a death-blow to the hopes of Velasquez. Exasperated by the failure of his schemes, impoverished by the expense of expeditions of which others had reaped the fruits, he had still looked forward to eventual redress, and cherished the sweet hope of vengeance,—long delayed. That hope was now gone. There was slight chance of redress, he well knew, in the tedious and thorny litigation of the Castilian courts. Ruined in fortune, dishonored before the nation, the haughty spirit of the governor was humbled in the dust. He

[20] The character of Fonseca has been traced by the same hand which has traced that of Columbus. (Irving's Life and Voyages of Columbus, Appendix, No. 32.) Side by side they will go down to posterity in the beautiful page of the historian, though the characters of the two individuals have been inscribed with pens as different from each other as the golden and iron pen which Paolo Giovio tells us he employed in his compositions.

would take no comfort, but fell into a sullen melancholy, and in a few months died—if report be true—of a broken heart.[21]

The portrait usually given of Velasquez is not favorable. Yet Las Casas speaks kindly of him, and, when his prejudices are not involved, there can be no better authority. But Las Casas knew him when, in his earlier days, the missionary first landed in Cuba. The governor treated him with courtesy, and even confidence; and it was natural that the condescension of a man of high family and station should have made its impression on the feelings of the poor ecclesiastic. In most accounts he is depicted as a haughty, irascible person, jealous of authority and covetous of wealth. He quarrelled with Grijalva, Cortés' predecessor, apparently without cause. With as little reason, he broke with Cortés before he left the port. He proposed objects to himself in their nature incompatible. He proposed that others should fight his battles, and that he should win the laurels; that others should make discoveries, and that he should reap the fruits of them. None but a weak mind would have conformed to his conditions, and a weak mind could not have effected his objects. His appointment of Cortés put him in a false position for the rest of his life. His efforts to retrieve his position only made things worse. The appointment of Cortés to the command was scarcely a greater error than the subsequent appointment of Narvaez and of Tápia. The life of Velasquez was a series of errors.

Narvaez had no better fate than his friend the gov-

[21] Bernal Diaz, Hist. de la Conquista, cap. 158.

ernor of Cuba. In the hope of retrieving his fortunes, he continued to pursue his adventurous career, and embarked in an expedition to Honduras. It was his last; and Las Casas, who had little love for the Conquerors, and who had watched the acts of cruelty perpetrated by Narvaez, concludes the notice of his death with the assurance that the " devil took possession of his soul."

The announcement of the emperor's commission confirming Cortés in the supreme authority of New Spain was received there with general acclamation. The army rejoiced in having at last secured not merely an amnesty for their irregular proceedings, but a distinct acknowledgment of their services. The nomination of Cortés to the supreme command put his mind at ease as to the past, and opened to him a noble theatre for future enterprise. The soldiers congratulated themselves on the broad powers conferred on their commander, and, as they reckoned up their scars and their services, indulged in golden dreams and the most vague and visionary expectations. It is not strange that their expectations should have been disappointed.

CHAPTER II.

MODERN MEXICO. — SETTLEMENT OF THE COUNTRY. —
CONDITION OF THE NATIVES. — CHRISTIAN MISSION-
ARIES. — CULTIVATION OF THE SOIL. — VOYAGES AND
EXPEDITIONS.

1522–1524.

IN less than four years from the destruction of Mexico, a new city had risen on its ruins, which, if inferior
to the ancient capital in extent, surpassed it in magnificence and strength. It occupied so exactly the
same site as its predecessor, that the *plaza mayor*, or
great square, was the same spot which had been covered
by the huge *teocalli* and the palace of Montezuma;
while the principal streets took their departure as
before from this central point, and, passing through
the whole length of the city, terminated at the principal causeways. Great alterations, however, took
place in the fashion of the architecture. The streets
were widened, many of the canals were filled up, and
the edifices were constructed on a plan better accom-
modated to European taste and the wants of a European population.

On the site of the temple of the Aztec war-god rose
the stately cathedral dedicated to St. Francis;[1] and, as

[1] [According to Señor Alaman, the cathedral, instead of being dedicated to Saint Francis, was consecrated to the Assumption of the
Virgin. Conquista de Méjico (trad. de Vega), tom. ii. p. 254.]

if to complete the triumphs of the Cross, the foundations were laid with the broken images of the Aztec
gods.[2]   In a corner of the square, on the ground once
covered by the House of Birds, stood a Franciscan
convent, a magnificent pile, erected a few years after
the Conquest by a lay brother, Pedro de Gante, a
natural son, it is said, of Charles the Fifth.[3]   In an
opposite quarter of the same square Cortés caused his
own palace to be constructed.   It was built of hewn
stone, and seven thousand cedar beams are said to have
been used for the interior.[4]   The government afterwards appropriated it to the residence of the viceroys;
and the Conqueror's descendants, the dukes of Monteleone, were allowed to erect a new mansion in another
part of the *plaza*, on the spot which, by an ominous coincidence, had been covered by the palace of Montezuma.[5]

The houses occupied by the Spaniards were of stone,
combining with elegance a solid strength which made
them capable of defence like so many fortresses.[6]   The
Indian buildings were for the most part of an inferior
quality.   They were scattered over the ancient district
of Tlatelolco, where the nation had made its last stand
for freedom.   This quarter was also provided with a
spacious cathedral;[7] and thirty inferior churches at-
tested the care of the Spaniards for the spiritual welfare

[2] Herrera, Hist. general, dec. 3, lib. 4, cap. 8.

[3] Clavigero, Stor. del Messico, tom. i. p. 271.—Humboldt, Essai
politique, tom. ii. p. 58.

[4] Herrera, Hist. general, ubi supra.

[5] Humboldt, Essai politique, tom. ii. p. 72.

[6] Rel. d'un gentil' huomo, ap. Ramusio, tom. iii. fol. 309.

[7] [Alaman asserts that there was no cathedral in Tlatelolco, but a
Franciscan convent, dedicated to St. James, which still exists.   Conquista de Méjico (trad. de Vega), tom. ii. p. 255.]

of the natives.[8] It was in watching over his Indian flock, and in the care of the hospitals with which the new capital was speedily endowed, that the good Father Olmedo, when oppressed by growing infirmities, spent the evening of his days.[9]

To give greater security to the Spaniards, Cortés caused a strong fortress to be erected in a place since known as the *Matadero*.[10] It was provided with a dock-yard, and the brigantines which had served in the siege of Mexico were long preserved there as memorials of the Conquest. When the fortress was completed, the general, owing to the evil offices of Fonseca, found himself in want of artillery and ammunition for its defence. He supplied the former deficiency by causing cannon to be cast in his own founderies, made of the copper which was common in the country, and tin which he obtained with more difficulty from the mines of Tasco. By this means, and a contribution which he received from the shipping, he contrived to mount his walls with seventy pieces of ordnance. Stone balls, much used in that age, could easily be made; but for the manufacture of his powder, although there was nitre in abundance, he was obliged to seek the sulphur by a perilous expedition into the bowels of the great *volcan*.[11] Such were the resources displayed by Cortés, enabling him to supply every deficiency, and to triumph over every obstacle which the malice of his enemies had thrown in his path.

[8] Rel. d'un gentil' huomo, ap. Ramusio, ubi supra.

[9] Bernal Diaz, Hist. de la Conquista, cap. 177.

[10] Rel. Quarta de Cortés, ap. Lorenzana, p. 376, nota.

[11] For an account of this singular enterprise, see *ante*, vol. ii. p. 46.

The general's next care was to provide a population for the capital. He invited the Spaniards thither by grants of lands and houses, while the Indians, with politic liberality, were permitted to live under their own chiefs as before, and to enjoy various immunities. With this encouragement, the Spanish quarter of the city in the neighborhood of the great square could boast in a few years two thousand families; while the Indian district of Tlatelolco included no less than thirty thousand.[12] The various trades and occupations were resumed; the canals were again covered with barges; two vast markets in the respective quarters of the capital displayed all the different products and manufactures of the surrounding country; and the city swarmed with a busy, industrious population, in which the white man and the Indian, the conqueror and the conquered, mingled together promiscuously in peaceful and picturesque confusion. Not twenty years had elapsed since the Conquest, when a missionary who visited it had the confidence, or the credulity, to assert that "Europe could not boast a single city so fair and opulent as Mexico."[13]

The metropolis of our day would seem to stand in a different situation from that reared by the Conquerors;

[12] Cortés, reckoning only the Indian population, says *treinta mil vecinos*. (Rel. Quarta, ap. Lorenzana, p. 375.) Gomara, speaking of Mexico some years later, estimates the number of Spanish householders as in the text. Crónica, cap. 162.

[13] Toribio, Hist. de los Indios, MS., Parte 3, cap. 7.—Yet this is scarcely stronger language than that of the Anonymous Conqueror: "Cosi ben ordinato et di si belle piazze et strade, quanto d' altre città che siano al mondo." Rel. d'un gentil' huomo, ap. Ramusio, tom. iii. fol. 309.

for the waters no longer flow through its streets, nor wash the ample circumference of its walls. These waters have retreated within the diminished basin of Tezcuco; and the causeways, which anciently traversed the depths of the lake, are not now to be distinguished from the other avenues to the capital. But the city, embellished, it is true, by the labors of successive viceroys, is substantially the same as in the days of the Conquerors; and the massive grandeur of the few buildings that remain of the primitive period, and the general magnificence and symmetry of its plan, attest the far-sighted policy of its founder, which looked beyond the present to the wants of coming generations.

The attention of Cortés was not confined to the capital. He was careful to establish settlements in every part of the country which afforded a favorable position for them. He founded Zacatula on the shores of the miscalled Pacific, Coliman in the territory of Michoacán, San Estevan on the Atlantic coast, probably not far from the site of Tampico, Medellin (so called after his own birthplace) in the neighborhood of the modern Vera Cruz, and a port near the river Antigua, from which it derived its name. It was designed to take the place of Villa Rica, which, as experience had shown, from its exposed situation, afforded no protection to shipping against the winds that sweep over the Mexican Gulf. Antigua, sheltered within the recesses of a bay, presented a more advantageous position. Cortés established there a board of trade, connected the settlement by a highway with the capital, and fondly predicted that his new city would become the great emporium of the country.[14] But in this he was mistaken. From some cause, not very obvious, the port of entry was removed, at the close of the sixteenth century, to the modern Vera Cruz, which, without any superiority, probably, of topographical position, or even of salubrity of climate, has remained ever since the great commercial capital of New Spain.

Cortés stimulated the settlement of his several colonies by liberal grants of land and municipal privileges. The great difficulty was to induce women to reside in the country; and without them he felt that the colonies, like a tree without roots, must soon perish. By a singular provision, he required every settler, if a married man, to bring over his wife within eighteen months, on pain of forfeiting his estate. If he were too poor to do this himself, the government would assist him. Another law imposed the same penalty on all bachelors who did not provide themselves with wives within the same period. The general seems to have considered celibacy as too great a luxury for a young country.[15]

[14] "Y tengo por cierto, que aquel Pueblo ha de ser, despues de esta Ciudad, el mejor que obiere en esta Nueva España." (Rel. Quarta, ap. Lorenzana, p. 382.) The archbishop confounds this town with the modern Vera Cruz. But the general's description of the port refutes this supposition, and confirms our confidence in Clavigero's statement that the present city was founded by the Conde de Monterey, at the time mentioned in the text. See ante, vol. i. p. 345, note.

[15] Ordenanzas municipales, Tenochtitlan, Marzo, 1524, MS.*—The

* [The exact date is given at the close of the document—" fecha en esta dicha ciudad [de Temixtitan] á veinte dias del mes de marzo de mil y quinientos é veinte y cuatro años." Sir Arthur Helps says a

His own wife, Doña Catalina Xuarez, was among
those who came over from the Islands to New Spain.

Ordinances made by Cortés for the government of the country during
his viceroyalty are still preserved in Mexico; and the copy in my
possession was transmitted to me from that capital. They give
ample evidence of the wise and penetrating spirit which embraced
every object worthy of the attention of an enlightened ruler; and I
will quote, in the original, the singular provisions mentioned in the
text:

" Item. Por que mas se manifieste la voluntad que los pobladores
de estas partes tienen de residir y permanecer en ellas, mando que
todas las personas que tuvieren Indios, que fueren casados en Castilla
ó en otras partes, que traigan sus mugeres dentro de un año y medio
primero siguientes de como estas ordenanzas fueren pregonadas, so
pena de perder los Indios, y todo lo con ellos adquirido é grangeado;
y por que muchas personas podrian poner por achaque aunque tuviesen aparejo de decir que no tienen dineros para enviar por ellas, por
hende las tales personas que tuvieran esta necesidad parescan ante el
Ro. Pe. Fray Juan de Tecto y ante Alonso de Estrada, tesorero de su
Magestad, á les informar de su necesidad, para que ellos la comuni-
quen á mí, y su necesidad se remedie; y si algunas personas hay que
casados y no tienen sus mugeres en esta tierra, y quisieran traerlas,
sepan que trayéndolas serán ayudadas así mismo para las traer, dando
fianzas.

" Item. Por quanto en esta tierra hay muchas personas que tienen
Indios de encomienda y no son casados, por hende por que conviene
así para *la salud de sus conciencias de los tales* por estar en buen estado, como por la poblacion é noblecimiento de sus tierras, mando
que las tales personas se casen, traigan y tengan sus mugeres en esta
tierra dentro de un año y medio, despues que fueren pregonadas estas
dichas Ordenanzas, é que no haciendo lo por el mismo caso sean pri-
vados y pierdan los tales Indios que así tienen."

---

copy sent by Cortés to the emperor in October of the same year " has
been lost, but the orders manifestly related to this subject of *encomiendas.*" The original seems also to have disappeared. But an ancient
copy of these, as well as of subsequent ordinances and instructions
of a similar nature, is preserved in the archives of the duke of Terra-

According to Bernal Diaz, her coming gave him no
particular satisfaction.[16]   It is possible; since his marriage with her seems to have been entered into with
reluctance, and her lowly condition and connections
stood somewhat in the way of his future advancement.
Yet they lived happily together for several years, according to the testimony of Las Casas;[17] and, whatever he may have felt, he had the generosity, or the
prudence, not to betray his feelings to the world.   On
landing, Doña Catalina was escorted by Sandoval to

[16] Bernal Diaz, Hist. de la Conquista, cap. 160.
[17] *Ante*, vol. i. p. 242.

nova y Monteleone in the Hospital of Jesus at Mexico, and the whole
series was published, so far back as 1844, by Señor Alaman, in his
Disertaciones históricas, tom. i. pp. 105-143.   The contents, therefore,
are not a matter of inference.   They do not relate chiefly or directly
to the *encomiendas*, that system having been already established and
become, in the language of Alaman, "the basis of the whole organization of the country."   The "Ordenanzas," while they incidentally
modify the system, consist for the most part of regulations suggested
by the general condition and circumstances of a new colony.   They
make provision for the military equipment and inspection of the
settlers, with a view to their readiness for service; for their permanent
residence in the country, which is made a condition of their holding
repartimientos; for the conversion of the natives, their protection
against robbery and oppression, and the education of the children of
their chiefs; for the cultivation of imported plants and grain, and the
raising of cattle, sheep, and swine; for facilitating traffic by the establishment of markets, adjustment of prices, etc.; and for the organization of the municipalities, prescribing their powers and forms of administration.   Some of these provisions are still in force, while others,
though obsolete, indicate the origin of certain existing customs.   Taken
together, they contain, in the opinion of Alaman, the foundation of
all the later institutions of the country,—"el fundamento de todas
nuestras instituciones."—ED.]

the capital, where she was kindly received by her husband, and all the respect paid to her to which she was entitled by her elevated rank. But the climate of the table-land was not suited to her constitution, and she died in three months after her arrival.[18] An event so auspicious to his worldly prospects did not fail, as we shall see hereafter, to provoke the tongue of scandal to the most malicious, but, it is scarcely necessary to say, unfounded, inferences.

In the distribution of the soil among the Conquerors, Cortés adopted the vicious system of *repartimientos*, universally practised among his countrymen. In a letter to the emperor, he states that the superior capacity of the Indians in New Spain had made him regard it as a grievous thing to condemn them to servitude, as had been done in the Islands. But, on further trial, he had found the Spaniards so much harassed and impoverished that they could not hope to maintain themselves in the land without enforcing the services of the natives, and for this reason he had at length waived his own scruples in compliance with their repeated remonstrances.[19] This was the wretched pretext used on the like occasions by his countrymen to cover up this flagrant act of injustice. The crown, however, in its instructions to the general, disavowed the act and annulled the *repartimientos*.[20] It was all in vain. The necessities, or rather the cupidity, of the colonists,

[18] Of asthma, according to Bernal Diaz (Hist. de la Conquista, cap. 160); but her death seems to have been too sudden to be attributed to that disease. I shall return to the subject hereafter.

[19] Rel. Terc., ap. Lorenzana, pp. 319, 320.

[20] Herrera, Hist. general, dec. 3, lib. 5, cap. 1.

easily evaded the royal ordinances.*   The colonial
legislation of Spain shows, in the repetition of enact-

---

* [This remark would imply that the instructions were published
and some attempts at least made to enforce them.   That such was not
the case we learn from a remarkable private letter of Cortés to the
emperor, sent with the "Relacion Quarta," and bearing the same
date,—October 15, 1524.   Referring first to an order that the Spanish
settlers should be allowed to have free intercourse with the Indian
population as a means of promoting conversion, he declines to comply
with it, on the ground that the effects would be most pernicious.   The
natives, he says, would be subjected to violence, robbery, and vexa-
tions of all kinds.   Even with the present rigorous rule forbidding
any Spaniard to leave his settlement and go among the Indians without a special license, the evils resulting from this intercourse were so
great that if he and his officers should attend solely to their suppression
they would be unable to effect it, the territory being so vast.   If all
the Spaniards now in the country or on their way to it were friars engaged in the work of conversion, entire freedom of intercourse would
no doubt be profitable.   But, the reverse being the case, such also
would be the effect.   Most of the Spaniards who came were men of
base condition and manners, addicted to every sort of vice and sin;
and if free intercourse were allowed, the natives would be converted
to evil rather than to good, and, seeing the difference between what
was preached and what was practised, would make a jest of what was
taught them by the priests, thinking it was meant merely to bring them
into servitude.   The injuries done them would lead to rebellion; they
would profit by their acquired knowledge to arm themselves better,
and being so many and the Spaniards so few, the latter would be cut
off singly, as had already happened in many cases, and the greatest
work of conversion since the time of the apostles would come to a
stop.

Turning then to the emperor's prohibition of the *repartimientos*,
as a thing which his conscience would not suffer, the theologians having declared that since God had made the Indians free their liberty
ought not to be taken away, Cortés states that he has not only not
complied with this order, but he has kept it secret except from the
officials, whom he has forbidden to make it public.   His reasons for
thus acting are as follows: 1st. The Spaniards are unable to live

ments against slavery, the perpetual struggle that sub-
sisted between the crown and the colonists, and the
impotence of the former to enforce measures repugnant to the interests, at all events to the avarice, of
the latter. New Spain furnishes no exception to the
general fact.

The Tlascalans, in gratitude for their signal services,
were exempted, at the recommendation of Cortés, from
the doom of slavery. It should be added that the

---

except by the labor of the Indians, and if deprived of this they would
be obliged to leave the country. 2d. His system of *repartimientos* is
such that by it the Indians are in fact taken out of captivity, their condition under their former masters having been one of intolerable servitude, in which they were not only deprived of all but the barest means
of subsistence, but they and their children were sacrificed to the idols
in numbers horrible to hear of, it being a certified fact that in the
great temple of Mexico alone, at a single festival, one of many that
were held annually, eight thousand persons had been sacrificed; all
this, with innumerable other wrongs, had now ceased; and the surest
punishment which could be inflicted on the Indians was the threat to
send them back to their former masters. 3d. Enumerating the various
provisions he has made for obviating the evils of the system as practised in the Islands, where, during a residence of twenty years, he had
ample knowledge of its workings, he asserts that, in the mode in
which it has been established and regulated by him, it will lead not to
the diminution but to the preservation and increase of the natives,
besides securing a provision for the settlers and large revenues to the
crown, and he contends that the *repartimientos*, instead of being
abrogated, should be made hereditary, so that the possessors might
have a stronger interest in the proper cultivation of the soil, instead of seeking to extract from it the most that was possible in a
given time.

The letter, which concludes by noticing and rejecting some minor
points in the emperor's instructions, has been recently discovered, and
is perhaps the ablest document that has come down to us with the
signature of Cortés. It has been published by Señor Icazbalceta, in
his Col. de Doc. para la Hist. de México, tom. i.—ED.]

L*

general, in granting the *repartimientos*, made many humane regulations for limiting the power of the master, and for securing as many privileges to the natives as were compatible with any degree of compulsory service.[21] These limitations, it is true, were too often disregarded ; and in the mining districts, in particular, the situation of the poor Indian was often deplorable. Yet the Indian population, clustering together in their own villages and living under their own magistrates, have continued to prove by their numbers, fallen as these have below their primitive amount, how far superior was their condition to that in most other parts of the vast colonial empire of Spain.[22] This condition has been gradually ameliorated, under the influence of higher moral views and larger ideas of government, until the servile descendants of the ancient lords of the soil have been permitted, in republican Mexico, to rise—nominally, at least—to a level with the children of their conquerors.

Whatever disregard he may have shown to the political rights of the natives, Cortés manifested a commendable solicitude for their spiritual welfare. He requested the emperor to send out holy men to the country ; not

[21] Herrera, Hist. general, dec. 4, lib. 6, cap. 5.—Ordenanzas, MS. —The ordinances prescribe the service of the Indians, the hours they may be employed, their food, compensation, and the like. They require the *encomendero* to provide them with suitable means of religious instruction and places of worship. But what avail good laws, which in their very nature imply the toleration of a great abuse ?

[22] The whole population of New Spain in 1810 is estimated by Don Fernando Navarro y Noriega at about 6,000,000 ; of whom more than half were pure Indians. The author had the best means for arriving at a correct result. See Humboldt, Essai politique, tom. i. pp. 318, 319, note.

bishops and pampered prelates, who too often squandered the substance of the Church in riotous living, but godly persons, members of religious fraternities, whose lives might be a fitting commentary on their teaching. Thus only, he adds,—and the remark is worthy of note,—can they exercise any influence over the natives, who have been accustomed to see the least departure from morals in their own priesthood punished with the utmost rigor of the law.[23] In obedience to these suggestions, twelve Franciscan friars embarked for New Spain, which they reached early in 1524. They were men of unblemished purity of life, nourished with the learning of the cloister, and, like many others whom the Romish Church has sent forth on such apostolic missions, counted all personal sacrifices as little in the sacred cause to which they were devoted.[24]

[23] Rel. Quarta, ap. Lorenzana, pp. 391–394.—The petition of the Conquerors was acceded to by the government, which further prohibited " attorneys and men learned in the law from setting foot in the country, on the ground that experience had shown they would be sure by their evil practices to disturb the peace of the community." (Herrera, Hist. general, dec. 3, lib. 5, cap. 2.) These enactments are but an indifferent tribute to the character of the two professions in Castile.

[24] Toribio, Hist. de los Indios, MS., Parte 1, cap. 1.—Camargo, Hist. de Tlascala, MS. [My views of the character of the Spanish missionaries find favor with Señor Alaman, who warmly eulogizes the spirit of self-sacrifice and the untiring zeal which they showed in propagating the gospel among the natives : " El Sr. Prescott hace de los misioneros el justo aprecio que sus virtudes merecieron, y sus elogios son tanto mas recomendables, cuanto que sus opiniones religiosas parece deberian hacerle contrario á ellos. En efecto, solo la iglesia católica ha producido misioneros inflamados de un verdadero celo religioso, que los ha hecho sacrificar su vida por la propagacion de la religion y en beneficio de la humanidad." Conquista de Méjico

The presence of the reverend fathers in the country
was greeted with general rejoicing.   The inhabitants
of the towns through which they passed came out in a
body to welcome them; processions were formed of
the natives bearing wax tapers in their hands, and the
bells of the churches rang out a joyous peal in honor
of their arrival.   Houses of refreshment were provided
for them along their route to the capital; and when
they entered it they were met by a brilliant cavalcade
of the principal cavaliers and citizens, with Cortés at
their head.   The general, dismounting, and bending
one knee to the ground, kissed the robes of Father
Martin of Valencia, the principal of the fraternity.
The natives, filled with amazement at the viceroy's
humiliation before men whose naked feet and tattered
garments gave them the aspect of mendicants, henceforth regarded them as beings of a superior nature.
The Indian chronicler of Tlascala does not conceal his
admiration of this edifying condescension of Cortés,
which he pronounces " one of the most heroical acts
of his life !'' 25

(trad. de Vega), tom. ii. p. 255.   Mr. Gallatin, also, in his " Notes on
the Semi-civilized Nations of America," pays a hearty tribute to the
labors of the Roman Catholic missionaries in the New World: "The
Dominican monks, though inquisitors and relentless persecutors in
Spain, became in America the protectors of the Indians. . . . The
praise must be extended to all the Catholic priests, whether Franciscans or Jesuits, monks or curates.   All, from the beginning, were,
have ever been, and continue to be, the protectors and the friends of
the Indian race."   Transactions of the American Ethnological Society, i. 213.]

25 " Cuyo hecho del rotísimo y humilde recebimiento fué uno de los
heroicos hechos que este Capitan hizo, porque fué documento para
que con mayor fervor los naturales desta tierra viniesen á la conver-

The missionaries lost no time in the good work of conversion. They began their preaching through interpreters, until they had acquired a competent knowledge of the language themselves. They opened schools and founded colleges, in which the native youth were instructed in profane as well as Christian learning.*

sion de nuestra fee." (Camargo, Hist. de Tlascala, MS.—See also Bernal Diaz, Hist. de la Conquista, cap. 171.) Archbishop Lorenzana falls nothing short of the Tlascalan historian in his admiration of the religious zeal of the great *Conquistador*, which, he assures us, "entirely overwhelms him, as savoring so much more of the apostolic missionary than of the soldier!" Lorenzana, p. 393, nota.

---

* [A singular tribute to the thoroughness of the instruction thus given, and the facility with which it was imbibed, is rendered in a long complaint on the subject addressed to the emperor by Gerónimo Lopez, under date of October 20, 1541. The writer, a person evidently commissioned to send home reports on the condition of the country, denounces the system of education instituted by the Franciscan monks as diabolically pernicious,—"muy dañoso como el diablo." He considers that the Indians should at the most be taught to repeat the Pater Noster and Ave Maria, the Creed and the Commandments, without any expositions, or any distinction of the persons of the Trinity and their attributes, above all without learning to read and write. Instead of this, they are taught not only these pernicious branches of knowledge, but punctuation, music,—nay, even grammar! Their natural ability is so great, and the devil is so largely interested in the matter, that they have acquired a skill in forming different kinds of letters which is marvellous, and a great number of them are thus enabled to carry on a correspondence and learn what is going on in the country from one sea to the other. There are boys among them who speak as elegant Latin as Tullius. They have translated and read the whole of the Scriptures,—the same thing that has ruined so many in Spain and given birth to a thousand heresies. A secular ecclesiastic told him that, having visited one of the colleges, he found there two hundred students, who stunned him with questions about religion, till the place seemed to him hell, and its inmates disciples of Satan.—Icazbalceta, Col. de Doc. para la Hist. de México, tom. ii.—ED.]

The ardor of the Indian neophyte emulated that of his teacher. In a few years every vestige of the primitive *teocallis* was effaced from the land. The uncouth idols of the country, and, unhappily, the hieroglyphical man-uscripts, shared the same fate. Yet the missionary and the convert did much to repair these losses by their copious accounts of the Aztec institutions, collected from the most authentic sources.[26]

The business of conversion went on prosperously among the several tribes of the great Nahuatlac family. In about twenty years from the first advent of the mis-sionaries, one of their body could make the pious vaunt that nine millions of converts—a number prob-ably exceeding the population of the country—had been admitted within the Christian fold![27] The Aztec worship was remarkable for its burdensome ceremonial, and prepared its votaries for the pomp and splendors of the Romish ritual. It was not difficult to pass from

[26] Toribio, Hist. de los Indios, MS., Parte 3, cap. 1.—Father Saha-gun, who has done better service in this way than any other of his order, describes with simple brevity the rapid process of demolition. "We took the children of the caciques," he says, "into our schools, where we taught them to read and write, and to chant. The children of the poorer natives were brought together in the court-yard, and instructed there in the Christian faith. After our teaching, one or two brethren took the pupils to some neighboring *teocalli*, and, by work-ing at it for a few days, they levelled it to the ground. In this way they demolished, in a short time, all the Aztec temples, great and small, *so that not a vestige of them remained.*" (Hist. de Nueva-España, tom. iii. p. 77.) This passage helps to explain why so few architectural relics of the Indian era still survive in Mexico.

[27] "De manera que á mi juicio y verdaderamente serán bautizados en este tiempo que digo, que serán quince años, mas de nueve millo-nes de ánimas de Indios." Toribio, Hist. de los Indios, MS., Parte 2, cap. 3.

the fasts and festivals of the one religion to the fasts and festivals of the other ; to transfer their homage from the fantastic idols of their own creation to the beautiful forms in sculpture and in painting which decorated the Christian cathedral. It is true, they could have comprehended little of the dogmas of their new faith, and little, it may be, of its vital spirit. But, if the philosopher may smile at the reflection that conversion, under these circumstances, was one of form rather than of substance, the philanthropist will console himself by considering how much the cause of humanity and good morals must have gained by the substitution of these unsullied rites for the brutal abominations of the Aztecs.

The Conquerors settled in such parts of the country as best suited their inclinations. Many occupied the southeastern slopes of the Cordilleras towards the rich valley of Oaxaca. Many more spread themselves over the broad surface of the table-land, which, from its elevated position, reminded them of the plateau of their own Castiles. Here, too, they were in the range of those inexhaustible mines which have since poured their silver deluge over Europe. The mineral re sources of the land were not, indeed, fully explored or comprehended till at a much later period ; but some few, as the mines of Zacatecas, Guanaxuato, and Tasco,—the last of which was also known in Montezuma's time,—had begun to be wrought within a generation after the Conquest.[28]

[28] Clavigero, Stor. del Messico, tom. i. p. 43.—Humboldt, Essai politique, tom. iii. pp. 115, 145.— Esposicion de Don Lúcas Alaman (México, 1828), p. 59.

But the best wealth of the first settlers was in the vegetable products of the soil, whether indigenous, or introduced from abroad by the wise economy of Cortés. He had earnestly recommended the crown to require all vessels coming to the country to bring over a certain quantity of seeds and plants.[29] He made it a condition of the grants of land on the plateau, that the proprietor of every estate should plant a specified number of vines in it.[30] He further stipulated that no one should get a clear title to his estate until he had occupied it eight years.[31] He knew that permanent residence could alone create that interest in the soil which would lead to its efficient culture, and that the opposite system had caused the impoverishment of the best plantations in the Islands. His various regulations, some of them not a little distasteful to the colonists, augmented the agricultural resources of the country by the addition of the most important European grains and other vegetables, for which the diversified climate of New Spain was admirably adapted. The sugar-cane was transplanted from the neighboring islands to the lower level of the country, and, together with indigo, cotton, and cochineal, formed a more desirable staple for the colony than its precious metals.

[29] " Páraque cada Navío traiga cierta cantidad de Plantas, y que no pueda salir sin ellas, porque será mucha causa para la Poblacion, y perpetuacion de ella." Rel. Quarta de Cortés, ap. Lorenzana, p. 397.

[30] " Item, que cualquier vecino que tubiere Indios de repartimiento sea obligado á poner en ellos en cada un año con cada cien Indios de los que tuvieren de repartimiento mil sarmientos aunque sean de la planta de su tierra, escogiendo la mejor que pudiesse hallar." Ordenanzas municipales, año de 1524, MS.

[31] Ordenanzas municipales, año de 1524, MS.

Under the sun of the tropics, the peach, the almond, the orange, the vine, and the olive, before unknown there, flourished in the gardens of the table-land, at an elevation twice as great as that at which the clouds are suspended in summer above our heads. The importation of a European fruit or vegetable was hailed by the simple colonists with delight. The first produce of the exotic was celebrated by a festival, and the guests greeted each other, as on the appearance of an old familiar friend, who called up the remembrance of the past and the tender associations of their native land.[32]

While thus occupied with the internal economy of the country, Cortés was still bent on his great schemes of discovery and conquest. In the preceding chapter we have seen him fitting out a little fleet at Zacatula to explore the shores of the Pacific. It was burnt in the dock-yard when nearly completed. This was a serious calamity, as most of the materials were to be transported across the country from Villa Rica. Cortés, however, with his usual promptness, took measures to repair the loss. He writes to the emperor that another squadron will soon be got ready at the same port, and, "he doubts not, will put his Majesty in possession of more lands and kingdoms than the nation has ever heard of"![33] This magnificent vaunt shows

[32] ["No general interest would attach to the private undertakings of Cortés, if the sole object of them had been the aggrandizement of his own fortune. But they were in fact the germs of what are now the most important branches of the national wealth; and they prove the grandeur of those views which in the times of the Conquest gave an impulse to whatever promised to contribute to the prosperity of the country." Alaman, Disertaciones históricas, tom. ii. p. 63.]

[33] "Tengo de ser causa, que Vuestra Cesarea Magestad sea en estas

22*

the common sentiment of the Spaniards at that time, who looked on the Pacific as the famed Indian Ocean, studded with golden islands and teeming with the rich treasures of the East.

A principal object of this squadron was the discovery of a strait which should connect the Atlantic with the Pacific. Another squadron, consisting of five vessels, was fitted out in the Gulf of Mexico, to take the direction of Florida, with the same view of detecting a strait. For Cortés trusted—we at this day may smile at the illusion—that one might be found in that direction which should conduct the navigator to those waters which had been traversed by the keels of Magellan ![34]

The discovery of a strait was the great object to which nautical enterprise in that day was directed, as it had been ever since the time of Columbus. It was in the sixteenth century what the discovery of the Northwest passage has been in our own age,—the *ignis fatuus* of navigators. The vast extent of the American continent had been ascertained by the voyages of Cabot in the North, and of Magellan very recently in the South. The proximity, in certain quarters, of the two great oceans that washed its eastern and western shores had been settled by the discoveries both of Balboa and of Cortés. European scholars could not

partes Señor de mas Reynos, y Señoríos que los que hasta hoy en nuestra Nacion se tiene noticia." Rel. Quarta de Cortés, ap. Lorenzana, p. 374.

[34] " Much as I esteem Hernando Cortés," exclaims Oviedo, " for the greatest captain and most practised in military matters of any we have known, I think such an opinion shows he was no great cosmographer." (Hist. de las Ind., MS., lib. 33, cap. 41.) Oviedo had lived to see its fallacy.

believe that Nature had worked on a plan so repugnant, apparently, to the interests of humanity, as to
interpose, through the whole length of the great continent, such a barrier to communication between the
adjacent waters. The correspondence of men of
science,[35] the instructions of the Court, the letters of
Cortés, like those of Columbus, touch frequently on
this favorite topic. "Your Majesty may be assured,"
he writes, "that, as I know how much you have at
heart the discovery of *this great secret of a strait*, I
shall postpone all interests and projects of my own,
some of them of the highest moment, for the fulfilment
of this great object."[36]

It was partly with the same view that the general
caused a considerable armament to be equipped and
placed under the command of Cristóval de Olid, the
brave officer who, as the reader will remember, had
charge of one of the great divisions of the besieging
army. He was to steer for Honduras and plant a
colony on its northern coast. A detachment of Olid's
squadron was afterwards to cruise along its southern
shore towards Darien in search of the mysterious strait.
The country was reported to be full of gold; so full
that "the fishermen used gold weights for their nets."
The life of the Spanish discoverers was one long day-
dream. Illusion after illusion chased one another like
the bubbles which the child throws off from his pipe,
as bright, as beautiful, and as empty. They lived in a
world of enchantment.[37]

---

35 Martyr, Opus Epist., ep. 811.
36 Rel. Quarta, ap. Lorenzana, p. 385.
37 The illusion at home was kept up, in some measure, by the daz-

Together with these maritime expeditions, Cortés
fitted out a powerful expedition by land.   It was intrusted to Alvarado, who, with a large force of Spaniards and Indians, was to descend the southern slant
of the Cordilleras and penetrate into the countries that
lay beyond the rich valley of Oaxaca.   The campaigns of this bold and rapacious chief terminated in
the important conquest of Guatemala.   The general
required his captains to send him minute accounts of
the countries which they visited, the productions of
the soil, and their general resources.   The result was
several valuable and interesting communications.[38]   In
his instructions for the conduct of these expeditions,
he enjoined a considerate treatment of the natives,
and inculcated a policy which may be called humane,
as far as humanity is compatible with a system of subjugation.[39]   Unfortunately, the character of his officers
too often rendered these instructions unavailing.

In the prosecution of his great enterprises, Cortés,
within three short years after the Conquest, had re-

zling display of gold and jewels remitted from time to time, wrought
into fanciful and often fantastic forms.   One of the articles sent home
by Cortés was a piece of ordnance, made of gold and silver, of very
fine workmanship, the metal of which alone cost 25,000 *pesos de oro.*
Oviedo, who saw it in the palace, speaks with admiracion of this
magnificent toy.   Hist. de las Ind., MS., lib. 33, cap. 41.

[38] Among these may be particularly mentioned the Letters of Alvarado and Diego de Godoy, transcribed by Oviedo in his Hist. de las
Ind., MS. (lib. 33, cap. 42–44), and translated by Ramusio for his
rich collection, Viaggi, tom. iii.

[39] See, among others, his orders to his kinsman, Francisco Cortés,—
" Instruccion civil y militar por la Expedicion de la Costa de Colima.'
The paper is dated in 1524, and forms part of the Muñoz collection
of MSS.

duced under the dominion of Castile an extent of country more than four hundred leagues in length, as he affirms, on the Atlantic coast, and more than five hundred on the Pacific, and, with the exception of a few interior provinces of no great importance, had brought them to a condition of entire tranquillity.[40] In accomplishing this, he had freely expended the revenues of the crown, drawn from tributes similar to those which had been anciently paid by the natives to their own sovereigns; and he had, moreover, incurred a large debt on his own account, for which he demanded remuneration from the government. The celebrity of his name, and the dazzling reports of the conquered countries, drew crowds of adventurers to New Spain, who furnished the general with recruits for his various enterprises.

Whoever would form a just estimate of this remarkable man must not confine himself to the history of the Conquest. His military career, indeed, places him on a level with the greatest captains of his age. But the period subsequent to the Conquest affords different, and in some respects nobler, points of view for the study of his character. For we then see him devising a system of government for the motley and antagonist races, so to speak, now first brought under a common dominion; repairing the mischiefs of war; and employing his efforts to detect the latent resources of the

[40] Rel. Quarta, ap. Lorenzana, p. 371.—" Well may we wonder," exclaims his archiepiscopal editor, " that Cortés and his soldiers could have overrun and subdued, in so short a time, countries, many of them so rough and difficult of access that even at the present day we can hardly penetrate them !" Ibid., nota.

country and to stimulate it to its highest power of production. The narrative may seem tame, after the recital of exploits as bold and adventurous as those of a paladin of romance. But it is only by the perusal of this narrative that we can form an adequate conception of the acute and comprehensive genius of Cortés.

CHAPTER III.

DEFECTION OF OLID.—DREADFUL MARCH TO HONDURAS.
— EXECUTION OF GUATEMOZIN. — DOÑA MARINA.—
ARRIVAL AT HONDURAS.

1524–1526.

IN the last chapter we have seen that Cristóval de
Olid was sent by Cortés to plant a colony in Honduras.
The expedition was attended with consequences which
had not been foreseen. Made giddy by the possession
of power, Olid, when he had reached his place of destination, determined to assert an independent jurisdiction for himself. His distance from Mexico, he
flattered himself, might enable him to do so with im-
punity. He misunderstood the character of Cortés,
when he supposed that any distance would be great
enough to shield a rebel from his vengeance.

It was long before the general received tidings of
Olid's defection. But no sooner was he satisfied of this
than he despatched to Honduras a trusty captain and
kinsman, Francisco de las Casas, with directions to
arrest his disobedient officer. Las Casas was wrecked
on the coast, and fell into Olid's hands, but eventually
succeeded in raising an insurrection in the settlement,
seized the person of Olid, and beheaded that unhappy
delinquent in the market-place of Naco.[1]

[1] Carta Quinta de Cortés, MS.

Of these proceedings, Cortés learned only what related to the shipwreck of his lieutenant.   He saw all
the mischievous consequences that must arise from
Olid's example, especially if his defection were to go
unpunished.   He determined to take the affair into
his own hands, and to lead an expedition in person to
Honduras.   He would thus, moreover, be enabled to
ascertain from personal inspection the resources of the
country, which were reputed great on the score of
mineral wealth, and would perhaps detect the point
of communication between the great oceans, which had
so long eluded the efforts of the Spanish discoverers.
He was still further urged to this step by the uncom-
fortable position in which he had found himself of late
in the capital.   Several functionaries had recently been
sent from the mother country for the ostensible purpose of administering the colonial revenues.   But they
served as spies on the general's conduct, caused him
many petty annoyances, and sent back to court the
most malicious reports of his purposes and proceedings.
Cortés, in short, now that he was made Governor-
General of the country, had less real power than when
he held no legal commission at all.

The Spanish force which he took with him did not
probably exceed a hundred horse and forty or perhaps
fifty foot ; to which were added about three thousand
Indian auxiliaries.[2]   Among them were Guatemozin
and the cacique of Tacuba, with a few others of highest

[2] Carta de Albornos, MS., Mexico, Dec. 15, 1525.—Carta Quinta
de Cortés, MS.—The authorities do not precisely agree as to the
numbers, which were changing, probably, with every step of their
march across the table-land.

rank, whose consideration with their countrymen would make them an obvious nucleus round which disaffection might gather. The general's personal retinue consisted of several pages, young men of good family, and among them Montejo, the future conqueror of Yucatan; a butler and steward; several musicians, dancers, jugglers, and buffoons, showing, it might seem, more of the effeminacy of an Oriental satrap than the hardy valor of a Spanish cavalier.[3] Yet the imputation of effeminacy is sufficiently disproved by the terrible march which he accomplished.

Towards the end of October, 1524, Cortés began his march. As he descended the sides of the Cordilleras, he was met by many of his old companions in arms, who greeted their commander with a hearty welcome, and some of them left their estates to join the expedition.[4] He halted in the province of Coatzacualco (Huazacualco) until he could receive intelligence respecting his route from the natives of Tabasco. They furnished him with a map, exhibiting the principal places whither the Indian traders who wandered over these wild regions were in the habit of resorting. With the aid of this map, a compass, and such guides as from time to time he could pick up on his journey, he proposed to traverse that broad and level tract which forms the base of Yucatan and spreads from the Coatzacualco River to the head of the Gulf of Honduras.

[3] Bernal Diaz, Hist. de la Conquista, cap. 175.

[4] Among these was Captain Diaz, who, however, left the pleasant farm, which he occupied in the province of Coatzacualco, with a very ill grace, to accompany the expedition. " But Cortés commanded it, and we dared not say no," says the veteran. Ibid., cap. 174.

"I shall give your Majesty," he begins his celebrated Letter to the emperor, describing this expedition, "an account, as usual, of the most remarkable events of my journey, every one of which might form the subject of a separate narration." Cortés did not exaggerate.[5]

The beginning of the march lay across a low and marshy level, intersected by numerous little streams,

[5] This celebrated Letter, which has never been published, is usually designated as the *Carta Quinta*, or "Fifth Letter," of Cortés. It is nearly as long as the longest of the printed letters of the Conqueror, is written in the same clear, simple, business-like manner, and is as full of interest as any of the preceding. It gives a minute account of the expedition to Honduras, together with events that occurred in the year following. It bears no date, but was probably written in that year from Mexico. The original manuscript is in the Imperial Library at Vienna, which, as the German sceptre was swayed at that time by the same hand which held the Castilian, contains many documents of value for the illustration of Spanish history.*

---

* [It is scarcely credible that a long and important document in an official form should have borne no date, and we may therefore suspect that the manuscript at Vienna, if unmutilated, is *not* the original. A copy in the Royal Library at Madrid, purporting to have been made "from the original" by Alonso Diaz, terminates as follows: "De la cibdad de Temixtitan, desta Nueva España á *tres del mes de setiembre del nascimiento de nuestro Señor é Salvador Jesu-Cristo de* 1526." This date is confirmed by a passage in a letter which will be found cited in the notes to the next chapter with the date of Sept. 11, but of which there are in fact two originals, the duplicate being dated Sept. 3. It gives a summary, for the emperor's own perusal, of the matters narrated at length in the *Carta Quinta*, which it thus describes: "Así mesmo *envio agora* á V. M. *con lo presente* una relacion bien larga y particular de todo lo que me subcedió en el camino que hice á las Hibueras, y al cabo della hago saber á V. M. muy por extenso lo que ha pasado y se ha hecho en esta Nueva España despues que yo parté de la isla de Cuba para ella." See Col. de Doc. inéd. para la Historia de España, tom. i.—ED.]

which form the head-waters of the Rio de Tabasco, and of the other rivers that discharge themselves, to the north, into the Mexican Gulf. The smaller streams they forded, or passed in canoes, suffering their horses to swim across as they held them by the bridle. Rivers of more formidable size they crossed on floating bridges. It gives one some idea of the difficulties they had to encounter in this way, when it is stated that the Spaniards were obliged to construct no less than fifty of these bridges in a distance of less than a hundred miles![6] One of them was more than nine hundred paces in length. Their troubles were much augmented by the difficulty of obtaining subsistence, as the natives frequently set fire to the villages on their approach, leaving to the way-worn adventurers only a pile of smoking ruins.

It would be useless to encumber the page with the names of Indian towns which lay in the route of the army, but which may be now obsolete, and, at all events, have never found their way into a map of the country.[7]

---

[6] "Es tierra mui baja y de muchas sienegas, tanto que en tiempo de invierno no se puede andar, ni se sirve sino en canoas, y con pasarla yo en tiempo de seca, desde la entrada hasta la salida de ella, que puede aver veinti leguas, se hiziéron mas de cinquenta puentes, que sin se hazer, fuera imposible pasar." Carta Quinta de Cortés, MS.

[7] I have examined some of the most ancient maps of the country, by Spanish, French, and Dutch cosmographers, in order to determine the route of Cortés. An inestimable collection of these maps, made by the learned German Ebeling, is to be found in the library of Harvard University. I can detect on them only four or five of the places indicated by the general. They are the places mentioned in the text, and, though few, may serve to show the general direction of the march of the army.

The first considerable place which they reached was Iztapan, pleasantly situated in the midst of a fruitful region, on the banks of one of the tributaries of the Rio de Tabasco. Such was the extremity to which the Spaniards had already, in the course of a few weeks, been reduced by hunger and fatigue, that the sight of a village in these dreary solitudes was welcomed by his followers, says Cortés, "with a shout of joy that was echoed back from all the surrounding woods." The army was now at no great distance from the ancient city of Palenque, the subject of so much speculation in our time. The village of *Las Tres Cruzes*, indeed, situated between twenty and thirty miles from Palenque, is said still to commemorate the passage of the Conquerors by the existence of three crosses which they left there. Yet no allusion is made to the ancient capital. Was it then the abode of a populous and flourishing community, such as once occupied it, to judge from the extent and magnificence of its remains? Or was it, even then, a heap of mouldering ruins, buried in a wilderness of vegetation, and thus hidden from the knowledge of the surrounding country? If the former, the silence of Cortés is not easy to be explained.

On quitting Iztapan, the Spaniards struck across a country having the same character of a low and marshy soil, checkered by occasional patches of cultivation, and covered with forests of cedar and Brazil wood, which seemed absolutely interminable. The overhanging foliage threw so deep a shade that, as Cortés says, the soldiers could not see where to set their feet.[8] To

[8] "Donde se ponian los pies en el suelo açia arriba la claridad del

add to their perplexity, their guides deserted them; and, when they climbed to the summits of the tallest trees, they could see only the same cheerless, interminable line of waving woods. The compass and the map furnished the only clue to extricate them from this gloomy labyrinth; and Cortés and his officers, among whom was the constant Sandoval, spreading out their chart on the ground, anxiously studied the probable direction of their route. Their scanty supplies meanwhile had entirely failed them, and they appeased the cravings of appetite by such roots as they dug out of the earth, or by the nuts and berries that grew wild in the woods. Numbers fell sick, and many of the Indians sank by the way, and died of absolute starvation.

When at length the troops emerged from these dismal forests, their path was crossed by a river of great depth, and far wider than any which they had hitherto traversed. The soldiers, disheartened, broke out into murmurs against their leader, who was plunging them deeper and deeper in a boundless wilderness, where they must lay their bones. It was in vain that Cortés encouraged them to construct a floating bridge, which might take them to the opposite bank of the river. It seemed a work of appalling magnitude, to which their wasted strength was unequal. He was more successful in his appeal to the Indian auxiliaries, till his own men, put to shame by the ready obedience of the latter, engaged in the work with a hearty good will, which enabled them, although ready to drop from fatigue, to

cielo no se veia, tanta era la espesura y alteza de los árboles, que aunque se subian en algunos, no podian descubrir un tiro de piedra." Carta Quinta de Cortés, MS.

accomplish it at the end of four days. It was, indeed, the only expedient by which they could hope to extricate themselves from their perilous situation. The bridge consisted of one thousand pieces of timber, each of the thickness of a man's body and full sixty feet long.[9] When we consider that the timber was all standing in the forest at the commencement of the labor, it must be admitted to have been an achievement worthy of the Spaniards. The well-compacted beams presented a solid structure which nothing, says Cortés, but fire could destroy. It excited the admiration of the natives, who came from a great distance to see it; and "the bridge of Cortés" remained for many a year the enduring monument of that commander's energy and perseverance.

The arrival of the army on the opposite bank of the river involved them in new difficulties. The ground was so soft and saturated with water that the horses floundered up to their girths, and, sometimes plunging into quagmires, were nearly buried in the mud. It was with the greatest difficulty that they could be extricated by covering the wet soil with the foliage and the boughs of trees, when a stream of water, which forced its way through the heart of the morass, furnished the jaded animals with the means of effecting their escape by swimming.[10] As the Spaniards emerged from these

[9] "Porque lleva mas que mil bigas, que la menor es casi tan gorda como un cuerpo de un hombre, y de nueve y diez brazas en largo." Carta Quinta de Cortés, MS.

[10] "Pasada toda la gente y cavallos de la otra parte del alcon dimos luego en una gran çienega, que durava bien tres tiros de ballesta, la cosa mas espantosa que jamas las gentes viéron, donde todos los cavallos desençillados se sumiéron hasta las orejas sin parecerse otra

slimy depths, they came on a broad and rising ground, which, by its cultivated fields teeming with maize, *agi*, or pepper of the country, and the *yuca* plant, intimated their approach to the capital of the fruitful province of Aculan. It was in the beginning of Lent, 1525, a period memorable for an event of which I shall give the particulars from the narrative of Cortés.

The general at this place was informed, by one of the Indian converts in his train, that a conspiracy had been set on foot by Guatemozin, with the cacique of Tacuba, and some other of the principal Indian nobles, to massacre the Spaniards. They would seize the moment when the army should be entangled in the passage of some defile, or some frightful morass like that from which it had just escaped, where, taken at disadvantage, it could be easily overpowered by the superior number of the Mexicans. After the slaughter of the troops, the Indians would continue their march to Honduras and cut off the Spanish settlements there. Their success would lead to a rising in the capital, and, indeed, throughout the land, until every Spaniard should be exterminated, and the vessels in the ports be seized, and secured from carrying the tidings across the waters.

cosa, y querer forçeiar á salir, sumianse mas, de manera que allí per-dímos toda la esperanza de poder escapar cavallos ningunos, pero todavía comenzámos á trabajar y componerles haçes de yerba y ramas grandes de bajo, sobre que se sostuviesen y no se sumiesen, remediá-vanse algo, y andando trabajando y yendo y viniendo de la una parte á la otra, abrióse por medio de un calejon de agua y çieno, que los cavallos comenzáron algo á nadar, y con esto plugo á nuestro Señor que saliéron todos sin peligro ninguno." Carta Quinta de Cortés MS.

No sooner had Cortés learned the particulars of this formidable plot than he arrested Guatemozin and the principal Aztec lords in his train. The latter admitted the fact of the conspiracy, but alleged that it had been planned by Guatemozin and that they had refused to come into it. Guatemozin and the chief of Tacuba neither admitted nor denied the truth of the accusation, but maintained a dogged silence. Such is the statement of Cortés.[11] Bernal Diaz, however, who was present in the expedition, assures us that both Guatemozin and the cacique of Tacuba declared their innocence. They had indeed, they said, talked more than once together of the sufferings they were then enduring, and had said that death was preferable to seeing so many of their poor followers dying daily around them. They admitted, also, that a project for rising on the Spaniards had been discussed by some of the Aztecs; but Guatemozin had discouraged it from the first, and no scheme of the kind could have been put into execution without his knowledge and consent.[12] These protestations did not avail the unfortunate princes; and Cortés, having satisfied, or affected to satisfy, himself of their guilt, ordered them to immediate execution.

When brought to the fatal tree, Guatemozin displayed the intrepid spirit worthy of his better days. "I knew what it was," said he, "to trust to your false promises, Malinche; I knew that you had destined me to this fate, since I did not fall by my own hand when you entered my city of Tenochtitlan. Why do you

[11] Carta Quinta de Cortés, MS.
[12] Hist. de la Conquista, cap. 177.

slay me so unjustly? God will demand it of you!" [13]
The cacique of Tacuba, protesting his innocence, declared that he desired no better lot than to die by the
side of his lord. The unfortunate princes, with one
or more inferior nobles (for the number is uncertain), were then executed by being hung from the
huge branches of a *ceiba*-tree which overshadowed
the road. [14]

Such was the sad end of Guatemozin, the last emperor of the Aztecs, if we might not rather call him
"the last of the Aztecs;" since from this time, broken
in spirit and without a head, the remnant of the nation
resigned itself, almost without a struggle, to the stern
yoke of its oppressors. Among all the names of barbarian princes, there are few entitled to a higher place
on the roll of fame than that of Guatemozin. He was
young, and his public career was not long; but it was
glorious. He was called to the throne in the convulsed
and expiring hours of the monarchy, when the banded
nations of Anahuac and the fierce European were
thundering at the gates of the capital. It was a post
of tremendous responsibility; but Guatemozin's conduct fully justified the choice of him to fill it. No
one can refuse his admiration to the intrepid spirit

[13] Bernal Diaz, Hist. de la Conquista, ubi supra.

[14] According to Diaz, both Guatemozin and the prince of Tacuba
had embraced the religion of their conquerors, and were confessed by
a Franciscan friar before their execution. We are further assured by
the same authority that " they were, *for Indians*, very good Christians,
and believed well and truly." (Ibid., loc. cit.) One is reminded of
the last hours of Caupolican, converted to Christianity by the same
men who tied him to the stake. See the scene, painted in the frightful
coloring of a master-hand, in the Araucana, Canto 34.

M*

which could prolong a defence of his city while one
stone was left upon another; and our sympathies, for
the time, are inevitably thrown more into the scale
of the rude chieftain, thus battling for his country's
freedom, than into that of his civilized and successful
antagonist.[15]

In reviewing the circumstances of Guatemozin's
death, one cannot attach much weight to the charge
of conspiracy brought against him. That the Indians,
brooding over their wrongs and present sufferings,
should have sometimes talked of revenge, would not
be surprising. But that any chimerical scheme of an
insurrection, like that above mentioned, should have
been set on foot, or even sanctioned, by Guatemozin,
is altogether improbable. That prince's explanation
of the affair, as given by Diaz, is, to say the least,
quite as deserving of credit as the accusation of the
Indian informer.[16] The defect of testimony and the

[15] Guatemozin's beautiful wife, the princess Tecuichpo, the daughter
of Montezuma, lived long enough after his death to give her hand to
four Castilians, all of noble descent. (See *ante*, vol. ii. p. 339, note
36.) She is described as having been as well instructed in the Catholic
faith as any woman in Castile, as most gracious and winning in her
deportment, and as having contributed greatly, by her example, and
the deference with which she inspired the Aztecs, to the tranquillity of
the conquered country. This pleasing portrait, it may be well enough
to mention, is by the hand of her husband, Don Thoan Cano. See
Appendix, Part 2, No. 11.

[16] The Indian chroniclers regard the pretended conspiracy of Guatemozin as an invention of Cortés. The informer himself, when afterwards put to the torture by the cacique of Tezcuco, declared that he
had made no revelation of this nature to the Spanish commander.
Ixtlilxochitl vouches for the truth of this story. (Venida de los Españoles, pp. 83-93.) But who will vouch for Ixtlilxochitl?

distance of time make it difficult for us, at the present
day, to decide the question. We have a surer criterion
of the truth in the opinion of those who were eye-
witnesses of the transaction. It is given in the words
of the old chronicler so often quoted. "The execution of Guatemozin," says Diaz, "was most unjust,
and was thought wrong by all of us."[17]

The most probable explanation of the affair seems to
be that Guatemozin was a troublesome and, indeed,
formidable captive. Thus much is intimated by Cortés
himself, in his Letter to the emperor.[18] The fallen
sovereign of Mexico, by the ascendency of his character, as well as by his previous station, maintained
an influence over his countrymen which would have
enabled him with a breath, as it were, to rouse their
smothered, not extinguished, animosity into rebellion. The Spaniards, during the first years after the
Conquest, lived in constant apprehension of a rising
of the Aztecs. This is evident from numerous passages in the writings of the time. It was under the
same apprehension that Cortés consented to embarrass
himself with his royal captive on this dreary expedition. And in such distrust did he hold him that,
even while in Mexico, he neither rode abroad, nor
walked to any great distance, according to Gomara,
without being attended by Guatemozin.[19]

[17] "Y fué esta muerte que les diéron muy injustamente dada, y
pareció mal á todos los que ibamos aquella jornada." Hist. de la
Conquista, cap. 177.

[18] "Guatemozin, Señor que fué de esta Ciudad de Temixtitan, á
quien yo despues que la gané he tenido siempre preso, teniéndole por
hombre bullicioso, y le llevé conmigo." Carta Quinta, MS.

[19] "Y le hacian aquella mesma reverencia, i ceremonias, que á

Parties standing in such relations to each other could have been the objects only of mutual distrust and aversion. The forlorn condition of the Spaniards on the present march, which exposed them in a peculiar degree to any sudden assault from their wily Indian vassals, increased the suspicions of Cortés. Thus predisposed to think ill of Guatemozin, the general lent a ready ear to the first accusation against him. Charges were converted into proofs, and condemnation followed close upon the charges. By a single blow he proposed to rid himself and the state forever of a dangerous enemy,—the more dangerous, that he was an enemy in disguise. Had he but consulted his own honor and his good name, Guatemozin's head was the last on which he should have suffered an injury to fall. "He should have cherished him," to borrow the homely simile of his encomiast, Gomara, "like gold in a napkin, as the best trophy of his victories." [20]

Whatever may have been the real motives of his conduct in this affair, it seems to have left the mind of Cortés but ill at ease. For a long time he was moody and irritable, and found it difficult to sleep at night. On one occasion, as he was pacing an upper chamber of a *teocalli* in which he was quartered, he missed his footing in the dark, and was precipitated from a height of some twelve feet to the ground, which occasioned him a severe contusion on the head,—a

Moteçuma, i creo que por eso le llevaba siempre consigo por la Ciudad á Caballo si cavalgaba, i sino á pie como él iba." Crónica, cap. 170.

[20] " I Cortés debiera guardarlo vivo, como Oro en paño, que era el triumpho, i gloria de sus Victorias." Crónica, cap. 170.

thing too palpable to be concealed, though he endeavored, says the gossiping Diaz, to hide the knowledge
of it, as well as he could, from the soldiers.[21]

It was not long after the sad scene of Guatemozin's
execution that the wearied troops entered the head
town of the great province of Aculan ; a thriving community of traders, who carried on a profitable traffic
with the farthest quarters of Central America. Cortés
notices in general terms the excellence and beauty of
the buildings, and the hospitable reception which he
experienced from the inhabitants.

After renewing their strength in these comfortable
quarters, the Spaniards left the capital of Aculan, the
name of which is to be found on no map, and held on
their toilsome way in the direction of what is now
called the Lake of Peten. It was then the property
of an emigrant tribe of the hardy Maya family, and
their capital stood on an island in the lake, "with its
houses and lofty *teocallis* glistening in the sun," says
Bernal Diaz, "so that it might be seen for the distance
of two leagues."[22] These edifices, built by one of the
races of Yucatan, displayed, doubtless, the same peculiarities of construction as the remains still to be seen
in that remarkable peninsula. But, whatever may have
been their architectural merits, they are disposed of in
a brief sentence by the Conquerors.

The inhabitants of the island showed a friendly
spirit, and a docility unlike the warlike temper of their
countrymen of Yucatan. They willingly listened to
the Spanish missionaries who accompanied the expedi-

[21] Hist. de la Conquista, ubi supra.
[22] Ibid., cap. 178.

tion, as they expounded the Christian doctrines through the intervention of Marina. The Indian interpreter was present throughout this long march, the last in which she remained at the side of Cortés. As this, too, is the last occasion on which she will appear in these pages, I will mention, before parting with her, an interesting circumstance that occurred when the army was traversing the province of Coatzacualco. This, it may be remembered, was the native country of Marina, where her infamous mother sold her, when a child, to some foreign traders, in order to secure her inheritance to a younger brother. Cortés halted for some days at this place, to hold a conference with the surrounding caciques on matters of government and religion. Among those summoned to this meeting was Marina's mother, who came, attended by her son. No sooner did they make their appearance than all were struck with the great resemblance of the cacique to her daughter. The two parties recognized each other, though they had not met since their separation. The mother, greatly terrified, fancied that she had been decoyed into a snare in order to punish her inhuman conduct. But Marina instantly ran up to her, and endeavored to allay her fears, assuring her that she should receive no harm, and, addressing the by-standers, said "that she was sure her mother knew not what she did when she sold her to the traders, and that she forgave her." Then, tenderly embracing her unnatural parent, she gave her such jewels and other little ornaments as she wore about her own person, to win back, as it would seem, her lost affection. Marina added that "she felt much happier than before, now that she had been instructed in the Christian faith and given up the bloody worship of the Aztecs."[23]

In the course of the expedition to Honduras, Cortés gave Marina away to a Castilian knight, Don Juan Xaramillo,[24] to whom she was wedded as his lawful wife. She had estates assigned to her in her native province, where she probably passed the remainder of her days.[25] From this time the name of Marina disappears from the page of history. But it has been always held in grateful remembrance by the Spaniards, for the important aid which she gave them in effecting the Conquest, and by the natives, for the kindness and sympathy which she showed them in their misfortunes. Many an Indian ballad commemorates the gentle virtues of Malinche,—her Aztec epithet. Even now her spirit, if report be true, watches over the capital which

[23] Diaz, who was present, attests the truth of this account by the most solemn adjuration: "Y todo esto que digo, se lo oí muy certificadamente y se lo juro, amen." Hist. de la Conquista, cap. 37.

[24] [Alaman, from an examination of the municipal archives of Mexico, finds that Juan de Jaramillo was commander of one of the brigantines in the siege of Mexico. He subsequently filled the office of royal standard-bearer of the city, and was several times chosen to represent it in the assemblies of the cities of New Spain. Conquista de Méjico (trad. de Vega), tom. ii. p. 269.]

[25] [The Spanish government showed its sense of the services of Marina by the grant of several estates both in the town and country. The house in which she usually resided in Mexico was in the street of Medinas, as it is now called, which then bore the name of her husband, Jaramillo. She had a pleasure-house at Chapultepec, and in Cuyoacan a garden that had belonged to Montezuma. She lived in the enjoyment of wealth and much consideration from her countrymen; and, as we see mention made of her grandchild during her lifetime, we may presume she reached a good old age. Conquista de Méjico (trad. de Vega), tom. ii. p. 269.—Alaman, Disertaciones históricas, tom. ii. p. 293.]

she helped to win; and the peasant is occasionally startled by the apparition of an Indian princess, dimly seen through the evening shadows, as it flits among the groves and grottos of the royal Hill of Chapoltepec.[26]

By the Conqueror, Marina left one son, Don Martin Cortés. He rose to high consideration, and was made a *comendador* of the order of St. Jago. He was subsequently suspected of treasonable designs against the government; and neither his parents' extraordinary services, nor his own deserts, could protect him from a cruel persecution; and in 1568 the son of Hernando Cortés was shamefully subjected to the torture in the very capital which his father had acquired for the Castilian crown!

The inhabitants of the isles of Peten—to return from our digression—listened attentively to the preaching of the Franciscan friars, and consented to the instant demolition of their idols, and the erection of the Cross upon their ruins.[27] A singular circumstance showed the value of these hurried conversions. Cortés, on his departure, left among this friendly people one of his horses, which had been disabled by an injury in the foot. The Indians felt a reverence for the animal, as in some way connected with the mysterious power of

[26] Life in Mexico, let. 8.—The fair author does not pretend to have been favored with a sight of the apparition.

[27] Villagutierre says that the Iztacs, by which name the inhabitants of these islands were called, did not destroy their idols while the Spaniards remained there. (Historia de la Conquista de la Provincia de el Itza (Madrid, 1701), pp. 49, 50.) The historian is wrong, since Cortés expressly asserts that the images were broken and burnt in his presence. Carta Quinta, MS.

the white men. When their visitors had gone, they offered flowers to the horse, and, as it is said, prepared for him many savory messes of poultry, such as they would have administered to their own sick. Under this extraordinary diet the poor animal pined away and died. The affrighted Indians raised his effigy in stone, and, placing it in one of their *teocallis*, did homage to it, as to a deity. In 1618, when two Franciscan friars came to preach the gospel in these regions, then scarcely better known to the Spaniards than before the time of Cortés, one of the most remarkable objects which they found was this statue of a horse, receiving the homage of the Indian worshippers, as the god of thunder and lightning ! [28]

It would be wearisome to recount all the perils and hardships endured by the Spaniards in the remainder of their journey. It would be repeating only the incidents of the preceding narrative, the same obstacles in their path, the same extremities of famine and fatigue, —hardships more wearing on the spirits than encounters with an enemy, which, if more hazardous, are also more exciting. It is easier to contend with man than with Nature. Yet I must not omit to mention the passage of the *Sierra de los Pedernales*, "the Mountain of Flints," which, though only twenty-four miles in extent, consumed no less than twelve days in crossing it ! The sharp stones cut the horses' feet to pieces, while many were lost down the precipices and ravines ; so that when they had reached the opposite side sixty-eight of these valuable animals had perished, and the

[28] The fact is recorded by Villagutierre, Conquista de el Itza, pp. 100–102, and Cojullado, Hist. de Yucathan, lib. 1, cap. 16.

remainder were, for the most part, in an unserviceable condition ! [29]

The rainy season had now set in, and torrents of water, falling day and night, drenched the adventurers to the skin, and added greatly to their distresses. The rivers, swollen beyond their usual volume, poured along with a terrible impetuosity that defied the construction of bridges; and it was with the greatest difficulty that, by laying trunks of trees from one huge rock to another, with which these streams were studded, they effected a perilous passage to the opposite banks.[30]

At length the shattered train drew near the Golfo Dolce, at the head of the Bay of Honduras. Their route could not have been far from the site of Copan, the celebrated city whose architectural ruins have furnished such noble illustrations for the pencil of Catherwood. But the Spaniards passed on in silence. Nor, indeed, can we wonder that at this stage of the enterprise they should have passed on without heeding the vicinity of a city in the wilderness, though it were as glorious as the capital of Zenobia; for they were arrived almost within view of the Spanish settlements, the object of their long and wearisome pilgrimage.

[29] " Y querer dezir la aspereza y fragosidad de este Puerto y sierras, ni quien lo dixese lo sabria significar, ni quien lo oyese podria entender, sino que sepa V. M. que en ocho leguas que duró hasta este puerto estuvímos en las andar doze dias, digo los postreros en llegar al cabo de él, en que muriéron sesenta y ocho cavallos despeñados y desxaretados, y todos los demas viniéron heridos y tan lastimados que no pensámos aprovecharnos de ninguno." Carta Quinta de Cortés, MS.

[30] " If any unhappy wretch had become giddy in this transit," says Cortés, " he must inevitably have been precipitated into the gulf and perished. There were upwards of twenty of these frightful passes." Carta Quinta, MS.

The place which they were now approaching was Naco, or San Gil de Buena Vista, a Spanish settlement on the Golfo Dolce. Cortés advanced cautiously, prepared to fall on the town by surprise. He had held on his way with the undeviating step of the North American Indian, who, traversing morass and mountain and the most intricate forests, guided by the instinct of revenge, presses straight towards the mark, and, when he has reached it, springs at once on his unsuspecting victim. Before Cortés made his assault, his scouts fortunately fell in with some of the inhabitants of the place, from whom they received tidings of the death of Olid, and of the re-establishment of his own authority. Cortés, therefore, entered the place like a friend, and was cordially welcomed by his countrymen, greatly astonished, says Diaz, "by the presence among them of the general so renowned throughout these countries." [31]

The colony was at this time sorely suffering from famine; and to such extremity was it soon reduced that the troops would probably have found a grave in the very spot to which they had looked forward as the goal of their labors, but for the seasonable arrival of a vessel with supplies from Cuba. With a perseverance which nothing could daunt, Cortés made an examination of the surrounding country, and occupied a month more in exploring dismal swamps, steaming with unwholesome exhalations, and infected with bilious fevers and with swarms of venomous insects which left peace

[31] "Espantáronse en gran manera, y como supiéron que era Cortés q̃ tan nombrado era en todas estas partes de las Indias, y en Castilla, no sabiã que se hazer de placer." Hist. de la Conquista, cap. 179.

neither by day nor night. At length he embarked with a part of his forces on board of two brigantines, and, after touching at one or two ports in the bay, anchored off Truxillo, the principal Spanish settlement on that coast. The surf was too high for him easily to effect a landing; but the inhabitants, overjoyed at his arrival, rushed into the shallow water and eagerly bore back the general in their arms to the shore.[32]

After he had restored the strength and spirits of his men, the indefatigable commander prepared for a new expedition, the object of which was to explore and to reduce the extensive province of Nicaragua. One may well feel astonished at the adventurous spirit of the man who, unsubdued by the terrible sufferings of his recent march, should so soon be prepared for another enterprise equally appalling. It is difficult, in this age of sober sense, to conceive the character of a Castilian cavalier of the sixteenth century, a true counterpart of which it would not have been easy to find in any other nation, even at that time,—or anywhere, indeed, save in those tales of chivalry, which, however wild and extravagant they may seem, were much more true to character than to situation. The mere excitement of exploring the strange and the unknown was a sufficient compensation to the Spanish adventurer for all his toils and trials. It seems to have been ordered by Providence that such a race of men should exist contemporaneously with the discovery of the New World, that those regions should be brought to light which were beset with dangers and difficulties so appalling as might

[32] Bernal Diaz, Hist. de la Conquista, cap. 179, et seq.—Herrera, Hist. general, dec. 3, lib. 8, cap.3, 4.—Carta Quinta de Cortés, MS.

have tended to overawe and to discourage the ordinary spirit of adventure. Yet Cortés, though filled with this spirit, proposed nobler ends to himself than those of the mere vulgar adventurer. In the expedition to Nicaragua he designed, as he had done in that to Honduras, to ascertain the resources of the country in general, and, above all, the existence of any means of communication between the great oceans on its borders. If none such existed, it would at least establish this fact, the knowledge of which, to borrow his own language, was scarcely less important.

The general proposed to himself the further object of enlarging the colonial empire of Castile. The conquest of Mexico was but the commencement of a series of conquests. To the warrior who had achieved this, nothing seemed impracticable; and scarcely would any thing have been so, had he been properly sustained. It is no great stretch of imagination to see the Conqueror of Mexico advancing along the provinces of the vast Isthmus,—Nicaragua, Costa Rica, and Darien,—until he had planted his victorious banner on the shores of the Gulf of Panamá; and, while it was there fanned by the breezes from the golden South, the land of the Incas, to see him gathering such intelligence of this land as would stimulate him to carry his arms still farther, and to anticipate, it might be, the splendid career of Pizarro!

But from these dreams of ambition Cortés was suddenly aroused by such tidings as convinced him that his absence from Mexico was already too far prolonged, and that he must return without delay, if he would save the capital or the country.

CHAPTER IV.

1526–1530.

THE intelligence alluded to in the preceding chapter
was conveyed in a letter to Cortés from the licentiate
Zuazo, one of the functionaries to whom the general
had committed the administration of the country
during his absence. It contained full particulars of
the tumultuous proceedings in the capital. No sooner
had Cortés quitted it, than dissensions broke out
among the different members of the provisional government. The misrule increased as his absence was
prolonged. At length tidings were received that Cortés
with his whole army had perished in the morasses
of Chiapa. The members of the government showed
no reluctance to credit this story. They now openly
paraded their own authority; proclaimed the general's
death; caused funeral ceremonies to be performed in
his honor; took possession of his property wherever
they could meet with it, piously devoting a small part
of the proceeds to purchasing masses for his soul, while
the remainder was appropriated to pay off what was
called his debt to the state. They seized, in like

manner, the property of other individuals engaged in the expedition. From these outrages they proceeded to others against the Spanish residents in the city, until the Franciscan missionaries left the capital in disgust, while the Indian population were so sorely oppressed that great apprehensions were entertained of a general rising. Zuazo, who communicated these tidings, implored Cortés to quicken his return. He was a temperate man, and the opposition which he had made to the tyrannical measures of his comrades had been rewarded with exile.[1]

The general, greatly alarmed by this account, saw that no alternative was left but to abandon all further schemes of conquest, and to return at once, if he would secure the preservation of the empire which he had won. He accordingly made the necessary arrangements for settling the administration of the colonies at Honduras, and embarked with a small number of followers for Mexico.

He had not been long at sea when he encountered such a terrible tempest as seriously damaged his vessel and compelled him to return to port and refit. A second attempt proved equally unsuccessful ; and Cortés, feeling that his good star had deserted him, saw in this repeated disaster an intimation from Heaven that he was not to return.[2] He contented himself, therefore, with sending a trusty messenger to advise his friends of his personal safety in Honduras. He then instituted processions and public prayers to

[1] Carta Quinta de Cortés, MS.—Bernal Diaz, Hist. de la Conquista, cap. 185.—Relacion del Tesorero Strada, MS., México, 1526.

[2] Carta Quinta de Cortés, MS.

ascertain the will of Heaven and to deprecate its anger. His health now showed the effects of his recent sufferings, and declined under a wasting fever. His spirits sank with it, and he fell into a state of gloomy despondency. Bernal Diaz, speaking of him at this time, says that nothing could be more wan and emaciated than his person, and that so strongly was he possessed with the idea of his approaching end that he procured a Franciscan habit,—for it was common to be laid out in the habit of some one or other of the monastic orders,—in which to be carried to the grave.[3]

From this deplorable apathy Cortés was roused by fresh advices urging his presence in Mexico, and by the judicious efforts of his good friend Sandoval, who had lately returned, himself, from an excursion into the interior. By his persuasion, the general again consented to try his fortunes on the seas. He embarked on board of a brigantine, with a few followers, and bade adieu to the disastrous shores of Honduras, April 25, 1526. He had nearly made the coast of New Spain, when a heavy gale threw him off his course and drove him to the island of Cuba. After staying there some time to recruit his exhausted strength, he again put to sea, on the 16th of May, and in eight days landed near San Juan de Ulua, whence he proceeded about five leagues on foot to Medellin.

Cortés was so much changed by disease that his person was not easily recognized. But no sooner was it known that the general had returned than crowds of people, white men and natives, thronged from all the neigh-

[3] Hist. de la Conquista, cap. 184. et seq.—Carta Quinta de Cortés, MS.

boring country to welcome him. The tidings spread
far and wide on the wings of the wind, and his progress
to the capital was a triumphal procession. The inhabitants came from the distance of eighty leagues to have
a sight of him; and they congratulated one another
on the presence of the only man who could rescue the
country from its state of anarchy. It was a resurrection of the dead,—so industriously had the reports of
his death been circulated, and so generally believed.[4]

At all the great towns where he halted he was sump-
tuously entertained. Triumphal arches were thrown
across the road, and the streets were strewed with
flowers as he passed. After a night's repose at Tezcuco, he made his entrance in great state into the
capital. The municipality came out to welcome him,
and a brilliant cavalcade of armed citizens formed his
escort; while the lake was covered with barges of the
Indians, all fancifully decorated with their gala dresses,
as on the day of his first arrival among them. The
streets echoed to music, and dancing, and sounds of
jubilee, as the procession held on its way to the great
convent of St. Francis, where thanksgivings were
offered up for the safe return of the general, who then
proceeded to take up his quarters once more in his
own princely residence.[5] It was in June, 1526, when
Cortés re-entered Mexico; nearly two years had elapsed
since he had left it, on his difficult march to Honduras,
—a march which led to no important results, but which

[4] Carta Quinta de Cortés, MS.—Bernal Diaz, Hist. de la Conquista,
cap. 189, 190.—Carta de Cortés al Emperador, MS., México, Sept.
11, 1526.

[5] Carta de Ocaña, MS., Agosto 31, 1526.—Carta Quinta de Cortés,
MS.

consumed nearly as much time, and was attended with sufferings quite as severe, as the Conquest of Mexico itself.[6]

Cortés did not abuse his present advantage. He, indeed, instituted proceedings against his enemies; but he followed them up so languidly as to incur the imputation of weakness. It is the only instance in which he has been accused of weakness; and, since it was shown in redressing his own injuries, it may be thought to reflect no discredit on his character.[7]

He was not permitted long to enjoy the sweets of triumph. In the month of July he received advices of the arrival of a *juez de residencia* on the coast, sent by the court of Madrid to supersede him temporarily in the government. The crown of Castile, as its colonial empire extended, became less and less capable of watching over its administration. It was therefore

6 " What Cortés suffered," says Dr. Robertson, " on this march,—a distance, according to Gomara, of 3000 miles" (the distance must be greatly exaggerated),—" from famine, from the hostility of the natives, from the climate, and from hardships of every species, has nothing in history parallel to it, but what occurs in the adventures of the other discoverers and conquerors of the New World. Cortés was employed in this dreadful service above two years; and, though it was not distinguished by any splendid event, he exhibited, during the course of it, greater personal courage, more fortitude of mind, more perseverance and patience, than in any other period or scene in his life." (Hist. of America, note 96.) The historian's remarks are just; as the passages which I have borrowed from the extraordinary record of the Conqueror may show. Those who are desirous of seeing something of the narrative told in his own way will find a few pages of it translated in the Appendix, Part 2, No. 14.

7 " Y esto yo lo oí dezir á los del Real Consejo de Indias, estando presente el señor Obispo Fray Bartolomé de las Casas, que se descuidó mucho Cortés en ello, y se lo tuviéron á floxedad." Bernal Diaz, Hist. de la Conquista, cap. 190.

obliged to place vast powers in the hands of its vice-roys; and, as suspicion naturally accompanies weak-ness, it was ever prompt to listen to accusations against these powerful vassals. In such cases the government adopted the expedient of sending out a commissioner, or *juez de residencia*, with authority to investigate the conduct of the accused, to suspend him in the mean while from his office, and, after a judicial examination, to reinstate him in it or to remove him altogether, according to the issue of the trial. The enemies of Cortés had been for a long time busy in undermining his influence at court, and in infusing suspicions of his loyalty in the bosom of the emperor. Since his elevation to the government of the country they had redoubled their mischievous activity, and they assailed his character with the foulest imputations. They charged him with appropriating to his own use the gold which belonged to the crown, and especially with secreting the treasures of Montezuma. He was said to have made false reports of the provinces he had con-quered, that he might defraud the exchequer of its lawful revenues. He had distributed the principal offices among his own creatures, and had acquired an unbounded influence, not only over the Spaniards, but the natives, who were all ready to do his bidding. He had expended large sums in fortifying both the capital and his own palace; and it was evident, from the mag-nitude of his schemes and his preparations, that he designed to shake off his allegiance and to establish an independent sovereignty in New Spain.[8]

[8] Memorial de Luis Cardenas, MS.—Carta de Diego de Ocaña, MS.—Herrera, Hist. general, dec. 3, lib. 8, cap. 14, 15.

The government, greatly alarmed by these formidable charges, the probability of which they could not estimate, appointed a commissioner with full powers to investigate the matter. The person selected for this delicate office was Luis Ponce de Leon, a man of high family, young for such a post, but of a mature judgment and distinguished for his moderation and equity. The nomination of such a minister gave assurance that the crown meant to do justly by Cortés.

The emperor wrote at the same time with his own hand to the general, advising him of this step, and assuring him that it was taken, not from distrust of his integrity, but to afford him the opportunity of placing that integrity in a clear light before the world.[9]

Ponce de Leon reached Mexico in July, 1526. He was received with all respect by Cortés and the municipality of the capital; and the two parties interchanged those courtesies with each other which gave augury that the future proceedings would be conducted in a spirit of harmony. Unfortunately, this fair beginning was blasted by the death of the commissioner in a few weeks after his arrival, a circumstance which did not fail to afford another item in the loathsome mass of accusation heaped upon Cortés. The commissioner fell the victim of a malignant fever, which carried off a number of those who had come over in the vessel with him.[10]

On his death-bed, Ponce de Leon delegated his authority to an infirm old man, who survived but a few

9 Carta del Emperador, MS., Toledo, Nov. 4, 1525.
10 Bernal Diaz, Hist. de la Conquista, cap. 192.—Carta de Cortés al Emperador, MS., México, Set. 11, 1526.

months,* and transmitted the reins of government to a
person named Estrada, or Strada, the royal treasurer,

* [This person, the licentiate Marcos de Aguilar, showed, during
his short tenure of office, much greater zeal and activity than would
be inferred from the slight mention of him by historians. Prescott has
omitted to state that a principal point in the instructions given to
Ponce de Leon related to the question of the *repartimientos* and other
methods of treating the Indians, in regard to which he was to obtain
the opinions of the authorities and other principal persons and of the
Dominican and Franciscan friars. Sir Arthur Helps, who notices this
fact, adds that it "led to no result," the instructions on this subject to
Ponce de Leon being on his death "forgotten or laid aside." But a
series of documents published by Señor Icazbalceta (Col. de Doc.
para la Hist. de México, tom. ii.) shows, on the contrary, that they
were promptly and fully carried out by Aguilar, who considered this
to be the principal business of the commission, and one, as he wrote
to the emperor, requiring despatch, since the very existence of the
native population depended on immediate action. He accordingly
consulted all the officials, Cortés himself included, the other chief
residents of the city, such as Alvarado and Sandoval, and the members
of the two religious orders, obtaining written opinions, individual as
well as collective, which he transmitted with his own report to the
emperor. The great majority of the persons consulted, including all
the monks, while differing on some matters of detail, concurred in
urging the necessity of the *repartimientos* and in recommending that
they should be made hereditary.

The same result followed an inquiry instituted in 1532 and the following years. Among the opinions delivered on that occasion is one
deserving of particular notice, both for the manner in which it is enforced and the character of the writer,—Fray Domingo de Batanzos,
whose career has been agreeably sketched, though his views on the
present matter have been misapprehended, by Sir Arthur Helps. The
three objects to be kept in view, he begins by remarking, are the
good treatment and preservation of the natives, the establishment and
security of the Spanish settlers, and the augmentation of the royal
revenues. The proper means to be adopted are also threefold: the
repartimientos extended and perpetuated, the abandonment of the
idea of reserving certain *pueblos* to be held by the crown and managed
by its officers, and the appointment of good governors, since the best

one of the officers sent from Spain to take charge of the finances, and who was personally hostile to Cortés.

measures are of no avail if not ably administered. The objections to the crown's reserving any *pueblos* for itself are, that the officers will be employed solely in collecting the tribute, the Indians will receive no protection or religious instruction, and the cultivation of the soil will be always degenerating, since no one will have an interest in maintaining or improving its condition. The *repartimientos*, on the contrary, by giving the holders a direct interest in the better cultivation of the soil and the increase of the people, will insure both these results; and though under this system the royal revenues may be diminished for a time, they will in the end be greatly augmented through the general improvement of the country. The great misfortune has been that the authorities at home pursue a policy which directly contravenes their own intentions: wishing to benefit, they destroy; wishing to enrich, they impoverish; wishing to save the Indians, they exterminate them. There is needed a man with the mind and resolution of Charlemagne or Cæsar, to adopt a plan and carry it out. Instead of this, the course pursued is that of endless changes and experiments, like a perpetual litigation. It is a sure sign that God intends destruction when men are unable to find a remedy. In the present case, well-meaning and holy men have sought one in vain. In his opinion, which he knows will be unheeded, the system which has in it the least evil and the most good is that of hereditary *repartimientos*, which should be established once for all. In a later letter he says, "The person least deceived about the affairs of this country is I, who know its fate as if I saw it with my eyes and touched it with my hands." He predicts the extermination of the Indians within fifty years. He has always believed and asserted that they would perish, and the laws and measures founded on any other supposition have all been bad. The wonderful thing is, he remarks, with an apparent allusion to Las Casas, that the men of greatest sanctity and zeal for good are those who have done the most harm. (Icazbalceta, Col. de Doc. para la Hist. de México, tom. ii.) That the prediction of Batanzos has been falsified by the event may be attributed to a variety of causes: the vastness of the country and the comparative density of the native population; the social and industrial habits of the latter, so different from those of more northern tribes; the decline of the Spanish power and of that spirit of conquest which, by keeping up a con-

The Spanish residents would have persuaded Cortés to assert for himself at least an equal share of the authority, to which they considered Estrada as having no sufficient title. But the general, with singular moderation, declined a competition in this matter, and determined to abide a more decided expression of his sovereign's will. To his mortification, the nomination of Estrada was confirmed; and this dignitary soon contrived to inflict on his rival all those annoyances by which a little mind in possession of unexpected power endeavors to assert superiority over a great one. The recommendations of Cortés were disregarded, his friends mortified and insulted, his attendants outraged by injuries. One of the domestics of his friend Sandoval, for some slight offence, was sentenced to lose his hand; and when the general remonstrated against these acts of violence he was peremptorily commanded to leave the city! The Spaniards, indignant at this outrage, would have taken up arms in his defence; but Cortés would allow no

stant stream of emigration and ardor of enterprise, might have led to a conflict of races; and the sedulous protection afforded to the Indians by the government and the church. Their welfare was the object of constant investigation and a long series of enactments. Slavery was in their case entirely abolished. The *repartimientos* were made hereditary, but the rights and power of the *encomenderos* were carefully restricted, and the personal services at first exacted were ultimately commuted for a fixed tribute. Living together in communities which resembled so many small republics, governed by their own laws and chiefs, guided and protected by the priests, exempt from military service and all the burdens imposed by the state on the rest of the population, the Indians constituted, down to the period of Independence, a separate and privileged class, despised, it is true, but not oppressed, by the superior race.—ED.]

resistance, and, simply remarking "that it was well that those who at the price of their blood had won the capital should not be allowed a footing in it," withdrew to his favorite villa of Cojohuacan, a few miles distant, to await there the result of these strange proceedings.[11]

The suspicions of the court of Madrid, meanwhile, fanned by the breath of calumny, had reached the most preposterous height. One might have supposed that it fancied the general was organizing a revolt throughout the colonies and meditated nothing less than an invasion of the mother country. Intelligence having been received that a vessel might speedily be expected from New Spain, orders were sent to the different ports of the kingdom, and even to Portugal, to sequestrate the cargo, under the expectation that it contained remittances to the general's family which belonged to the crown; while his letters, affording the most luminous account of all his proceedings and discoveries, were forbidden to be printed. Fortunately, however, three letters, constituting the most important part of the Conqueror's correspondence, had been given to the public, some years previous, by the indefatigable press of Seville.

The court, moreover, made aware of the incompetency of the treasurer, Estrada, to the present delicate conjuncture, now intrusted the whole affair of the inquiry to a commission dignified with the title of the Royal Audience of New Spain. This body was clothed with full powers to examine into the charges against

[11] Bernal Diaz, Hist. de la Conquista, cap. 194.—Carta de Cortés al Emperador, MS., Set. 11, 1526.

Cortés, with instructions to send him back, as a preliminary measure, to Castile,—peacefully if they could, but forcibly if necessary. Still afraid that its belligerent vassal might defy the authority of this tribunal, the government resorted to artifice to effect his return. The president of the Indian Council was commanded to write to him, urging his presence in Spain to vindicate himself from the charges of his enemies, and offering his personal co-operation in his defence. The emperor further wrote a letter to the Audience, containing his commands for Cortés to return, as the government wished to consult him on matters relating to the Indies, and to bestow on him a recompense suited to his high deserts. This letter was intended to be shown to Cortés.[12]

But it was superfluous to put in motion all this complicated machinery to effect a measure on which Cortés was himself resolved. Proudly conscious of his own unswerving loyalty, and of the benefits he had rendered to his country, he was deeply sensible to this unworthy requital of them, especially on the very theatre of his achievements. He determined to abide no longer where he was exposed to such indignities, but to proceed at once to Spain, present himself before his sovereign, boldly assert his innocence, and claim redress for his wrongs and a just reward for his services. In the close of his letter to the emperor, detailing the painful expedition to Honduras, after enlarging on the magnificent schemes he had entertained of discovery in the South Sea, and vindicating himself from the

---

[12] Herrera, Hist. general, dec. 4, lib. 2, cap. 1; and lib. 3, cap. 8.

N*

charge of a too lavish expenditure, he concludes with the lofty yet touching declaration "that he trusts his Majesty will in time acknowledge his deserts; but, if that unhappily shall not be, the world at least will be assurêd of his loyalty, and he himself shall have the conviction of having done his duty; and no better inheritance than this shall he ask for his children." [13]

No sooner was the intention of Cortés made known, than it excited a general sensation through the country. Even Estrada relented; he felt that he had gone too far, and that it was not his policy to drive his noble enemy to take refuge in his own land. Negotiations were opened, and an attempt at a reconciliation was made, through the bishop of Tlascala. Cortés received these overtures in a courteous spirit, but his resolution was unshaken. Having made the necessary arrangements, therefore, in Mexico, he left the Valley, and proceeded at once to the coast. Had he entertained the criminal ambition imputed to him by his enemies, he might have been sorely tempted by the repeated offers of support which were made to him, whether in good or in bad faith, on the journey, if he would but reassume the government and assert his independence of Castile. But these disloyal advances he rejected with the scorn they merited. [14]

[13] "Todas estas entradas están ahora para partir casi á una, plega á Dios de los guiar como él se sirva, que yo aunque V. M. mas me mande desfavoreçer no tengo de dejar de servir, que no es posible que por tiempo V. M. no conosca mis servicios, y ya que esto no sea, yo me satisfago con hazer lo que debo, y con saber que á todo el mundo tengo satisfecho, y les son notorios mis servicios y lealdad, con que los hago, y no quiero otro mayorazgo sino este." Carta Quinta, MS.

[14] Bernal Diaz, Hist. de la Conquista, cap. 194.—Carta de Ocaña, MS., Agosto 31, 1526.

On his arrival at Villa Rica he received the painful tidings of the death of his father, Don Martin Cortés, whom he had hoped so soon to embrace after his long and eventful absence. Having celebrated his obsequies with every mark of filial respect, he made preparations for his speedy departure. Two of the best vessels in the port were got ready and provided with everything requisite for a long voyage. He was attended by his friend the faithful Sandoval, by Tápia, and some other cavaliers most attached to his person. He also took with him several Aztec and Tlascalan chiefs, and among them a son of Montezuma, and another of Maxixca, the friendly old Tlascalan lord, both of whom were desirous to accompany the general to Castile. He carried home a large collection of plants and minerals, as specimens of the natural resources of the country; several wild animals, and birds of gaudy plumage; various fabrics of delicate workmanship, especially the gorgeous feather-work; and a number of jugglers, dancers, and buffoons, who greatly astonished the Europeans by the marvellous facility of their performances, and were thought a suitable present for his Holiness the Pope.[15] Lastly, Cortés displayed his magnificence in a rich treasure of jewels, among which were emeralds of extraordinary size and lustre, gold

[15] The Pope, who was of the joyous Medici family, Clement VII., and the cardinals, were greatly delighted with the feats of the Indian jugglers, according to Diaz; and his Holiness, who, it may be added, received at the same time from Cortés a substantial donative of gold and jewels, publicly testified, by prayers and solemn processions, his great sense of the services rendered to Christianity by the Conquerors of Mexico, and generously requited them by bulls granting plenary absolution from their sins. Hist. de la Conquista. cap. 195.

to the amount of two hundred thousand *pesos de oro*, and fifteen hundred marks of silver. "In fine," says Herrera, "he came in all the state of a great lord." [16]

After a brief and prosperous voyage, Cortés came in sight once more of his native shores, and, crossing the bar of Saltes, entered the little port of Palos in May, 1528,—the same spot where Columbus had landed five-and-thirty years before, on his return from the discovery of the Western World. Cortés was not greeted with the enthusiasm and public rejoicings which welcomed the great navigator ; and, indeed, the inhabitants were not prepared for his arrival. From Palos he soon proceeded to the convent of La Rabida, the same place, also, within the hospitable walls of which Columbus had found a shelter. An interesting circumstance is mentioned by historians, connected with his short stay at Palos. Francisco Pizarro, the Conqueror of Peru, had arrived there, having come to Spain to solicit aid for his great enterprise.[17] He was then in the commencement of his brilliant career, as Cortés might be said to be at the close of his. He was an old acquaintance, and a kinsman, as is affirmed, of the general, whose mother was a Pizarro.[18] The meeting of these two extraordinary men, the Conquerors of the North and of the South in the New World, as they set foot, after their eventful absence, on the shores of their native land, and that, too, on the spot consecrated by

[16] "Y en fin venia como gran Señor." Hist. gen., dec. 4, lib. 3, cap. 8.

[17] Herrera, Hist. general, dec. 4, lib. 4, cap. 1.—Cavo, Los tres Siglos de México, tom. i. p. 78.

[18] Pizarro y Orellana, Varones ilustres, p. 121.

the presence of Columbus, has something in it striking
to the imagination. It has accordingly attracted the
attention of one of the most illustrious of living poets,
who, in a brief but beautiful sketch, has depicted the
scene in the genuine coloring of the age.[19]

While reposing from the fatigues of his voyage, at
La Rabida, an event occurred which afflicted Cortés
deeply and which threw a dark cloud over his return.
This was the death of Gonzalo de Sandoval, his trusty
friend, and so long the companion of his fortunes.
He was taken ill in a wretched inn at Palos, soon after
landing; and his malady gained ground so rapidly
that it was evident his constitution, impaired, probably,
by the extraordinary fatigues he had of late years undergone, would be unable to resist it. Cortés was
instantly sent for, and arrived in time to administer
the last consolations of friendship to the dying cavalier.
Sandoval met his approaching end with composure,
and, having given the attention which the short interval allowed to the settlement of both his temporal and
spiritual concerns, he breathed his last in the arms of
his commander.

Sandoval died at the premature age of thirty-one.[20]
He was in many respects the most eminent of the great
captains formed under the eye of Cortés. He was of
good family, and a native of Medellin, also the birthplace of the general, for whom he had the warmest
personal regard. Cortés soon discerned his uncommon
qualities, and proved it by uniformly selecting the

[19] See the conclusion of Rogers's Voyage of Columbus.

[20] Bernal Diaz says that Sandoval was twenty-two years old when
he first came to New Spain, in 1519.—Hist. de la Conquista, cap. 205.

young officer for the most difficult commissions. His conduct on these occasions fully justified the preference. He was a decided favorite with the soldiers; for, though strict in enforcing discipline, he was careful of their comforts and little mindful of his own. He had nothing of the avarice so common in the Castilian cavalier, and seemed to have no other ambition than that of faithfully discharging the duties of his profession. He was a plain man, affecting neither the showy manners nor the bravery in costume which distinguished Alvarado, the Aztec *Tonatiuh.* The expression of his countenance was open and manly; his chestnut hair curled close to his head; his frame was strong and sinewy. He had a lisp in his utterance, which made his voice somewhat indistinct. Indeed, he was no speaker; but, if slow of speech, he was prompt and energetic in action. He had precisely the qualities which fitted him for the perilous enterprise in which he had embarked. He had accomplished his task; and, after having escaped death, which lay waiting for him in every step of his path, had come home, as it would seem, to his native land, only to meet it there.

His obsequies were performed with all solemnity by the Franciscan friars of La Rabida, and his remains were followed to their final resting-place by the comrades who had so often stood by his side in battle. They were laid in the cemetery of the convent, which, shrouded in its forest of pines, stood, and may yet stand, on the bold eminence that overlooks the waste of waters so lately traversed by the adventurous soldier.[21]

[21] Bernal Diaz, Hist. de la Conquista, cap. 195.

It was not long after this melancholy event that Cortés and his suite began their journey into the interior. The general stayed a few days at the castle of the duke of Medina Sidonia, the most powerful of the Andalusian lords, who hospitably entertained him, and, at his departure, presented him with several noble Arabian horses. Cortés first directed his steps towards Guadalupe, where he passed nine days, offering up prayers and causing masses to be performed at Our Lady's shrine for the soul of his departed friend.

Before his departure from La Rabida, he had written to the court, informing it of his arrival in the country. Great was the sensation caused there by the intelligence; the greater, that the late reports of his treasonable practices had made it wholly unexpected. His arrival produced an immediate change of feeling. All cause of jealousy was now removed; and, as the clouds which had so long settled over the royal mind were dispelled, the emperor seemed only anxious to show his sense of the distinguished services of his so dreaded vassal. Orders were sent to different places on the route to provide him with suitable accommodations, and preparations were made to give him a brilliant reception in the capital.

Meanwhile, Cortés had formed the acquaintance at Guadalupe of several persons of distinction, and among them of the family of the *comendador* of Leon, a nobleman of the highest consideration at court. The general's conversation, enriched with the stores of a life of adventure, and his manners, in which the authority of habitual command was tempered by the frank and careless freedom of the soldier, made a most favorable impression on his new friends; and their letters to the court, where he was yet unknown, heightened the interest already felt in this remarkable man. The tidings of his arrival had by this time spread far and wide throughout the country; and, as he resumed his journey, the roads presented a spectacle such as had not been seen since the return of Columbus. Cortés did not usually affect an ostentation of dress, though he loved to display the pomp of a great lord in the number and magnificence of his retainers. His train was now swelled by the Indian chieftains, who by the splendors of their barbaric finery gave additional brilliancy, as well as novelty, to the pageant. But his own person was the object of general curiosity. The houses and the streets of the great towns and villages were thronged with spectators, eager to look on the hero who with his single arm, as it were, had won an empire for Castile, and who, to borrow the language of an old historian, "came in the pomp and glory, not so much of a great vassal, as of an independent monarch." [22]

As he approached Toledo, then the rival of Madrid, the press of the multitude increased, till he was met by the duke de Bejar, the count de Aguilar, and others of his steady friends, who, at the head of a large body of the principal nobility and cavaliers of the city, came out to receive him, and attended him to the quarters

[22] "Vino de las Indias despues de la conquista de Mexico, con tanto acompañamiento y magestad, que mas parecia de Príncipe, ó señor poderosíssimo, que de Capitan y vasallo de algun Rey ó Emperador." Lanuza, Historias ecclesiásticas y seculares de Aragon (Zaragoza, 1622), lib. 3, cap. 14.

prepared for his residence. It was a proud moment for Cortés; and distrusting, as he well might, his reception by his countrymen, it afforded him a greater satisfaction than the brilliant entrance which, a few years previous, he had made into the capital of Mexico.

The following day he was admitted to an audience by the emperor, and Cortés, gracefully kneeling to kiss the hand of his sovereign, presented to him a memorial which succinctly recounted his services and the requital he had received for them. The emperor graciously raised him, and put many questions to him respecting the countries he had conquered. Charles was pleased with the general's answers, and his intelligent mind took great satisfaction in inspecting the curious specimens of Indian ingenuity which his vassal had brought with him from New Spain. In subsequent conversations the emperor repeatedly consulted Cortés on the best mode of administering the government of the colonies, and by his advice introduced some important regulations, especially for ameliorating the condition of the natives and for encouraging domestic industry.

The monarch took frequent opportunity to show the confidence which he now reposed in Cortés. On all public occasions he appeared with him by his side; and once, when the general lay ill of a fever, Charles paid him a visit in person, and remained some time in the apartment of the invalid. This was an extraordinary mark of condescension in the haughty court of Castile; and it is dwelt upon with becoming emphasis by the historians of the time, who seem to regard it as an ample compensation for all the sufferings and services of Cortés.[23]

The latter had now fairly triumphed over opposition. The courtiers, with that ready instinct which belongs to the tribe, imitated the example of their master; and even envy was silent, amidst the general homage that was paid to the man who had so lately been a mark for the most envenomed calumny. Cortés, without a title, without a name but what he had created for himself, was at once, as it were, raised to a level with the proudest nobles in the land.

He was so still more effectually by the substantial honors which were accorded to him by his sovereign in the course of the following year. By an instrument dated July 6th, 1529, the emperor raised him to the dignity of the Marquis of the Valley of Oaxaca;[24] and the title of "marquis," when used without the name of the individual, has been always appropriated in the colonies, in an especial manner, to Cortés, as the title of "admiral" was to Columbus.[25]

Two other instruments, dated in the same month of July, assigned to Cortés a vast tract of land in the rich province of Oaxaca, together with large estates in the

[23] Gomara, Crónica, cap. 183.—Herrera, Hist. general, dec. 4, lib. 4, cap. 1.—Bernal Diaz, Hist. de la Conquista, cap. 195.

[24] Título de Marques, MS., Barcelona, 6 de Julio, 1529.

[25] Humboldt, Essai politique, tom. ii. p. 30, note.—According to Lanuza, he was offered by the emperor the Order of St. Jago, but declined it, because no *encomienda* was attached to it. (Hist. de Aragon, tom. i. lib. 3, cap. 14.) But Caro de Torres, in his History of the Military Orders of Castile, enumerates Cortés among the members of the Compostellan fraternity. Hist. de las Órdenes militares (Madrid, 1629), fol. 103, et seq.

city of Mexico, and other places in the Valley.[26]   The
princely domain thus granted comprehended more than
twenty large towns and villages, and twenty-three thousand vassals.   The language in which the gift was
made greatly enhanced its value.   The preamble of the
instrument, after enlarging on the "good services
rendered by Cortés in the Conquest, and the great
benefits resulting therefrom, both in respect to the
increase of the Castilian empire and the advancement
of the Holy Catholic Faith," acknowledges "the sufferings he had undergone in accomplishing this glorious
work, and the fidelity and obedience with which, as a
good and trusty vassal, he had ever served the crown."[27]
It declares, in conclusion, that it grants this recompense of his deserts because it is "the duty of princes
to honor and reward those who serve them well and
loyally, in order that the memory of their great deeds
should be perpetuated, and others be incited by their
example to the performance of the like illustrious exploits."   The unequivocal testimony thus borne by his
sovereign to his unwavering loyalty was most gratifying
to Cortés,—how gratifying, every generous soul who has

[26] Merced de Tierras inmediatas á Mexico, MS., Barcelona, 23 de
Julio, 1529.—Merced de los Vasallos, MS., Barcelona, 6 de Julio,
1529.

[27] " É nos habemos recibido y tenemos de vos por bien servido en
ello, y acatando los grandes provechos que de vuestros servicios han
redundado, ansí para el servicio de Nuestro Señor y aumento de su
santa fé católica, y en las dichas tierras que estaban sin conocimiento
ni fé se han plantado, como el acrecentamiento que dello ha redundado á nuestra corona real destos reynos, y los trabajos que en ello
habeis pasado, y la fidelidad y obediencia con que siempre nos habeis
servido como bueno é fiel servidor y vasallo nuestro, de que somos
ciertos y confiados."   Merced de los Vasallos, MS.

been the subject of suspicion undeserved will readily estimate. The language of the general in after-time shows how deeply he was touched by it.[28]

Yet there was one degree in the scale, above which the royal gratitude would not rise. Neither the solicitations of Cortés, nor those of the duke de Bejar and his other powerful friends, could prevail on the emperor to reinstate him in the government of Mexico. The country, reduced to tranquillity, had no longer need of his commanding genius to control it; and Charles did not care to place again his formidable vassal in a situation which might revive the dormant spark of jealousy and distrust. It was the policy of the crown to employ one class of its subjects to effect its conquests, and another class to rule over them. For the latter it selected men in whom the fire of ambition was tempered by a cooler judgment naturally, or by the sober influence of age. Even Columbus, notwithstanding the terms of his original "capitulation" with the crown, had not been permitted to preside over the colonies; and still less likely would it be to concede this power to one possessed of the aspiring temper of Cortés.

But, although the emperor refused to commit the civil government of the colony into his hands, he reinstated him in his military command. By a royal ordi-

[28] "The benignant reception which I experienced, on my return, from your Majesty," says Cortés, "your kind expressions and generous treatment, make me not only forget all my toils and sufferings, but even cause me regret that I have not been called to endure more in your service." (Carta de Cortés al Lic. Nuñez, MS., 1535.) This memorial, addressed to his agent in Castile, was designed for the emperor.

nance, dated also in July, 1529, the marquis of the
Valley was named Captain-General of New Spain and
of the coasts of the South Sea. He was empowered
to make discoveries in the Southern Ocean, with the
right to rule over such lands as he should colonize,[29]
and by a subsequent grant he was to become proprietor
of one-twelfth of all his discoveries.[30] The government had no design to relinquish the services of so able
a commander. But it warily endeavored to withdraw
him from the scene of his former triumphs, and to
throw open a new career of ambition, that might stimulate him still further to enlarge the dominions of the
crown.

Thus gilded by the sunshine of royal favor, " rival-
ling," to borrow the homely comparison of an old
chronicler, "Alexander in the fame of his exploits, and
Crassus in that of his riches," [31] with brilliant manners,
and a person which, although it showed the effects of
hard service, had not yet lost all the attractions of
youth, Cortés might now be regarded as offering an
enviable alliance for the best houses in Castile. It was
not long before he paid his addresses, which were
favorably received, to a member of that noble house

[29] Titulo de Capitan General de la Nueva-España y Costa del Sur,
MS., Barcelona, 6 de Julio, 1529.

[30] Asiento y Capitulacion que hizo con el Emperador Don H. Cortés,
MS., Madrid, 27 de Oct., 1529.

[31] " Que, segun se dezia, excedia en las hazañas á Alexandro Magno, y en las riquezas á Crasso." (Lanuza, Hist. de Aragon, lib. 3,
cap. 14.) The rents of the marquis of the Valley, according to L.
Marineo Siculo, who lived at the court at this time, were about 60,000
ducats a year. Cosas memorables de España (Alcalá de Henares,
1539), fol. 24.

which had so steadily supported him in the dark hour of his fortunes. The lady's name was Doña Juana de Zuñiga, daughter of the second count de Aguilar, and niece of the duke de Bejar.[32] She was much younger than himself, beautiful, and, as events showed, not without spirit. One of his presents to his youthful bride excited the admiration and envy of the fairer part of the court. This was five emeralds, of wonderful size and brilliancy. These jewels had been cut by the Aztecs into the shapes of flowers, fishes, and into other fanciful forms, with an exquisite style of workmanship which enhanced their original value.[33] They were, not improbably, part of the treasure of the unfortunate Montezuma, and, being easily portable, may have escaped the general wreck of the *noche triste.* The queen of Charles the Fifth, it is said,—it may be the idle gossip of a court,—had intimated a willingness to become proprietor of some of these magnificent

[32] Doña Juana was of the house of Arellano, and of the royal lineage of Navarre. Her father was not a very wealthy noble. L. Marineo Siculo, Cosas memorables, fol. 24, 25.

[33] One of these precious stones was as valuable as Shylock's turquoise. Some Genoese merchants in Seville offered Cortés, according to Gomara, 40,000 ducats for it. The same author gives a more particular account of the jewels, which may interest some readers. It shows the ingenuity of the artist, who, without steel, could so nicely cut so hard a material. One emerald was in the form of a rose; the second, in that of a horn; a third, like a fish, with eyes of gold; the fourth was like a little bell, with a fine pearl for the tongue, and on the rim was this inscription, in Spanish: *Blessed is he who created thee.* The fifth, which was the most valuable, was a small cup with a foot of gold, and with four little chains, of the same metal, attached to a large pearl as a button. The edge of the cup was of gold, on which was engraven this Latin sentence: *Inter natos mulierum non surrexit major.* Gomara, Crónica, cap. 184.

baubles ; and the preference which Cortés gave to his fair bride caused some feelings of estrangement in the royal bosom, which had an unfavorable influence on the future fortunes of the Marquis.

Late in the summer of 1529, Charles the Fifth left his Spanish dominions for Italy. Cortés accompanied him on his way, probably to the place of embarkation ; and in the capital of Aragon we find him, according to the national historian, exciting the same general interest and admiration among the people as he had done in Castile. On his return, there seemed no occasion for him to protract his stay longer in the country. He was weary of the life of idle luxury which he had been leading for the last year, and which was so foreign to his active habits and the stirring scenes to which he had been accustomed. He determined, therefore, to return to Mexico, where his extensive property required his presence, and where a new field was now opened to him for honorable enterprise.

CHAPTER V.

1530–1547.

EARLY in the spring of 1530, Cortés embarked for
New Spain. He was accompanied by the marchioness,
his wife, together with his aged mother, who had the
good fortune to live to see her son's elevation, and by
a magnificent retinue of pages and attendants, such as
belonged to the household of a powerful noble. How
different from the forlorn condition in which, twenty-
six years before, he had been cast loose, as a wild adventurer, to seek his bread upon the waters!

The first point of his destination was Hispaniola,
where he was to remain until he received tidings of
the organization of the new government that was to
take charge of Mexico.[1] In the preceding chapter it
was stated that the administration of the country had
been intrusted to a body called the Royal Audience;
one of whose first duties it was to investigate the
charges brought against Cortés. Nuñez de Guzman,
his avowed enemy, was placed at the head of this
board; and the investigation was conducted with all

[1] Carta de Cortés al Emperador, MS., Tezcuco, 10 de Oct., 1530.

the rancor of personal hostility. A remarkable document still exists, called the *Pesquisa Secreta*, or " Secret Inquiry," which contains a record of the proceedings against Cortés. It was prepared by the secretary of the Audience, and signed by the several members. The document is very long, embracing nearly a hundred folio pages. The name and·the testimony of every witness are given, and the whole forms a mass of loathsome details, such as might better suit a prosecution in a petty municipal court than that of a great officer of the crown.

The charges are eight in number; involving, among other crimes, that of a deliberate design to cast off his allegiance to the crown; that of the murder of two of the commissioners who had been sent out to supersede him; of the murder of his own wife, Catalina Xuarez;[2] of extortion, and of licentious practices,—

[2] Doña Catalina's death happened so opportunely for the rising fortunes of Cortés, that this charge of murder by her husband has found more credit with the vulgar than the other accusations brought against him. Cortés, from whatever reason, perhaps from the conviction that the charge was too monstrous to obtain credit, never condescended to vindicate his innocence. But, in addition to the arguments mentioned in the text for discrediting the accusation generally, we should consider that this particular charge attracted so little attention in Castile, where he had abundance of enemies, that he found no difficulty, on his return there, seven years afterwards, in forming an alliance with one of the noblest houses in the kingdom; that no writer of that day (except Bernal Diaz, who treats it as a base calumny), not even Las Casas, the stern accuser of the Conquerors, intimates a suspicion of his guilt; and that, lastly, no allusion whatever is made to it in the suit instituted, some years after her death, by the relatives of Doña Catalina, for the recovery of property from Cortés, pretended to have been derived through her marriage with him,—a suit conducted with acrimony and protracted for several years.

of offences, in short, which, from their private nature, would seem to have little to do with his conduct as a public man. The testimony is vague and often contradictory; the witnesses are for the most part obscure individuals, and the few persons of consideration among them appear to have been taken from the ranks of his decided enemies. When it is considered that the inquiry was conducted in the absence of Cortés, before a court the members of which were personally unfriendly to him, and that he was furnished with no specification of the charges, and had no opportunity, consequently, of disproving them, it is impossible, at this distance of time, to attach any importance to this paper as a legal document. When it is added that no action was taken on it by the government to whom it was sent, we may be disposed to regard it simply as a monument of the malice of his enemies. It has been drawn by the curious antiquary from the obscurity to which it had been so long consigned in the Indian archives at Seville ; but it can be of no further use to the historian than to show that a great name in the sixteenth century exposed its possessor to calumnies as malignant as it has at any time since.[3]

I have not seen the documents connected with this suit, which are still preserved in the archives of the house of Cortés, but the fact has been communicated to me by a distinguished Mexican who has carefully examined them, and I cannot but regard it as of itself conclusive that the family at least of Doña Catalina did not attach credit to the accusation. Yet so much credit has been given to this in Mexico, where the memory of the old Spaniards is not held in especial favor at the present day, that it has formed the subject of an elaborate discussion in the public periodicals of that city.

[3] This remarkable paper, forming part of the valuable collection of Don Vargas Ponçe, is without date. It was doubtless prepared in

The high-handed measures of the Audience, and the oppressive conduct of Guzman, especially towards the Indians, excited general indignation in the colony and led to serious apprehensions of an insurrection. It became necessary to supersede an administration so reckless and unprincipled. But Cortés was detained two months at the island, by the slow movements of the Castilian court, before tidings reached him of the appointment of a new Audience for the government of the country. The person selected to preside over it was the bishop of St. Domingo, a prelate whose acknowledged wisdom and virtue gave favorable augury for the conduct of his administration. After this, Cortés resumed his voyage, and landed at Villa Rica on the 15th of July, 1530.

After remaining for a time in the neighborhood, where he received some petty annoyances from the Audience, he proceeded to Tlascala, and publicly proclaimed his powers as Captain-General of New Spain and the South Sea. An edict issued by the empress

1529, during the visit of Cortés to Castile. The following Title is prefixed to it:

"Pesquisa secreta.

"Relacion de los cargos que resultan de la pesquisa secreta contra Don Hernando Cortés, de los quales no se le dió copia ni traslado á la parte del dicho Don Hernando, así por ser los dichos cargos de la calidad que son, como por estar la persona del dicho Don Hernando ausente como está. Los quales yo Gregorio de Saldaña, escribano de S. M. y escribano de la dicha Residencia, saqué de la dicha pesquisa secreta por mandado de los Señores, Presidente y Oidores de la Audiencia y Chancillería Real que por mandado de S. M. en esta Ñueva España reside. Los quales dichos Señores, Presidente y Oidores, envian á S. M. para que los mande ver, y vistos mande proveer lo que á su servicio convenga." MS.

during her husband's absence had interdicted Cortés from approaching within ten leagues of the Mexican capital while the present authorities were there.[4] The empress was afraid of a collision between the parties. Cortés, however, took up his residence on the opposite side of the lake, at Tezcuco.

No sooner was his arrival there known in the metropolis than multitudes, both of Spaniards and natives, crossed the lake to pay their respects to their old commander, to offer him their services, and to complain of their manifold grievances. It seemed as if the whole population of the capital was pouring into the neighboring city, where the Marquis maintained the state of an independent potentate. The members of the Audience, indignant at the mortifying contrast which their own diminished court presented, imposed heavy penalties on such of the natives as should be found in Tezcuco, and, affecting to consider themselves in danger, made preparations for the defence of the city. But these belligerent movements were terminated by the arrival of the new Audience; though Guzman had the address to maintain his hold on a northern province, where he earned a reputation for cruelty and extortion unrivalled even in the annals of the New World.

Everything seemed now to assure a tranquil residence to Cortés. The new magistrates treated him with marked respect, and took his advice on the most important measures of government. Unhappily, this state of things did not long continue; and a misunderstanding arose between the parties, in respect to the

4 MS., Tordelaguna, 22 de Marzo, 1530.

enumeration of the vassals assigned by the crown to
Cortés, which the marquis thought was made on principles prejudicial to his interests and repugnant to the
intentions of the grant.[5]   He was still further displeased by finding that the Audience were intrusted,
by their commission, with a concurrent jurisdiction
with himself in military affairs.[6]   This led occasionally
to an interference, which the proud spirit of Cortés, so
long accustomed to independent rule, could ill brook.
After submitting to it for a time, he left the capital in
disgust, no more to return there, and took up his residence in his city of Cuernavaca.

It was the place won by his own sword from the
Aztecs previous to the siege of Mexico.   It stood on
the southern slope of the Cordilleras, and overlooked a
wide expanse of country, the fairest and most flourishing portion of his own domain.[7]   He had erected a
stately palace on the spot, and henceforth made this
city his favorite residence.[8]   It was well situated for

[5] The principal grievance alleged was that slaves, many of them
held temporarily by their masters, according to the old Aztec usage,
were comprehended in the census.   The complaint forms part of a
catalogue of grievances embodied by Cortés in a memorial to the
emperor.   It is a clear and business-like paper.   Carta de Cortés á
Nuñez, MS.

[6] Ibid., MS.

[7] [" Dominando una vista muy extensa sobre el valle hácia el Sur, lo
que al Norte y Oriente se termina con la magestuosa cordillera que
separa el valle de Cuernavaca del de Méjico." Alaman, Disertaciones
históricas, tom. ii. p. 35.]

[8] The palace has crumbled into ruins, and the spot is now only remarkable for its natural beauty and its historic associations.   " It was
the capital," says Madame de Calderon, " of the Tlahuica nation,
and, after the Conquest, Cortés built here a splendid palace, a church,
and a convent for Franciscans, believing that he had laid the foun-

superintending his vast estates, and he now devoted himself to bringing them into proper cultivation. He introduced the sugar-cane from Cuba, and it grew luxuriantly in the rich soil of the neighboring lowlands. He imported large numbers of merino sheep and other cattle, which found abundant pastures in the country around Tehuantepec. His lands were thickly sprinkled with groves of mulberry-trees, which furnished nourishment for the silk-worm. He encouraged the cultivation of hemp and flax, and, by his judicious and enterprising husbandry, showed the capacity of the soil for the culture of valuable products before unknown in the land; and he turned these products to the best account, by the erection of sugar-mills, and other works for the manufacture of the raw material. He thus laid the foundation of an opulence for his family, as substantial, if not as speedy, as that derived from the mines. Yet this latter source of wealth was not neglected by him, and he drew gold from the region of Tehuantepec, and silver from that of Zacatecas. The amount derived from these mines was not so abundant as at a later day. But the expense of working them, on the other hand, was much less in the earlier stages

dation of a great city. . . . It is, however, a place of little importance, though so favored by nature; and the Conqueror's palace is a half-ruined barrack, though a most picturesque object, standing on a hill, behind which starts up the great white volcano." Life in Mexico, vol. ii. let. 31. [The beautiful church of San Francisco, now the parish church, was constructed by Cortés, and enriched with jewels and sacred vessels by his wife, manifesting, says Alaman, the good taste and the piety of *the marquis* and *the marchioness*,—as, in consequence of their being the first and at that time the only persons who bore the title in Mexico, they were styled and always subscribed themselves. Disertaciones históricas, tom. ii. p. 35.]

of the operation, when the metal lay so much nearer the surface.[9]

But this tranquil way of life did not long content his restless and adventurous spirit; and it sought a vent by availing itself of his new charter of discovery to explore the mysteries of the great Southern Ocean. In 1527, two years before his return to Spain, he had sent a little squadron to the Moluccas. The expedition was attended with some important consequences; but, as they do not relate to Cortés, an account of it will find a more suitable place in the maritime annals of Spain, where it has been given by the able hand which has done so much for the country in this department.[10]

Cortés was preparing to send another squadron of four vessels in the same direction, when his plans were interrupted by his visit to Spain; and his unfinished little navy, owing to the malice of the Royal Audience, who drew off the hands employed in building it, went to pieces on the stocks. Two other squadrons were now fitted out by Cortés, in the years 1532 and 1533, and sent on a voyage of discovery to the Northwest.[11] They were unfortunate, though in the latter expedition the Californian peninsula was reached, and a landing

9 These particulars respecting the agricultural economy of Cortés I have derived in part from a very able argument, prepared, in January, 1828, for the Mexican Chamber of Deputies, by Don Lúcas Alaman, in defence of the territorial rights possessed at this day by the Conqueror's descendant, the duke of Monteleone.

10 Navarrete, Coleccion de los Viages y Descubrimientos (Madrid, 1837), tom. v., Viages al Maluco.

11 Instruccion que dió el Marques del Valle á Juan de Avellaneda, etc., MS.

effected on its southern extremity at Santa Cruz, probably the modern port of La Paz. One of the vessels, thrown on the coast of New Galicia, was seized by Guzman, the old enemy of Cortés, who ruled over that territory, the crew were plundered, and the ship was detained as a lawful prize. Cortés, indignant at the outrage, demanded justice from the Royal Audience ; and, as that body was too feeble to enforce its own decrees in his favor, he took redress into his own hands.[12]

He made a rapid but difficult march on Chiametla, the scene of Guzman's spoliation ; and, as the latter did not care to face his incensed antagonist, Cortés recovered his vessel, though not the cargo. He was then joined by the little squadron which he had fitted out from his own port of Tehuantepec,—a port which in the sixteenth century promised to hold the place since occupied by that of Acapulco.[13] The vessels were provided with everything requisite for planting a colony in the newly-discovered region, and transported four hundred Spaniards and *three hundred negro slaves*, which Cortés had assembled for that purpose. With this intention he crossed the Gulf, the Adriatic—to which an old writer compares it—of the Western World.

Our limits will not allow us to go into the details of this disastrous expedition, which was attended with no

[12] Provision sobre los Descubrimientos del Sur, MS., Setiembre, 1534.

[13] The river Huasacualco furnished great facilities for transporting across the isthmus, from Vera Cruz, materials to build vessels on the Pacific. Humboldt, Essai politique, tom. iv. p. 50.

important results either to its projector or to science. It may suffice to say that, in the prosecution of it, Cortés and his followers were driven to the last extremity by famine; that he again crossed the Gulf, was tossed about by terrible tempests, without a pilot to guide him, was thrown upon the rocks, where his shattered vessel nearly went to pieces, and, after a succession of dangers and disasters as formidable as any which he had ever encountered on land, succeeded, by means of his indomitable energy, in bringing his crazy bark safe into the same port of Santa Cruz from which he had started.

While these occurrences were passing, the new Royal Audience, after a faithful discharge of its commission, had been superseded by the arrival of a viceroy, the first ever sent to New Spain. Cortés, though invested with similar powers, had the title only of Governor. This was the commencement of the system, afterwards pursued by the crown, of intrusting the colonial administration to some individual whose high rank and personal consideration might make him the fitting representative of majesty. The jealousy of the court did not allow the subject clothed with such ample authority to remain long enough in the same station to form dangerous schemes of ambition, but at the expiration of a few years he was usually recalled, or transferred to some other province of the vast colonial empire. The person now sent to Mexico was Don Antonio de Mendoza, a man of moderation and practical good sense, and one of that illustrious family who in the preceding reign furnished so many distinguished ornaments to the Church, to the camp, and to letters.

o*

The long absence of Cortés had caused the deepest anxiety in the mind of his wife, the marchioness of the Valley. She wrote to the viceroy immediately on his arrival, beseeching him to ascertain, if possible, the fate of her husband, and, if he could be found, to urge his return. The viceroy, in consequence, despatched two ships in search of Cortés, but whether they reached him before his departure from Santa Cruz is doubtful. It is certain that he returned safe, after his long absence, to Acapulco, and was soon followed by the survivors of his wretched colony.

Undismayed by these repeated reverses, Cortés, still bent on some discovery worthy of his reputation, fitted out three more vessels, and placed them under the command of an officer named Ulloa. This expedition, which took its departure in July, 1539, was attended with more important results. Ulloa penetrated to the head of the Gulf, then, returning and winding round the coast of the peninsula, doubled its southern point. and ascended as high as the twenty-eighth or twenty-ninth degree of north latitude on its western borders. After this, sending home one of the squadron, the bold navigator held on his course to the north, but was never more heard of.[14]

[14] Instruccion del Marques del Valle, MS.—The most particular and authentic account of Ulloa's cruise will be found in Ramusio. (Tom. iii. pp. 340–354.) It is by one of the officers of the squadron. My limits will not allow me to give the details of the voyages made by Cortés, which, although not without interest, were attended with no permanent consequences.* A good summary of his expeditions in

* [The restless and determined spirit with which Cortés pursued his mainly ineffectual projects of discovery is exemplified by a letter

Thus ended the maritime enterprises of Cortés, sufficiently disastrous in a pecuniary view, since they cost
him three hundred thousand *castellanos* of gold, without the return of a ducat.[15]   He was even obliged to
borrow money, and to pawn his wife's jewels, to procure funds for the last enterprise;[16] thus incurring a
debt which, increased by the great charges of his
princely establishment, hung about him during the
remainder of his life.   But, though disastrous in an
economical view, his generous efforts added important
contributions to science.   In the course of these expeditions, and those undertaken by Cortés previous to
his visit to Spain, the Pacific had been coasted from
the Bay of Panamá to the Rio Colorado.   The great
peninsula of California had been circumnavigated as
far as to the isle of Cedros, or Cerros, into which the
name has since been corrupted.   This vast tract, which

the Gulf has been given by Navarrete in the Introduction to his Relacion del Viage hecho por las Goletas Sutil y Mexicana (Madrid,
1802), pp. vi.–xxvi.; and the English reader will find a brief account
of them in Greenhow's valuable Memoir on the Northwest Coast of
North America (Washington, 1840), pp. 22–27.

[15] Memorial al Rey del Marques del Valle, MS., 25 de Junio, 1540.
[16] Provision sobre los Descubrimientos del Sur, MS.

----

to the Council of the Indies, September 20, 1538, begging that body
to assist his agents in procuring pilots for him.   He has at present, he
says, nine vessels, very good and well equipped, and is only waiting
for pilots, having tried in vain to obtain some from Panamá and Leon.
Though he has not yet secured the fruits he had expected from his
expeditions, he trusts in God that they will be henceforth attended
with better fortune.   Col. de Doc. inéd. relativos al Descubrimiento,
Conquista y Colonizacion de las Posesiones españolas en América y
Oceanía, tom. iii.—ED.]

had been supposed to be an archipelago of islands, was now discovered to be a part of the continent; and its general outline, as appears from the maps of the time, was nearly as well understood as at the present day.[17] Lastly, the navigator had explored the recesses of the Californian Gulf, or *Sea of Cortés*, as, in honor of the great discoverer, it is with more propriety named by the Spaniards; and he had ascertained that, instead of the outlet before supposed to exist towards the north, this unknown ocean was locked up within the arms of the mighty continent. These were results that might have made the glory and satisfied the ambition of a common man; but they are lost in the brilliant renown of the former achievements of Cortés.

Notwithstanding the embarrassments of the marquis of the Valley, he still made new efforts to enlarge the limits of discovery, and prepared to fit out another squadron of five vessels, which he proposed to place under the command of a natural son, Don Luis. But the viceroy Mendoza, whose imagination had been inflamed by the reports of an itinerant monk respecting an *El Dorado* in the north, claimed the right of discovery in that direction. Cortés protested against this, as an unwarrantable interference with his own powers. Other subjects of collision arose between them; till the marquis, disgusted with this perpetual check on his authority and his enterprises, applied for redress to Castile.[18] He finally determined to go there

[17] See the map prepared by the pilot Domingo del Castillo, in 1541, ap. Lorenzana, p. 328.

[18] In the collection of Vargas Ponçe is a petition of Cortés, setting forth his grievances, and demanding an investigation of the viceroy's

to support his claims in person, and to obtain, if possible, remuneration for the heavy charges he had incurred by his maritime expeditions, as well as for the spoliation of his property by the Royal Audience during his absence from the country; and, lastly, to procure an assignment of his vassals on principles more conformable to the original intentions of the grant. With these objects in view, he bade adieu to his family, and, taking with him his eldest son and heir, Don Martin, then only eight years of age, he embarked at Mexico in 1540, and, after a favorable voyage, again set foot on the shores of his native land.

The emperor was absent from the country. But Cortés was honorably received in the capital, where ample accommodations were provided for him and his retinue. When he attended the Royal Council of the Indies to urge his suit, he was distinguished by uncommon marks of respect. The president went to the door of the hall to receive him, and a seat was provided for him among the members of the Council.[19] But all evaporated in this barren show of courtesy. Justice, proverbially slow in Spain, did not mend her gait for Cortés; and at the expiration of a year he found himself no nearer the attainment of his object than on the first week after his arrival in the capital.

In the following year, 1541, we find the marquis of the Valley embarked as a volunteer in the memorable expedition against Algiers. Charles the Fifth, on his return to his dominions, laid siege to that stronghold

conduct. It is without date. Peticion contra Don Antonio de Mendoza Virrey, pediendo residencia contra él, MS.

[19] Bernal Diaz, Hist. de la Conquista, cap. 200.

326 SUBSEQUENT CAREER OF CORTÉS.

of the Mediterranean corsairs. Cortés accompanied
the forces destined to meet the emperor, and embarked
on board the vessel of the Admiral of Castile. But a
furious tempest scattered the navy, and the admiral's
ship was driven a wreck upon the coast. Cortés and
his son escaped by swimming, but the former, in the
confusion of the scene, lost the inestimable set of jewels
noticed in the preceding chapter; "a loss," says an
old writer, "that made the expedition fall more heavily
on the marquis of the Valley than on any other man
in the kingdom, except the emperor." [20]

It is not necessary to recount the particulars of this
disastrous siege, in which Moslem valor, aided by the
elements, set at defiance the combined forces of the
Christians. A council of war was called, and it was
decided to abandon the enterprise and return to Castile. This determination was indignantly received by
Cortés, who offered, with the support of the army, to
reduce the place himself; and he only expressed the
regret that he had not a handful of those gallant veterans by his side who had served him in the Conquest
of Mexico. But his offers were derided, as those of
a romantic enthusiast. He had not been invited to
take part in the discussions of the council of war. It
was a marked indignity; but the courtiers, weary of
the service, were too much bent on an immediate return to Spain, to hazard the opposition of a man who,
when he had once planted his foot, was never known
to raise it again till he had accomplished his object. [21]

[20] Gomara, Crónica, cap. 237.
[21] Sandoval, Hist. de Cárlos V., lib. 12, cap. 25.—Ferreras (trad.
d'Hermilly), Hist. d'Espagne, tom. ix. p. 231.

On arriving in Castile, Cortés lost no time in laying his suit before the emperor. His applications were received by the monarch with civility,—a cold civility, which carried no conviction of its sincerity. His position was materially changed since his former visit to the country. More than ten years had elapsed, and he was now too well advanced in years to give promise of serviceable enterprise in future. Indeed, his undertakings of late had been singularly unfortunate. Even his former successes suffered the disparagement natural to a man of declining fortunes. They were already eclipsed by the magnificent achievements in Peru, which had poured a golden tide into the country, that formed a striking contrast to the streams of wealth that as yet had flowed in but scantily from the silver-mines of Mexico. Cortés had to learn that the gratitude of a court has reference to the future much more than to the past. He stood in the position of an importunate suitor whose claims, however just, are too large to be readily allowed. He found, like Columbus, that it was possible to deserve too greatly.[22]

In the month of February, 1544, he addressed a letter to the emperor,—it was the last he ever wrote him,—soliciting his attention to his suit. He begins by proudly alluding to his past services to the crown.

[22] Voltaire tells us that, one day, Cortés, unable to obtain an audience of the emperor, pushed through the press surrounding the royal carriage, and mounted the steps; and, when Charles inquired "who that man was," he replied, "One who has given you more kingdoms than you had towns before." (Essai sur les Mœurs, chap. 147.) For this most improbable anecdote I have found no authority whatever. It served, however, very well to point a moral,—the main thing with the philosopher of Ferney.

" He had hoped that the toils of youth would have secured him repose in his old age. For forty years he had passed his life with little sleep, bad food, and with his arms constantly by his side. He had freely exposed his person to peril, and spent his substance in exploring distant and unknown regions, that he might spread abroad the name of his sovereign and bring under his sceptre many great and powerful nations. All this he had done, not only without assistance from home, but in the face of obstacles thrown in his way by rivals and by enemies who thirsted like leeches for his blood. He was now old, infirm, and embarrassed with debt. Better had it been for him not to have known the liberal intentions of the emperor, as intimated by his grants ; since he should then have devoted himself to the care of his estates, and not have been compelled, as he now was, to contend with the officers of the crown, against whom it was more difficult to defend himself than to win the land from the enemy." He concludes with beseeching his sovereign to " order the Council of the Indies, with the other tribunals which had cognizance of his suits, to come to a decision ; since he was too old to wander about like a vagrant, but ought rather, during the brief remainder of his life, to stay at home and settle his account with Heaven, occupied with the concerns of his soul, rather than with his substance." [23]

This appeal to his sovereign, which has something in it touching from a man of the haughty spirit of Cortés, had not the effect to quicken the determination of his

[23] The Letter, dated February 3, 1544, Valladolid, may be found entire, in the original, in Appendix, Part 2, No. 15.

suit. He still lingered at the court from week to week, and from month to month, beguiled by the deceitful hopes of the litigant, tasting all that bitterness of the soul which arises from hope deferred. After three years more, passed in this unprofitable and humiliating occupation, he resolved to leave his ungrateful country and return to Mexico.

He had proceeded as far as Seville, accompanied by his son, when he fell ill of an indigestion, caused, probably, by irritation and trouble of mind. This terminated in dysentery, and his strength sank so rapidly under the disease that it was apparent his mortal career was drawing towards its close. He prepared for it by making the necessary arrangements for the settlement of his affairs. He had made his will some time before; and he now executed it. It is a very long document, and in some respects a remarkable one.

The bulk of his property was entailed to his son, Don Martin, then fifteen years of age. In the testament he fixes his majority at twenty-five; but at twenty his guardians were to allow him his full income, to maintain the state becoming his rank. In a paper accompanying the will, Cortés specified the names of the agents to whom he had committed the management of his vast estates scattered over many different provinces; and he requests his executors to confirm the nomination, as these agents have been selected by him from a knowledge of their peculiar qualifications. Nothing can better show the thorough supervision which, in the midst of pressing public concerns, he had given to the details of his widely-extended property.

He makes a liberal provision for his other children,

and a generous allowance to several old domestics and retainers in his household. By another clause he gives away considerable sums in charity, and he applies the revenues of his estates in the city of Mexico to establish and permanently endow three public institutions,—a hospital in the capital, which was to be dedicated to Our Lady of the Conception, a college in Cojohuacan for the education of missionaries to preach the gospel among the natives, and a convent, in the same place, for nuns. To the chapel of this convent, situated in his favorite town, he orders that his own body shall be transported for burial, in whatever quarter of the world he may happen to die.

After declaring that he has taken all possible care to ascertain the amount of the tributes formerly paid by his Indian vassals to their native sovereigns, he enjoins on his heir that, in case those which they have hitherto paid shall be found to exceed the right valuation, he shall restore them a full equivalent. In another clause he expresses a doubt whether it is right to exact personal service from the natives, and commands that a strict inquiry shall be made into the nature and value of such services as he had received, and that in all cases a fair compensation shall be allowed for them. Lastly, he makes this remarkable declaration : "It has long been a question whether one can conscientiously hold property in Indian slaves. Since this point has not yet been determined, I enjoin it on my son Martin and his heirs that they spare no pains to come to an exact knowledge of the truth; as a matter which deeply concerns the conscience of each of them, no less than mine." [24]

[24] " Item. Porque acerca de los esclavos naturales de la dicha

Such scruples of conscience, not to have been expected in Cortés, were still less likely to be met with in the Spaniards of a later generation. The state of opinion in respect to the great question of slavery, in the sixteenth century, at the commencement of the system, bears some resemblance to that which exists in our time, when we may hope it is approaching its conclusion. Las Casas and the Dominicans of the former age, the abolitionists of their day, thundered out their uncompromising invectives against the system on the broad ground of natural equity and the rights of man. The great mass of proprietors troubled their heads little about the question of right, but were satisfied with the expediency of the institution. Others, more considerate and conscientious, while they admitted the evil, found an argument for its toleration in the plea of necessity, regarding the constitution of the white man as unequal, in a sultry climate, to the labor of cultivating the soil.[25] In one important respect the condition of slavery in the sixteenth century differed materially from its condition in the nineteenth. In

Nueva España, así de guerra como de rescate, ha habido y hay muchas dudas y opiniones sobre si se han podido tener con buena conciencia ó no, y hasta ahora no está determinado : Mando que todo aquello que generalmente se averiguare, que en este caso se debe hacer para descargo de las conciencias en lo que toca á estos esclavos de la dicha Nueva España, que se haya y cumpla en todos los que yo tengo, é encargo y mando á D. Martin mi hijo subcesor, y á los que despues dél subcedieren en mi Estado, que para averiguar esto hagan todas las diligencias que combengan al descargo de mi conciencia y suyas." Testamento de Hernan Cortés, MS.

[25] This is the argument controverted by Las Casas in his elaborate Memorial addressed to the government, in 1542, on the best method of arresting the destruction of the aborigines.

the former, the seeds of the evil, but lately sown, might have been, with comparatively little difficulty, eradicated. But in our time they have struck their roots deep into the social system, and cannot be rudely handled without shaking the very foundations of the political fabric. It is easy to conceive that a man who admits all the wretchedness of the institution and its wrong to humanity may nevertheless hesitate to adopt a remedy until he is satisfied that the remedy itself is not worse than the disease. That such a remedy will come with time, who can doubt, that has confidence in the ultimate prevalence of the right and the progressive civilization of his species?

Cortés names as his executors, and as guardians of his children, the duke of Medina Sidonia, the marquis of Astorga, and the count of Aguilar. For his executors in Mexico, he appoints his wife, the marchioness, the archbishop of Toledo, and two other prelates. The will was executed at Seville, October 11th, 1547.[26]

Finding himself much incommoded, as he grew weaker, by the presence of visitors, to which he was necessarily exposed at Seville, he withdrew to the neighboring village of Castilleja de la Cuesta, attended by his son, who watched over his dying parent with filial solicitude.[27] Cortés seems to have contemplated

[26] This interesting document is in the Royal Archives of Seville; and a copy of it forms part of the valuable collection of Don Vargas Ponçe.

[27] [My friend Mr. Picard has furnished me with the copy of an inscription which may be seen, or could a few years since, on the house in which Cortés expired. "Here died, on the second of September, 1544, victim of sorrow and misfortune, the renowned Hernan Cortés,

his approaching end with a composure not always to
be found in those who have faced death with indifference on the field of battle. At length, having de-
voutly confessed his sins and received the sacrament,
he expired on the 2d of December, 1547, in the sixty-
third year of his age.[28]

The inhabitants of the neighboring country were
desirous to show every mark of respect to the memory
of Cortés. His funeral obsequies were celebrated with
due solemnity by a long train of Andalusian nobles
and of the citizens of Seville, and his body was transported to the chapel of the monastery of San Isidro,
in that city, where it was laid in the family vault of the
duke of Medina Sidonia.[29] In the year 1562 it was
removed, by order of his son, Don Martin, to New
Spain, not, as directed by his will, to Cojohuacan,*
but to the monastery of St. Francis, in Tezcuco, where
it was laid by the side of a daughter, and of his

the glory of our country and the conqueror of the Mexican empire."
It is strange that the author of the inscription should have made a
blunder of more than three years in the date of the hero's death.]

[28] Zuñiga, Annales de Sevilla, p. 504.—Gomara, Crónica, cap. 237.
—In his last letter to the emperor, dated in February, 1544, he speaks
of himself as being "sixty years of age." But he probably did not
mean to be exact to a year. Gomara's statement, that he was born
in the year 1485 (Crónica, cap. 1), is confirmed by Diaz, who tells us
that Cortés used to say that when he first came over to Mexico, in
1519, he was thirty-four years old. (Hist. de la Conquista, cap. 205.)
This would coincide with the age mentioned in the text.

[29] Noticia del Archivero de la Santa Eclesia de Sevilla, MS.

---

* [This may be accounted for by the fact that his intention to found
a convent at Cuyoacan, as the place is now called, had, according to
Alaman, never been carried out.—ED.]

mother, Doña Catalina Pizarro. In 1629 the remains of Cortés were again removed; and on the death of Don Pedro, fourth marquis of the Valley, it was decided by the authorities of Mexico to transfer them to the church of St. Francis, in that capital. The ceremonial was conducted with the pomp suited to the occasion. A military and religious procession was formed, with the archbishop of Mexico at its head. He was accompanied by the great dignitaries of church and state, the various associations with their respective banners, the several religious fraternities, and the members of the Audience. The coffin, containing the relics of Cortés, was covered with black velvet, and supported by the judges of the royal tribunals. On either side of it was a man in complete armor, bearing, on the right, a standard of pure white, with the arms of Castile embroidered in gold, and, on the left, a banner of black velvet, emblazoned in like manner with the armorial ensigns of the house of Cortés. Behind the corpse came the viceroy and a numerous escort of Spanish cavaliers, and the rear was closed by a battalion of infantry, armed with pikes and arquebuses, and with their banners trailing on the ground. With this funeral pomp, by the sound of mournful music, and the slow beat of the muffled drum, the procession moved forward, with measured pace, till it reached the capital, when the gates were thrown open to receive the mortal remains of the hero who, a century before, had performed there such prodigies of valor.

Yet his bones were not permitted to rest here undisturbed; and in 1794 they were removed to the Hospital of Jesus of Nazareth. It was a more fitting place, since it was the same institution which, under the name of "Our Lady of the Conception," had been founded and endowed by Cortés, and which, with a fate not too frequent in similar charities, has been administered to this day on the noble principles of its foundation. The mouldering relics of the warrior, now deposited in a crystal coffin secured by bars and plates of silver, were laid in the chapel, and over them was raised a simple monument, displaying the arms of the family, and surmounted by a bust of the Conqueror, executed in bronze by Tolsa, a sculptor worthy of the best period of the arts.[30]

Unfortunately for Mexico, the tale does not stop here. In 1823, the patriot mob of the capital, in their zeal to commemorate the era of the national independence, and their detestation of the "old Spaniards," prepared to break open the tomb which held the ashes of Cortés, and to scatter them to the winds ! The authorities declined to interfere on the occasion ; but the friends of the family, as is commonly reported, entered the vault by night, and, secretly removing the relics, prevented the commission of a sacrilege which must have left a stain, not easy to be effaced, on the scutcheon of the fair city of Mexico.[31]   Humboldt,

[30] The full particulars of the ceremony described in the text may be found in Appendix, Part 2, No. 16, translated into English from a copy of the original document, existing in the Archives of the Hospital of Jesus, in Mexico.

[31] [The bust of Cortés and the arms of gilt bronze were secretly removed from his monument, and sent to his descendant, the duke of Monteleone, at Palermo. The remains of the Conqueror were soon after sent in the same direction, according to Doctor Mora, cited by Alaman, who does not contradict it : " Aun se habrian profanado las

forty years ago, remarked that "we may traverse Spanish America from Buenos Ayres to Monterey, and in
no quarter shall we meet with a national monument
which the public gratitude has raised to Christopher
Columbus or Hernando Cortés."[32]   It was reserved
for our own age to conceive the design of violating
the repose of the dead and insulting their remains!
Yet the men who meditated this outrage were not the
descendants of Montezuma, avenging the wrongs of
their fathers and vindicating their own rightful inheritance.   They were the descendants of the old
Conquerors, and their countrymen, depending on
the right of conquest for their ultimate title to the
soil.[33]

Cortés had no children by his first marriage.   By his
second he left four; a son, Don Martin,—the heir of
his honors, and of persecutions even more severe than
those of his father,[34]—and three daughters, who formed

cenizas del héroe, sin la precaucion de personas despreocupadas, que
deseando evitar el deshonor de su patria por tan reprensible é irre-
flexivo procedimiento, lograron ocultarlas de pronto y despues las re-
mitieron á Italia á su familia." Disertaciones históricas, tom. ii. p.
61.]

[32] Essai politique, tom. ii. p. 60.

[33] [They entertained, says Alaman, the rather extravagant idea that,
as descendants of the conquering nation, they were the heirs of the
rights of the conquered, and bound to avenge their wrongs. Conquista de Méjico (trad. de Vega), tom. ii. p. 309.]

[34] Don Martin Cortés, second marquis of the Valley, was accused,
like his father, of an attempt to establish an independent sovereignty
in New Spain. His natural brothers, Don Martin and Don Luis,
were involved in the same accusation with himself, and the former—
as I have elsewhere remarked—was in consequence subjected to the
torture. Several others of his friends, on charge of abetting his treasonable designs, suffered death. The marquis was obliged to remove

splendid alliances. He left, also, five natural children, whom he particularly mentions in his testament and honorably provides for. Two of these, Don Martin, the son of Marina, and Don Luis Cortés, attained considerable distinction, and were created *comendadores* of the Order of St. Jago.[35]

The male line of the marquises of the Valley became extinct in the third generation. The title and estates descended to a female, and by her marriage were united with those of the house of Terranova, descendants of the "Great Captain," Gonsalvo de Cordova.[36] By a subsequent marriage they were carried into the family of the duke of Monteleone, a Neapolitan noble. The present proprietor of these princely honors and of vast domains, both in the Old and the New World, dwells in Sicily, and boasts a descent—such as few princes can boast—from two

with his family to Spain, where the investigation was conducted; and his large estates in Mexico were sequestered until the termination of the process, a period of seven years, from 1567 to 1574, when he was declared innocent. But his property suffered irreparable injury, under the wretched administration of the royal officers, during the term of sequestration.

[35] [The illegitimate children were Don Martin Cortés, Don Luis Cortés, Doña Catalina Pizarro (daughter of Doña Leonor Pizarro), also two other daughters, Leonor and María, born of two Indian women of noble birth. Alaman, Disertaciones históricas, tom. ii. p. 48.]

[36] [Señor Alaman, in reference to this passage, says, " It is a mistake to suppose that the heirs of Cortés and Gonsalvo de Cordova were ever united by marriage. The fact appears to be that the title of duke of Terranova was held by the descendants of both; but the Terranova assigned to the Great Captain was in Calabria, while the place from which the descendants of Cortés took the title was in Sicily. Conquista de Méjico (trad. de Vega), tom. ii. p. 308.]

of the most illustrious commanders of the sixteenth century, the "Great Captain," and the Conqueror of Mexico.

The personal history of Cortés has been so minutely detailed in the preceding narrative that it will be only necessary to touch on the more prominent features of his character. Indeed, the history of the Conquest, as I have already had occasion to remark, is necessarily that of Cortés, who is, if I may so say, not merely the soul, but the body, of the enterprise, present everywhere in person, in the thick of the fight or in the building of the works, with his sword or with his musket, sometimes leading his soldiers, and sometimes directing his little navy. The negotiations, intrigues, correspondence, are all conducted by him; and, like Cæsar, he wrote his own Commentaries in the heat of the stirring scenes which form the subject of them. His character is marked with the most opposite traits, embracing qualities apparently the most incompatible. He was avaricious, yet liberal; bold to desperation, yet cautious and calculating in his plans; magnanimous, yet very cunning; courteous and affable in his deportment, yet inexorably stern; lax in his notions of morality, yet (not uncommon) a sad bigot. The great feature in his character was constancy of purpose; a constancy not to be daunted by danger, nor baffled by disappointment, nor wearied out by impediments and delays.

He was a knight-errant, in the literal sense of the word. Of all the band of adventurous cavaliers whom Spain, in the sixteenth century, sent forth on the

career of discovery and conquest, there was none more
deeply filled with the spirit of romantic enterprise than
Hernando Cortés. Dangers and difficulties, instead
of deterring, seemed to have a charm in his eyes.
They were necessary to rouse him to a full conscious-
ness of his powers. He grappled with them at the
outset, and, if I may so express myself, seemed to prefer to take his enterprises by the most difficult side.
He conceived, at the first moment of his landing in
Mexico, the design of its conquest. When he saw the
strength of its civilization, he was not turned from his
purpose. When he was assailed by the superior force
of Narvaez, he still persisted in it; and when he was
driven in ruin from the capital, he still cherished his
original idea. How successfully he carried it into execution, we have seen. After the few years of repose
which succeeded the Conquest, his adventurous spirit
impelled him to that dreary march across the marshes
of Chiapa, and, after another interval, to seek his
fortunes on the stormy Californian Gulf. When he
found that no other continent remained for him to
conquer, he made serious proposals to the emperor to
equip a fleet at his own expense, with which he would
sail to the Moluccas and subdue the Spice Islands for
the crown of Castile ![37]

[37] " Yo me ofresco á descubrir por aquí toda la espeçería, y otras
Islas si huviere cerca de Moluco, ó Melaca, y la China, y aun de dar
tal órden que V. M. no aiga la espeçería por via de rescate, como la
ha el Rey de Portugal, sino que la tenga por cosa propria, y los naturales de aquellas Islas le reconoscan y sirvan como á su Rey y señor
natural, porque yo me ofresco con el dicho additamento de embiar á
ellas tal armada, ó *ir yo con mi persona por manera que la sojusge y
pueble.*" Carta Quinta de Cortés, MS.

This spirit of knight-errantry might lead us to under-value his talents as a general and to regard him merely in the light of a lucky adventurer. But this would be doing him injustice; for Cortés was certainly a great general, if that man be one who performs great achievements with the resources which his own genius has created. There is probably no instance in history where so vast an enterprise has been achieved by means apparently so inadequate. He may be truly said to have effected the Conquest by his own re-sources. If he was indebted for his success to the co-operation of the Indian tribes, it was the force of his genius that obtained command of such materials. He arrested the arm that was lifted to smite him, and made it do battle in his behalf. He beat the Tlascalans, and made them his stanch allies. He beat the soldiers of Narvaez, and doubled his effective force by it. When his own men deserted him, he did not desert himself. He drew them back by degrees, and compelled them to act by his will, till they were all as one man. He brought together the most miscellaneous collection of mercenaries who ever fought under one standard : ad-venturers from Cuba and the Isles, craving for gold; hidalgos, who came from the old country to win laurels; broken-down cavaliers, who hoped to mend their fortunes in the New World; vagabonds flying from justice; the grasping followers of Narvaez, and his own reckless veterans,—men with hardly a common tie, and burning with the spirit of jealousy and faction; wild tribes of the natives from all parts of the country, who had been sworn enemies from their cradles, and who had met only to cut one another's throats and to

procure victims for sacrifice; men, in short, differing
in race, in language, and in interests, with scarcely
anything in common among them. Yet this motley
congregation was assembled in one camp, compelled to
bend to the will of one man, to consort together in
harmony, to breathe, as it were, one spirit, and to
move on a common principle of action! It is in this
wonderful power over the discordant masses thus
gathered under his banner that we recognize the genius
of the great commander, no less than in the skill of his
military operations.

His power over the minds of his soldiers was a
natural result of their confidence in his abilities. But
it is also to be attributed to his popular manners,—
that happy union of authority and companionship
which fitted him for the command of a band of roving
adventurers. It would not have done for him to
fence himself round with the stately reserve of a commander of regular forces. He was embarked with his
men in a common adventure, and nearly on terms of
equality, since he held his commission by no legal
warrant. But, while he indulged this freedom and
familiarity with his soldiers, he never allowed it to interfere with their strict obedience nor to impair the
severity of discipline. When he had risen to higher
consideration, although he affected more state, he still
admitted his veterans to the same intimacy. "He
preferred," says Diaz, "to be called 'Cortés' by us,
to being called by any title; and with good reason,"
continues the enthusiastic old cavalier, "for the name
of Cortés is as famous in our day as was that of Cæsar
among the Romans, or of Hannibal among the Cartha-

ginians." [38]   He showed the same kind regard towards
his ancient comrades in the very last act of his life.
For he appropriated a sum by his will for the celebration of two thousand masses for the souls of
those who had fought with him in the campaigns of
Mexico. [39]

His character has been unconsciously traced by the
hand of a master:

> " And oft *the chieftain* deigned to aid
> And mingle in the mirth they made;
> For, though with men of high degree
> The proudest of the proud was he,
> Yet, trained in camps, he knew the art
> To win the soldiers' hardy heart.
> They love a captain to obey,
> Boisterous as March, yet fresh as May:
> With open hand, and brow as free,
> Lover of wine and minstrelsy;

[38] The comparison to Hannibal is better founded than the old
soldier probably imagined.   Livy's description of the Carthaginian
warrior has a marvellous application to Cortés,—better, perhaps, than
that of the imaginary personage quoted a few lines below in the text.
" Plurimum audaciæ ad pericula capessenda, plurimum consilii inter
ipsa pericula erat: nullo labore aut corpus fatigari, aut animus vinci
poterat.   Caloris ac frigoris patientia par: cibi potionisque desiderio
naturali, non voluptate, modus finitus : vigiliarum somnique nec die,
nec nocte discriminata tempora.   Id, quod gerendis rebus superesset,
quieti datum ; ea neque molli strato, neque silentio arcessita.   Multi
sæpe militari sagulo opertum, humi jacentem, inter custodias statio-
nesque militum, conspexerunt. Vestitus nihil inter æquales excellens;
arma atque equi conspiciebantur.   Equitum peditumque idem longe
primus erat; princeps in prœlium ibat; ultimus conserto prœlio ex-
cedebat."   (Hist., lib. xxi. sec. 5.)   The reader who reflects on the
fate of Guatemozin may possibly think that the extract should have
embraced the "perfidia plus quám Punica," in the succeeding sentence.
[39] Testamento de Hernan Cortés, MS.

Ever the first to scale a tower,
As venturous in a lady's bower ;—
Such buxom chief shall lead his host
From India's fires to Zembla's frost."

Cortés, without much violence, might have sat for this portrait of Marmion.

Cortés was not a vulgar conqueror. He did not conquer from the mere ambition of conquest. If he destroyed the ancient capital of the Aztecs, it was to build up a more magnificent capital on its ruins. If he desolated the land and broke up its existing institutions, he employed the short period of his administration in digesting schemes for introducing there a more improved culture and a higher civilization. In all his expeditions he was careful to study the resources of the country, its social organization, and its physical capacities. He enjoined it on his captains to attend particularly to these objects. If he was greedy of gold, like most of the Spanish cavaliers in the New World, it was not to hoard it, nor merely to lavish it in the support of a princely establishment, but to secure funds for prosecuting his glorious discoveries. Witness his costly expeditions to the Gulf of California. His enterprises were not undertaken solely for mercenary objects ; as is shown by the various expeditions he set on foot for the discovery of a communication between the Atlantic and the Pacific. In his schemes of ambition he showed a respect for the interests of science, to be referred partly to the natural superiority of his mind, but partly, no doubt, to the influence of early education. It is, indeed, hardly possible that a person of his wayward and mercurial temper should have improved his advantages at the University; but he brought away from it a tincture of scholarship seldom found among the cavaliers of the period, and which had its influence in enlarging his own conceptions. His celebrated Letters are written with a simple elegance that, as I have already had occasion to remark, have caused them to be compared to the military narrative of Cæsar. It will not be easy to find in the chronicles of the period a more concise yet comprehensive statement, not only of the events of his campaigns, but of the circumstances most worthy of notice in the character of the conquered countries.

Cortés was not cruel; at least, not cruel as compared with most of those who followed his iron trade. The path of the conqueror is necessarily marked with blood. He was not too scrupulous, indeed, in the execution of his plans. He swept away the obstacles which lay in his track; and his fame is darkened by the commission of more than one act which his boldest apologists will find it hard to vindicate. But he was not wantonly cruel. He allowed no outrage on his unresisting foes. This may seem small praise; but it is an exception to the usual conduct of his countrymen in their conquests, and it is something to be in advance of one's time. He was severe, it may be added, in enforcing obedience to his orders for protecting their persons and their property. With his licentious crew, it was, sometimes, not without a hazard that he was so. After the Conquest, he sanctioned the system of *repartimientos;* but so did Columbus. He endeavored to regulate it by the most humane laws, and continued to suggest many important changes for ameliorating the condition of the natives. The best commentary on his conduct in this respect is the deference that was shown him by the Indians, and the confidence with which they appealed to him for protection in all their subsequent distresses.

In private life he seems to have had the power of attaching to himself warmly those who were near his person. The influence of this attachment is shown in every page of Bernal Diaz, though his work was written to vindicate the claims of the soldiers in opposition to those of the general. He seems to have led a happy life with his first wife, in their humble retirement in Cuba, and regarded the second, to judge from the expressions in his testament, with confidence and love. Yet he cannot be acquitted from the charge of those licentious gallantries which entered too generally into the character of the military adventurer of that day. He would seem also, by the frequent suits in which he was involved, to have been of an irritable and contentious spirit. But much allowance must be made for the irritability of a man who had been too long accustomed to independent sway, patiently to endure the checks and control of the petty spirits who were incapable of comprehending the noble character of his enterprises. "He thought," says an eminent writer, "to silence his enemies by the brilliancy of the new career on which he had entered. He did not reflect that these enemies had been raised by the very grandeur and rapidity of his success." [40] He was rewarded for his efforts by the misinterpretation of his motives; by the calumnious charges of squandering the public

---

[40] Humboldt, Essai politique, tom. ii. p. 267.

P*

revenues and of aspiring to independent sovereignty. But, although we may admit the foundation of many of the grievances alleged by Cortés, yet, when we consider the querulous tone of his correspondence and the frequency of his litigation, we may feel a natural suspicion that his proud spirit was too sensitive to petty slights and too jealous of imaginary wrongs.

One trait more remains to be noticed in the character of this remarkable man ; that is, his bigotry, the failing of the age,—for surely it should be termed only a failing.[41] When we see the hand, red with the blood of the wretched native, raised to invoke the blessing of Heaven on the cause which it maintains, we experience something like a sensation of disgust at the act, and a doubt of its sincerity. But this is unjust. We should throw ourselves back (it cannot be too often repeated) into the age,—the age of the Crusades. For every Spanish cavalier, however sordid and selfish might be his private motives, felt himself to be the soldier of the Cross. Many of them would have died in defence of it. Whoever has read the correspondence of Cortés, or, still more, has attended to the circumstances of his career, will hardly doubt that he would have been among the first to lay down his life for the

[41] An extraordinary anecdote is related by Cavo of this bigotry (shall we call it policy ?) of Cortés. " In Mexico," says the historian, "it is commonly reported that after the Conquest he commanded that on Sundays and holidays all should attend, under pain of a certain number of stripes, to the expounding of the Scriptures. The general was himself guilty of an omission on one occasion, and, after having listened to the admonition of the priest, submitted, with edifying humility, to be chastised by him, to the unspeakable amazement of the Indians." Hist. de los tres Siglos, tom. i. p. 151.

Faith. He more than once perilled life, and fortune, and the success of his whole enterprise, by the premature and most impolitic manner in which he would have forced conversion on the natives.[42] To the more rational spirit of the present day, enlightened by a purer Christianity, it may seem difficult to reconcile gross deviations from morals with such devotion to the cause of religion. But the religion taught in that day was one of form and elaborate ceremony. In the punctilious attention to discipline, the spirit of Christianity was permitted to evaporate. The mind, occupied with forms, thinks little of substance. In a worship that is addressed too exclusively to the senses, it is often the case that morality becomes divorced from religion, and the measure of righteousness is determined by the creed rather than by the conduct.

In the earlier part of the History I have given a description of the person of Cortés.[43] It may be well to close this review of his character by the account of his manners and personal habits left us by Bernal Diaz, the old chronicler, who has accompanied us through the whole course of our narrative, and who may now fitly furnish the conclusion of it. No man knew his commander better; and, if the avowed object of his work might naturally lead to a disparagement of Cortés, this is more than counterbalanced by the warmth of his personal attachment, and by that *esprit de corps*

[42] " Al Rey infinitas tierras,
      Y á Dios infinitas almas,"

says Lope de Vega, commemorating in this couplet the double glory of Cortés. It is the light in which the Conquest was viewed by every devout Spaniard of the sixteenth century.

[43] *Ante*, vol. i. p. 257.

which leads him to take a pride in the renown of his general.

"In his whole appearance and presence," says Diaz, "in his discourse, his table, his dress, in everything, in short, he had the air of a great lord. His clothes were in the fashion of the time; he set little value on silk, damask, or velvet, but dressed plainly and exceedingly neat;[44] nor did he wear massy chains of gold, but simply a fine one, of exquisite workmanship, from which was suspended a jewel having the figure of our Lady the Virgin and her precious Son, with a Latin motto cut upon it. On his finger he wore a splendid diamond ring; and from his cap, which, according to the fashion of that day, was of velvet, hung a medal, the device of which I do not remember. He was magnificently attended, as became a man of his rank, with chamberlains and major-domos and many pages; and the service of his table was splendid, with a quantity of both gold and silver plate. At noon he dined heartily, drinking about a pint of wine mixed with water. He supped well, though he was not dainty in regard to his food, caring little for the delicacies of the table, unless, indeed, on such occasions as made attention to these matters of some consequence.[45]

"He was acquainted with Latin, and, as I have understood, was made Bachelor of Laws; and when he conversed with learned men who addressed him in Latin, he answered them in the same language. He

[44] So Gomara: "He dressed neatly rather than richly, and was always scrupulously clean." *Crónica*, cap. 238.

[45] "Fué mui gran comedor, i templado en el beber, teniendo abundancia. Sufria mucho la hambre con necesidad." *Ibid., ubi supra.*

was also something of a poet; his conversation was agreeable, and he had a pleasant elocution. In his attendance on the services of the Church he was most punctual, devout in his manner, and charitable to the poor.[46]

"When he swore, he used to say, 'On my conscience;' and when he was vexed with any one, 'Evil betide you.' With his men he was very patient; and they were sometimes impertinent and even insolent. When very angry, the veins in his throat and forehead would swell, but he uttered no reproaches against either officer or soldier.

"He was fond of cards and dice, and, when he played, was always in good humor, indulging freely in jests and repartees. He was affable with his followers, especially with those who came over with him from Cuba. In his campaigns he paid strict attention to discipline, frequently going the rounds himself during the night, and seeing that the sentinels did their duty. He entered the quarters of his soldiers without ceremony, and chided those whom he found without their arms and accoutrements, saying, 'It was a bad sheep that could not carry its own wool.' On the expedition to Honduras he acquired the habit of sleeping after his meals, feeling unwell if he omitted it; and, however sultry or stormy the weather, he caused a carpet or his cloak to be thrown under a tree, and slept soundly for some time. He was frank and exceedingly liberal in his disposition, until the last few years of his life, when

[46] He dispensed a thousand ducats every year in his ordinary charities, according to Gomara. "Grandísimo limosnero; daba cada un año mil ducados de limosna ordinaria." Crónica, cap. 238.

he was accused of parsimony. But we should consider that his funds were employed on great and costly enterprises, and that none of these, after the Conquest, neither his expedition to Honduras nor his voyages to California, were crowned with success. It was perhaps intended that he should receive his recompense in a better world; and I fully believe it; for he was a good cavalier, most true in his devotions to the Virgin, to the Apostle St. Peter, and to all the other Saints." [47]

Such is the portrait, which has been left to us by the faithful hand most competent to trace it, of Hernando Cortés, the Conqueror of Mexico.

[47] Hist. de la Conquista, cap. 203.

APPENDIX.

PART I.

ORIGIN OF THE MEXICAN CIVILIZATION.

(351)

PRELIMINARY NOTICE.

THE following Essay was originally designed to close the Introductory Book, to which it properly belongs. It was written three years since, at the same time with that part of the work. I know of no work of importance, having reference to the general subject of discussion, which has appeared since that period, except Mr. Bradford's valuable treatise on *American Antiquities*. But in respect to that part of the discussion which treats of American Architecture a most important contribution has been made by Mr. Stephens's two works, containing the account of his visits to Central America and Yucatan, and especially by the last of these publications. Indeed, the ground, before so imperfectly known, has now been so diligently explored that we have all the light, which we can reasonably expect, to aid us in making up our opinion in regard to the mysterious monuments of Yucatan. It only remains that the exquisite illustrations of Mr. Catherwood should be published on a larger scale, like the great works on the subject in France and England, in order to exhibit to the eye a more adequate representation of these magnificent ruins than can be given in the limited compass of an octavo page.

But, notwithstanding the importance of Mr. Stephens's researches, I have not availed myself of them to make any additions to the original draft of this Essay, nor have I rested my conclusions in any instance on his authority. These conclusions had been formed from a careful study of the narratives of Dupaix and Waldeck, together with that of their splendid illustrations of the remains of Palenque and Uxmal, two of the principal places explored by Mr. Stephens; and the additional facts collected by him from the vast field which he has surveyed, so far from shaking my previous deductions, have only served to confirm them. The only object of my own speculations on these remains was to ascertain their probable origin, or rather to see what light, if any, they could throw on the origin of Aztec Civilization. The reader, on comparing my reflections with those of Mr. Stephens in the closing chapters of his two works, will see that I have arrived at inferences, as to the origin and probable antiquity of these structures, precisely the same as his. Conclusions formed under such different circumstances serve to corroborate each other; and, although the reader will find here some things which would have been different had I been guided by the light now thrown on the path, yet I prefer not to disturb the foundations on which the argument stands, nor to impair its value—if it has any—as a distinct and independent testimony.

APPENDIX, PART I.

_____

ORIGIN OF THE MEXICAN CIVILIZATION.— ANALOGIES WITH THE OLD WORLD.

WHEN the Europeans first touched the shores of America, it was as if they had alighted on another planet,—every thing there was so different from what they had before seen. They were introduced to new varieties of plants, and to unknown races of animals; while man, the lord of all, was equally strange, in complexion, language, and institutions.[1] It was what they emphatically styled it,—a New World. Taught by their faith to derive all created beings from one source, they felt a natural perplexity as to the manner in which these distant and insulated regions could have obtained their inhabitants. The same curiosity was felt by their countrymen at home, and the European scholars bewildered their brains with speculations on the best way of solving this interesting problem.

[1] The names of many animals in the New World, indeed, have been frequently borrowed from the Old; but the species are very different. "When the Spaniards landed in America," says an eminent naturalist, "they did not find a single animal they were acquainted with; not one of the quadrupeds of Europe, Asia, or Africa." Lawrence, Lectures on Physiology, Zoology, and the Natural History of Man (London, 1819), p. 250.

(355)

In accounting for the presence of animals there, some imagined that the two hemispheres might once have been joined in the extreme north, so as to have afforded an easy communication.[2] Others, embarrassed by the difficulty of transporting inhabitants of the tropics across the Arctic regions, revived the old story of Plato's Atlantis, that huge island, now submerged, which might have stretched from the shores of Africa to the eastern borders of the new continent;[*] while

---

[2] Acosta, lib. i, cap. 16.

---

[*] [The existence at some former period of such an island, or rather continent, seems to be regarded by geologists as a well-attested fact. But few would admit that its subsidence can have taken place through any sudden convulsion or within the period of human existence. Such, however, is the theory maintained by M. Brasseur de Bourbourg, who dates the event " six or seven thousand years ago," and believes that the traditions of it have been faithfully preserved. This is the great cataclysm with which all mythology begins. It may be traced through the myths of Greece, Egypt, India, and America, all being identical and having a common origin. It is the subject of the *Teo-Amoxtli*, of which several of the Mexican manuscripts, the Borgian and Dresden Codices in particular, are the hieroglyphical transcriptions, and of which " the actual letter," " in the Nahuatlac language," is found in a manuscript in Boturini's Collection. This manuscript is " in appearance" a history of the Toltecs and of the kings of Colhuacan and Mexico; but " under the ciphers of a fastidious chronology, under the recital more or less animated of the Toltec history, are concealed the profoundest mysteries concerning the geological origin of the world in its existing form and the cradle of the religions of antiquity." The Toltecs are " telluric powers, agents of the subterranean fire;" they are identical with the Cabiri, who reappear as the Cyclops, having " hollowed an eye in their forehead; that is to say, raised themselves with masses of earth above the surface and filled the craters of the volcanoes with fire." " The Chichimecs and the Aztecs are also symbolical names, borrowed from the forces of nature." Tollan, " the marshy or reedy place," was " the

they saw vestiges of a similar convulsion of nature in the green islands sprinkled over the Pacific, once the mountain summits of a vast continent, now buried beneath the waters.[3] Some, distrusting the existence of revolutions of which no record was preserved, supposed that animals might have found their way across the ocean by various means; the birds of stronger wing by flight over the narrowest spaces; while the tamer kinds of quadrupeds might easily have been transported by men in boats, and even the more ferocious, as tigers, bears, and the like, have been brought over, in the same manner, when young, "for amusement and the pleasure of the chase"![4] Others, again, maintained the equally probable opinion that angels, who had, doubtless, taken charge of them in the ark,

[3] Count Carli shows much ingenuity and learning in support of the famous Egyptian tradition, recorded by Plato in his "Timæus,"— of the good faith of which the Italian philosopher nothing doubts. Lettres Améric., tom. ii. let. 36–39.

[4] Garcia, Orígen de los Indios de el nuevo Mundo (Madrid, 1729), cap. 4.

---

low fertile region" now covered by the Gulf of Mexico. Quetzalcoatl is "merely the personification of the land swallowed up by the ocean." Tlapallan, Aztlan, and other names are similarly explained. Osiris, Pan, Hercules, and Bacchus have their respective parts assigned to them; for "not only all the sources of ancient mythology, but even the most mysterious details, even the obscurest enigmas, with which that mythology is enveloped, are to be sought in the two mediterraneans hollowed out by the cataclysm, and in the islands, great and small, which separate them from the ocean." (Quatre Lettres sur le Mexique.) There can be no refutation of such a theory, or of the assumptions on which it rests; but it may be proper to remark that its author has not succeeded in deciphering a single hieroglyphical character, and has published no translation of the real or supposed *Teo-Amoxtli*,—a point on which some misapprehension seems to exist.—ED.]

had also superintended their distribution afterwards over the different parts of the globe.[5] Such were the extremities to which even thinking minds were reduced, in their eagerness to reconcile the literal interpretation of Scripture with the phenomena of nature! The philosophy of a later day conceives that it is no departure from this sacred authority to follow the suggestions of science, by referring the new tribes of animals to a creation, since the deluge, in those places for which they were clearly intended by constitution and habits.[6]

Man would not seem to present the same embarrassments, in the discussion, as the inferior orders. He is fitted by nature for every climate, the burning sun of the tropics and the icy atmosphere of the North. He wanders indifferently over the sands of the desert, the waste of polar snows, and the pathless ocean. Neither mountains nor seas intimidate him, and, by the aid of mechanical contrivances, he accomplishes journeys which birds of boldest wing would perish in attempting. Without ascending to the high northern latitudes, where the continents of Asia and America approach within fifty miles of each other, it would be easy for the inhabitant of Eastern Tartary or Japan to

[5] Torquemada, Monarch. Ind., lib. 1, cap. 8.

[6] Prichard, Researches into the Physical History of Mankind (London, 1826), vol. i. p. 81, et seq.—He may find an orthodox authority of respectable antiquity, for a similar hypothesis, in St. Augustine, who plainly intimates his belief that, " as by God's command, at the time of the creation, the earth brought forth the living creature after his kind, so a similar process must have taken place after the deluge, in islands too remote to be reached by animals from the continent." De Civitate Dei, ap. Opera (Parisiis, 1636), tom. v. p. 987.

steer his canoe from islet to islet, quite across to the American shore, without ever being on the ocean more than two days at a time.[7] The communication is somewhat more difficult on the Atlantic side. But even there, Iceland was occupied by colonies of Europeans many hundred years before the discovery by Columbus; and the transit from Iceland to America is comparatively easy.[8] Independently of these channels, others were opened in the Southern hemisphere, by means of the numerous islands in the Pacific. The population of America is not nearly so difficult a problem as that of these little spots. But experience shows how practicable the communication may have been, even with such sequestered places.[9] The savage has been picked up in his canoe, after drifting hundreds of leagues on the open ocean, and sustaining life, for months, by the rain from heaven, and such fish as he could catch.[10]

[7] Beechey, Voyage to the Pacific and Beering's Strait (London, 1831), Part 2, Appendix.—Humboldt, Examen critique de l'Histoire de la Géographie du Nouveau-Continent (Paris, 1837), tom. ii. p. 58.

[8] Whatever skepticism may have been entertained as to the visit of the Northmen, in the eleventh century, to the coasts of the great continent, it is probably set at rest in the minds of most scholars since the publication of the original documents by the Royal Society at Copenhagen. (See, in particular, Antiquitates Americanæ (Hafniæ, 1837), pp. 79–200.) How far south they penetrated is not so easily settled.

[9] The most remarkable example, probably, of a direct intercourse between remote points is furnished us by Captain Cook, who found the inhabitants of New Zealand not only with the same religion, but speaking the same language, as the people of Otaheite, distant more than 2000 miles. The comparison of the two vocabularies establishes the fact. Cook's Voyages (Dublin, 1784), vol. i. book 1, chap. 8.

[10] The eloquent Lyell closes an enumeration of some extraordinary and well-attested instances of this kind with remarking, "Were the

The instances are not very rare; and it would be strange if these wandering barks should not sometimes have been intercepted by the great continent which stretches across the globe, in unbroken continuity, almost from pole to pole. No doubt, history could reveal to us more than one example of men who, thus driven upon the American shores, have mingled their blood with that of the primitive races who occupied them.

The real difficulty is not, as with the animals, to explain how man could have reached America, but from what quarter he actually has reached it. In surveying the whole extent of the New World, it was found to contain two great families, one in the lowest stage of civilization, composed of hunters, and another nearly as far advanced in refinement as the semi-civilized empires of Asia. The more polished races were probably unacquainted with the existence of each other on the different continents of America, and had as little intercourse with the barbarian tribes by whom they were surrounded. Yet they had some things in common both with these last and with one another, which remarkably distinguished them from the inhabitants of the Old World. They had a common complexion and physical organization,—at least, bearing a more

whole of mankind now cut off, with the exception of one family, inhabiting the old or new continent, or Australia, or even some coral islet of the Pacific, we should expect their descendants, though they should never become more enlightened than the South Sea Islanders or the Esquimaux, to spread, in the course of ages, over the whole earth, diffused partly by the tendency of population to increase beyond the means of subsistence in a limited district, and partly by the accidental drifting of canoes by tides and currents to distant shores." *Principles of Geology* (London, 1832), vol. ii. p. 121.

uniform character than is found among the nations of any other quarter of the globe. They had some usages and institutions in common, and spoke languages of similar construction, curiously distinguished from those in the Eastern hemisphere.

Whence did the refinement of these more polished races come? Was it only a higher development of the same Indian character which we see, in the more northern latitudes, defying every attempt at permanent civilization? Was it engrafted on a race of higher order in the scale originally, but self-instructed, working its way upward by its own powers? Was it, in short, an indigenous civilization? or was it borrowed in some degree from the nations in the Eastern World? If indigenous, how are we to explain the singular coincidence with the East in institutions and opinions? If Oriental, how shall we account for the great dissimilarity in language, and for the ignorance of some of the most simple and useful arts, which, once known, it would seem scarcely possible should have been forgotten? This is the riddle of the Sphinx, which no Œdipus has yet had the ingenuity to solve. It is, however, a question of deep interest to every curious and intelligent observer of his species. And it has accordingly occupied the thoughts of men, from the first discovery of the country to the present time ; when the extraordinary monuments brought to light in Central America have given a new impulse to inquiry, by suggesting the probability—the possibility, rather— that surer evidences than any hitherto known might be afforded for establishing the fact of a positive communication with the other hemisphere.

It is not my intention to add many pages to the volumes already written on this inexhaustible topic. The subject—as remarked by a writer of a philosophical mind himself, and who has done more than any other for the solution of the mystery—is of too speculative a nature for history, almost for philosophy.[11] But this work would be incomplete without affording the reader the means of judging for himself as to the true sources of the peculiar civilization already described, by exhibiting to him the alleged points of resemblance with the ancient continent. In doing this, I shall confine myself to my proper subject, the Mexicans, or to what, in some way or other, may have a bearing on this subject; proposing to state only real points of resemblance, as they are supported by evidence, and stripped, as far as possible, of the illusions with which they have been invested by the pious credulity of one party, and the visionary system-building of another.

An obvious analogy is found in *cosmogonal traditions* and *religious usages.* The reader has already been made acquainted with the Aztec system of four great cycles, at the end of each of which the world was destroyed, to be again regenerated.[12] The belief in these periodical convulsions of nature, through the agency of some one or other of the elements, was familiar to many countries in the Eastern hemisphere;

---

[11] " La question générale de la première origine des habitans d'un continent est au-delà des limites prescrites à l'histoire : peut-être même n'est-elle pas une question philosophique." Humboldt, Essai politique, tom. i. p. 349.

[12] *Ante*, vol. i. p. 64.

and, though varying in detail, the general resemblance of outline furnishes an argument in favor of a common origin.[13]

No tradition has been more widely spread among nations than that of a Deluge. Independently of tradition, indeed, it would seem to be naturally suggested by the interior structure of the earth, and by the elevated places on which marine substances are found to be deposited. It was the received notion, under some form or other, of the most civilized people in the Old World, and of the barbarians of the New.[14] The Aztecs combined with this some particular circumstances of a more arbitrary character, resembling the accounts of the East. They believed that two persons survived the Deluge,—a man, named Coxcox, and his wife. Their heads are represented in ancient paintings,

[13] The fanciful division of time into four or five cyles or ages was found among the Hindoos (Asiatic Researches, vol. ii. mem. 7), the Thibetians (Humboldt, Vues des Cordillères, p. 210), the Persians (Bailly, Traité de l'Astronomie (Paris, 1787), tom. i. discours préliminaire), the Greeks (Hesiod, 'Εργα καὶ 'Ημέραι, v. 108, et seq.), and other people, doubtless. The five ages in the Grecian cosmogony had reference to moral rather than physical phenomena,—a proof of higher civilization.

[14] The Chaldean and Hebrew accounts of the Deluge are nearly the same. The parallel is pursued in Palfrey's ingenious Lectures on the Jewish Scriptures and Antiquities (Boston, 1840), vol. ii. lect. 21, 22. Among the pagan writers, none approach so near to the Scripture narrative as Lucian, who, in his account of the Greek traditions, speaks of the ark, and the pairs of different kinds of animals. (De Deâ Syriâ, sec. 12.) The same thing is found in the Bhagawatn Purana, a Hindoo poem of great antiquity. (Asiatic Researches, vol. ii. mem. 7.) The simple tradition of a universal inundation was preserved among most of the aborigines, probably, of the Western World. See McCulloh, Researches, p. 147.

together with a boat floating on the waters, at the foot
of a mountain. A dove is also depicted, with the
hieroglyphical emblem of languages in his mouth,
which he is distributing to the children of Coxcox,
who were born dumb.[15] The neighboring people of
Michoacán, inhabiting the same high plains of the
Andes, had a still further tradition, that the boat in which
Tezpi, their Noah, escaped, was filled with various
kinds of animals and birds. After some time, a vul-
ture was sent out from it, but remained feeding on the
dead bodies of the giants, which had been left on the
earth, as the waters subsided. The little humming-
bird, *huitzitzilin,* was then sent forth, and returned with
a twig in its mouth. The coincidence of both these
accounts with the Hebrew and Chaldean narratives is
obvious. It were to be wished that the authority for
the Michoacán version were more satisfactory.[16]

[15] This tradition of the Aztecs is recorded in an ancient hieroglyphical map, first published in Gemelli Carreri's Giro del Mondo. (See
tom. vi. p. 38, ed. Napoli, 1700.) Its authenticity, as well as the integrity of Carreri himself, on which some suspicions have been thrown
(see Robertson's America (London, 1796), vol. iii. note 26), has been
successfully vindicated by Boturini, Clavigero, and Humboldt, all of
whom trod in the steps of the Italian traveller. (Boturini, Idea, p. 54.
—Humboldt, Vues des Cordillères, pp. 223, 224.—Clavigero, Stor.
del Messico, tom. i. p. 24.) The map is a copy from one in the curious
collection of Siguenza. It has all the character of a genuine Aztec
picture, with the appearance of being retouched, especially in the
costumes, by some later artist. The painting of the four ages, in the
Vatican Codex, No. 3730, represents, also, the two figures in the boat,
escaping the great cataclysm. Antiq. of Mexico, vol. i. Pl. 7.

[16] I have met with no other voucher for this remarkable tradition
than Clavigero (Stor. del Messico, dissert. 1), a good, though certainly not the best, authority, when he gives us no reason for our
faith. Humboldt, however, does not distrust the tradition. (See Vues

On the way between Vera Cruz and the capital, not far from the modern city of Puebla, stands the venerable relic—with which the reader has become familiar in the course of the narrative—called the temple of Cholula. It is, as he will remember, a pyramidal mound, built, or rather cased, with unburnt brick, rising to the height of nearly one hundred and eighty feet. The popular tradition of the natives is that it was erected by a family of giants, who had escaped the great inundation and designed to raise the building to the clouds; but the gods, offended with their presumption, sent fires from heaven on the pyramid, and compelled them to abandon the attempt.[17] The partial coincidence of this legend with the Hebrew account of the tower of Babel, received also by other nations of the East, cannot be denied.[18] But one who has not

des Cordillères, p. 226.) He is not so skeptical as Vater; who, in allusion to the stories of the Flood, remarks, " I have purposely omitted noticing the resemblance of religious notions, for I do not see how it is possible to separate from such views every influence of Christian ideas, if it be only from an imperceptible confusion in the mind of the narrator." Mithridates, oder allgemeine Sprachenkunde (Berlin, 1812), Theil iii. Abtheil. 3, p. 82, note.

[17] This story, so irreconcilable with the vulgar Aztec tradition, which admits only two survivors of the Deluge, was still lingering among the natives of the place on M. de Humboldt's visit there. (Vues des Cordillères, pp. 31, 32.) It agrees with that given by the interpreter of the Vatican Codex (Antiq. of Mexico, vol. vi. p. 192, et seq.); a writer—probably a monk of the sixteenth century—in whom ignorance and dogmatism contend for mastery. See a precious specimen of both, in his account of the Aztec chronology, in the very pages above referred to.

[18] A tradition, very similar to the Hebrew one, existed among the Chaldeans and the Hindoos. (Asiatic Researches, vol. iii. mem. 16.) The natives of Chiapa, also, according to the bishop Nuñez de la

examined the subject will scarcely credit what bold hypotheses have been reared on this slender basis.

Another point of coincidence is found in the goddess Cioacoatl, " our lady and mother;" " the first goddess who brought forth;" " who bequeathed the sufferings of childbirth to women, as the tribute of death;" " by whom sin came into the world." Such was the remarkable language applied by the Aztecs to this venerated deity. She was usually represented with a serpent near her; and her name signified the " serpent-woman." In all this we see much to remind us of the mother of the human family, the Eve of the Hebrew and Syrian nations.[19]

Vega, had a story, cited as genuine by Humboldt (Vues des Cordillères, p. 148), which not only agrees with the Scripture account of the manner in which Babel was built, but with that of the subsequent dispersion and the confusion of tongues. A very marvellous coincidence! But who shall vouch for the authenticity of the tradition? The bishop flourished towards the close of the seventeenth century. He drew his information from hieroglyphical maps, and an Indian MS., which Boturini in vain endeavored to recover. In exploring these, he borrowed the aid of the natives, who, as Boturini informs us, frequently led the good man into errors and absurdities ; of which he gives several specimens. (Idea, p. 116, et seq.)—Boturini himself has fallen into an error equally great, in regard to a map of this same Cholulan pyramid, which Clavigero shows, far from being a genuine antique, was the forgery of a later day. (Stor. del Messico, tom. i. p. 130, nota.) It is impossible to get a firm footing in the quicksands of tradition. The further we are removed from the Conquest, the more difficult it becomes to decide what belongs to the primitive Aztec and what to the Christian convert.

[19] Sahagun, Hist. de Nueva-España, lib. 1, cap. 6; lib. 6, cap. 28, 33. —Torquemada, not content with the honest record of his predecessor, whose MS. lay before him, tells us that the Mexican Eve had two sons, Cain and Abel. (Monarch. Ind., lib. 6, cap. 31.) The ancient interpreters of the Vatican and Tellerian Codices add the further tradition

But none of the deities of the country suggested such astonishing analogies with Scripture as Quetzalcoatl, with whom the reader has already been made acquainted.[20] He was the white man, wearing a long beard, who came from the East, and who, after presiding over the golden age of Anahuac, disappeared as mysteriously as he had come, on the great Atlantic Ocean. As he promised to return at some future day, his reappearance was looked for with confidence by each succeeding generation. There is little in these circumstances to remind one of Christianity. But the curious antiquaries of Mexico found out that to this god were to be referred the institution of ecclesiastical communities, reminding one of the monastic societies of the Old World ; that of the rites of confession and penance ; and the knowledge even of the great doctrines of the Trinity and the Incarnation![21] One party, with pious industry, accumulated proofs to establish his identity with the Apostle St. Thomas ;[22] while

of her bringing sin and sorrow into the world by plucking the forbidden *rose* (Antiq. of Mexico, vol. vi., explan. of Pl. 7, 20) ; and Veytia remembers to have seen a Toltec or Aztec map representing a garden with a single tree in it, round which was coiled the serpent with a human face ! (Hist. antig., lib. 1, cap. 1.) After this we may be prepared for Lord Kingsborough's deliberate conviction that the " Aztecs had a clear knowledge of the Old Testament, and, most probably, of the New, though somewhat corrupted by time and hieroglyphics" ! Antiq. of Mexico, vol. vi. p. 409.

[20] *Ante*, vol. i. pp. 60, 61.

[21] Veytia, Hist. antig., lib. 1, cap. 15.

[22] Ibid., lib. 1, cap. 19.—A sorry argument, even for a casuist. See, also, the elaborate dissertation of Dr. Mier (apud Sahagun, lib. 3, Suplem.), which settles the question entirely to the satisfaction of his reporter, Bustamante.

another, with less scrupulous faith, saw, in his anticipated advent to regenerate the nation, the type, dimly
veiled, of the Messiah![23]

Yet we should have charity for the missionaries who
first landed in this world of wonders, where, while
man and nature wore so strange an aspect, they were
astonished by occasional glimpses of rites and ceremonies which reminded them of a purer faith. In their
amazement, they did not reflect whether these things
were not the natural expression of the religious feeling
common to all nations who have reached even a moderate civilization. They did not inquire whether the
same things were not practised by other idolatrous
people. They could not suppress their wonder, as they
beheld the Cross, the sacred emblem of their own faith,
raised as an object of worship in the temples of Anahuac.
They met with it in various places; and the image of
a cross may be seen at this day, sculptured in bas-
relief, on the walls of one of the buildings of Palenque,
while a figure bearing some resemblance to that of a
child is held up to it, as if in adoration.[24]

[23] See, among others, Lord Kingsborough's reading of the Borgian
Codex, and the interpreters of the Vatican (Antiq. of Mexico, vol. vi..
explan. of Pl. 3, 10, 41), equally well skilled with his lordship—and
Sir Hudibras—in unravelling mysteries

> "Whose primitive tradition reaches
> As far as Adam's first green breeches."

[24] Antiquités Mexicaines, exped. 3, Pl. 36.—The figures are surrounded by hieroglyphics of most arbitrary character, perhaps phonetic. (See, also, Herrera, Hist. general, dec. 2, lib. 3, cap. 1.—
Gomara, Crónica de la Nueva-España, cap. 15, ap. Barcia, tom. ii.)
Mr. Stephens considers that the celebrated " Cozumel Cross," preserved at Merida, which claims the credit of being the same originally

Their surprise was heightened when they witnessed a religious rite which reminded them of the Christian communion. On these occasions an image of the tutelary deity of the Aztecs was made of the flour of maize, mixed with blood, and, after consecration by the priests, was distributed among the people, who, as they ate it, "showed signs of humiliation and sorrow, declaring it was the flesh of the deity!" [25] How could the Roman Catholic fail to recognize the awful ceremony of the Eucharist?

With the same feelings they witnessed another ceremony, that of the Aztec baptism; in which, after a solemn invocation, the head and lips of the infant were touched with water, and a name was given to it; while the goddess Cioacoatl, who presided over childbirth, was implored "that the sin which was given to us be-

---

worshipped by the natives of Cozumel, is, after all, nothing but a cross that was erected by the Spaniards in one of their own temples in that island after the Conquest. This fact he regards as "completely invalidating the strongest proof offered at this day that the Cross was recognized by the Indians as a symbol of worship." (Travels in Yucatan, vol. ii. chap. 20.) But, admitting the truth of this statement, that the Cozumel Cross is only a Christian relic, which the ingenious traveller has made extremely probable, his inference is by no means admissible. Nothing could be more natural than that the friars in Merida should endeavor to give celebrity to their convent by making it the possessor of so remarkable a monument as the very relic which proved, in their eyes, that Christianity had been preached at some earlier date among the natives. But the real proof of the existence of the Cross, as an object of worship, in the New World, does not rest on such spurious monuments as these, but on the unequivocal testimony of the Spanish discoverers themselves.

[25] "Lo recibian con gran reverencia, humiliacion, y lágrimas, diciendo que comian la carne de su Dios." Veytia, Hist. antig., lib. 1 cap. 18.—Also, Acosta, lib. 5, cap. 24.

Q*

fore the beginning of the world might not visit the child, but that, cleansed by these waters, it might live and be born anew !'' [26]

It is true, these several rites were attended with

[26] *Ante*, vol. i. p. 67.—Sahagun, Hist. de Nueva-España, lib. 6, cap. 37.—That the reader may see for himself how like, yet how unlike, the Aztec rite was to the Christian, I give the translation of Sahagun's account, at length : " When everything necessary for the baptism had been made ready, all the relations of the child were assembled, and the midwife, who was the person that performed the rite of baptism, was summoned. At early dawn, they met together in the court-yard of the house. When the sun had risen, the midwife, taking the child in her arms, called for a little earthen vessel of water, while those about her placed the ornaments which had been prepared for the baptism in the midst of the court. To perform the rite of baptism, she placed herself with her face towards the west, and immediately began to go through certain ceremonies. . . . After this she sprinkled water on the head of the infant, saying, ' O my child ! take and receive the water of the Lord of the world, which is our life, and is given for the increasing and renewing of our body. It is to wash and to purify. I pray that these heavenly drops may enter into your body, and dwell there ; that they may destroy and remove from you all the evil and sin which was given to you before the beginning of the world ; since all of us are under its power, being all the children of Chalchivitlycue' [the goddess of water]. She then washed the body of the child with water, and spoke in this manner : ' Whencesoever thou comest, thou that art hurtful to this child, leave him and depart from him, for he now liveth anew, and is born anew ; now is he purified and cleansed afresh, and our mother Chalchivitlycue again bringeth him into the world.' Having thus prayed, the midwife took the child in both hands, and, lifting him towards heaven, said, ' O Lord, thou seest here thy creature, whom thou hast sent into this world, this place of sorrow, suffering, and penitence. Grant him, O Lord, thy gifts, and thine inspiration, for thou art the great God, and with thee is the great goddess.' Torches of pine were kept burning during the performance of these ceremonies. When these things were ended, they gave the child the name of some one of his ancestors, in the hope that he might shed a new lustre over it. The name was given by the same midwife, or priestess, who baptized him."

many peculiarities, very unlike those in any Christian church. But the fathers fastened their eyes exclusively on the points of resemblance. They were not aware that the Cross was a symbol of worship, of the highest antiquity, in Egypt and Syria, [27] and that rites resembling those of communion [28] and baptism were practised by pagan nations on whom the light of Christianity had never shone. [29] In their amazement, they not only magnified what they saw, but were perpetually cheated by the illusions of their own heated imaginations. In this they were admirably assisted by their Mexican converts, proud to establish—and half

[27] Among Egyptian symbols we meet with several specimens of the Cross. One, according to Justus Lipsius, signified "life to come." (See his treatise, De Cruce (Lutetiæ Parisiorum, 1598), lib. 3, cap. 8.) We find another in Champollion's catalogue, which he interprets "support or saviour." (Précis, tom. ii., Tableau gén., Nos. 277, 348.) Some curious examples of the reverence paid to this sign by the ancients have been collected by McCulloh (Researches, p. 330, et seq.), and by Humboldt, in his late work, Géographie du Nouveau-Continent, tom. ii. p. 354, et seq.

[28] "Ante, Deos homini quod conciliare valeret
        Far erat,"

says Ovid. (Fastorum, lib. 1, v. 337.) Count Carli has pointed out a similar use of consecrated bread, and wine or water, in the Greek and Egyptian mysteries. (Lettres Améric., tom. i. let. 27.) See, also, McCulloh, Researches, p. 240, et seq.

[29] Water for purification and other religious rites is frequently noticed by the classical writers. Thus Euripides:

"Ἁγνοῖς καθαρμοῖς πρῶτά νιν νίψαι θέλω.
Θάλασσα κλύζει πάντα τἀνθρώπων κακά."
                IPHIG. IN TAUR., vv. 1192, 1194.

The notes on this place, in the admirable Variorum edition of Glasgow, 1821, contain references to several passages of similar import in different authors.

believing it themselves—a correspondence between their own faith and that of their conquerors.[30]

The ingenuity of the chronicler was taxed to find out analogies between the Aztec and Scripture histories, both old and new. The migration from Aztlan to Anahuac was typical of the Jewish exodus.[31] The places where the Mexicans halted on the march were identified with those in the journey of the Israelites;[32] and the name of Mexico itself was found to be nearly identical with the Hebrew name for the Messiah.[33] The Mexican hieroglyphics afforded a boundless field for the display of this critical acuteness. The most remarkable passages in the Old and New Testaments were read in their mysterious characters; and the eye of faith could trace there the whole story of the Pas-

[30] The difficulty of obtaining anything like a faithful report from the natives is the subject of complaint from more than one writer, and explains the great care taken by Sahagun to compare their narratives with each other. See Hist. de Nueva-España, Prólogo,—Ixtlilxochitl, Hist. Chich., MS., Pról.,—Boturini, Idea, p. 116.

[31] The parallel was so closely pressed by Torquemada that he was compelled to suppress the chapter containing it, on the publication of his book. See the Proemio to the edition of 1723, sec. 2.

[32] "The devil," says Herrera, "chose to imitate, in everything, the departure of the Israelites from Egypt, and their subsequent wanderings." (Hist. general, dec. 3, lib. 3, cap. 10.) But all that has been done by monkish annalist and missionary to establish the parallel with the children of Israel falls far short of Lord Kingsborough's learned labors, spread over nearly two hundred folio pages. (See Antiq. of Mexico, tom. vi. pp. 282-410.) *Quantum inane!*

[33] The word משיח, from which is derived *Christ*, "the anointed," is still more nearly—not "precisely," as Lord Kingsborough states (Antiq. of Mexico, vol. vi. p. 186)—identical with that of Mexi, or Mesi, the chief who was said to have led the Aztecs on the plains of Anahuac.

sion, the Saviour suspended from the cross, and the Virgin Mary with her attendant angels ![34]

The Jewish and Christian schemes were strangely mingled together, and the brains of the good fathers were still further bewildered by the mixture of heathenish abominations which were so closely intertwined with the most orthodox observances. In their perplexity, they looked on the whole as the delusion of the devil, who counterfeited the rites of Christianity and the traditions of the chosen people, that he might allure his wretched victims to their own destruction.[35]

But, although it is not necessary to resort to this startling supposition, nor even to call up an apostle from the dead, or any later missionary, to explain the coincidences with Christianity, yet these coincidences must be allowed to furnish an argument in favor of some primitive communication with that great brotherhood of nations on the old continent, among whom similar ideas have been so widely diffused. The probability of such a communication, especially with Eastern Asia, is much strengthened by the resemblance of sacerdotal institutions, and of some religious rites, as those of marriage,[36] and the burial of

[34] Interp. of Cod. Tel.-Rem. et Vat., Antiq. of Mexico, vol. vi.-Sahagun, Hist. de Nueva-España, lib. 3, Suplem. — Veytia, Hist. antig., lib. 1, cap. 16.

[35] This opinion finds favor with the best Spanish and Mexican writers, from the Conquest downwards. Solís sees nothing improbable in the fact that "the malignant influence, so frequently noticed in sacred history, should be found equally in profane." Hist. de la Conquista, lib. 2, cap. 4.

[36] The bridal ceremony of the Hindoos, in particular, contains curious points of analogy with the Mexican (See Asiatic Researches

the dead;[37] by the practice of human sacrifices, and
even of cannibalism, traces of which are discernible in
the Mongol races;[38] and, lastly, by a conformity of
social usages and manners, so striking that the description of Montezuma's court may well pass for that of the
Grand Khan's, as depicted by Maundeville and Marco
Polo.[39] It would occupy too much room to go into
details in this matter, without which, however, the
strength of the argument cannot be felt, nor fully established. It has been done by others; and an occasional
coincidence has been adverted to in the preceding
chapters.

It is true, we should be very slow to infer identity,
or even correspondence, between nations, from a partial resemblance of habits and institutions. Where

vol. vii. mem. 9.) The institution of a numerous priesthood, with the
practices of confession and penance, was familiar to the Tartar people.
(Maundeville, Voiage, chap. 23.) And monastic establishments were
found in Thibet and Japan from the earliest ages. Humboldt, Vues
des Cordillères, p. 179.

[37] "Doubtless," says the ingenious Carli, "the fashion of burning
the corpse, collecting the ashes in a vase, burying them under pyramidal mounds, with the immolation of wives and servants at the funeral,
all remind one of the customs of Egypt and Hindostan." Lettres
Améric., tom. ii. let. 10.

[38] Marco Polo notices a civilized people in Southeastern China, and
another in Japan, who drank the blood and ate the flesh of their captives, esteeming it the most savory food in the world,—" la più saporita
et migliore, che si possa truovar al mondo." (Viaggi, lib. 2, cap. 75; lib.
3, 13, 14.) The Mongols, according to Sir John Maundeville, regarded
the ears " sowced in vynegre" as a particular dainty. Voiage, chap. 23.

[39] Marco Polo, Viaggi, lib. 2, cap. 10.—Maundeville, Voiage, cap.
20, et alibi.—See, also, a striking parallel between the Eastern Asiatics
and Americans, in the Supplement to Ranking's "Historical Researches;" a work embodying many curious details of Oriental
history and manners in support of a whimsical theory.

this relates to manners, and is founded on caprice, it is not more conclusive than when it flows from the spontaneous suggestions of nature, common to all. The resemblance, in the one case, may be referred to accident; in the other, to the constitution of man. But there are certain arbitrary peculiarities, which, when found in different nations, reasonably suggest the idea of some previous communication between them. Who can doubt the existence of an affinity, or, at least, intercourse, between tribes who had the same strange habit of burying the dead in a sitting posture, as was practised to some extent by most, if not all, of the aborigines, from Canada to Patagonia?[40] The habit of burning the dead, familiar to both Mongols and Aztecs, is in itself but slender proof of a common origin. The body must be disposed of in some way; and this, perhaps, is as natural as any other. But when to this is added the circumstance of collecting the ashes in a vase and depositing the single article of a precious stone along with them, the coincidence is remarkable.[41]

[40] Morton, Crania Americana (Philadelphia, 1839), pp. 224-246.—The industrious author establishes this singular fact by examples drawn from a great number of nations in North and South America.

[41] Gomara, Crónica de la Nueva-España, cap. 202, ap. Barcia, tom. ii.—Clavigero, Stor. del Messico, tom. i. pp. 94, 95.—McCulloh (Researches, p. 198), who cites the Asiatic Researches.—Dr. McCulloh, in his single volume, has probably brought together a larger mass of materials for the illustration of the aboriginal history of the continent than any other writer in the language. In the selection of his facts he has shown much sagacity, as well as industry; and, if the formal and somewhat repulsive character of the style has been unfavorable to a popular interest, the work must always have an interest for those who are engaged in the study of the Indian antiquities. His fanciful speculations on the subject of Mexican mythology may amuse those whom they fail to convince.

Such minute coincidences are not unfrequent; while the accumulation of those of a more general character, though individually of little account, greatly strengthens the probability of a communication with the East.

A proof of a higher kind is found in the analogies of *science*. We have seen the peculiar chronological system of the Aztecs; their method of distributing the years into cycles, and of reckoning by means of periodical series, instead of numbers. A similar process was used by the various Asiatic nations of the Mongol family, from India to Japan. Their cycles, indeed, consisted of sixty, instead of fifty-two, years; and for the terms of their periodical series they employed the names of the elements and the signs of the zodiac, of which latter the Mexicans, probably, had no knowledge. But the principle was precisely the same.[42]

A correspondence quite as extraordinary is found between the hieroglyphics used by the Aztecs for the signs of the days, and those zodiacal signs which the Eastern Asiatics employed as one of the terms of their series. The symbols in the Mongolian calendar are borrowed from animals. Four of the twelve are the same as the Aztec. Three others are as nearly the same as the different species of animals in the two hemispheres would allow. The remaining five refer to no creature then found in Anahuac.[43] The resemblance went as

[42] *Ante*, vol. i. p. 114, et seq.

[43] This will be better shown by enumerating the zodiacal signs, used as the *names of the years* by the Eastern Asiatics. Among the Mongols, these were—1, mouse; 2, ox; 3, leopard; 4, hare; 5, crocodile; 6, serpent; 7, horse; 8, sheep; 9, monkey; 10, hen; 11, dog; 12, hog. The Mantchou Tartars, Japanese, and Thibetians have nearly the same terms, substituting, however, for No. 3, tiger; 5, dragon;

far as it could.[44] The similarity of these conventional symbols among the several nations of the East can hardly fail to carry conviction of a common origin for the system, as regards them. Why should not a similar conclusion be applied to the Aztec calendar, which, although relating to days instead of years, was, like the Asiatic, equally appropriated to chronological uses and to those of divination?[45]

I shall pass over the further resemblance to the Per-

8, goat. In the Mexican signs for the names of the days we also meet with *hare, serpent, monkey, dog.* Instead of the "leopard," "crocodile," and "hen,"—neither of which animals was known in Mexico at the time of the Conquest,—we find the *ocelotl*, the *lizard*, and the *eagle.*—The lunar calendar of the Hindoos exhibits a correspondence equally extraordinary. Seven of the terms agree with those of the Aztecs, namely, *serpent, cane, razor, path of the sun, dog's tail, house.* (Humboldt, Vues des Cordillères, p. 152.) These terms, it will be observed, are still more arbitrarily selected, not being confined to animals; as, indeed, the hieroglyphics of the Aztec calendar were derived indifferently from them, and other objects, like the signs of our zodiac. These scientific analogies are set in the strongest light by M. de Humboldt, and occupy a large and, to the philosophical inquirer, the most interesting portion of his great work. (Vues des Cordillères, pp. 125-194.) He has not embraced in his tables, however, the Mongol calendar, which affords even a closer approximation to the Mexican than that of the other Tartar races. Comp. Ranking, Researches, pp. 370, 371, note.

[44] There is some inaccuracy in Humboldt's definition of the *ocelotl* as "the tiger," "the jaguar." (Ibid., p. 159.) It is smaller than the jaguar, though quite as ferocious, and is as graceful and beautiful as the leopard, which it more nearly resembles. It is a native of New Spain, where the tiger is not known. (See Buffon, Histoire naturelle (Paris, An VIII), tom. ii., *vox Ocelotl.*) The adoption of this latter name, therefore, in the Aztec calendar, leads to an inference somewhat exaggerated.

[45] Both the Tartars and the Aztecs indicated the year by its sign; as the "year of the hare" or "rabbit," etc. The Asiatic signs, like-

sians, shown in the adjustment of time by a similar system of intercalation; [46] and to the Egyptians, in the celebration of the remarkable festival of the winter solstice; [47] since, although sufficiently curious, the co-incidences might be accidental, and add little to the weight of evidence offered by an agreement in com-binations of so complex and artificial a character as those before stated.

Amid these intellectual analogies, one would expect to meet with that of *language*, the vehicle of intellect-ual communication, which usually exhibits traces of its origin even when the science and literature that are embodied in it have widely diverged. No inquiry, however, has led to less satisfactory results. The lan-guages spread over the Western continent far exceed in number those found in any equal population in the Eastern. [48] They exhibit the remarkable anomaly of

wise, far from being limited to the years and months, presided also over days, and even hours. (Humboldt, Vues des Cordillères, p. 165.) The Mexicans had also astrological symbols appropriated to the hours. Gama, Descripcion, Parte 2, p. 117.

[46] *Ante*, vol. i. p. 115, note.

[47] Achilles Tatius notices a custom of the Egyptians,—who, as the sun descended towards Capricorn, put on mourning, but, as the days lengthened, their fears subsided, they robed themselves in white, and, crowned with flowers, gave themselves up to jubilee, like the Aztecs. This account, transcribed by Carli's French translator, and by M. de Humboldt, is more fully criticised by M. Jomard in the Vues des Cordillères, p. 309, et seq.

[48] Jefferson (Notes on Virginia (London, 1787), p. 164), confirmed by Humboldt (Essai politique, tom. i. p. 353). Mr. Gallatin comes to a different conclusion. (Transactions of American Antiquarian Society (Cambridge, 1836), vol. ii. p. 161.) The great number of American dialects and languages is well explained by the unsocial nature of a hunter's life, requiring the country to be parcelled out into small and separate territories for the means of subsistence.

differing as widely in etymology as they agree in organization; and, on the other hand, while they bear some slight affinity to the languages of the Old World in the former particular, they have no resemblance to them whatever in the latter.[49]   The Mexican was spoken for an extent of three hundred leagues.   But within the boundaries of New Spain more than twenty languages were found; not simply dialects, but, in many instances, radically different.[50]   All these idioms, however, with one exception, conformed to that peculiar synthetic structure by which every Indian dialect appears to have been fashioned, from the land of the Esquimaux to Terra del Fuego;[51] a system which, bringing the greatest number of ideas within the smallest possible compass, condenses whole sentences into a single word,[52] displaying a curious mechanism,

[49] Philologists have, indeed, detected two curious exceptions, in the Congo and primitive Basque; from which, however, the Indian languages differ in many essential points.   See Du Ponceau's Report, ap. Transactions of the Lit. and Hist. Committee of the Am. Phil. Society, vol. i.

[50] Vater (Mithridates, Theil iii. Abtheil. 3, p. 70), who fixes on the Rio Gila and the Isthmus of Darien as the boundaries within which traces of the Mexican language were to be discerned.   Clavigero estimates the number of dialects at thirty-five.   I have used the more guarded statement of M. de Humboldt, who adds that fourteen of these languages have been digested into dictionaries and grammars. Essai politique, tom. i. p. 352.

[51] No one has done so much towards establishing this important fact as that estimable scholar, Mr. Du Ponceau.   And the frankness with which he has admitted the exception that disturbed his favorite hypothesis shows that he is far more wedded to science than to system. See an interesting account of it, in his prize essay before the Institute, Mémoire sur le Système grammaticale des Langues de quelques Nations Indiennes de l'Amérique.   (Paris, 1838.)

[52] The Mexican language, in particular, is most flexible; admitting

in which some discern the hand of the philosopher, and others only the spontaneous efforts of the savage.[53]

The etymological affinities detected with the ancient continent are not very numerous, and they are drawn indiscriminately from all the tribes scattered over America. On the whole, more analogies have been found with the idioms of Asia than of any other quarter. But their amount is too inconsiderable to balance the opposite conclusion inferred by a total dissimilarity of structure.[54] A remarkable exception is found in the Othomi or Otomi language, which covers a wider territory than any other but the Mexican in New Spain,[55] and which, both in its monosyllabic composition, so different from those around it, and in its vo-

of combinations so easily that the most simple ideas are often buried under a load of accessories. The forms of expression, though picturesque, were thus made exceedingly cumbrous. A "priest," for example, was called *notlazomahuizteopixcatatzin*, meaning "venerable minister of God, that I love as my father." A still more comprehensive word is *amatlacuilolitquitcatlaxtlahuitli*, signifying "the reward given to a messenger who bears a hieroglyphical map conveying intelligence."

[53] See, in particular, for the latter view of the subject, the arguments of Mr. Gallatin, in his acute and masterly disquisition on the Indian tribes; a disquisition that throws more light on the intricate topics of which it treats than whole volumes that have preceded it. Transactions of the American Antiquarian Society, vol. ii., Introd., sec. 6.

[54] This comparative anatomy of the languages of the two hemispheres, begun by Barton (Origin of the Tribes and Nations of America (Philadelphia, 1797)), has been extended by Vater (Mithridates, Theil iii. Abtheil. 1, p. 348, et seq.). A selection of the most striking analogies may be found, also, in Malte Brun, book 75, table.

[55] *Othomi*, from *otho*, "stationary," and *mi*, "nothing." (Najera, Dissert., *ut infra*.) The etymology intimates the condition of this rude nation of warriors, who, imperfectly reduced by the Aztec arms, roamed over the high lands north of the Valley of Mexico.

cabulary, shows a very singular affinity to the Chinese.[56] The existence of this insulated idiom in the heart of this vast continent offers a curious theme for speculation, entirely beyond the province of history.

The American languages, so numerous and widely diversified, present an immense field of inquiry, which, notwithstanding the labors of several distinguished philologists, remains yet to be explored. It is only after a wide comparison of examples that conclusions founded on analogy can be trusted. The difficulty of making such comparisons increases with time, from the facility which the peculiar structure of the Indian languages affords for new combinations; while the insensible influence of contact with civilized man, in producing these, must lead to a still further distrust of our conclusions.

The theory of an Asiatic origin for Aztec civilization derives stronger confirmation from the light of *tradition*, which, shining steadily from the far Northwest, pierces through the dark shadows that history and mythology have alike thrown around the traditions of the country. Traditions of a Western or Northwestern origin were found among the more barbarous tribes,[57] and by the Mexicans were preserved

[56] See Najera's Dissertatio De Lingua Othomitorum, ap. Transactions of the American Philosophical Society, vol. v. New Series.— The author, a learned Mexican, has given a most satisfactory analysis of this remarkable language, which stands alone among the idioms of the New World, as the Basque—the solitary wreck, perhaps, of a primitive age—exists among those of the Old.

[57] Barton, p. 92.—Heckewelder, chap. 1, ap. Transactions of the Hist. and Lit. Committee of the Am. Phil. Soc., vol. i.—The various traditions have been assembled by M. Warden, in the Antiquités Mexicaines, part 2, p. 185, et seq.

both orally and in their hieroglyphical maps, where the different stages of their migration are carefully noted. But who, at this day, shall read them?[58] They are admitted to agree, however, in representing the populous North as the prolific hive of the American races.[59] In this quarter were placed their Aztlan and their Huehuetlapallan,—the bright abodes of their ancestors, whose warlike exploits rivalled those which the Teutonic nations have recorded of Odin and the mythic heroes of Scandinavia. From this quarter the

[58] The recent work of Mr. Delafield (Inquiry into the Origin of the Antiquities of America (Cincinnati, 1839)) has an engraving of one of these maps, said to have been obtained by Mr. Bullock from Boturini's collection. Two such are specified on page 10 of that antiquary's Catalogue. This map has all the appearance of a genuine Aztec painting, of the rudest character. We may recognize, indeed, the symbols of some dates and places, with others denoting the aspect of the country, whether fertile or barren, a state of war or peace, etc. But it is altogether too vague, and we know too little of the allusions, to gather any knowledge from it of the course of the Aztec migration.— Gemelli Carreri's celebrated chart contains the names of many places on the route, interpreted, perhaps, by Siguenza himself, to whom it belonged (Giro del Mondo, tom. vi. p. 56); and Clavigero has endeavored to ascertain the various localities with some precision. (Stor. del Messico, tom. i. p. 160, et seq.) But, as they are all within the boundaries of New Spain, and, indeed, south of the Rio Gila, they throw little light, of course, on the vexed question of the primitive abodes of the Aztecs.

[59] This may be fairly gathered from the agreement of the *traditionary* interpretations of the maps of the various people of Anahuac, according to Veytia; who, however, admits that it is "next to impossible," with the lights of the present day, to determine the precise route taken by the Mexicans. (Hist. antig., tom. i. cap. 2.) Lorenzana is not so modest. "Los Mexicanos por tradicion viniéron por el norte," says he, "y se saben ciertamente sus mansiones." (Hist. de Nueva-España, p. 81, nota.) There are some antiquaries who see best in the dark.

Toltecs, the Chichimecs, and the kindred races of the Nahuatlacs came successively up the great plateau of the Andes, spreading over its hills and valleys, down to the Gulf of Mexico.[60]

Antiquaries have industriously sought to detect some still surviving traces of these migrations. In the northwestern districts of New Spain, at the distance of a thousand miles from the capital, dialects have been discovered showing intimate affinity with the Mexican.[61] Along the Rio Gila, remains of populous towns are to be seen, quite worthy of the Aztecs in their style of architecture.[62] The country north of the great Rio Colorado has been imperfectly explored; but in the

[60] Ixtlilxochitl, Hist. Chich., MS., cap. 2, et seq.—Idem, Relaciones, MS.—Veytia, Hist. antig., ubi supra.—Torquemada, Monarch. Ind., tom. i. lib. 1.

[61] In the province of Sonora, especially along the Californian Gulf. The Cora language, above all, of which a regular grammar has been published, and which is spoken in New Biscay, about 30° north, so much resembles the Mexican that Vater refers them both to a common stock. Mithridates, Theil iii. Abtheil. 3, p. 143.

[62] On the southern bank of this river are ruins of large dimensions, described by the missionary Pedro Font on his visit there in 1775. (Antiq. of Mexico, vol. vi. p. 538.)—At a place of the same name, Casas Grandes, about 33° north, and, like the former, a supposed station of the Aztecs, still more extensive remains are to be found ; large enough, indeed, according to a late traveller, Lieut. Hardy, for a population of 20,000 or 30,000 souls. The country for leagues is covered with these remains, as well as with utensils of earthen-ware, obsidian, and other relics. A drawing which the author has given of a painted jar or vase may remind one of the Etruscan. "There were, also, good specimens of earthen images in the Egyptian style," he observes, "which are, *to me at least, so perfectly uninteresting* that I was at no pains to procure any of them." (Travels in the Interior of Mexico (London, 1829), pp. 464-466.) The lieutenant was neither a Boturini nor a Belzoni.

higher latitudes, in the neighborhood of Nootka, tribes still exist whose dialects, both in the termination and general sound of the words, bear considerable resemblance to the Mexican.[63] Such are the vestiges, few, indeed, and feeble, that still exist to attest the truth of traditions which themselves have remained steady and consistent through the lapse of centuries and the migrations of successive races.

The conclusions suggested by the intellectual and moral analogies with Eastern Asia derive considerable support from those of a *physical nature.* The aborigines of the Western World were distinguished by certain peculiarities of organization, which have led physiologists to regard them as a separate race. These peculiarities are shown in their reddish complexion, approaching a cinnamon color; their straight, black, and exceedingly glossy hair; their beard thin, and usually eradicated;[64] their high cheek-bones, eyes obliquely directed towards the temples, prominent noses, and narrow foreheads falling backwards with a greater inclination than those of any other race except the African.[65] From this general standard, however, there

[63] Vater has examined the languages of three of these nations, between 50° and 60° north, and collated their vocabularies with the Mexican, showing the probability of a common origin of many of the words in each. Mithridates, Theil iii. Abtheil. 3, p. 212.

[64] The Mexicans are noticed by M. de Humboldt as distinguished from the other aborigines whom he had seen, by the quantity both of beard and moustaches. (Essai politique, tom. i. p. 361.) The modern Mexican, however, broken in spirit and fortunes, bears as little resemblance, probably, in physical as in moral characteristics to his ancestors, the fierce and independent Aztecs.

[65] Prichard, Physical History, vol. i. pp. 167–169, 182, et seq.—

are deviations, in the same manner, if not to the same extent, as in other quarters of the globe, though these deviations do not seem to be influenced by the same laws of local position.[66] Anatomists, also, have discerned in crania disinterred from the mounds, and in those of the inhabitants of the high plains of the Cordilleras, an obvious difference from those of the more barbarous tribes. This is seen especially in the ampler forehead, intimating a decided intellectual superiority.[67] These characteristics are found to bear a close resemblance to those of the Mongolian family, and especially to the people of Eastern Tartary;[68] so that, notwithstanding certain differences recognized by physiologists, the skulls of the two races could not be readily

—Morton, Crania Americana, p. 66.—McCulloh, Researches, p. 18. —Lawrence, Lectures, pp. 317, 565.

[66] Thus we find, amidst the generally prevalent copper or cinnamon tint, nearly all gradations of color, from the European white, to a black, almost African; while the complexion capriciously varies among different tribes in the neighborhood of each other. See examples in Humboldt (Essai politique, tom. i. pp. 358, 359), also Prichard (Physical History, vol. ii. pp. 452, 522, et alibi), a writer whose various research and dispassionate judgment have made his work a text-book in this department of science.

[67] Such is the conclusion of Dr. Warren, whose excellent collection has afforded him ample means for study and comparison. (See his Remarks before the British Association for the Advancement of Science, ap. London Athenæum, Oct. 1837.) In the specimens collected by Dr. Morton, however, the barbarous tribes would seem to have a somewhat larger facial angle, and a greater quantity of brain, han the semi-civilized. Crania Americana, p. 259.

[68] "On ne peut se refuser d'admettre que l'espèce humaine n'offre pas de races plus voisines que le sont celles des Américains, des Mongols des Mantchoux, et des Malais." Humboldt, Essai politique, tom. i. p. 367.—Also, Prichard, Physical History, vol. i. pp. 184-186 vol. ii. pp. 365-367.—Lawrence, Lectures, p. 365.

distinguished from one another by a common observer. No inference can be surely drawn, however, without a wide range of comparison. That hitherto made has been chiefly founded on specimens from the barbarous tribes.[69] Perhaps a closer comparison with the more civilized may supply still stronger evidence of affinity.[70]

In seeking for analogies with the Old World, we should not pass by in silence the *architectural remains* of the country, which, indeed, from their resemblance

---

[69] Dr. Morton's splendid work on American crania has gone far to supply the requisite information. Out of about one hundred and fifty specimens of skulls, of which he has ascertained the dimensions with admirable precision, one-third belong to the semi-civilized races; and of them thirteen are Mexican. The number of these last is too small to found any general conclusions upon, considering the great diversity found in individuals of the same nation, not to say kindred.— Blumenbach's observations on American skulls were chiefly made, according to Prichard (Physical History, vol. i. pp. 183, 184), from specimens of the Carib tribes, as unfavorable, perhaps, as any on the continent.

[70] Yet these specimens are not so easy to be obtained. With uncommon advantages for procuring these myself in Mexico, I have not succeeded in obtaining any specimens of the genuine Aztec skull. The difficulty of this may be readily comprehended by any one who considers the length of time that has elapsed since the Conquest, and that the burial-places of the ancient Mexicans have continued to be used by their descendants. Dr. Morton more than once refers to his specimens as those of the " genuine Toltec skull, from cemeteries in Mexico, older than the Conquest." (Crania Americana, pp. 152, 155, 231, et alibi.) But how does he know that the heads are Toltec? That nation is reported to have left the country about the middle of the eleventh century, nearly eight hundred years ago,—according to Ixtlilxochitl, indeed, a century earlier; and it seems much more probable that the specimens now found in these burial-places should belong to some of the races who have since occupied the country, than to one so far removed. The presumption is manifestly too feeble to authorize any positive inference.

to the pyramidal structures of the East, have suggested to more than one antiquary the idea of a common origin.[71] The Spanish invaders, it is true, assailed the Indian buildings, especially those of a religious character, with all the fury of fanaticism. The same spirit survived in the generations which succeeded. The war has never ceased against the monuments of the country; and the few that fanaticism has spared have been nearly all demolished to serve the purposes of utility. Of all the stately edifices, so much extolled by the Spaniards who first visited the country, there are scarcely more vestiges at the present day than are to be found in some of those regions of Europe and Asia which once swarmed with populous cities, the great marts of luxury and commerce.[72] Yet some of these remains, like the temple of Xochicalco,[73] the

[71] The tower of Belus, with its retreating stories, described by Herodotus (Clio, sec. 181), has been selected as the model of the *teocalli;* which leads Vater somewhat shrewdly to remark that it is strange no evidence of this should appear in the erection of similar structures by the Aztecs in the whole course of their journey to Anahuac. (Mithridates, Theil iii. Abtheil. 3, pp. 74, 75.) The learned Niebuhr finds the elements of the Mexican temple in the mythic tomb of Porsenna. (Roman History, Eng. trans. (London, 1827), vol. i. p. 88.) The resemblance to the accumulated pyramids composing this monument is not very obvious. Comp. Pliny (Hist. Nat., lib. 36, sec. 19). Indeed, the antiquarian may be thought to encroach on the poet's province when he finds in Etruscan *fable*—" cum omnia excedat fabulositas," as Pliny characterizes this—the origin of Aztec science.

[72] See the powerful description of Lucan, Pharsalia, lib. 9, v. 966.—The Latin bard has been surpassed by the Italian, in the beautiful stanza beginning *Giace l' alta Cartago* (Gierusalemme Liberata, c. 15, s. 20), which may be said to have been expanded by Lord Byron into a canto,—the fourth of Childe Harold.

[73] The most remarkable remains on the proper Mexican soil are the

palaces of Tezcotzinco,[74] the colossal calendar-stone in the capital, are of sufficient magnitude, and wrought with sufficient skill, to attest mechanical powers in the Aztecs not unworthy to be compared with those of the ancient Egyptians.

But, if the remains on the Mexican soil are so scanty, they multiply as we descend the southeastern

temple or fortress of Xochicalco, not many miles from the capital. It stands on a rocky eminence, nearly a league in circumference, cut into terraces faced with stone. The building on the summit is seventy-five feet long and sixty-six broad. It is of hewn granite, put together without cement, but with great exactness. It was constructed in the usual pyramidal, terraced form, rising by a succession of stories, each smaller than that below it. The number of these is now uncertain; the lower one alone remaining entire. This is sufficient, however, to show the nice style of execution, from the sharp, salient cornices, and the hieroglyphical emblems with which it is covered, all cut in the hard stone. As the detached blocks found among the ruins are sculptured with bas-reliefs in like manner, it is probable that the whole building was covered with them. It seems probable, also, as the same pattern extends over different stones, that the work was executed after the walls were raised.—In the hill beneath, subterraneous galleries, six feet wide and high, have been cut to the length of one hundred and eighty feet, where they terminate in two halls, the vaulted ceilings of which connect by a sort of tunnel with the buildings above. These subterraneous works are also lined with hewn stone. The size of the blocks, and the hard quality of the granite of which they consist, have made the buildings of Xochicalco a choice quarry for the proprietors of a neighboring sugar-refinery, who have appropriated the upper stories of the temple to this ignoble purpose ! The Barberini at least built palaces, beautiful themselves, as works of art, with the plunder of the Coliseum. See the full description of this remarkable building, both by Dupaix and Alzate. (Antiquités Mexicaines, tom. i. Exp. I, pp. 15–20; tom. iii. Exp. I, Pl. 33.) A recent investigation has been made by order of the Mexican government, the report of which differs, in some of its details, from the preceding. Revista Mexicana, tom. i. mem. 5.

[74] *Ante*, vol. i. pp. 183–185.

slope of the Cordilleras, traverse the rich Valley of
Oaxaca, and penetrate the forests of Chiapa and Yucatan. In the midst of these lonely regions we meet
with the ruins, recently discovered, of several ancient
cities, Mitla, Palenque, and Itzalana or Uxmal,[75] which
argue a higher civilization than anything yet found on
the American continent; and, although it was not the
Mexicans who built these cities, yet, as they are probably the work of cognate races, the present inquiry
would be incomplete without some attempt to ascertain what light they can throw on the origin of the
Indian, and consequently of the Aztec, civilization.[76]

Few works of art have been found in the neighborhood of any of the ruins. Some of them, consisting
of earthen or marble vases, fragments of statues, and
the like, are fantastic, and even hideous; others show
much grace and beauty of design, and are apparently

[75] It is impossible to look at Waldeck's finished drawings of
buildings, where Time seems scarcely to have set his mark on
the nicely chiselled stone, and the clear tints are hardly defaced by
a weather-stain, without regarding the artist's work as a *restoration;*
a picture true, it may be, of those buildings in the day of their
glory, but not of their decay. — Cogolludo, who saw them in the
middle of the seventeenth century, speaks of them with admiration, as works of " accomplished architects," of whom history has
preserved no tradition. Historia de Yucatan (Madrid, 1688), lib.
4, cap. 2.

[76] In the original text is a description of some of these ruins, especially of those of Mitla and Palenque. It would have had novelty
at the time in which it was written, since the only accounts of these
buildings were in the colossal publications of Lord Kingsborough,
and in the Antiquités Mexicaines, not very accessible to most readers.
But it is unnecessary to repeat descriptions now familiar to every one,
and so much better executed than they can be by me, in the spirited
pages of Stephens.

well executed.[77] It may seem extraordinary that no
iron in the buildings themselves, nor iron tools, should
have been discovered, considering that the materials
used are chiefly granite, very hard, and carefully hewn
and polished. Red copper chisels and axes have been
picked up in the midst of large blocks of granite imperfectly cut, with fragments of pillars and architraves,
in the quarries near Mitla.[78] Tools of a similar kind
have been discovered, also, in the quarries near Thebes;
and the difficulty, nay, impossibility, of cutting such
masses from the living rock with any tools which we
possess, except iron, has confirmed an ingenious writer
in the supposition that this metal must have been employed by the Egyptians, but that its tendency to decomposition, especially in a nitrous soil, has prevented
any specimens of it from being preserved.[79] Yet iron
has been found, after the lapse of some thousands of
years, in the remains of antiquity; and it is certain
that the Mexicans, down to the time of the Conquest,
used only copper instruments, with an alloy of tin,
and a silicious powder, to cut the hardest stones,
some of them of enormous dimensions.[80] This fact,
with the additional circumstance that only similar

[77] See, in particular, two terra-cotta busts with helmets, found in
Oaxaca, which might well pass for Greek, both in the style of the
heads and the casques that cover them. Antiquités Mexicaines, tom.
iii. Exp. 2, Pl. 36.

[78] Dupaix speaks of these tools as made of pure copper. But doubtless there was some alloy mixed with it, as was practised by the Aztecs
and Egyptians; otherwise their edges must have been easily turned
by the hard substances on which they were employed.

[79] Wilkinson, Ancient Egyptians, vol. iii. pp. 246–254.

[80] *Ante*, vol. i. p. 142.

tools have been found in Central America, strengthens the conclusion that iron was neither known there nor in ancient Egypt.

But what are the nations of the Old Continent whose style of architecture bears most resemblance to that of the remarkable monuments of Chiapa and Yucatan? The points of resemblance will probably be found neither numerous nor decisive. There is, indeed, some analogy both to the Egyptian and Asiatic style of architecture in the pyramidal, terrace-formed bases on which the buildings repose, resembling also the Toltec and Mexican *teocalli*. A similar care, also, is observed in the people of both hemispheres to adjust the position of their buildings by the cardinal points. The walls in both are covered with figures and hieroglyphics, which, on the American as on the Egyptian, may be designed, perhaps, to record the laws and historical annals of the nation. These figures, as well as the buildings themselves, are found to have been stained with various dyes, principally vermilion;[81] a favorite color with the Egyptians also, who painted their colossal statues and temples of granite.[82] Notwithstanding these points of similarity, the Palenque architecture has little to remind us of the Egyptian or of the Oriental. It is, indeed, more conformable, in

[81] Waldeck, Atlas pittoresque, p. 73.—The fortress of Xochicalco was also colored with a red paint (Antiquités Mexicaines, tom. i. p. 20); and a cement of the same color covered the Toltec pyramid at Teotihuacan, according to Mr. Bullock, Six Months in Mexico, vol. ii. p. 143.

[82] Description de l'Égypte, Antiq., tom. ii. cap. 9, sec. 4.—The huge image of the Sphinx was originally colored red. (Clarke's Travels, vol. v. p. 202.) Indeed, many of the edifices, as well as statues, of ancient Greece, also, still exhibit traces of having been painted.

the perpendicular elevation of the walls, the moderate size of the stones, and the general arrangement of the parts, to the European. It must be admitted, however, to have a character of originality peculiar to itself.

More positive proofs of communication with the East might be looked for in their sculpture and in the conventional forms of their hieroglyphics. But the sculptures on the Palenque buildings are in relief, unlike the Egyptian, which are usually in *intaglio*. The Egyptians were not very successful in their representations of the human figure, which are on the same invariable model, always in profile, from the greater facility of execution this presents over the front view; the full eye is placed on the side of the head, while the countenance is similar in all, and perfectly destitute of expression.[83] The Palenque artists were equally awkward in representing the various attitudes of the body, which they delineated also in profile. But the parts are executed with much correctness, and sometimes gracefully; the costume is rich and various; and the ornamented head-dress, typical, perhaps, like the Aztec, of the name and condition of the person represented, conforms in its magnificence to the Oriental taste. The countenance is various, and often expressive. The contour of the head is, indeed, most extraordinary, describing almost a semicircle from the forehead to the tip of the nose, and contracted towards the crown,

[83] The various causes of the stationary condition of art in Egypt, for so many ages, are clearly exposed by the duke di Serradifalco, in his *Antichità della Sicilia* (Palermo, 1834, tom. ii. pp. 33, 34); a work in which the author, while illustrating the antiquities of a little island, has thrown a flood of light on the arts and literary culture of ancient Greece.

whether from the artificial pressure practised by many
of the aborigines, or from some preposterous notion
of ideal beauty.[84]   But, while superior in the execution of the details, the Palenque artist was far inferior
to the Egyptian in the number and variety of the
objects displayed by him, which on the Theban temples comprehend animals as well as men, and almost
every conceivable object of use or elegant art.

The hieroglyphics are too few on the American
buildings to authorize any decisive inference.   On
comparing them, however, with those of the Dresden
Codex, probably from this same quarter of the country,[85] with those on the monument of Xochicalco, and
with the ruder picture-writing of the Aztecs, it is not
easy to discern any thing which indicates a common
system.   Still less obvious is the resemblance to the
Egyptian characters, whose refined and delicate abbre-
viations approach almost to the simplicity of an alpha-
bet.   Yet the Palenque writing shows an advanced

[84] "The ideal is not always the beautiful," as Winckelmann truly
says, referring to the Egyptian figures. (Histoire de l'Art chez les
Anciens, liv. 4, chap. 2, trad. Fr.)   It is not impossible, however, that
the portraits mentioned in the text may be copies from life.   Some of
the rude tribes of America distorted their infants' heads into forms
quite as fantastic ; and Garcilaso de la Vega speaks of a nation discovered by the Spaniards in Florida, with a formation apparently not
unlike the Palenque: "*Tienen cabezas increiblemente largas, y ahu-
sadas para arriba*, que las ponen así con artificio, atándoselas desde el
punto, que nascen las criaturas, hasta que son de nueve ó diez años."
La Florida (Madrid, 1723), p. 190.

[85] For a notice of this remarkable codex, see *ante*, vol. i. p. 107.
There is, indeed, a resemblance, in the use of straight lines and dots,
between the Palenque writing and the Dresden MS.   Possibly these
dots denoted years, like the rounds in the Mexican system.

R*

stage of the art, and, though somewhat clumsy, intimates, by the conventional and arbitrary forms of the hieroglyphics, that it was symbolical, and perhaps phonetic, in its character.[86] That its mysterious import will ever be deciphered is scarcely to be expected. The language of the race who employed it, the race itself, is unknown. And it is not likely that another Rosetta stone will be found, with its trilingual inscription, to supply the means of comparison, and to guide the American Champollion in the path of discovery.

It is impossible to contemplate these mysterious monuments of a lost civilization without a strong feeling of curiosity as to who were their architects and what is their probable age. The data on which to rest our conjectures of their age are not very substantial; although some find in them a warrant for an antiquity of thousands of years, coeval with the architecture of Egypt and Hindostan.[87] But the interpretation of

[86] The hieroglyphics are arranged in perpendicular lines. The heads are uniformly turned towards the right, as in the Dresden MS.

[87] " Les ruines," says the enthusiastic chevalier Le Noir, "sans nom, à qui l'on a donné celui de *Palenque*, peuvent remonter comme les plus anciennes ruines du monde à trois mille ans. Ceci n'est point mon opinion seule ; c'est celle de *tous* les voyageurs qui ont vu les ruines dont il s'agit, de *tous* les archéologues qui en ont examiné les dessins ou lu les descriptions, enfin des historiens qui ont fait des recherches, et qui n'ont rien trouvé dans les annales du monde qui fasse soupçonner l'époque de la fondation de tels monuments, dont l'origine se perd dans la nuit des temps." (Antiquités Mexicaines, tom. ii., Examen, p. 73.) Colonel Galindo, fired with the contemplation of the American ruins, pronounces this country the true cradle of civilization, whence it passed over to China, and latterly to Europe, which, whatever " its foolish vanity" may pretend, has but just started in the march of improvement ! See his Letter on Copan, ap. Trans. of Am. Ant. Soc., vol. ii.

hieroglyphics, and the apparent duration of trees, are vague and unsatisfactory.[88] And how far can we derive an argument from the discoloration and dilapidated condition of the ruins, when we find so many structures of the Middle Ages dark and mouldering with decay, while the marbles of the Acropolis and the gray stone of Pæstum still shine in their primitive splendor?

There are, however, undoubted proofs of considerable age to be found there. Trees have shot up in the midst of the buildings, which measure, it is said, more than nine feet in diameter.[89] A still more striking fact is the accumulation of vegetable mould in one of the courts, to the depth of nine feet above the pavement.[90] This in our latitude would be decisive of a very great antiquity. But in the rich soil of Yucatan, and under the ardent sun of the tropics, vegetation bursts forth with irrepressible exuberance, and generations of plants succeed each other without intermission, leaving an accumulation of deposits that would have perished under a northern winter. Another evi-

[88] From these sources of information, and especially from the number of the concentric rings in some old trees, and the incrustation of stalactites found on the ruins of Palenque, M. Waldeck computes their age at between two and three thousand years. (Voyage en Yucatan, p. 78.) The criterion, as far as the trees are concerned, cannot be relied on in an advanced stage of their growth; and as to the stalactite formations, they are obviously affected by too many casual circumstances, to afford the basis of an accurate calculation.

[89] Waldeck, Voyage en Yucatan, ubi supra.

[90] Antiquités Mexicaines, Examen, p. 76.—Hardly deep enough, however, to justify Captain Dupaix's surmise of the antediluvian existence of these buildings; especially considering that the accumulation was in the sheltered position of an interior court.

dence of their age is afforded by the circumstance that in one of the courts of Uxmal the granite pavement, on which the figures of tortoises were raised in relief, is worn nearly smooth by the feet of the crowds who have passed over it ;[91] a curious fact, suggesting inferences both in regard to the age and population of the place. Lastly, we have authority for carrying back the date of many of these ruins to a certain period, since they were found in a deserted, and probably dilapidated, state by the first Spaniards who entered the country. Their notices, indeed, are brief and casual, for the old Conquerors had little respect for works of art ;[92] and it is fortunate for these structures that they

[91] Waldeck, Voyage en Yucatan, p. 97.

[92] The chaplain of Grijalva speaks with admiration of the "lofty towers of stone and lime, some of them very ancient," found in Yucatan. (Itinerario, MS. (1518).) Bernal Diaz, with similar expressions of wonder, refers the curious antique relics found there to the Jews. (Hist. de la Conquista, cap. 2, 6.) Alvarado, in a letter to Cortés, expatiates on the "maravillosos et grandes edificios" to be seen in Guatemala. (Oviedo, Hist. de las Ind., MS., lib. 33, cap. 42.) According to Cogolludo, the Spaniards, who could get no tradition of their origin, referred them to the Phœnicians or Carthaginians. (Hist. de Yucatan, lib. 4, cap. 2.) He cites the following emphatic notice of these remains from Las Casas: "Ciertamente la tierra de Yucathan da á entender cosas mui especiales, y de mayor antiguedad, por las grandes, admirables, y excessivas maneras de edificios, y letreros de ciertos caracteres, que en otra ninguna parte se hallan." (Loc. cit.) Even the inquisitive Martyr has collected no particulars respecting them, merely noticing the buildings of this region with general expressions of admiration. (De Insulis nuper Inventis, pp. 334-340.) What is quite as surprising is the silence of Cortés, who traversed the country forming the base of Yucatan, in his famous expedition to Honduras, of which he has given many details we would gladly have exchanged for a word respecting these interesting memorials. Carta Quinta de Cortés, MS.—I must add that some remarks in the above

had ceased to be the living temples of the gods, since no merit of architecture, probably, would have availed to save them from the general doom of the monuments of Mexico.

If we find it so difficult to settle the age of these buildings, what can we hope to know of their architects? Little can be gleaned from the rude people by whom they are surrounded. The old Tezcucan chronicler so often quoted by me, the best authority for the traditions of his country, reports that the Toltecs, on the breaking up of their empire,—which he places, earlier than most authorities, in the middle of the tenth century,—migrating from Anahuac, spread themselves over Guatemala, Tehuantepec, Campeachy, and the coasts and neighboring isles on both sides of the Isthmus.[93] This assertion, important, considering its source, is confirmed by the fact that several of the nations in that quarter adopted systems of astronomy and chronology, as well as sacerdotal institutions, very similar to the Aztec,[94] which, as we have seen, were

paragraph in the text would have been omitted, had I enjoyed the benefit of Mr. Stephens's researches when it was originally written. This is especially the case with the reflections on the probable condition of these structures at the time of the Conquest; when some of them would appear to have been still used for their original purposes.

[93] "Asimismo los Tultecas que escapáron se fuéron por las costas del Mar del Sur y Norte, como son Huatimala, Tecuantepec, Cuauh-zacualco, Campechy, Tecolotlan, y los de las Islas y Costas de una mar y otra, que despues se viniéron á multiplicar." Ixtlilxochitl, Relaciones, MS., No. 5.

[94] Herrera, Hist. general, dec. 4, lib. 10, cap. 1–4.—Cogolludo, Hist. de Yucatan, lib. 4, cap. 5.—Pet. Martyr, De Insulis, ubi supra.—M. Waldeck comes to just the opposite inference, namely, that the inhabitants of Yucatan were the true sources of the Toltec and Aztec

also probably derived from the Toltecs, their more polished predecessors in the land.

If so recent a date for the construction of the American buildings be thought incompatible with this oblivion of their origin, it should be remembered how treacherous a thing is tradition, and how easily the links of the chain are severed. The builders of the pyramids had been forgotten before the time of the earliest Greek historians.[95] The antiquary still disputes whether the frightful inclination of that architectural miracle, the tower of Pisa, standing as it does in the heart of a populous city, was the work of accident or design. And we have seen how soon the Tezcucans, dwelling amidst the ruins of their royal palaces, built just before the Conquest, had forgotten their history, while the more inquisitive traveller refers their construction to some remote period before the Aztecs.[96]

The reader has now seen the principal points of coincidence insisted on between the civilization of ancient Mexico and the Eastern hemisphere. In presenting them to him, I have endeavored to confine myself to such as rest on sure historic grounds, and not so much to offer my own opinion as to enable him to form one for himself. There are some material embarrassments in the way to this, however, which must

civilization. (Voyage en Yucatan, p. 72.) "Doubt must be our lot in everything," exclaims the honest Captain Dupaix,—"*the true faith always excepted.*" Antiquités Mexicaines, tom. i. p. 21.

[95] "Inter omnes eos non constat a quibus factæ sint, justissimo casu, obliteratis tantæ vanitatis auctoribus." Pliny, Hist. Nat., lib. 36, cap. 17.

[96] *Ante*, vol. i. p. 186.

not be passed over in silence. These consist, not in explaining the fact that, while the mythic system and the science of the Aztecs afford some striking points of analogy with the Asiatic, they should differ in so many more; for the same phenomenon is found among the nations of the Old World, who seem to have borrowed from one another those ideas, only, best suited to their peculiar genius and institutions. Nor does the difficulty lie in accounting for the great dissimilarity of the American languages to those in the other hemisphere; for the difference with these is not greater than what exists among themselves; and no one will contend for a separate origin for each of the aboriginal tribes.[97] But it is scarcely possible to reconcile the knowledge of Oriental science with the total ignorance of some of the most serviceable and familiar arts, as the use of milk and iron, for example; arts so simple, yet so important to domestic comfort, that when once acquired they could hardly be lost.

The Aztecs had no useful domesticated animals. And we have seen that they employed bronze, as a substitute for iron, for all mechanical purposes. The bison, or wild cow of America, however, which ranges in countless herds over the magnificent prairies of the west, yields milk like the tame animal of the same species in Asia and Europe;[98] and iron was scattered

[97] At least, this is true of the etymology of these languages, and, as such, was adduced by Mr. Edward Everett, in his Lectures on the Aboriginal Civilization of America, forming part of a course delivered some years since by that acute and highly accomplished scholar.

[98] The mixed breed, from the buffalo and the European stock, was known formerly in the northwestern counties of Virginia, says Mr. Gallatin (Synopsis, sec. 5); who is, however, mistaken in asserting

in large masses over the surface of the table-land. Yet there have been people considerably civilized in Eastern Asia who were almost equally strangers to the use of milk.[99] The buffalo range was not so much on the western coast as on the eastern slopes of the Rocky Mountains;[100] and the migratory Aztec might well doubt whether the wild, uncouth monsters whom he occasionally saw bounding with such fury over the distant plains were capable of domestication, like the meek animals which he had left grazing in the green pastures of Asia. Iron, too, though met with on the surface of the ground, was more tenacious, and harder to work, than copper, which he also found in much greater quantities on his route. It is possible, more-

that " the bison is not known to have ever been domesticated by the Indians." (Ubi supra.) Gomara speaks of a nation, dwelling about 40° north latitude, on the northwestern borders of New Spain, whose chief wealth was in droves of these cattle (*buyes con una giba sobre la cruz*, " oxen with a hump on the shoulders"), from which they got their clothing, food, and drink, which last, however, appears to have been only the blood of the animal. Historia de las Indias, cap. 214, ap. Barcia, tom. ii.

[99] The people of parts of China, for example, and, above all, of Cochin China, who never milk their cows, according to Macartney, cited by Humboldt, Essai politique, tom. iii. p. 58, note. See, also, p. 118.

[100] The native regions of the buffalo were the vast prairies of the Missouri, and they wandered over the long reach of country east of the Rocky Mountains, from 55° north, to the headwaters of the streams between the Mississippi and the Rio del Norte. The Columbia plains, says Gallatin, were as naked of game as of trees. (Synopsis, sec. 5.) That the bison was sometimes found also on the other side of the mountains, is plain from Gomara's statement. (Hist. de las Ind., loc. cit.) See, also, Laet, who traces their southern wanderings to the river Vaquimi (?), in the province of Cinaloa, on the Californian Gulf. Novus Orbis (Lugd. Bat , 1633), p. 286.

over, that his migration may have been previous to the
time when iron was used by his nation; for we have
seen more than one people in the Old World employing bronze and copper with entire ignorance, apparently, of any more serviceable metal.[101]—Such is the
explanation, unsatisfactory, indeed, but the best that
suggests itself, of this curious anomaly.

The consideration of these and similar difficulties
has led some writers to regard the antique American
civilization as purely indigenous. Whichever way we
turn, the subject is full of embarrassment. It is easy,
indeed, by fastening the attention on one portion of
it, to come to a conclusion. In this way, while some
feel little hesitation in pronouncing the American
civilization original, others, no less certainly, discern
in it a Hebrew, or an Egyptian, or a Chinese, or a
Tartar origin, as their eyes are attracted by the light

---

[101] *Ante*, vol. i. p. 142.
Thus Lucretius:

> " Et prior æris erat, quam ferri cognitus usus,
> Quo facilis magis est natura, et copia major.
> Ære solum terræ tractabant, æreque belli
> Miscebant fluctus."
>
> DE RERUM NATURA, lib. 5.

According to Carli, the Chinese were acquainted with iron 3000
years before Christ. (Lettres Améric., tom. ii. p. 63.) Sir J. G.
Wilkinson, in an elaborate inquiry into its first appearance among the
people of Europe and Western Asia, finds no traces of it earlier than
the sixteenth century before the Christian era. (Ancient Egyptians.
vol. iii. pp. 241–246.) The origin of the most useful arts is lost in
darkness. Their very utility is one cause of this, from the rapidity
with which they are diffused among distant nations. Another cause
is, that in the first ages of the discovery men are more occupied with
availing themselves of it than with recording its history; until time
turns history into fiction. Instances are familiar to every school-boy.

of analogy too exclusively to this or the other quarter. The number of contradictory lights, of itself, perplexes the judgment and prevents us from arriving at a precise and positive inference. Indeed, the affectation of this, in so doubtful a matter, argues a most unphilosophical mind. Yet where there is most doubt there is often the most dogmatism.

The reader of the preceding pages may perhaps acquiesce in the general conclusions,—not startling by their novelty,—

First, that the coincidences are sufficiently strong to authorize a belief that the civilization of Anahuac was in some degree influenced by that of Eastern Asia.

And, secondly, that the discrepancies are such as to carry back the communication to a very remote period; so remote that this foreign influence has been too feeble to interfere materially with the growth of what may be regarded in its essential features as a peculiar and indigenous civilization.

APPENDIX.

PART II.

ORIGINAL DOCUMENTS.

(403)

APPENDIX, PART II.

ORIGINAL DOCUMENTS.

No. 1.—See vol. i. p. 153.

ADVICE OF AN AZTEC MOTHER TO HER DAUGHTER;
TRANSLATED FROM SAHAGUN'S "HISTORIA DE NUEVA-
ESPAÑA," LIB. VI. CAP. XIX.

[I have thought it best to have this translation made
in the most literal manner, that the reader may have a
correct idea of the strange mixture of simplicity, approaching to childishness, and moral sublimity, which
belongs to the original. It is the product of the twilight
of civilization.]

My beloved daughter, very dear little dove, you have already
heard and attended to the words which your father has told you.
They are precious words, and such as are rarely spoken or listened
to, and which have proceeded from the bowels and heart in which
they were treasured up; and your beloved father well knows that you
are his daughter, begotten of him, are his blood, and his flesh; and
God our Lord knows that it is so. Although you are a woman, and
are *the image of your father*, what more can I say to you than has already been said? What more can you hear than what you have heard
from your lord and father? who has fully told you what it is becoming
for you to do and to avoid; nor is there anything remaining, which
concerns you, that he has not touched upon. Nevertheless, that I
may do towards you my whole duty, I will say to you some few words.

—The first thing that I earnestly charge upon you is, that you observe and do not forget what your father has now told you, since it is all very precious; and persons of his condition rarely publish such things; for they are the words which belong to the noble and wise,—valuable as rich jewels. See, then, that you take them and lay them up in your heart, and write them in your bowels. If God gives you life, with these same words will you teach your sons and daughters, if God shall give you them.—The second thing that I desire to say to you is, that I love you much, that you are my dear daughter. Remember that nine months I bore you in my womb, that you were born and brought up in my arms. I placed you in your cradle, and in my lap, and with my milk I nursed you. This I tell you, in order that you may know that I and your father are the source of your being; it is we who now instruct you. See that you receive our words, and treasure them in your breast.—Take care that your garments are such as are decent and proper; and observe that you do not adorn yourself with much finery, since this is a mark of vanity and of folly. As little becoming is it, that your dress should be very mean, dirty, or ragged; since rags are a mark of the low, and of those who are held in contempt. Let your clothes be becoming and neat, that you may neither appear fantastic nor mean. When you speak, do not hurry your words from uneasiness, but speak deliberately and calmly. Do not raise your voice very high, nor speak very low, but in a moderate tone. Neither mince, when you speak, nor when you salute, nor speak through your nose; but let your words be proper, of a good sound, and your voice gentle. Do not be nice in the choice of your words. In walking, my daughter, see that you behave becomingly, neither going with haste, nor too slowly; since it is an evidence of being puffed up, to walk too slowly, and walking hastily causes a vicious habit of restlessness and instability. Therefore neither walk very fast, nor very slow; yet, when it shall be necessary to go with haste, do so,—in this use your discretion. And when you may be obliged to jump over a pool of water, do it with decency, that you may neither appear clumsy nor light. When you are in the street, do not carry your head much inclined, or your body bent; nor as little go with your head very much raised; since it is a mark of ill breeding; walk erect, and with your head slightly inclined. Do not have your mouth covered, or your face, from shame, nor go looking like a near-sighted person, nor, on your way, make fantastic movements with your feet. Walk through the street quietly, and with propriety. Another thing that you must attend to, my daughter, is, that when you are in the street you do not go looking hither and thither, nor turning your head to look at this and that; walk neither looking at the skies nor on the ground. Do not look upon those whom you meet with the eyes of an offended person, nor have the appearance of being uneasy; but of one who looks upon all with a serene countenance; doing this, you will give no one occasion of being offended with you. Show a becoming countenance; that you m1y neither appear morose, nor, on the other hand, too complaisant. See, my daughter, that you give yourself no concern about the words you may hear, in going through the street, nor pay any regard to them, let those who come and go say what they will. Take care that you neither answer nor speak, but act as if you neither heard nor understood them; since, doing in this manner, no one will be able to say with truth that you have said anything amiss. See, likewise, my daughter, that you never paint your face, or stain it or your lips with colors, in order to appear well; since this is a mark of vile and unchaste women. Paints and coloring are things which bad women use,—the immodest, who have lost all shame and even sense, who are like fools and drunkards, and are called *rameras* [prostitutes]. But, that your husband may not dislike you, adorn yourself, wash yourself, and cleanse your clothes; and let this be done with moderation; since if every day you wash yourself and your clothes it will be said of you that you are over-nice,—too delicate; they will call you *tapepetzon tinemaxoch.*—My daughter, this is the course you are to take; since in this manner the ancestors from whom you spring brought us up. Those noble and venerable dames, your grandmothers, told us not so many things as I have told you,—they said but few words, and spoke thus: " Listen, my daughters; in this world it is necessary to live with much prudence and circumspection. Hear this allegory, which I shall now tell you, and preserve it, and take from it a warning and example for living aright. Here, in this world, we travel by a very narrow, steep, and dangerous road, which is as a lofty mountain ridge, on whose top passes a narrow path; on either side is a great gulf without bottom; and if you deviate from the path you will fall into it. There is need, therefore, of much discretion in pursuing the road." My tenderly loved daughter, my little dove, keep this illustration in your heart, and see that you do not forget it,—it will be to you as a lamp and a beacon so long as you shall live in this world. Only one thing remains to be said, and I have done. If God shall give you life, if you shall continue some years upon the earth, see that you guard yourself carefully, that no stain come upon you; should you forfeit your chastity and afterwards be asked in marriage and should marry any one, yo: will never be fortunate, nor have true love,—he will always remembe: that you were not a virgin, and this will be the cause of great affliction and distress; you will never be at peace, for your husband will always be suspicious of you. O my dearly beloved daughter, if you shall live upon the earth, see that not more than one man approaches you; and observe what I now shall tell you, as a strict command. When it shall please God that you receive a husband, and you are placed under his authority, be free from arrogance, see that you do not neglect him, nor allow your heart to be in opposition to him. Be not disrespectful to him. Beware that in no time or place you commit the treason against him called adultery. See that you give no favor to another; since this, my dear and much-loved daughter, is to fall into a pit without bottom, from which there will be no escape. According to the custom of the world, if it shall be known, for this crime they will kill you, they will throw you into the street, for an example to all the people, where your head will be crushed and dragged upon the ground. Of these says a proverb, "You will be stoned and dragged upon the earth, and others will take warning at your death." From this will arise a stain and dishonor upon our ancestors, the nobles and senators from whom we are descended. You will tarnish their illustrious fame, and their glory, by the filthiness and impurity of your sin. You will, likewise, lose your reputation, your nobility, and honor of birth; your name will be forgotten and abhorred. Of you will it be said that you were buried in the dust of your sins. And remember, my daughter, that, though no man shall see you, nor your husband ever know what happens, *God, who is in every place, sees you*, will be angry with you, and will also excite the indignation of the people against you, and will be avenged upon you as he shall see fit. By his command, you shall either be maimed, or struck blind, or your body will wither, or you will come to extreme poverty, for daring to injure your husband. Or perhaps he will give you to death, and put you under his feet, sending you to the place of torment. Our Lord is compassionate; but, if you commit treason against your husband, God, who is in every place, shall take vengeance on your sin, and will permit you to have neither contentment, nor repose, nor a peaceful life; and he will excite your husband to be always unkind towards you, and always to speak to you with anger. My dear daughter, whom I tenderly love, see that you live in the world in peace, tranquillity, and contentment, all the days that you shall live. See that you disgrace not yourself, that you stain not your honor, nor pollute the lustre and fame of your ancestors. See that you honor me and your father, and reflect glory on us by your good life. May God prosper you, my first-born, and may you come to God, who is in every place.

No. II.—See vol. i. p. 175.

A CASTILIAN AND AN ENGLISH TRANSLATION OF A POEM ON THE MUTABILITY OF LIFE, BY NEZAHUALCOYOTL, LORD OF TEZCUCO.

[This poem was fortunately rescued from the fate of too many of the Indian MSS., by the chevalier Boturini, and formed part of his valuable *Muséo*. It was subsequently incorporated in the extensive collection of documents made by Father Manuel de la Vega, in Mexico, 1792. This magnificent collection was made in obedience to an enlightened order of the Spanish government, "that all such MSS. as could be found in New Spain, fitted to illustrate the antiquities, geography, civil, ecclesiastical, and natural history of America, should be copied and transmitted to Madrid." This order was obeyed, and the result was a collection of thirty-two volumes in folio, which, amidst much that is trivial and of little worth, contains also a mass of original materials, of inestimable value to the historian of Mexico and of the various races who occupied the country of New Spain.]

Un rato cantar quiero,
pues la ocasion y el tiempo se ofrece;

ser admitido espero,
si intento lo merece;
y comienzo mi canto,
aunque fuera mejor llamarle llanto,
    Y tú, querido Amigo,
goza la amenidad de aquestas flores,
alégrate conmigo;
desechemos de pena los temores,
que el gusto trae medida,
por ser al fin con fin la mala vida.

    Io tocaré cantando
el músico instrumento sonoroso,
tú de flores gozando
danza, y festeja á Dios que es Poderoso,
gocemos de esta gloria,
porque la humana vida es transitoria.

    De Ocblehacan pusiste
en esta noble Corte, y siendo tuyo,
tus sillas, y quisiste
vestirlas; donde arguyo,
que con grandeza tanta
el Imperio se aumenta y se levanta.

    Oyoyotzin prudente,
famoso Rey y singular Monarca,
goza del bien presente,
que lo presente lo florido abarca;
porque vendrá algun dia
que busques este gusto y alegría.

    Entonces tu Fortuna
te ha de quitar el Cetro de la mano,
ha de menguar tu Luna
no te verás tan fuerte y tan ufano;
entonces tus criados
de todo bien serán desamparados.

    Y en tan triste suceso
los nobles descendientes de tu nido,
de Príncipes el peso,
los que de nobles Padres han nacido,
faltando tú Cabeza,
gustarán la amargura de pobreza.

Y traerán á la memoria
quien fuíste en pompa de todos envidiada
tus triunfos y victoria;
y con la gloria y Magestad pasada
ootcjando pesares,
de lágrimas harán crecidas Mares.

Y estos tus descendientes,
que te sirven de pluma y de corona
de tí viéndose ausentes,
de Culhuacan estrañarán la cuna,
y tenidos por tales
con sus desdichas crecerán sus males.

Y de esta grandeza rara,
digna de mil coronas y blasones,
será la fama avara;
solo se acordarán en las naciones,
lo bien que governáron,
las tres Cabezas que el imperio honráron.

En México famosa
Moctezumá, valor de pecho Indiano;
á Culhuacan dichosa
de Neçahualcoyotl rigió la mano;
Acatlapan la fuerte
Totoquilhuastli le salió por suerte.

Y ningun olvido temo
de lo bien que tu reyno dispusíste,
estando en el supremo
lugar, que de la mano recibíste
de aquel Señor del Mundo,
factor de aquestas cosas sin segundo.

Y goza pues muy gustoso,
O Neçahualcoyotl, lo que agora tienes
con flores de este hermoso
jardin corona tus ilustres sienes;
oye mi canto, y lira
que á darte gustos y placeres tira.

Y los gustos de esta vida,
sus riquezas, y mandos son prestados,
son sustancia fingida,
con apariencias solo matizados;

y es tan gran verdad esta,
que á una pregunta me has de dar respuesta,
    ¿Y que es de Cihuapan,
y Quantzintecomtzin el valiente,
y Conahuatzin;
que es de toda esa gente?
sus voces; ¡agora acaso!
ya están en la otra vida, este es el caso.
    ¡Ojala los, que agora
juntos los tiene del amor el hilo,
que amistad atesora,
vieramos de la muerte el duro filo!
porque no hay bien seguro,
que siempre trae mudanza á lo futuro,

Now would I sing, since time and place
    Are mine,—and oh! with thee
May this my song obtain the grace
    My purpose claims for me.
I wake these notes on song intent,
But call it rather a lament.
Do thou, beloved, now delight
In these my flowers, pure and bright,
    Rejoicing with thy friend;
Now let us banish pain and fear,
For, if our joys are measured here,
    Life's sadness hath its end.

And I will strike, to aid my voice,
    The deep, sonorous chord;
Thou, dancing, in these flowers rejoice,
    And feast Earth's mighty Lord;
Seize we the glories of to-day,
For mortal life fleets fast away.—
In Ocblehacan, all thine own,
Thy hand hath placed the noble throne

Which thou hast richly dressed ;
From whence I argue that thy sway
Shall be augmented day by day,
  In rising greatness blessed.

Wise Oyoyotzin ! prudent king !
  Unrivalled Prince, and great !
Enjoy the fragrant flowers that spring
  Around thy kingly state ;
A day will come which shall destroy
Thy present bliss,—thy present joy,—
When fate the sceptre of command
Shall wrench from out thy royal hand,—
  Thy moon diminished rise ;
And, as thy pride and strength are quenched,
From thy adherents shall be wrenched
  All that they love or prize.

When sorrow shall my truth attest,
  And this thy throne decline,—
The birds of thy ancestral nest,
  The princes of thy line,—
The mighty of thy race,—shall see
The bitter ills of poverty ;—
And then shall memory recall
Thy envied greatness, and on all
  Thy brilliant triumphs dwell ;
And as they think on by-gone years,
Compared with present shame, their tears
  Shall to an ocean swell.

And those who, though a royal band,
  Serve thee for crown, or plume,
Remote from Culhuacan's land
  Shall find the exile's doom.
Deprived of thee,—their rank forgot,—
Misfortune shall o'erwhelm their lot.
Then fame shall grudgingly withhold
Her meed to greatness, which of old
  Blazons and crowns displayed ;

35*

The people will retain alone
Remembrance of that *triple throne*
   Which this our land obeyed.

Brave Moctezuma's Indian land
   Was Mexico the great,
And Nezahualcoyotl's hand
   Blessed Culhuacan's state,
Whilst Totoquil his portion drew
In Acatlapan, strong and true;
But no oblivion can I fear,
Of good by thee accomplished here,
   Whilst high upon thy throne;
That station, which, to match thy worth,
Was given by the Lord of Earth,
   Maker of good alone.

Then, Nezahualcoyotl,—now,
   In what thou *hast*, delight;
And wreathe around thy royal brow
   Life's garden blossoms bright;
List to my lyre and my lay,
Which aim to please thee, and obey.
The pleasures which our lives present—
Earth's sceptres, and its wealth—are lent,
   Are shadows fleeting by;
Appearance colors all our bliss;
A truth so great, that now to this
   One question, make reply.

What has become of Cihuapan,
   Quantzintecomtzin brave,
And Conahuatzin, mighty man;
   Where are they?   In the grave!
Their names remain, but they are fled,
Forever numbered with the dead.
Would that those now in friendship bound,
We whom Love's thread encircles round,
   Death's cruel edge might see!
Since good on earth is insecure,
And all things must a change endure
   In dark futurity!

No. III.—See vol. i. p. 178.

DESCRIPTION OF THE RESIDENCE OF NEZAHUALCOYOTL AT TEZCOTZINCO, EXTRACTED FROM IXTLILXOCHITL'S "HISTORIA CHICHIMECA," MS., CAP. XLII.

De los jardines el mas ameno y de curiosidades fué el Bosque de Tezcotzinco; porque demas de la cerca tan grande que tenia, para subir á la cumbre de él, y andarlo todo, tenia sus gradas, parte de ellas de argamasa, parte labrada en la misma peña; y el agua que se trahia para las Fuentes, Pilas, y Baños, y los caños que se repartian para el riego de las Flores y arboledas de este Bosque, para poderla traer desde su Nacimiento, fué menester hacer fuertes y altíssimas murallas de argamasa desde unas sierras á otras, de increible grandeza; sobre la qual hizo una Fargea hasta venir á dar á la mas alta del Bosque, y á las espaldas de la cumbre de él. En el primer Estanque de Agua estaba una Peña esculpida en ella en circunferencia los años desde que havia nacido el Rey Nezahualcoiotzin hasta la edad de aquel tiempo; y por la parte de afuera los años en fin de cada uno de ellos, así mismo esculpidas las cosas mas memorables que hizo: y por dentro de la rueda esculpidas sus Armas, que eran una casa, que estaba ardiendo, en llamas y desaciéndose; otra que estaba muy ennoblecida de edificios: y en medio de las dos un pie de venado, atada en él una piedra preciosa, y salian del pie unos penachos de plumas preciosas, y así mismo una cierva, y en ella un Brazo asido de un Arco con unas Flechas, y como un Hombre armado con su Morrion y oregeras, coselete, y dos tigres á los Lados, de cuias bocas salian agua y fuego, y por orla, doce cabezas de Reyes y Señores, y otras cosas que el primer Arzobispo de México, Don Fray Juan de Zumarraga, mandó hacer pedazos, entendiendo ser algunos Ídolos; y todo lo referido era la etimología de sus Armas. Y de allí se partia esta agua en dos partes, que la una iba cercando y rodeando el Bosque por la parte del Norte, y la otra por la parte del Sur. En la cumbre de este Bosque estaban edificadas unas casas á manera de torre, y por remate y Chapitel estaba hecha de cantería una como á manera de Mazeta, y dentra de ella salian unos Penachos y plumeros, que era la etimología del nombre del Bosque; y luego mas abajo, hecho de una Peña, un Leon de mas de dos brazas de largo con sus alas y plumas: estaba hechado y mirando á la parte del Oriente, en cuia boca asomaba un rostro, que era el mismo retrato del Rey, el qual Leon estaba de ordinario debajo de un palio hecho de oro y plumería. Un poquito mas abajo estaban tres Albercas de agua, y en la de en medio estaban en sus Bordos tres Damas esculpidas y labradas en la misma Peña, que significaban la gran Laguna y las Ramas las cabezas del Imperio; y por un lado (que era hacia la parte del Norte) otra Alberca, y en una Peña esculpido el nombre y Escudo de Armas de la Ciudad de Tolan, que fué cabecera de los Tultecas; y por el lado izquierdo, que caia hacia la parte del Sur, estaba la otra Alberca, y en la peña esculpido el Escudo de Armas y nombre de la Ciudad de Tenaiocan, que fué la cabecera del Imperio de los Chichimecas; y de esta Alberca salia un caño de Agua, que saltando sobre unas peñas salpicaba el Agua, que iba á caer á un Jardin de todas flores olorosas de Tierra caliente, que parecia que llovia con la precipitacion y golpe que daba el agua sobre la peña. Tras este jardin se seguian los Baños hechos y labrados de peña viva, que con dividirse en dos Baños eran de una pieza; y por aquí se bajaba por una peña grandísima de unas gradas hechas de la misma peña, tan bien gravadas y lizas, que parecian Espejos; y por el pretil de estas gradas estaba esculpido el dia, mes, y año, y hora, en que se le dió aviso al Rey Nezahualcoiotzin de la muerte de un Señor de Huexotzinco, á quien quisó y amó notablemente, y le cojió esta nueva quando se estaban haciendo estas gradas. Luego consecutivamente estaba el Alcazar y Palacio que el Rey tenia en el Bosque, en los quales havia, entre otras muchas salas, aposentos, y retretes, una muy grandísima, y delante de ella un Patio, en la qual recivia á los Reyes de México y Tlacopan, y á otros Grandes Señores, quando se iban á holgar con él, y en el Patio se hacian las Damas, y algunas representaciones de gusto y entretenimiento. Estaban estos alcazares con tan admirable y maravillosa hechura, y con tanta diversidad de piedras, que no parecian ser hechos de industria humana. El Aposento donde el Rey dormia era redondo; todo lo demas de este Bosque, como dicho tengo, estaba plantado de diversidad de Árboles, y flores odoríferas, y en ellos diversidad de Aves, sin las que el Rey tenia en jaulas, traidas de diversas partes, que hacian una armonia, y canto, que no se oian las Gentes. Fuera de las florestas, que las dividia, una Pared entraba la Montaña, en que havia muchos venados, conejos, y liebres, que si de cada cosa muy particular se describiese, y de los demas Bosques de este Reyno, era menester hacer Historia muy particular.

No. IV.—See vol. i. p. 201.

TRANSLATION FROM IXTLILXOCHITL'S "HISTORIA CHICHI-MECA," MS., CAP. LXIV.

OF THE EXTRAORDINARY SEVERITY WITH WHICH THE KING
NEZAHUALPILLI PUNISHED THE MEXICAN QUEEN FOR HER
ADULTERY AND TREASON.

When Axaiacatzin, king of Mexico, and other lords, sent their
daughters to king Nezahualpilli, for him to choose one to be his queen
and lawful wife, whose son might succeed to the inheritance, she who
had highest claims among them, from nobility of birth and rank, was
Chachiuhnenetzin, daughter of the Mexican king. But, being at that
time very young, she was brought up by the monarch in a separate
palace, with great pomp and numerous attendants, as became the
daughter of so great a king. The number of servants attached to
her household exceeded two thousand. Young as she was, she was
yet exceedingly artful and vicious; so that, finding herself alone, and
seeing that her people feared her, on account of her rank and importance, she began to give way to the unlimited indulgence of her lust.
Whenever she saw a young man who pleased her fancy, she gave
secret orders to have him brought to her, and, having satisfied her
desires, caused him to be put to death. She then ordered a statue or
effigy of his person to be made, and, adorning it with rich clothing,
gold, and jewelry, had it placed in the apartment in which she lived.
The number of statues of those whom she thus put to death was so
great as almost to fill the apartment. When the king came to visit
her, and inquired respecting these statues, she answered that they
were her gods; and he, knowing how strict the Mexicans were in
the worship of their false deities, believed her. But, as no iniquity
can be long committed with entire secrecy, she was finally found out
in this manner. Three of the young men, for some reason or other,
she had left alive. Their names were Chicuhcoatl, Huitzilimitzin, and
Maxtla, one of whom was lord of Tesoyucan, and one of the grandees
of the kingdom; and the other two, nobles of high rank. It happened that one day the king recognized on one of these a very precious
jewel, which he had given to the queen; and, although he had no fear
of treason on her part, it gave him some uneasiness. Proceeding to
visit her that night, her attendants told him that she was asleep, sup-

s*

posing that the king would then return, as he had done at other times. But the affair of the jewel made him insist on entering the chamber in which she slept; and, going to awake her, he found only a statue in the bed, adorned with her hair, and closely resembling her. This being seen by the king, and also that the attendants around were in much trepidation and alarm, he called his guards, and, assembling all the people of the house, made a general search for the queen, who was shortly found, at an entertainment with the three young lords, who were likewise arrested with her. The king referred the case to the judges of his court, in order that they might make an inquiry into the matter and examine the parties implicated. These discovered many individuals, servants of the queen, who had in some way or other been accessory to her crimes, workmen who had been engaged in making and adorning the statues, others who had aided in introducing the young men into the palace, and others again who had put them to death and concealed their bodies. The case having been sufficiently investigated, he despatched ambassadors to the kings of Mexico and Tlacopan, giving them information of the event, and signifying the day on which the punishment of the queen and her accomplices was to take place; and he likewise sent through the empire to summon all the lords to bring their wives and their daughters, however young they might be, to be witnesses of a punishment which he designed for a great example. He also made a truce with all the enemies of the empire, in order that they might come freely to see it. The time being arrived, so great was the concourse of people gathered on the occasion, that, large as was the city of Tezcuco, they could scarcely all find room in it. The execution took place publicly, in sight of the whole city. The queen was put to the *garrote* [a method of strangling by means of a rope twisted round a stick], as well as her three gallants; and, from their being persons of high birth, their bodies were burned, together with the effigies before mentioned. The other parties who had been accessory to the crime, who were more than two thousand persons, were also put to the *garrote*, and buried in a pit made for the purpose in a ravine near a temple of the Idol of Adulterers. All applauded so severe and exemplary a punishment, except the Mexican lords, the relations of the queen, who were much incensed at so public an example, and, although for the present they concealed their resentment, meditated future revenge. It was not without cause that the king experienced this disgrace in his household, since he was thus punished for the unworthy means made use of by his father to obtain his mother as a wife.

No. V.—See vol. i. p. 248.

INSTRUCTIONS GIVEN BY VELASQUEZ, GOVERNOR OF CUBA, TO CORTÉS ON HIS TAKING COMMAND OF THE EXPEDITION ; DATED AT FERNANDINA, OCTOBER 23, 1518.

[The instrument forms part of the Muñoz collection.]

Por quanto yo Diego Velasquez, Alcalde, capitan general, é repartidor de los caciques é yndios de esta isla Fernandina por sus Altezas, &c., embié los dias pasados, en nombre é servicio de sus Altezas, aver é bojar la ysla de Yucatan Sta María de los remedios, que nuevamente habia descubierto, é á descobrir lo demas que Dios N^{ro} S^{or} fuese servido, y en nombre de sus Altezas tomar la posesion de todo, una armada con la gente necesaria, en que fué é nombre por capitan della á Juan de Grijalva, vezino de la villa de la Trinidad desta ysla, el qual me embió una caravela de las que llevava, porque le facia mucha agua, é en ella cierta gente, que los Indios en la dicha Sta María de los remedios le habian herido, é otros adolecido, y con la razon de todo lo que le habia ocurrido hasta otras yslas é tierras que de nuebo descubrió ; que la una es una ysla que se dice Cozumel, é le puso por nombre Sta Cruz ; y la otra es una tierra grande, que parte della se llama Ulua, que puso por nombre Sta María de las Niebes ; desde donde me embió la dicha caravela é gente, é me escribió como iba siguiendo su demanda principalmente á saber si aquella tierra era Isla, ó tierra firme ; é ha muchos dias que de razon habia de haber sabido nueva dél, de que se presume, pues tal nueva dél fasta oy no se sabe, que debe de tener ó estar en alguna ó estrema necesidad de socorro : é así mesmo porque una caravela, que yo embié al dicho Juan de Grijalva desdel puerto desta cibdad de Santiago, para que con él é la armada que lleva se juntase en el puerto de S^{n} Cristóbal de la Havana, porque muy mas proveido de todo é como al servicio de sus Altezas convenia fuesen, quando llegó donde pensó fallarle, el d^{ho} Juan de Grijalva se habia fecho á la bela é hera ido con toda la dicha armada, puesto que dejó abiso del viage que la d^{ha} carabela habia de llebar ; é como la d^{ha} carabela, en que iban ochenta, ó noventa hombres, no falló la d^{ha} armada, tomó el dicho aviso, y fué en seguimiento del d^{ho} Juan de Grijalva ; y segun paresze é se ha sabido por informacion de las

personas feridas é dolientes, que el d^ho Juan de Grijalva me embió, no
se habia juntado con él, ni della habia habido ninguna nueba, ni los
d^hos dolientes ni feridos la supiéron á la buelta, puesto que viniéron
mucha parte del biage costa á costa de la ysla de Sta M^a de los remedios por donde habian ydo; de que se presume que con tiempo for-
zoso podria de caer acia tierra firme, ó llegar á alguna parte donde los
dichos ochenta ó noventa ombres españoles corran detrimento por el
nabío, ó por ser pocos, ó por andar perdidos en busca del d^ho Juan de
Grijalva, puesto que iban muy bien pertrechados de todo lo necesario:
ademas de esto porque despues que con el d^ho Juan de Grijalva embié
la dicha armada he sido informado de muy cierto por un yndio de los
de la d^ha ysla de Yucatan Sta María de los remedios, como en poder
de ciertos Caciques principales della están seis cristianos cautibos, y
los tienen por esclabos, é se sirben dellos en sus haciendas, que los
tomáron muchos dias ha de una carabela que con tiempo por allí diz
que aportó perdida, que se cree que alguno dellos deve ser Nicuesa
capitan, que el católico Rey D^n Fernando de gloriosa memoria mandó
ir á tierra firme, é redimirlos seria grandísimo servicio de Dios N^ro S^or é
de sus Altezas: por todo lo qual pareciéndome que al servicio de Dios
N^ro S^nr é de sus Altezas convenia inhiar así en seguimiento é socorro
de la d^ha armada quel d^ho Juan de Grijalva llebó, y busca de la carabela que tras él en su seguimiento fué como á redimir si posible fuese
los d^hos cristianos que en poder de los d^hos Indios están cabtivos;
acordé, habiendo muchas veces pensado, é pesado, é platicadolo con
personas cuerdas, de embiar otra armada tal, é tambien
bastecida é aparejada ansí de nabíos é mantenimientos como de gente
é todo lo demas para semejante negocio necesario; que si por caso á
la gente de la otra primera armada, ó de la d^ha carabela que fué en su
seguimiento hallase en alguna parte cerca de infieles, sea bastante
para los socorrer ó descercar; é si ansí no los hallare, por sí sola
pueda seguramente andar é calar en su busca todas aquellas yslas
tierras, é saber el secreto dellas, y faser todo lo demas que al servicio
è de Dios N^ro S^or cumpla é al de sus Altezas combenga: é para ello
he acordado de la encomendar á vos Fernando Cortés, é os imbiar
por capitan della, por la esperiencia que de vos tengo del tiempo que
ha que en esta ysla en mi compañia habeis servido á sus Altezas, confiando que soys persona cuerda, y que con toda pendencia é zelo de
su real servicio daréis buena razon é quenta de todo lo que por mí en
nombre de sus Altezas os fuere mandado acerca de la dicha negocia-
cion, y la guiaréis ó encaminaréis como mas al servicio ae Dios N^ro

S^{or} é de sus Altezas combenga; y porque mejor guiada la negocia-
cion de todo vaya, lo que habeis de fazer, y mirar, é con mucha vigilancia y deligencia ynquirir é saber, es lo siguiente.

1. Hágase el servicio de Dios en todo, y quien saltaré castiga con
rigor.

2. Castigaréis en particular la fornicacion.

3. Proibiréis dados y naipes, ocasion de discordias y otros excesos.

4. Ya salido la armada del p^{to} desta ciud^d de Santiago en los otros,
dotaréis desta esta cuidado no se haga agravio á Españoles ni Indios.

5. Tomados los bastimentos necesarios en d^{hos} puertos, partiréis á
v^{ro} destino, haciendo antes alarde de gente ó armas.

6. No consentiréis vaya ningun Indio ni India.

7. Salido al mar y metidas las barcas, en la de v^{ro} navío visitaréis
los otros, y reconoceréis otra vez la gente con las copias [las listas] de
cada uno.

8. Apercibiréis á los capitanes y Maestres de los otros navíos que
jamas se aparten de v^{ra} conserva, y haréis quanto convenga para
llegar todos juntos á la ysla de Cozumel Santa Cruz, donde será vuestra derecha derrota.

9. Si por algun caso llegaren antes que vos, les mandaréis que nadie
sea osado á tratar mal á los Indios, ni les diga la causa porque vais, ni
les demande ó interrogue por los cristianos captivos en la Isla de Sta
María de los remedios: digan solo que vos hablaréis en llegando.

10. Llegado á d^{ha} ysla de Sta Cruz veréis y sondearéis los puertos,
entradas, y aguadas, así della como de Sta María de los remedios, y la
punta de Sta María de las Nieves, para dar cumplida relacion de todo.

11. Diréis á los Indios de Cozumel, Sta Cruz, y demas partes, que vais
por mandado del Rey á visitarles; hablaréis de su poder y conquistas,
individuando las hechas en estas Islas y Tierra firme, de sus mercedes
á quantos le sirven; que ellos se vengan á su obediencia y den muestras dello, regalándole, como los otros han hecho, con oro, perlas,
&c., para que eche de ver su buena voluntad y les favorezca y defi-
enda: que yo les aseguro de todo en su nombre, que me pesó mucho
de la batalla que con ellos ovo Francisco Hernandez, y os embió para
darles á entender como Su Alteza quiere que sean bien tratados, &c.

12. Tomaréis entera informacion de las cruces que diz se hallan en
d^{ha} Isla Sta Cruz adoradas por los Indios, del orígen y causas de
semejante costumbre.

13. En general sabréis quanto concierne á la religion de la tierra.

14. Y cuidad mucho de doctrinarlos en la verdadera fee, pues esta

es la causa principal porque sus Altezas permiten estos descubrimientos.

15. Inquirid de la armada de Juan de Grijalva, y de la caravela que llevó en su seguimiento Cristóv. de Olid.

16. Caso de juntaros con la armada, búsquese la caravela, y concertad donde podréis juntaros otra vez todos.

17. Lo mismo haréis si 1º se halla la caravela.

18. Iréis por la costa de la Isla de Yucatan Sta María de los remedios, do están seis cristianos en poder de unos caciques á quienes dice conocer Melchor Indio de allí, que con vos llevais. Tratadlo con mucho amor, para que os le tenga y sirva fielmente. No sea que os suceda algun daño, por que los Indios de aquella tierra en caso de guerra son mañosos.

19. Donde quiera, trataréis muy bien á los Indios.

20. Quantos rescates hicieredes meteréis en arca de tres llaves de que tendréis vos una, las otras el Veedor y el Tesorero que nombraredes.

21. Quando se necesite hacer agua, ó leña, &c., embiaréis personas cuerdas al mando dél de mayor confianza, que ni causen escándalo ni se pongan en peligro.

22. Si adentro la tierra viereis alguna poblacion de Indios que ofrecieren amistad, podréis ir á ella con la gente mas pacífica y bien armada, mirando mucho en que ningun agravio se les haga en sus bienes y mugeres.

23. En tal caso dejaréis á mui buen recabdo los navíos; estaréis mui sobre aviso que no os engañen ni se entrometan muchos Indios entre los Españoles, &c.

24. Avisdo que placiendo á Dios N. S. ayais los Xnos que en la dha Isla de Sta Ma de los remedios están captivos, y buscado que por ella ayais la dha armada é la dha caravela, seguiréis vuestro viage á la punta llana ques el principio de la tierra grande que agora nuevamente el dho J. de Grijalva descubrió, y correréis en su busca por la costa della adelante buscando todos los rios é puertos della fasta llegar á la baia de S. Juan, y Sta Ma de los Nieves, que es desde donde el dho J. de Grijalva me embió los heridos é dolientes, é me escrivió lo que hasta allí le habia occurrido; é si allí hallaredes, juntaros é ir con el J.; porque entre los Españoles que llevais ó allá están no haya diferencias, ... cada uno tenga cargo de la gente que consigo lleva, ... y entramos mui conformes, consultaréis lo que mas convenga conforme á esta instruccion, y á la que Grijalva llevó de sus Paternidades y mias:

en tal caso los rescates todos se harán en presencia de Francisco de Peñalosa, veedor nombrado por sus Paternidades.

25. Inquiriréis las cosas de las tierras á do llegareis, así morales como físicas, si hai perlas, especiería, oro, &c., part^re en Sta M^a de las Nieves, de donde Grijalva me embió ciertos granos de oro por fundir é fundidos.

26. Quando salteis en tierra sea ante v^ro S^no y muchos testigos, y tomaréis posesion della con las solemnidades usadas: inquirid la calidad de las gentes: porque diz que hay gentes de orejas grandes y anchas, y otras que tienen las caras como perros, ... á que parte están las Amazonas, que dicen estos Indios que con vos llevais, que están cerca de allí.

27. Las demas cosas dejo á v^ra prudencia, confiando de vos que en todo tomeis el cuidadoso cuidado de hacer lo que mas cumpla al servicio de Dios y de SS. AA.

28. En todos los puertos de esta ysla do hallareis Españoles que quieran ir con vos, no lleveis á quien tuviere deudas, si antes no las paga ó da fianzas suficientes.

29. Luego en llegando á Sta M^a de las Nieves, me embiaréis en el navío que menos falta hiciere, quanto hubieredes rescatado y hallado de oro, perlas, especería, animales, aves, &c., con relacion de lo hecho y lo que pensais hacer, p^a que yo lo mande y diga al Rey.

30. Conoceréis conforme á derecho de las causas civiles y criminales que ocurran, como Capitan desta armada con todos los poderes, &c. &c. F^ha en esta cibdad de Santiago puerto desta isla Fernandina, á 23 Oct., 1518.

No. VI.—See vol. i. p. 270.

EXTRACT FROM LAS CASAS' "HISTORIA GENERAL DE LAS INDIAS," MS., LIB. III. CAP. CXVI.

[Few Spanish scholars have had access to the writings of Las Casas; and I have made this short extract from the original, as a specimen of the rambling but vigorous style of a work the celebrity of which has been much enhanced by the jealous reserve with which it has been withheld from publication.]

Esto es uno de los herrores y disparates que muchos han tenido y echo en estas partes; porque simprimero por mucho tiempo aver á los yndios y á qualquiera nacion ydolatria dotrinado es gran desvario quitarles los ýdolos; lo qual nunca se hace por voluntad sino contra de los ydólatras; porque ninguno puede dexar por su voluntad é de buena gana aquello que tiene de muchos años por Dios y en la leche mamado y autorizado por sus mayores, sin que primero tenga entendido que aquello que les dan ó en que les comutan su Dios, sea verdadero Dios. Mirad que doctrina les podian dar en dos ó en tres ó en quatro ó en diez dias, que allí estuviéron, y que mas estuvieran, del verdadero Dios, y tampoco les supieran dar para desarraygalles la opinion erronea de sus dioses, que en yéndose, que se fuéron, no tornáron á ydolatrar. Primero se han de rraer de los corazones los ydolos, conviene á saber el concepto y estima que tienen de ser aquellos Dios los ydólatras por diuturna y deligente é continua dotrina, ý pintalles en ellos el concepto y verdad del verdadero Dios, y despues ellos mismos viendo su engaño y error an de derrocar é destruir, con sus mismas manos y de toda su voluntad, los ýdolos que veneraban por Dios é por dioses. Y así lo enseña San Agustin en el sermon, *De puero centurionis, de verbis Domini.* Pero no fué aqueste el postrero disparate que en estas yndias cerca desta materia se a hecho poner cruces, ynduciendo á los yndios á la rreverencia dellas. Si ay tiempo para ello con sinificacion alguna del fruto que pueden sacar dello, si se lo pueden dar á entender para hacerse y bien hacerse, pero no aviendo tiempo ni lengua ni sazon, cosa superflua é ynútil parece. Porque pueden pensar los yndios que les dan algun ýdolo de aquella figura que tienen por Dios los chris-tianos, y así lo arán ydólatra adorando por Dios aquel palo. La mas cierta é conveniente regla é dotrina que por estas tierras y otras de ynfieles semejantes á estos los christianos deben dar é tener, quando van de pasada como estos yvan, é quando tambien quisieren morar entre ellas, es dalles muy buen exemplo de hobras virtuosas y chris-tianas, para que, como dice nuestro Redemptor, viéndolas alaben y den gloria al Dios é padre de los cristianos, é por ellas juzguen que quien tales cultores tiene no puede ser sino bueno é verdadero Dios.

No. VII.—See vol. i. p. 325.

DEPOSITION OF ALONSO HERNANDEZ DE PUERTO - CAR-RERO, MS.

[Puerto-Carrero and Montejo were the two officers sent home by Cortés from Villa Rica with despatches to the government. The emissaries were examined under oath before the venerable Dr. Carbajal, one of the Council of the Indies, in regard to the proceedings of Velasquez and Cortés; and the following is the deposition of Puerto-Carrero. He was a man of good family, superior in this respect to most of those embarked in the expedition. The original is in the Archives of Simancas.]

En la cibdad de la Coruña, á 30 dias del mes de Abril, de 1520 años, se tomó el d^{ho} é depusicion de Alonso Hernandez Puerto-Carrero por mí, Joan de Samano, del qual haviendo jurado en forma so cargo del juramento dijo lo sig^{te}.

Primeramente dijo, que en ell armada que hizo Fran^{co} Hernandez de Cordova é Caycedo é su compañero él no fué en ella; de la qual armada fué el d^{ho} Fran^{co} Hernandez de Cordova por Capitan General é principal armador; é que ha oido decir como estos descubrieron la Isla que se llama de Yucatan.

Item: dijo que en ell armada de que fué Cap^{n} General Joan de Grijalva este testigo no fué; pero que vido un Cap^{n}, que se dice Pedro de Alvarado, que embió Joan de Grijalva en una caravela con cierto oro é joyas á Diego Velasquez; é que oyó decir, que des que Diego Velasquez vido que traian tan poco oro, é el Capitan Joan de Grijalva se queria luego bolver é no hacer mas rescate, acordó de hablar á Hernandez Cortés para que hiciesen esta armada, por que al presente en Santiago no havia persona que mejor aparejo tuviese, i que mas bien quisto en la isla fuese, por que al presente tenia tres navíos; fuéle preguntado, como savia lo susod^{ho}; respondió, que porque lo avia oido decir á muchas personas de la isla.

Dice mas que se pregonó en el pueblo don este testigo vivia, que todas las personas que quisiesen ir en ell armada, de todo lo que se oviese ó rescátase habria la una tercera parte, é las otras dos partes eran para los armadores i navíos.

Fuéle preguntado, quien hizo dar el d^(ho) pregun, é en cuyo nombre se hacia, é quien se decia entonces que hacia la d^(ha) armada ; respondió, que oyó decir, que Hernando Cortés havia escripto una carta á un Alc^e de aquel pueblo para que hiciese á pregonarlo ; é que oyó decir, que Diego Velasquez habló con Hern^(do) Cortés para que juntam^(te) con él hiciesen la d^(ha) armada, por que al presente no habia otra persona que mejor aparejo en la dicha isla para ello tuviese, porque al presente tenia tres navíos, é era bien quisto en la isla ; é que oyó decir, que si él no fuera por Capitan, que no fuera la tercera parte de la gente que con él fué ; é que no sabe el concierto que entre sí tienen, mas de que oyó decir, que amvos hacian aquella armada, é que ponia Hern^(do) Cortés mas de las dos partes della, é que la otra parte cree este testigo que la puso Diego Velasquez, porque lo oyó decir, e despues que fué en la d^(ha) armada vido ciertos navíos que puso Hern^(do) Cortés, en lo que gastaba con la gente, que le pareció que ponia las dos partes ó mas, é que de diez navíos que fuéron en ell armada los tres puso Diego Velasquez, é los siete Cortés suyos é de sus amigos.

Dijo que le dijéron muchas personas que ivan en ell armada como Hern^(do) Cortés hizo pregonar, que todos los que quisiesen ir en su compañía, si toviesen nescésida de dineros así para comprar vestidos como provisiones ó armas para ellos, que fuesen á él, é que él les socoreria é les daria lo que hoviesen menester, é que á todos los que á él acodian que lo dava, é que esto sabe, porque muchas personas á quien el socorria con dineros que lo dijéron ; é que estando en la villa de la Trenidad, vió que él é sus amigos davan á toda la gente que allí estaba todo lo que havian menester ; é así mesmo estando en la villa de Sant Cristobal en la Havana, vió hacer lo mismo, é comprar muchos puercos é pan, que podian ser tres ó cuatro meses.

Fuéle preguntado, á quien tenian por principal armador desta armada, é quien era público que la hacia ; dijo que lo que oyó decir é vido, que Hern^(do) Cortés gastava las dos partes, é que los d^(hos) Diego Velasquez é Hern^(do) Cortés la hiciéron como d^(ho) tiene, é que no sabe mas en esto de este artículo.

Fuéle preguntado, si sabia quel d^(ho) Diego Velasquez fuese el principal por respecto de ser Governador por su Al en las tierras é islas que por su industria se descobriesen; que no lo sabe, por que no le eran entonces llegados Gonzalo de Guzman é Narvaez.

Fuéle preguntado, si sabe el d^ho Diego Velasquez sea lugar teniente de Governador é capitan de la isla de Cuba; dijo que ha oido decir, ques teniente de Almirante.

Fuéle preguntado, si sabia dellasi^to é capitulac^n que el dicho Diego Velasquez tomó con los Frailes Gerónimos en nombre de S. M., é de la instruccion que ellos para el descubrimiento le diéron; dijo que oyó decir, que les havia f^ho relacion que havia descovierto una t^rra que era mui rica, é les embió á pedir le diesen lic^a para vojallá é para rescatar en ella, é los Padres Gerónimos que la diéron, é que esto sabe por que lo oyó decir: fuéle preguntado, si vió este asiento ó poderes algunos de los d^hos Padres ó la d^ha instruccion; dijo que bien los puede haver visto, mas lo que en ellos iva, no se acuerda mas que lo arriva d^ho.

Fuéle preguntado, si vió ó oyó decir, que los dichos poderes é capitulac^n de los d^hos Padres Gerónimos fuese nombrado Diego Velasquez ó el d^ho Cortés; dijo que en los poderes que los P^es Gerónimos embiáron á Diego Velasquez que á él seria, é no há Hernando Cortés, por que el d^ho Diego Velasquez lo embió á pedir.

Fuéle preguntado, como é porque causa obedecia á Hern^do Cortés por Cap^n General de aquella armada; dijo que porque Diego Velasquez le dió su poder en nombre de su Al. para ir hacer aquel rescate; é que lo sabe, porque vió el poder é lo oyó decir á todos ellos.

Fuéle preguntado, que fué la causa por que no usáron con el d^ho Hern^do Cortés de los poderes que llevaba del d^ho Diego Velasquez; dijo que esta armada iva en achaque de buscar á Juan de Grijalva; que oyó decir, que no tenia poder Diego Velasquez de los P^res Gerónimos para hacer esta armada; é con este achaque que arriva dice hiciéron esta armada, é que él usó del poder que Diego Velasquez le dió, é allí rescató.

Fuéle preguntado, qué fué la causa porque, quando quisiéron poblar, le nombráron ellos por Capitan General é justicia mayor de nuevo; dijo que Hernando Cortés, desque havia rescatado é vido que tenia pocos vastim^tos, que no havia mas de para bolver tasadamente á la isla de Cuba, dijo que se queria bolver; é entonces toda la gente se juntaron é le requiriéron que poblase, pues los Yndios les tenian buena voluntad é mostravan que holgaban con ellos, é la t^rra era tan aparejada para ello, é S. M. seria dello mui servido; é respondió, que él no fraia poder para poblar, que él responderia; é respondió, que pues era servicio de S. M. poblar, otejaba que poblasen; é hiciéron Alc^s è Rexiaores, é se juntáron en su cabildo, é le proveyéron de Xusticia mayor é Capitan General en nombre de S. M.

Fuéle preguntado, que se hiciéron los navíos que llebáion; dijo que desque pobláron venian los maestres de los navíos, á decir al capitan que todos los navíos se ivan á fondo, que no los podian tener encima dell agua; i el d^ho Capitan mandó á ciertos maestres é pilotos que entrasen en los navíos é viesen los que estavan para poder navegar, é ver si se podiesen remediar; é los d^hos maestres é pilotos digéron, que no havia mas de tres navíos que pudiesen navegar é remediarse, é que havia de ser con mucha costa; é que los demas que no havia medio ninguno en ellos, é que alguno dellos se undió en la mar, estando echada el ancla; é que con los demas que no estavan para poder navegar é remediarse, los dejáron ir al traves; é que esta es la verdad, é firmólo de su nombre.

Dijo que se acuerda que oyó decir, que Hernando Cortés havia gastado en esta armada cinco mill ducados ó castellanos; é que Diego Velasquez oyó decir, que havia gastado mill é setecientos, poco mas ó menos; é que esto que gastó fué en vinos é aceites é vinagre é ropas de vestir, las que les vendió un factor que allá está de Diego Velasquez, en que les vendia el arroba de vino á cuatro castellanos que salia al respecto por una pipa cient. castellanos, el arroba del aceite á seis castellanos, é alomesmo la arrova del vinagre, é las camisas á dos pesos, y el par de los alpargates á castellano, é un mazo de cuentas de valoría á dos castellanos costándole á él á dos reales, é á este respecto fuéron todas las otras cosas; é que esto que gastó Diego Velasquez lo sabe, porque lo vido vender, é este testigo se le vendió hasta parte dello. —Alonso Hernandez Portocarrero declaró ante mí, Johan de Samano.

No. VIII.—See vol. i. p. 328.

EXTRACT FROM THE "CARTA DE VERA CRUZ," MS.

[The following extract from this celebrated letter of the Municipality of La Villa Rica de la Vera Cruz to the Emperor gives a succinct view of the foundation

of the first colony in Mexico, and of the appointment
of Cortés by that body as Chief Justice and Captain-
General. The original is preserved in the Imperial
Library at Vienna.]

Despues de se aver despedido de nosotros el dicho Caçique, y buelto
á su casa, en mucha conformidad, como en esta armada venimos, personas nobles, cavalleros, hijos dalgo, zelosos del servicio de n^{ro} Señor
y de V^{ras} Reales Altezas, y deseosos de ensalzar su Corona Real, de
acrecentar sus Señoríos, y de aumentar sus rentas, nos juntámos y
platicámos con el dicho capitan Fernando Cortés, diciendo que esta
tierra era buena, y que segun la muestra de oro que aquel Caçique
avia traido, se creia que debia de ser mui rica, y que segun las muestras que el dicho Caçique avia dado, era de creer que él y todos sus
Indios nos tenian muy buena voluntad; por tanto que nos pareçia
que nos convenia al servicio de V^{ras} Magestades, y que en tal tierra se
hiziese lo que Diego Velasquez avia mandado hacer al dicho Capitan
Fernando Cortés, que era rescatar todo el oro que pudiese, y rescatado
bolverse con todo ello á la Isla Fernandina, para gozar solamente de
ello el dicho Diego Velasquez y el dicho Capitan; y que lo mejor que
á todos nos parecia era, que en nombre de V^{ras} Reales Altezas se
poblase y fundase allí un pueblo en que huviese justicia, para que en
esta tierra tuviesen Señorío, como en sus Reinos y Señoríos lo tienen;
porque siendo esta tierra poblada de Españoles, de mas de acreçentar
los Reinos y Señoríos de V^{ras} Magestades, y sus rentas, nos podrian
hacer mercedes á nosotros y á los pobladores que de mas allá viniesen adelante; y acordado esto, nos juntámos todos en concordes
de un ánimo y voluntad, y hizímos un requerimiento al dicho capitan, en el qual diximos, que pues él veia quanto al servicio de
Dios n^{ro} Señor y al de V^{ras} Magestades convenia, que esta tierra
estuviese poblada, dándole las causas de que arriba á V^{ras} Altezas
se ha hecho relaçion, que le requerímos que luego cesase de hacer
rescates de la manera que los venia á hacer, porque seria destruir
la tierra en mucha manera, y V^{ras} Magestades serian en ellos muy
desservidos; y que ansí mismo le pedímos y requerímos que luego
nombrase para aquella villa, que se avia por nosotros de hacer y
fundar, Alcaldes y Regidores, en nombre de V^{ras} Reales Altezas, con
ciertas protestaciones, en forma que contra él protestámos si ansí no lo
hiziesen; y hecho este requerimiento al dicho Capitan, dixo que daria

su respuesta el dia siguiente; y viendo pues el dicho Capitan como convenia al servicio de V^{ras} Reales Altezas lo que le pediamos, luego otro dia nos respondió diciendo, que su voluntad estava mas inclinada al servicio de V^{ras} Magestades que á otra cosa alguna, y que no mirando al interese que á él se le siguiese, si prosiguiera en el rescate que traia propuesto de rehacer los grandes gastos que de su hacienda avia hecho en aquella armada juntamente con el dicho Diego Velasquez, antes poniéndolo todo le placia y era contento de hacer lo que por nosotros le era pedido, pues que tanto convenia al servicio de V^{ras} Reales Altezas; y luego comenzó con gran diligencia á poblar y á fundar una villa la qual puso por nombre la rica Villa de Vera Cruz, y nombrónos á los que lá delantes subscribímos, por Alcaldes y Regidores de la dicha Villa, y en nombre de V^{ras} Reales Altezas recibió de nosotros el juramento y solenidad que en tal caso se acostumbra y suele hacer; despues de lo qual otro dia siguiente entrámos en nuestro cabildo y ajuntamiento, y estando así juntos embiamos á llamar al dicho Capitan Fernando Cortés, y le pedímos en nombre de V^{ras} Reales Altezas que nos mostrase los poderes y instrucciones que el dicho Diego Velasquez le avia dado para venir á estas partes, el qual embió luego por ellos y nos los mostró; y vistos y leidos por nosotros, bien examinados segun lo que pudímos mejor entender, hallámos á nuestro parecer que por los dichos poderes y instrucciones no tenia mas poder el dicho capitan Fernando Cortés, y que por aver ya espirado no podia usar de justicia ni de Capitan de allí adelante; pareciéndonos pues, mui Excellentíssimos Príncipes! que para la pacificacion y concordia de entre nosotros, y para nos gobernar bien, convenia poner una persona para su Real servicio, que estuviese en nombre de V^{ras} Magestades en la dicha villa y en estas partes por justicia mayor y capitan y cabeza, á quien todos acatasemos hasta hacer relacion de ello á V^{ras} Reales Altezas para que en ello proveyesen lo que mas servidos fuesen, y visto que á ninguna persona se podria dar mejor el dicho cargo que al dicho Fernando Cortés, porque demas de ser persona tal qual para ello conviene, tiene muy gran zelo y deseo del servicio de V^{ras} Magestades, y ansí mismo por la mucha experiencia que de estas partes y Islas tiene, de causa de los quales ha siempre dado buena cuenta, y por haver gastado todo quanto tenia por venir como vino con esta armada en servicio de V^{ras} Magestades, y por aver tenido en poco, como hemos hecho relacion, todo lo que podia ganar y interese que se le podia seguir si rescatara como traia concertado, y le proveimos en nombre de V^{ras} Reales Altezas de

justicia y Alcalde mayor, del qual recibímos el juramento que en tal
caso se requiere, y hecho como convenia al Real servicio de V^{ra} Magestad, lo recibímos en su Real nombre en n^{ro} ajuntamiento y cabildo
por Justicia mayor y capitan de V^{ras} Reales armas, y ansí está y estará
hasta tanto que V^{ras} Magestades provean lo que mas á su servicio
convenga: hemos querido hacer de todo esto relaçion á V^{ras} Reales
Altezas, porque sepan lo que acá se ha hecho, y el estado y manera
en que quedamos.

No. IX.—See vol. i. p. 407.

EXTRACT FROM CAMARGO'S "HISTORIA DE TLASCALA," MS.

[This passage from the Indian chronicler relates to
the ceremony of inauguration of a Tecuhtle, or mer-
chant-knight, in Tlascala. One might fancy himself
reading the pages of Ste.-Palaye, or any other historian
of European chivalry.]

Esta ceremonia de armarse caballeros los naturales de México y
Tlaxcalla y otras provincias de la Laguna Mejicana es cosa muy
notoria; y así no nos detendrémos en ella, mas de pasar secunta-
mente. Es de saber, que cualquier Señor, ó hijos de Señores, que por
sus personas habian ganado alguna cosa en la guerra, ó que hubiesen
hecho ó emprendido cosas señaladas y aventajadas, como tubiese
indicios de mucho valoi, y que fuese de buen consejo y aviso en la
república, le armaban caballero; que como fuesen tan ricos que por
sus riquezas se enoblecian y hacian negocios de hijos y dalgo y
caballero, los armaban caballeros por dos, diferentemente que los
caballeros de linea recta, porque los llamaban Tepilhuan: Al Mercader que era armado caballero, y á los finos que por descendencia
lo eran, llamaban Tecuhtles. Estos Tecuhtles se armaban caballeros con muchas ceremonias. Ante todas cosas, estaban encer-
rados 40 ó 60 dias en un templo de sus ídolos, y ayunaban todo

este tiempo, y no trataban con gente mas que con aquellos que les
servian, y al cabo de los cuales eran llevados al templo mayor, y
allí se les daban grandes doctrinas de la vida que habian de tener y
guardar; y antes de todas estas cosas les daban grandes bejancnes
con muchas palabras afrentosas y satíricas, y les daban de puñadas
con grandes represiones, y aun en su propio rostro, segun atras dejámos tratado, y les horadaban las narices y labios y orejas; y la sangre
que de ellos salia la ofrecian á sus Ídolos. Allí les daban publicamente sus arcos y flechas y macanas y todo género de armas usadas
en su arte militar. Del templo era llevado por las calles y plazas
acostumbradas con gran pompa y regocijo y solemnidad: poníanles
en las orejas orejeras de oro, y bezotes de lo mismo, llevando adelante
muchos truhanes y chocarreros que decian grandes donaires, con que
hacian reir las gentes; pero como vamos tratando, se ponian en las
narices piedras ricas, oradábanles las orejas y narices y bezos, no con
yerros ni cosa de oro ni plata, sino con guesos de Tigres y leones y
águilas agudos. Este armado caballero hacia muy solemnes fiestas y
costosas, y daban muy grandes presentes á los antiguos Señores caballeros así de ropas como de esclavos, oro y piedras preciosas y plume-
rías ricas, y divisas, escudos, rodelas y arcos y flechas, á manera de
propinas cuando se doctoran nuestros letrados. Andan de casa en
casa de estos Tecuhtles dándoles estos presentes y dadivas, y lo propio
hacen con estos armados caballeros despues que lo eran, y se tenia
cuenta con todos ellos. Y era república; y así no se armaban muchos
caballeros hidalgos pobres, por su poca posibilidad, sino eran aquellos
que por sus nobles y loables hechos lo habian merecido, que en tal
caso los caciques cabeceros y los mas supremos Señores Reyes, pues
tenian meromixto imperio con sus tierras, y orca y cuchillo para eje-
cutar los casos de justicia, como en efecto era así. Finalmente, que
los que oradaban las orejas, bezos, y narices de estos, que así se
armaban caballeros, eran caballeros ancianos y muy antiguos, los
cuales estaban dedicados para esto; y así como para en los casos de
justicia y consejos de guerra. Servian estos caballeros veteranos en
la república, los cuales eran temidos, obedecidos, y reverenciados en
muy gran veneracion y estima. Y como atras dejámos dicho, que al
cabo de los 40 ó 60 dies de ayuno de los caballeros nobles los sacaban
de allí para llevarlos al templo mayor donde tenian sus simulacros;
no les oradaban entonces las orejas, narices, ni labios, que son los labios
de la parte de abajo, sino que cuando se ponian en el ayuno, entonces;
y ante todas cosas les hacian estos bestiales espectáculos; y en todo

el tiempo de ayuno estaba en cura, para que el dia de la mayor ceremonia fuese sano de las heridas, que pudiesen ponerle las orejeras y
bezotes sin ningun detrimento ni dolor; y en todo este tiempo no se
lavaban, antes estaban todo tiznados y embiajados de negro, y con
muestras de gran humildad para conseguir y alcanzar tan gran merced
y premio, velando las armas todo el tiempo del ayuno segun sus ordenanzas, constitutiones, y usos y costumbres entre ellos tan celebrados.
Tambien usaban tener las puertas donde estaban ayunando cerradas
con ramos de laurel, cuyo árbol entre los naturales era muy estimado.

No. X.—See vol. ii. p. 119.

EXTRACT FROM OVIEDO'S "HISTORIA DE LAS INDIAS," MS., LIB. XXXIII. CAP. XLVI.

[This chapter, which has furnished me with many
particulars for the narrative, contains a minute account
of Montezuma's household and way of life, gathered
by the writer, as he tells us, from the testimony of
different individuals of credit, who had the best means
of information. It affords a good specimen of the
historian's manner, and may have interest to the Castilian scholar, since the original has never been published, and, to judge from appearances, is not likely
to be so.]

Quando este gran Príncipe Montezuma comia, estaba en una gran
sala encalada é mui pintada de pinturas diversas; allí tenia enanos é
chocarreros que le decian gracias é donaires, é otros que jugaban con
vn palo puesto sobre los pies grande, é le traian é meneaban con tanta
facilidad é ligereza, que parecia cosa imposible; e otros hacian otros
juegos é cosas de mucho para se admirar los hombres. Á la puerta
de la sala estaba vn patio mui grande, en que habia cien aposentos de
25 ó 30 pies de largo, cada uno sobre sí, en torno de dicho patio, é

allí estaban los Señores principales aposentados como guardas del palacio ordinarias, y estos tales aposentos se llaman galpones, los quales á la contina ocupan mas de 600 hombres, que jamas se quitaban de allí, é cada vno de aquellos tenian mas de 30 servidores, de manera que á lo menos nunca faltaban 3000 hombres de guerra en esta guarda cotediana del palacio. Quando queria comer aquel príncipe grande, daban le agua á manos sus Mugeres, é salian allí hasta 20 dellas las mas queridas é mas hermosas é estaban en pie en tanto que él comia; É traíale vn Mayordomo ó Maestre-sala 3000 platos ó mas de diversos manjares de gallinas, codornices, palomas, tórtolas, é otras aves, é algunos platos de muchachos tiernos guisados á su modo, é todo mui lleno de axi, é el comia de lo que las mugeres le trahian ó queria. Despues que habia acabado de comer se tornaba á labar las manos, é las Mugeres se iban á su aposento dellas, donde eran mui bien servidas; É luego ante el señor allegábanse á sus burlas é gracias aquellos chocarreros é donosos, é mandaba les dar de comer sentados á vn cabo de la sala; é todo lo restante de la comida mandaba dar á la otra gente que se ha dicho que estaban en aquel gran patio; y luego venian 3000 Xicalos i cantaros ó ánforas de brevage, é despues que el señor habia comido ó bebido, é labádose las manos, íbanse las Mugeres, é acabadas de salir de la sala, entraban los negociantes de muchas partes, así de la misma cibdad como de sus señoríos; é los que le habian de hablar incábanse de rodillas quatro varas de medir ó mas, apartados dél é descalzos, é sin manta de algodon que algo valiese; é sin mirarle á la cara decian su razonamiento; é él proveia lo que le parecia; é aquellos se levantaban é tornaban atras retraiéndose sin volver las espaldas vn buen tiro de piedra, como lo acostumbraban hacer los Moros de Granada delante de sus señores é príncipes. Allí habia muchos jugadores de diversos juegos, en especial con vnos fesoles á manera de habas, é apuntadas como dados, que es cosa de ver; é juegan cuanto tienen los que son Tahures entrellos. Ivan los Españoles á ver á Montezuma, é mandábales dar duchos, que son vnos banquillos ó escabeles, en que se sentasen, mui lindamente labrados, é de gentil madera, é decíanles que querian, que lo pidiesen é dárselo han. Su persona era de pocas carnes, pero de buena gracia é afabil, é tenia cinco ó seis pelos en la barba tan luengos como un geme. Si le parecia buena alguna ropa que el Español tubiese, pedíasela, é si se la dada liberalmente sin le pedir nada por ella, luego se la cobria é la miraba mui particularmente, é con placer la loaba; mas si le pedian precio por ella hacíalo dar luego, é tomaba la ropa é tornábasela á dar á los christianos sin

se la cobrir é como descontento de la mala crianza dél que pedia el
precio, decia : Para mí no ha de haber precio alguno, porque yo soy
señor, é no me han de pedir nada deso ; que yo lo daré sin que me
den alguna cosa ; que es mui gran atrenta poner precio de ninguna
cosa á los que son señores, ni ser ellos Mercaderes. Con esto con-
cuerdan las palabras que de Scipion Africano, que de sí decian aquella
contienda de prestancia, que escrive Luciano, entre los tres capitanes
mas excelentes de los antiguos, que son Alexandro Magno, é Anibal,
é Scipion : Desde que nascí, ni vendí ni compré cosa ninguna. Así que
decia Montezuma quando así le pedian prescio : Otro dia no te pediré
cosa alguna, porque me has hecho mercader ; vete con Dios á tu casa,
é lo que obieses menester pídelo, é dársete ha : É no tornes acá, que no
soy amigo desos tratos, ni de los que en ellos entienden, para mas de
dexárselos vsar con otros hombres en mi Señorío. Tenia Montezuma
mas de 3000 señores que le eran subgetos, é aquellos tenian muchos
vasallos cada uno dellos ; É cada qual tenia casa principal en Temixtitan, é habia de residir en ella ciertos meses del año ; É quando se
habian de ir á su tierra con licencia de Montezuma, habia de quedar
en la casa su hijo ó hermano hasta quel señor della tornase. Esto
hacia Montezuma por tener su tierra segura, é que ninguno se le
alzase sin ser sentido. Tenia vna seña, que trahian sus Almoxarifes é
Mensageros quando recogian los tributos, é él que erraba lo mataban
á él é á quantos dél venian. Dábanle sus vasallos en tributo ordinario
de tres hijos uno, é él que no tenia hijos habia de dar vn Indio ó India
para sacrificar á sus Dioses, é sino lo daban, habian de sacrificarle á
él : Dábanle tres hanegas de mahiz vna, é de todo lo que grangeaban,
ó comian, ó bebian ; En fin, de todo se le daba el tercio ; É él que
desto faltaba pagaba con la cabeza. En cada pueblo tenian Mayordomo con sus libros del número de la gente é de todo lo demas asen-
tado por tales figuras é caracteres quellos se entendian sin discrepancia,
como entre nosotros con nuestras letras se entenderia vna cuenta mui
bien ordenada. É aquellos particulares Mayordomos daban quenta á
aquellos que residian en Temixtitan, é tenian sus alholíes é magazenes
é depósitos donde se recogian los tributos, é oficiales para ello, é
ponian en cárceles los que á su tiempo no pagaban, é dábanles término para la paga, é aquel pasado é no pagado, justiciaban al tal
deudor, ó le hacian esclavo.

    *   *   *   *   *   *   *   *   *

Dexemos esta materia, é volvamos á este gran Príncipe Montezuma,
el qual en vna gran sala de 150 pies de largo, é de 50 de ancho, de

grandes vigas é postes de madera que lo sostenian, encima de la qual, era todo vn terrado é azutea, é tenia dentro desta sala muchos géneros de aves, é de animales. Havia 50 águilas caudales en jaolas, tigres, lobos, culebras, tan gruesas como la pierna, de mucho espanto, é en sus jaolas así mismo, é allí se les llevaba la sangre de los hombres é mugeres é niños que sacrificaban, é cebaban con ella aquellas bestias ; é habia vn suelo hecho de la mesma sangre humana en toda la dicha sala, é si se metia vn palo ó vara temblaba el suelo. En entrando por la sala, el hedor era mucho é aborrecible é asqueroso ; las culebras daban grandes é horribles silvos, é los gemidos é tonos de los otros animales allí presos era una melodía infernal, é para poner espanto ; tenian 500 gallinas de racion cada dia para la sustentacion desos animales. En medio de aquella sala habia vna capilla á manera de vn horno grande, é por encima chapada de las minas de oro é plata é piedras de muchas maneras, como ágatas é cornesinas, nides, topacios, planas desmeraldas, é de otras suertes, muchas é mui bien engastadas. Allí entraba Montezuma é se retrahia á hablar con el Dieblo, al qual nombraban Atezcatepoca, que aquella gente tienen por Dios de la guerra, y él les daba á entender, que era Señor y criador de todo, y que en su mano era el vencer ; é los Indios en sus arreitos y cantares é hablas le dan gracias y lo invocan en sus necesidades. En aquel patio é sala habia continuamente 5000 hombres pintados de cierto betun ó tinta, los quales no llegan á mugeres é son castos ; llámanlos papas, é aquestos son religiosos.

* * * . * * * * * *

Tenia Montezuma vna casa mui grande en que estaban sus Mugeres, que eran mas de 4000 hijas de señores, que se las daban para ser sus Mugeres, é él lo mandaba hacer así ; é las tenia mui guardadas y servidas ; y algunas veces él daba algunas dellas á quien queria favorecer y honrar de sus principales : Ellos las recibian como vn don grandísimo. Habia en su casa muchos jardines é 100 vaños, ó mas, como los que vsan los Moros, que siempre estaban calientes, en que se bañaban aquellas sus Mugeres, las quales tenian sus guardas, é otras mugeres como Prioras que las governaban : É á estas mayores, que eran ancianas, acataban como á Madres, y ellas las trataban como á hijas. Tuvo su padre de Montezuma 150 hijos é hijas, de los quales los mas mató Montezuma, y las hermanas casó muchas dellas con quien le pareció ; y él tubo 50 hijos y hijas, ó mas ; y acaeció algunas veces tener 50 mugeres preñadas, y las mas dellas mataban las criaturas en el cuerpo, porque así dicen que se lo mandaba el Diablo, que

hablaba con ellas y decíales que se sacrificasen ellas las orejas y las
lenguas y sus naturas, é se sacasen mucha sangre é se la ofreciesen,
é así lo hacian en efeto. Parecia la casa de Montezuma vna cibdad
mui poblada. Tenia sus porteros en cada puerta. Tenia 20 puertas
de servicio; entraban nuchas calles de agua á ellas, por las quales
entraban é salian las canoas con mahiz, é otros bastimentos, é leña.
Entraba en esta casa vn caño de agua dulce, que venia de dos leguas
de allí, por encima de vna calzada de piedra, que venia de vna fuente,
que se dice chapictepeque, que nace en vn peñon, que está en la
Laguna salada, de mui excelente agua.

No. XI.—See vol. ii. p. 274, et alibi.

DIALOGUE OF OVIEDO WITH DON THOAN CANO, AP.
"HISTORIA DE LAS INDIAS," MS., LIB. XXXIII. CAP.
LIV.

[The most remarkable, in some respects, of Oviedo's compositions is his *Quincuagenas*, a collection of
imaginary dialogues with the most eminent persons of
his time, frequently founded, no doubt, on the personal
communications which he had held with them. In his
"History of the Indies" he has also introduced a
dialogue which he tells us he actually had with Don
Thoan Cano, a Castilian hidalgo, who married Guatemozin's widow, the lovely daughter of Montezuma.
He came into the country originally with Narvaez;
and, as he was a man of intelligence, according to
Oviedo, and his peculiar position both before and after
the Conquest opened to him the best sources of information, his testimony is of the highest value. As
such I have made frequent use of it in the preceding

37*

pages, and I now transcribe it entire, in the original, as an important document for the history of the Conquest.]

DIÁLOGO DEL ALCAYDE DE LA FORTALEZA DE LA CIBDAD É PUERTO DE SANTO DOMINGO DE LA ISLA ESPAÑOLA, AUTOR Y CHRONISTA DESTAS HISTORIAS, DE LA VNA PARTE, É DE LA OTRA, VN CABALLERO VECINO DE LA GRAND CIBDAD DE MÉXICO, LLAMADO THOAN CANO.

ALC. Señor, ayer supe que Vm. vive en la grand cibdad de México, y que os llamais Thoan Cano; y porque yo tube amistad con vn caballero llamado Diego Cano, que fué criado del sereníssimo Príncipe Don Thoan, mi señor, de gloriosa memoria, deseo saber si es vivo, é donde sois señor natural, é como quedástes avecindado en estas partes, é rescibiré merced, que no rescibais pesadumbre de mis preguntas; porque tengo necesidad de saber algunas cosas de la Nueva España, y es razon, que para mi satisfaccion yo procure entender lo que deseo de tales personas é hábito que merezcan crédito; y ansí, Señor, recibiré mucha merced de la vuestra en lo que digo.

THOAN CANO. Señor Alcayde, yo soy él que gaño mucho en conoceros; y tiempo ha que deseaba ver vuestra persona, porque os soi aficionado, y querria que mui de veras me tubiesedes por tan amigo é servidor como yo os lo seré. É satisfaciendo á lo que Vm. quiere saber de mí, digo, que Diego Cano, Escribano de Cámara del Príncipe Don Thoan, y camarero de la Tapicería de su Alteza, fué mi tio, é ha poco tiempo que murió en la cibdad de Caceres, donde vivia é yo soy natural: Y quanto á lo demas, yo, Señor, pasé desde la Isla de Cuba á la Nueva España con el capitan Pámphilo de Narvaez, é aunque mozo é de poco edad, yo me hallé cerca dél quando fué preso por Hernando Cortés é sus mañas; é en ese trance le quebráron vn ojo, peleando él como mui valiente hombre; pero como no le acudió su gente, é con él se halláron mui pocos, quedó preso é herido, é se hizo Cortés señor del campo, é truxo á su devocion la gente que con Pámphilo habia ido, é en rencuentros é en batallas de manos en México; y todo lo que ha sucedido despues yo me he hallado en ello. Mandais que diga como quedé avecindado en estas partes, y que no reciba pesadumbre de vuestras preguntas; satisfaciendo á mi asiento, digo, Señor, que yo me casé con una Señora hija legítima de Montezuma, llamada doña Isabel, tal persona, que aunque se hobiera criado en nuestra España, no estobiera mas enseñada é bien dotrinada é Católica, é de tal conversacion é arte,

que os satisfaria su manera é buena gracia; y no es poco útil é prove-
chosa al sosiego é contentamientos de los naturales de la tierra; porque,
como es Señora en todas sus cosas é amiga de los christianos, por su
respecto é exemplo mas quietud é reposo se imprime en los ánimos de
los Mexicanos. En lo demas que se me preguntare, é de que yo tenga
memoria, yo, Señor, diré lo que supiere conforme á la verdad.

ALC. Io acepto la merced que en eso recibiré; y quiero comenzar
á decir lo que me ocurre, porque me acuerdo, que fuí informado que
su padre de Montezuma tubo 150 hijos é hijas, ó mas, é que le acaeció
tener 50 mugeres preñadas; É ansí escrebí esto, é otras cosas á este
propósito en el capítulo 46, lo qual si así fué, queria saber, ¿como
podeis vos tener por legítima hija de Montezuma á la Srª Doña Isabel
vuestra Muger, é que forma tenia vuestro suegro para que se cono-
ciesen los hijos bastardos entre los legítimos ó espurios, é quales eran
mugeres legítimas é concubinas?

CAN. Fué costumbre vsada y guardada entre los Mexicanos, que
las mugeres legítimas que tomaban, era de la manera que agora se
dirá. Concertados el hombre é muger que habian de contraer matri-
monio, para le efectuar se juntaban los parientes de ambas partes é
hacian vn areito despues que habian comido ó cenado; é al tiempo
que los Novios se habian de acostar é dormir en vno, tomaban la halda
delantera de la camisa dè la Novia é atábanla á la manta de algodon
que tenia cubierto el Novio. É así ligados tomábanlos de las manos los
principales parientes de ambos, é metian los en una cámara, donde los
dejaban solos é oscuros por tres dias contiguos sin que de allí saliesen
él ni ella, ni allá entraba mas de vna India á los proveer de comer é
lo que habian menester; en el qual tiempo deste encerramiento siempre
habia bailes ó areitos, que ellos llaman mitote; é en fin de los tres dias
no hai mas fiesta. É los que sin esta cerimonia se casan no son habi-
dos por matrimonios, ni los hijos que proceden por legítimos, ni here-
dan. Ansí como murió Montezuma, quedáronle solamente por hijos
legítimos mi Muger é vn hermano suio, é muchachos ambos; á causa
de lo qual fué elegido por Señor vn hermano de Montezuma, que se
decia Cuitcavaci, Señor de Iztapalapa, el qual vivió despues de su
eleccion solos 60 dias, y murió de viruelas; á causa de lo qual vn
sobrino de Montezuma, que era Papa ó sacerdote maior entre los
Indios, que se llamaba Guatimuci, mató al primo hijo legítimo de
Montezuma, que se decia Asupacaci, hermano de padre é madre de
doña Isabel, é hizose señor, é fué mui valeroso. Este fué él que perdió
á Mexico, é fué preso, é despues injustamente muerto con otros prin-

cipales Señores é Indios; pues come Cortés é los christianos fuéron enseñoreados de Méxicó, ningun hijo quedó legítimo sino bastardos de Montezuma, ecepto mi Muger, que quedaba viuda, porque Guatimuci señor de Méxíco, su primo, por fixar mejor su estado, siendo ella mui muchacha, la tubo por muger con la cerimonia ya dicha del atar la camisa con la manta; é no obiéron hijos, ni tiempo para procreallos; é ella se convirtió á nuestra santa fee católica, é casóse con vn hombre de bien de los conquistadores primeros, que se llamaba Pedro Gallego, é ovo vn hijo en ella, que se llama Thoan Gallego Montezuma; é murió el dicho Pedro Gallego, é yo casé con la dicha doña Isabel, en la qual me ha dado Dios tres hijos é dos hijas, que se llaman Pedro Cano, Gonzalo Cano de Saavedra, Thoan Cano, doña Isabel, é doña Catalina.

ALC. Señor Thoan Cano, suplícoos que me digais porque mató Hernando Cortés á Guatimuci: ¿revelóse despues, ó que hizo para que muriese?

CAN. Habeis de saber, que así á Guatimuci, como al Rey de Tacuba, que se decia Tetepanquezal, é al Señor de Tezcuco, el capitan Hernando Cortés les hizo dar muchos tormentos é crudos, quemándoles los pies, é untándoles las plantas con aceite, é poniéndoselas cerca de las brasas, é en otras diversas maneras, porque les diesen sus tesoros; é teniéndolos en contiguas fatigas, supo como el capitan Cristóval de Olit se le habia alzado en puerto de Caballos é Honduras, la qual provincia los Indios llaman Guaimuras, é determinó de ir á buscar é castigar el dicho Christóval de Olit, é partió de México por tierra con mucha gente de Españoles, é de los naturales de la tierra; é llevóse consigo aquellos tres principales ya dichos, y despues los ahorcó en el camino; é ansí enviudó doña Isabel, é despuês ella se casó de la manera que he dicho con Pedro Gallego, é despues conmigo.

ALC. Pues en cierta informacion, que se envió al Emperador Nuestro Señor, dice Hernando Cortés, que habia sucedido Guatimuci en el Señorío de México tras Montezuma, porque en las puentes murió el hijo é heredero de Montezuma, é que otros dos hijos que quedáron vivos. el vno era loco ó mentecapto, é el otro paralítico, é ináviles por sus enfermedades: É yo lo he escripto así en el capítulo 16, pensando quello seria así.

CAN. Pues escriba Vm. lo que mandare, y el Marques Hernando Cortés lo que quisiere, que yo digo en Dios y en mi conciencia la verdad, y esto es mui notorio.

ALC. Señor Thoan Cano, dígame Vm ¿de que procedió el alza-

miento de los Indios de México en tanto que Hernando Cortés salió
de aquella cibdad é fué á buscar á Pámphilo de Narvaez, é dexó preso
á Montezuma en poder de Pedro de Alvarado? Porque he oido
sobre esto muchas cosas, é mui diferentes las vnas de las otras ; é yo
querria escrebir verdad, así Dios salve mi ánima.

CAN. Señor Alcayde, eso que preguntais es vn paso en que pocos
de los que hai en la tierra sabrán dar razon, aunque ello fué mui notorio, é mui manifiesta la sinrazon que á los Indios se les hizo, y de allí
tomáron tanto odio con los Christianos que no fiáron mas dellos, y se
siguiéron quantos males ovo despues, é la rebelion de México, y
pienso desta manera: Esos Mexicanos tenian entre las otras sus idolatrías ciertas fiestas del año en que se juntaban á sus ritos é cerimo-
nias ; y llegado el tiempo de vna de aquellas, estaba Alvarado en
guarda de Montezuma, é Cortés era ido donde habeis dicho, é muchos
Indios principales juntáronse é pidiéron licencia al capitan Alvarado,
para ir á celebrar sus fiestas en los patios de sus mezquitas ó qq.
maiores junto al aposento de los españoles, porque no pensasan que
aquel aiuntamiento se hacia á otro fin ; É el dicho Capitan les dió la
licencia. É así los Indios, todos Señores, mas de 600, desnudos, é
con muchas joyas de oro, é hermosos penachos, é muchas piedras
preciosas, é como mas aderezados é gentiles hombres se pudiéron é
supiéron aderezar, é sin arma alguna defensiva ni ofensiva, bailaban é
cantaban é hacian su areito é fiesta segund su costumbre ; é al mejor
tiempo que ellos estaban embebecidos en su regocijo, movido de cob-
dicia el Alvarado hizo poner en cinco puertas del patio cada 15 hombres, é en él entró con la gente restante de los Españoles, é comenzáron á acuchillar é matar los Indios sin perdonar á vno ni á ninguno,
hasta que á todos los acabáron en poco espacio de hora. I esta fué
la causa porque los de México, viendo muertos é robados aquellos
sobre seguro, é sin haber merecido que tal crueldad en ellos hobiese
fecho, se alzáron é hiciéron la guerra al dicho Alvarado, é á los christianos que con él estaban en guarda de Montezuma, é con mucha
razon que tenian para ello.

ALC. ¿Montezuma, como murió? porque diversamente lo he entendido, y ansí lo he yo escripto diferenciadamente.

CAN. Montezuma murió de vna pedrada que los de fuera tiráron,
lo qual no se hiciera, si delante dél no se pusiera vn rodelero, porque
como le vieran ninguno tirara ; y ansí por le cubrir con la rodela, é no
creer que allí estaba Montezuma, le diéron vna pedrada de que murió.
Pero quiero que sepais, Señor Alcayde, que desde la primera revelion

de los Indios hasta que el Marques volvió á la cibdad despues de preso Narvaez, non obstante la pelea ordinaria que con los christianos tenian, siempre Montezuma les hacia dar de comer; é despues que el Marques tornó se le hizo grand recebimiento, é le diéron á todos los Españoles mucha comida. Mas habeis de saber, que el capitan Alvarado, como le acusaba la conciencia, é no arrepentido de su culpa, mas queriéndole dar color, é por aplacar el ánimo de Montezuma, dixo á Hernando Cortés, que fingiese que le queria prender é castigar, porque Montezuma le rogase por él, é que se fuesen muertos por muertos; lo qual Hernando Cortés no quiso hacer, antes mui enojado dixo, que eran vnos perros, é que no habia necesidad de aquel cumplimiento; é envió á vn principal á que hiciesen el Franquez ó Mercado; el qual principal enojado de ver la ira de Cortés y la poca estimacion que hacia de los Indios vivos, y lo poco que se le daba de los muertos, desdeñado el principal é determinado en la venganza fué el primero que renovó la guerra contra los Españoles dentro de vna hora.

ALC. Siempre oí decir que es buena la templanza, é sancta la piedad, é abominable la soberbia. Dicen que fué grandísimo el tesoro que Hernando Cortés repartió entre sus mílites todos, quando determinó de dexar la cibdad é irse fuera della por consejo de vn Botello, que se preciaba de pronosticar lo que estaba por venir.

CAN. Bien sé quien era ese, y en verdad que él fué de parecer que Cortés y los Christianos se saliesen; y al tiempo del efectuarlo no lo hizo saber á todos, antes no lo supiéron, sino los que con él se halláron á esa plática; é los demas que estaban en sus aposentos é cuarteles se quedáron, que eran 270 hombres; los quales se defendiéron ciertos dias peleando hasta que de hambre se diéron á los Indios, é guardáronles la palabra de la manera que Alvarado la guardó á los que es dicho; é así los 270 Christianos, é los que dellos no habian sido muertos peleando todos, quando se rindiéron, fuéron cruelmente sacrificados: pero habeis, Señor, de saber, que desa liberalidad que Hernando Cortés vsó, como decis, entre sus mílites, los que mas parte alcanzáron della, é mas se cargáron de oro é joyas, mas presto los matáron; porque por salvar el albarda murió el Asno que mas pesado la tomó; é los que no la quisiéron, sino sus espaldas é armas, pasáron con menos ocupacion, haciéndose el camino con el espada.

ALC. Grand lástima fué perderse tanto Thesoro y 154 Españoles, è 45 yeguas, é mas de 2000 Indios, é entrellos al Hijo é Hijas de Montezuma, é á todos los otros Señores que trahian presos. Io así lo tengo escripto en el capítulo 14 de esta Historia.

CAN. Señor Alcayde, en verdad quien tal os dixo, ó no lo vidó, ni supo ó quiso callar la verdad. Io os certifico, que fuéron los Españoles muertos en eso, con los que como dixe de suso que quedáron en la cibdad y en los que se perdiéron en el camino siguiendo á Cortés, y continuándose nuestra fuga, mas de 1170; é ási pareció por alarde; è de los Indios nuestros amigos de Tascaltecle, que decis 2000, sin dubda fuéran mas de 8000.

ALC. Maravíllome como despues que Cortés se acogió, é los que escapáron á la tierra de Tascaltecle, como no acabáron á él é á los christianos dexando allá muertos á los amigos; y aun así diz, que no les daban de comer sino por rescate los de Guaulip, que es ya término de Tascaltecle, é el rescate no le querian sino era oro.

CAN. Tenedlo, Señor, por falso todo eso; porque en casa de sus Padres no pudiéron hallar mas buen acogimiento los Christianos, é todo quanto quisiéron, é aun sin pedirlo, se les dió gracioso é de mui buena voluntad.

ALC. Para mucho ha sido el Marques é digno es de quanto tiene, é de mucho mas. É tengo lástima de ver lisiado vn cavallero tan valeroso é manco de dos dedos de la mano izquierda, como lo escrebí é saqué de su relacion, é puse en el capítulo 15. Pero las cosas de la guerra ansí son, é los honores, é la palma de la victoria no se adquieren durmiendo.

CAN. Sin dubda, Señor, Cortés ha sido venturoso é sagaz capitan, é los principales suelen hacer mercedes á quien los sirve, y es bien las hagan á todos los que en su servicio real trabajan; pero algunos he visto yo que trabajan é sirven é nunca medran, é otros que no hacen tanto como aquellos son gratificados é aprovechados; pera ansí fuesen todos remunerados como el Marques lo ha sido en lo de sus dedos de lo que le habeis lástima. Tubo Dios poco que hacer en sanarlo; y salid, Señor, de ese cuidado, que así como los sacó de Castilla, quando pasó la primera vez á estas partes, así se los tiene agora en España; porque nunca fué manco dellos, ni le faltan; y ansí, ni hubo menester cirujano ni milagro para guarecer de ese trabajo.

ALC. Señor Thoan Cano, ¿es verdad aquella crueldad que dicen que el Marques vsó con Chulula, que es vna Cibdad por donde pasó la primera vez que fué á México?

CAN. Mui grand verdad es, pero eso yo no lo ví, porque aun no era yo ido á la tierra; pero supe lo despues de muchos que los viéron é se halláron en esa cruel hazaña.

ALC. ¿Como oístes decir que pasó?

CAN. Lo que oí por cosa mui notoria es, que en aquella cibdad pidió Hernando Cortés 3000 Indios para que llevasen el fardage, é se los diéron, é los hizo todos poner á cuchillo sin que escapase ninguno.

ALC. Razon tiene el Emperador Nuestro Señor de mandar quitar los Indios á todos los Christianos.

CAN. Hágase lo que S. M. mandare é fuese servido, que eso es lo que es mejor; pero yo no querria que padeciesen justos por pecadores: ¿quien hace crueldades paguelas, mas él que no comete delicto porque le han de castigar? Esto es materia para mas espacio; y yo me tengo de envarcar esta noche, é es ya quasi hora del Ave María. Mirad, Señor Alcayde, si hay en México en que pueda yo emplearme en vuestro servicio, que yo lo haré con entera voluntad é obra. Y en lo que toca á la libertad de los Indios, sin dubda á vnos se les habia de rogar con ellos á que los tuviesen é governasen, é los industrasen en las cosas de nuestra sancta fee Católica, é á otros se debian quitar: Pero pues aquí está el Obispo de Chiapa, Fr. Bartolomé de las Casas, que ha sido el movedor é inventor destas mudanzas, é va cargado de frailes mancebos de su órden, con él podeis, Señor Alcayde, desenvolver esta materia de Indios. É yo no me quiero mas entremeter ni hablar en ella, aunque sabria decir mi parte.

ALC. Sin dubda, Señor Thoan Cano, Vmd. habla como prudente, y estas cosas deben ser así ordenadas de Dios, y es de pensar, que este reverendo Obispo de Cibdad Real en la provincia de Chiapa, como celoso del servicio de Dios é de S. M., se ha movido á estas peregrinaciones en que anda, y plega á Dios qué él y sus Frailes acierten á servirles; pero él no está tan bien con migo como pensais, antes se ha quexado de mí por lo que escrebí cerca de aquellos Labradores é nuevos cavalleros que quiso hacer, y con sendas cruces, que querian parecer á las de Calatrava, siendo labradores é de otras mezclas é género de gente baxa, quando fué á Cubagua é á Cumaná, é lo dixo al Señor Obispo de S. Joan, don Rodrigo de Bastidas, para que me lo dixese, y ansí me lo dixo; y lo que yo respondí á su quexa no lo hice por satisfacer al Obispo de San Joan, é su sancta intencion; fué que le supliqué que le dixese, que en verdad yo no tube cuenta ni respecto, quando aquello escreví, á le hacer pesar ni placer, sino á decir lo que pasó; y que viese vn Libro, que es la primera parte destas Historias de Indias, que se imprimió el año de 1535, y allí estaba lo que escrebí; é que holgaba porque estabamos en parte que todo lo que dixe y lo que dexé de decir se provaria facilmerte; y que supiese que aquel Libro estaba ya en Lengua Toscana y Francesa é Alemana é Latina é Griega é Turca é Arábiga, aunque yo le escreví en Castellana; y que pues él continuaba nuevas empresas, y yo no habia de cesar de escrebir las materias de Indias en tanto que S. S. M. M. desto fuesen servidos, que yo tengo esperanza en Dios que le dexara mejor acertar en lo porvenir que en lo pasado, y ansí adelante le pareceria mejor mi pluma. Y como el Señor Obispo de San Joan es tan noble é le consta la verdad, y quan sin pasion yo escribo, el Obispo de Chiapa quedó satisfecho, aun yo no ando por satisfacer á su paladar ni otro, sino por cumplir con lo que debo, hablando con vos, Señor, lo cierto; y por tanto quanto á la carga de los muchos Frailes me parece en verdad que estas tierras manan, ó que llueven Frailes, pero pues son sin canas todos y de 30 años abajo, plega á Dios que todos acierten á servirle. Ya los ví entrar en esta Cibdad de dos en dos hasta 30 dellos, con sendos bordones, é sus sayas é escapularios é sombreros é sin capas, é el Obispo detras dellos. É no parecia vna devota farsa, é agora la comienzan no sabemos en que parará; el tiempo lo dirá, y esto haga Nuestra Señor al propósito de su sancto servicio. Pero pues van hacia aquellos nuevos vulcanes, decidme, Señor, ¿que cosa son, si los habeis visto, y que cosa es otro que teneis allá en la Nueva España, que se dice Guaxocingo?

CAN. El Vulcan de Chalco ó Guaxocingo todo es vna cosa, é alumbraba de noche 3 ó 4 leguas ó mas, é de dia salia continuo humo é á veces llamas de fuego, lo qual está en vn escollo de la sierra nevada, en la qual nunca falta perpetua nieve, é está á 9 leguas de México; pero este fuego é humo que he dicho turó hasta 7 años, poco mas ó menos, despues que Hernando Cortés pasó á aquellas partes, é ya no sale fuego alguno de allí; pero ha quedado mucho azufre é mui bueno, que se ha sacado para hacer pólvora, é hai quanto quisiéron sacar dello: pero en Guatimala hai dos volcanes é montes fogosos, é echan piedras mui grandísimas fuera de sí quemadas, é lanzan aquellas bocas mucho humo, é es cosa de mui horrible aspecto, en especial como le viéron quando murió la pecadora de doña Beatriz de la Cueva, Muger del Adelantado Don Pedro de Alvarado. Plega á nuestro Señor de quedar con Vmd., Señor Alcaide, é dadme licencia que atiende la Barca para irme á la Nao.

ALC. Señor Thoan Cano, el Espíritu Sancto vaya con Vm., y os dé tan próspero viage é navegacion, que en pocos dias y en salvamento llegueis á Vuestra Casa, y halleis á la Sra doña Isabel y los hijos é hijas con la salud que Vmd. y ellos os deseais.

No. XII.—See vol. ii. p. 333.

GRANT OF CORTÉS TO DOÑA ISABEL MONTEZUMA, DAUGH-
TER OF THE EMPEROR MONTEZUMA ; DATED AT MEX-
ICO, JUNE 27, 1526.

[Montezuma, on his death-bed, commended, as we
have seen in the History, three favorite daughters to
the protection of Cortés. After their father's death
they were baptized, and after the Conquest were married to Spaniards of honorable family, and from them
have descended several noble houses in Spain. Cortés
granted, by way of dowry, to the eldest, Doña Isabel,
the city of Tacuba and several other places, embracing
an extensive and very populous district. I have given
here the instrument containing this grant, which has
a singular degree of interest, from the notices it contains of Montezuma's last moments, and the strong
testimony it bears to his unswerving friendship for the
Spaniards. Some allowance must be made by the
reader for the obvious endeavor of Cortés to exhibit
Montezuma's conduct in so favorable a light to the
Castilian government as might authorize the extensive
grant to his daughter.

The instrument in the Muñoz collection was taken
from an ancient copy in the library of Don Rafael
Floranes of Valladolid.]

PRIVILEGIO DE DOÑA ISABEL MOTEZUMA, HIJA DEL GRAN MOTE-
ZUMA, ÚLTIMO REY INDIO DEL GRAN REYNO Y CIBDAD DE MÉ-
XICO, QUE BAUTIZADA Y SIENDO CHRISTIANA CASÓ CON ALONSO
GRADO, NATURAL DE LA VILLA DE ALCANTARA, HIDALGO, Y

CRIADO DE SU MAGESTAD, QUE HABIA SERVIDO Y SERVIA EN
MUCHOS OFFICIOS EN AQUEL REYNO.
OTORGADO POR DON HERNANDO CORTÉS, CONQUISTADOR DEL
DICHO REYNO, EN NOMBRE DE SU MAGESTAD, COMO SU CAPITAN
GENERAL Y GOVERNADOR DE LA NUEVA ESPAÑA.

Por quanto al tiempo que yo, Don Hernando Cortés, capitan general é Governador desta nueva España é sus provincias por S. Mag^d,
pasé á estas partes con ciertos Navíos é gente para las pacificar é poblar
y traher las gentes della al dominio y servidumbre de la Corona Imperial de S. M. como al presente está, y despues de á ellos benido
tuve noticia de un gran Señor, que en esta gran cibdad de Tenextitan
residió, y hera Señor della, y de todas las demas provincias y tierras á
ella comarcanas, que se llamaba Moteçuma, al qual hize saber mi
venida, y como lo supo por los Mensageros que le envié para que me
obedeciese en nombre de S. M. y se ofreciese por su vasallo: Tuvo
por bien la dicha mi venida, é por mejor mostrar su buen celo y voluntad de servir á S. M., y obedecer lo que por mí en su Real nombre le
fuese mandado, me mostró mucho amor, é mandó, que per todas las
partes que pasasen los Españoles hasta llegar á esta Cibdad se nos
hiciese mui buen acogimiento, y se nos diese todo lo que hubiesemos
menester, como siempre se hizo, y mui mejor despues que á esta cibdad llegámos, donde fuímos mui bien recevidos, yo y todos los que en
mi compañía benímos; y aun mostró haberle pesado mucho de algunos recuentros y batallas que en el camino se me ofreciéron antes de la
llegada á esta dicha cibdad, queriéndose él desculpar dello; y que de
lo demas dicho para efetuar y mostrar mejor su buen deseo, huvo por
bien el dicho Moteçuma de estar debajo de la obediencia de S. M., y
en mi poder á manera de preso asta que yo hiciese relacion á S. M.,
y del estado y cosas destas partes, y de la voluntad del dicho Moteçuma; y que estando en esta paz y sosiego, y teniendo yo pacificada
esta dicha tierra docientas leguas y mas hacia una parte y otra con
el sello y seguridad del dicho señor Moteçuma, por la voluntad y
amor que siempre mostró al servicio de S. M., y complacerme á mí
en su real nombre, hasta mas de un año, que se ofreció la venida de
Pánfilo de Narvaez, que los alborotó y escandalizó con sus dañadas
palabras y temores que les puso; por cuyo respeto se levantó contra
el dicho señor Moteçuma un hermano suyo, llamado Auit Lavaci,
Señor de Iztapalapa, y con mucha gente que traxo assí hizo mui
cruda guerra al dicho Moteçuma y a mí y á los Españoles que en mi
compañía estavan, poriéndonos mui recio cerco en los aposentos y

casas donde estavamos; y para quel dicho su hermano y los principales que con él venian cesasen la dicha guerra y alzasen el cerco, se
puso de una ventana el dicho Moteçuma, y estándoles mandando y
amonestando que no lo hiciesen, y que fuesen vasallos de S. M. y
obedeciesen los mandamientos que yo en su real nombre le mandaba,
le tiráron con muchas hondas, y le diéron con una piedra en la cabeza,
que le hiciéron mui gran herida; y temiendo de morir della, me hizo
ciertos razonamientos, trayéndome á la memoria que por el entraña-
ble amor que tenia al servicio de S. M. y á mí en su Real nombre y è
todos los Españoles, padecia tantas heridas y afrentas, lo qual daña por
bien empleado; y que si él de aquella herida fallecia, que me rogava
y encargaba muy afetuosamente, que aviendo respeto á lo mucho que
me queria y deseava complacer, tuviese por bien de tomar á cargo
tres hijas suyas que tenia, y que las hiciese bautizar y mostrar nuestra
doctrina, porque conocia que era mui buena; á las quales, despues
que yo gané esta dicha cibdad, hize luego bautizar, y poner por nom-
bres á la una que es la mayor, su legítima heredera, Doña Isabel, y á
las otras dos, Doña María y Doña Marina; y estando en finamiento
de la dicha herida me tornó á llamar y rogar mui ahincadamente, que
si él muriese, que quirase por aquellas hijas, que eran las mejores
joyas que él me daba, y que partiese con ellas de lo que tenia, por que
no quedasen perdidas, especialmente á la mayor, que esta queria
él mucho; y que si por ventura Dios le escapaba de aquella en-
fermedad, y le daba Victoria en aquel cerco, que él mostraria mas
largamente el deseo que tenia de servir á S. M. y pagarme con obras
la voluntad y amor que me tenia; y que demas desto yo hiciese relacion á su Magestad de como me dexaba estas sus hijas, y le suplicase
en su nombre se sirviese de mandarme que yo mirase por ellas y las
tuviese so mi amparo y administracion, pues él hera tan servidor y
vasallo de S. M. y siempre tuvo mui buena voluntad á los Españoles,
como yo havia visto y via, y por el amor que les tenia le havian dado
el pago que tenia, aunque no le pesaba dello. Y aun en su lengua
me dixo, y entre estos razonamientos que encargaba la conciencia
sobre ello.—Por ende acatando los muchos servicios que el dicho
Señor Moteçuma hizo á S. M. en las buenas obras que siempre en su
vida me hizo, y buenos tratamientos de los Españoles que en mi compañía yo tenia en su real nombre, y la voluntad que me mostró en su
real servicio; y que sin duda él no fué parte en el levantamiento desta
dicha cibdad, sino el dicho su hermano; antes se esperaba, como yo
tenia por cierto, que su vida fuera mucha ayuda para que la tierra es-

tuviera siempre mui pacífica, y vinieran los naturales della en verdadero conocimiento, y se sirviera S. M. con mucha suma de pesos de oro y joyas y otras cosas, y por causa de la venida del dicho Narvaez y de la guerra que el dicho su hermano Auit Lavaci levantó, se perdiéron; y considerando asi mismo que Dios nuestro señor y S. M. son mui servidos que en estas partes planté nuestra santíssima Religion, como de cada dia la en crecimiento: Y que las dichas hijas de Moteçuma y los demas Señores y principales y otras personas de los naturales desta Nueva España se les dé y muestre toda la mas y mejor Dotrina que fuere posible, para quitarlos de las idolatrías en que hasta aquí han estado, y traerlos al verdadero conocimiento de nuestra sancta fee cathólica, especialmente los hijos de los mas principales, como lo era este Señor Moteçuma, y que en esto se descargava la conciencia de S. M. y la mia; en su real nombre tuve por bien de azetar su ruego, y tener en mi casa á las dichas tres sus hijas, y hacer, como he hecho, que se les haga todo el mejor tratamiento y acogimiento que ha podido, haciéndoles administrar y enseñar los mandamientos de nuestra santa fe cathólica y las otras buenas costumbres de Christianos, para que con mejor voluntad y amor sirvan á Dios nuestro Señor y conozcan y los Artículos della, y que los demas naturales tomen exemplo. Me pareció que segun la calidad de la persona de la dicha Doña Isabel, que es la mayor y legítima heredera del dicho Señor Moteçuma, y que mas encargada me dejó, y que su edad requeria tener compañía, le he dado por marido y esposo á una persona de honra, Hijo-Dalgo, y que ha servido á S. M. en mi compañía dende el principio que á estas partes pasó, teniendo por mí y en nombre de S. M. cargos y oficios mui honrosos, así de Contador y mi lugartheniente de Capitan Governador como de otras muchas, y dado dellas mui buena cuenta, y al presente está á su administracion el cargo y oficio de visitador general de todos los Indios desta dicha Nueva España, el qual se dice y nombra Alonso Grado, natural de la villa de Alcantara. Con la qual dicha Doña Isabel le prometo y doi en dote y arras á la dicha Doña Isabel y sus descendientes, en nombre de S. M., como su Go-vernador y Capitan General destas partes, y porque de derecho le per-tenece de su patrimonio y legítima, el Señorío y naturales del Pueblo de Tacuba, que tiene ciento é veinte casas; y Yeteve, que es estancia que tiene quarenta casas; y Izqui Luca, otra estancia, que tiene otras ciento y veinte casas; y Chimalpan, otra estancia, que tiene quarenta casas; y Chapulma Loyan, que tiene otras quarenta casas; y Escapu-caltango, que tiene veinte casas; é Xiloango, que tiene quarenta

casas; y otra estancia que se dice Ocoiacaque, y otra que se dice
Castepeque, y otra que se dice Talanco, y otra estancia que se dice
Goatrizco, y otra estancia que se dice Duotepeque, y otra que se dice
Tacala, que podrá haver en todo mil y docientas y quarenta casas;
las quales dichas estancias y pueblos son subjetos al pueblo de Tacuba
y al Señor della. Lo qual, como dicho es, doy en nombre de S. M.
en dote y arras á la dicha Doña Isabel para que lo haya y tenga y goce
por juro de heredad, para agora y para siempre jamas, con título de
Señora de dicho Pueblo y de lo demas aquí contenido. Lo qual le
doy en nombre de S. M. por descargar su Real conciencia y la mia en
su nombre.—Por esta digo; que no le será quitado ni removido por
cosa alguna, en ningun tiempo, ni por alguna manera; y para mas
saneamiento prometo y doy mi fe en nombre de S. M., que si se lo
escriviese, le haré relacion de todo, para que S. M. se sirva de confirmar esta Merced de la dicha Doña Isabel y á los dichos sus here-
deros y subcesores del dicho Pueblo de Tacuba y lo demas aquí
contenido, y de otras estancias á él subjetas, que están en poder de
algunos Españoles, para que S. M. asimismo se sirva demandárselas
dar y confirmar juntamente con las que al presente le doy; que poi
estar, como dicho es, en poder de Españoles, no se las dí hasta ver si
S. M. es dello servido; y doy por ninguna y de ningun valor y efeto
qualquier cédula de encomienda y depósito que del dicho pueblo de
Tacuba y de las otras estancias aquí contenidas y declaradas yo aya
dado á qualquiera persona; por quanto yo en nombre de S. M. las
revoco y lo restituyo y doi á la dicha Doña Isabel, para que lo tenga
como cosa suya propia y que de derecho le pertenece. Y mando á
todas y qualesquier personas, vecinos y moradores desta dicha Nueva
España, estantes y habitantes en ella, que hayan y tengan á la dicha
Doña Isabel por Señora del dicho pueblo de Tacuba con las dichas
estancias, y que no le impidan ni estorven cosa alguna della, so pena
de quinientos pesos de oro para la cámara y fino de S. Mag^d.—Fecho
á veinte y siete dias del mes de Junio de mil y quinientos y veinte y
seis años.—Don Hernando de Cortés.—Por mandado del Governador
mi señor.—Alonso Baliente.

No. XIII.—See vol. ii. p. 442.

MILITARY CODE ; DATED AT TLASCALA, DEC. 22, 1520.

[These Regulations, proclaimed by Cortés at Tlascala on the eve of the final march against Mexico, show the careful discipline established in his camp, and, to some extent, the nature of his military policy. The Code forms part of the collection of Muñoz.]

ORDENANZAS MILITARES.

Este dia á voz de pregonero publicó sus Ordenanzas, cuyo proemio es este.

Porque por muchas escrituras y corónicas auténticas nos es notorio é manifiesto quanto los antiguos que siguiéron el exercicio de la guerra procuráron é travaxáron de introducir tales y tan buenas costumbres y ordenaciones, con las cuales y con su propia virtud y fortaleza pudiesen alcanzar y conseguir victoria y próspero fin en las conquistas y guerras, que hobiesen de hacer é seguir ; é por el contrario vemos haber sucedido grandes infortunios, desastres, é muertes á los que no siguiéron la buena costumbre y órden que en la guerra se debe tener ; e les haber sucedido semejantes casos con poca pujanza de los enemigos, segun parece claro por muchos exemplos antiguos é modernos, que aquí se podrian espresar ; é porque la órden es tan loable, que no tan solamente en las cosas humanas mas aun en las divinas se ama y sigue, y sin ella ninguna cosa puede haber cumplido efecto, como que ello sea un principio, medio, y fin para el buen reximiento de todas las cosas : Por ende yo, H. C., Capitan general é Justicia mayor en esta Nueva España del mar occéano por el mui alto, mui poderoso, é mui católico D. Cárlos nuestro Señor, electo Rey de Romanos, futuro Emperador semper Augusto, Rey de España é de otros muchos grandes reynos é Señoríos, considerando todo lo suso dicho, y que si los pasados falláron ser necesario hacer Ordenanzas é costumbres por donde se rigiesen é gobernasen aquellos que hubiesen de seguir y exercer el uso de la guerra, á los Españoles que en mi compañía agora están é estubiesen é á mí nos es mucho mas necesario é conveniente seguir y observar toda la mejor costumbre y órden que nos sea posible, así por lo que toca al servicio de Dios nuestro Señor y de la sacra Católica Magestad, como por tener por enemigos y contrarios á la mas belicosa y astuta gente en la guerra é de mas géneros de armas que ninguna otra generacion, especialmente por ser tanta que no tiene número, é nosotros tan pocos y tan apartados y destituidos de todo humano socorro; viendo ser mui necesario y cumplidero al servicio de su Cesarea Magestad é utilidad nuestra, Mandé hacer é hicemas Ordenanzas que de yuso serán contenidas é irán firmadas de mì nombre é del infrascrito en la manera siguiente.

PRIMERAMENTE, por quanto por la experiencia que habemos visto é cada dia vemos quanta solicitud y vigilancia los naturales de estas partes tienen en la cultura y veneracion de sus ídolos, de que á Dios nuestro Señor se hace gran deservicio, y el demonio por la ceguedad y engaño en que los trae es de ellos muy venerado; y en los apartar de tanto error é idolatría y en los reducir al conocimiento de nuestra Santa Fe católica nuestro Señor será muy servido, y demas de adquirir gloria para nuestras ánimas con ser causa que de aquí adelante no se pierdan ni condenen tantos, acá en lo temporal seria Dios siempre en nuestra ayuda y socorro: por ende, con toda la justicia que puedo y debo, exhorto y ruego á todos los Españoles que en mi compañía fuesen á esta guerra que al presente vamos, y á todas las otras guerras y conquistas que en nombre de S. M. por mi mandado hubiesen de ir, que su principal motivo é intencion sea apartar y desarraigar de las dichas idolatrías á todos los naturales destas partes, y reducillos, ó á lo menos desear su salvacion, y que sean reducidos al conocimiento de Dios y de su Santa Fe católica; porque si con otra intencion se hiciese la dicha guerra, seria injusta, y todo lo que en ella se oviese Onoloxio é obligado á restitucion, é S. M. no ternia razon de mandar gratificar á los que en ellas sìrviesen. É sobre ello encargo la conciencia á los dichos Españoles, é desde ahora protesto en nombre de S. M. que mi principal intencion é motivo en facer esta guerra é las otras que ficiese por traer y reducir á los dichos naturales al dicho conocimiento de nuestra Santa Fe é creencia; y despues por los sozjugar é supeditar debajo del yugo é dominio imperial é real de su Sacra Magestad, á quien juridicamente el Señorío de todas estas partes.

Yt. En por quanto de los reniegos é blasfemias Dios nuestro Señor es mucho deservido, y es la mayor ofensa que á su Santísimo nombre se puede hacer, y por eso permite en las gentes recios y duros castigos; y no basta que seamos tan malos que por los inmensos beneficios que de cada dia dél recibimos no le demos gracias, mas decimos mal é blasfemamos de su santo nombre; y por evitar tan aborrecible uso y pecado, mando que ninguna persona, de qualquiera condicion que sea, no sea osado decir, No creo en Dios, ni Pese, ni Reniego, ni Del cielo, ni No ha poder en Dios; y que lo mismo se entienda de Nuestra Señora y de todos los otros Santos: sopena que demas de ser executadas las penas establecidas por las leyes del reyno contra los blasfemos, la persona que en lo susodicho incurriese pague 15 caste-llanos de oro, la tercera parte para la primera Cofradía de Nuestra Señora que en estas partes se hiciese, y la otra tercera parte para el fisco de S. M., y la otra tercera parte para el juez que lo sentenciase.

Yt. Porque de los juegos muchas y las mas veces resultan reniegos y blasfemias, é nacen otros inconvenientes, é es justo que del todo se prohiban y defiendan; por ende mando que de aquí adelante ninguna persona sea osada de jugar á naypes ni á otros juegos vedados dineros ni preseas ni otra cosa alguna; sopena de perdimiento de todo lo que jugase é de 20 pesos de oro, la mitad de todo ello para la Cámara, é la otra mitad para el juez que lo sentenciase. Pero por quanto en las guerras es bien que tenga la gente algun exercicio, y se acostumbra y permítese que jueguen por que se eviten otros mayores inconveni-entes; permítese que en el aposento donde estubiese se jueguen naypes é otros juegos moderadamente, con tanto que no sea á los dados, porque allí es curarse han de no de decir mal, é á lo menos si lo dixesen serán castigados.

Yt. Que ninguno sea osado de echar mano á la espada ó puñal ó otra arma alguna para ofender á ningun Español; sopena que él que lo contrario hiciese, si fuese hidalgo, pague 100 pesos de oro, la mitad para el fisco de S. M., y la otra mitad para los gastos de la Xusticia; y al que no fuese hidalgo se le han de dar 100 azotes publicamente.

Yt. Por quanto acaese que algunos Españoles por no valar é hacer otras cosas se dexan de aputar en las copias de los Capitanes que tienen gente: por ende mando que todos se alisten en las Capitanías que yo tengo hechas é hiciese, excepto los que yo señalaré que queden fuera dellas, con apercibimiento que dende agora se les face, que él que ansí no lo hiciese, no se le dará parte ni partes algunas.

Otrosí, por quanto algunas veces suele acaecer, que en burlas é por pasar tiempo algunas personas que están en una capitanía burlan é porfian de algunos de las otras Capitanías, y los unos dicen de los otros, y los otros de los otros, de que se suelen recrecer quistiones é escándalos; por ende mando que de aquí adelante ninguno sea osado de burlar ni decir mal de ninguna Capitanía ni la perjudicar ; sopena de 20 pesos de oro, la mitad para la Cámara, y la otra mitad para los gastos de Xusticia.

Otrosí, que ninguno de los dichos Españoles no se aposente ni pose en ninguna parte, exepto en el lugar é parte donde estubiese aposentada su capitan ; supena de 12 pesos de oro, aplicados en la forma contenida en el capítulo antecedente.

Yt. Que ningun capitan se aposente en ninguna poblacion ó villa ó ciudad, sino en el pueblo que le fuese señalado por el Maestro de Campo, sopena de 10 pesos de oro, aplicados en la forma suso dicha.

Yt. Por quanto cada Capitan tenga mejor acaudillada su gente, mando que cada uno de los dichos Capitanes tenga sus cuadrillas de 20 en 20 Españoles, y con cada una quadrilla un quadrillero ó cabo de escuadra, que sea persona hábil y de quien se deba confiar ; so la dicha pena.

Otrosí, que cada uno de los dichos quadrilleros ó cabos desquadra ronden sobre las velas todos los quartos que les cupiese de velar, so la dicha pena ; é que la vela que hallasen durmiendo, ó ausente del lugar donde debiese velar, pague cuatro Castellanos, aplicados en la forma suso dicha, y demas que esté atado medio dia.

Otrosí, que los dichos quadrilleros tengan cuidado de avisar y avisen á las velas que hubiesen de poner, que puesto que recaudo en el Real no desamparen ni dexen los portillos ó calles ó pasos donde les fuese mandado velar y se vayan de allí á otra parte por ninguna necesidad que digan que les constriñó hasta que sean mandado ; sopena de 50 castellanos, aplicados en la forma suso dicha al que fuese hijo dalgo ; y sino lo fuese, que le sean dados 100 azotes publicamente.

Otrosí, que cada Capitan que por mí fuese nombrado tenga y traiga consigo su tambor é bandera para que rija y acaudille mejor la gente que tenga á su cargo ; sopena de 10 pesos de oro, aplicados en la forma suso dicha.

Otrosí, que cada Español que oyese tocar el atambor de su compañía sea obligado á salir e salga á acompañar su bandera con todas sus armas en forma y á punto de guerra ; sopena de 20 castellanos aplicados en la forma arriba declarada.

Otrosí, que todas las veces que yo mandase mover el Real para alguna parte cada Capitan sea obligado de llevar por el camino toda su gente junta y apartada de las otras Capitanías, sinque se entrometa en ella ningun Español de otra Capitanía ninguna ; y para ello constriñan é apremien á los que así llevasen debaxo de su bandera segun uso de guerra; sopena de 10 pesos de oro, aplicados en la forma suso declarada.

Yt. Por quanto acaece que antes ó al tiempo de romper en los enemigos algunos Españoles se meten entre el fardage, demas de ser pusilanimidad, es cosa fea el mal exemplo para los Indios nuestros amigos que nos acompañan en la guerra: por ende mando que ningun Español se entremeta ni vaya con el fardage, salvo aquellos que para ello fuesen dados é señalados: sopena de 20 pesos de oro, aplicados segun que de suso contiene.

Otrosí, por quanto acaece algunas veces que algunos Españoles fuera de órden y sin les ser mandado arremeten ó rompen en algun esquadron de los enemigos, é por se desmandar ansí se desbaratan y salen fuera de ordenanza, de que suele recrecerse peligro á los mas: por ende mando que ningun Capitan se desmande á romper por los enemigos sin que primeramente por mí le sea mandado; sopena de muerte. En otra persona se desmanda, si fuese hijodalgo, pena de 100 pesos, aplicados en la forma suso dicha; y si no fuese hidalgo, le sean dados 100 azotes publicamente.

Yt. Por quanto podria ser que al tiempo que entran á tomar por fuerza alguna poblacion ó villa ó ciudad á los enemigos, antes de ser del todo echados fuera, con codicia de robar, algun Español se entrase en alguna casa de los Enemigos, de que se podria seguir daño: por ende mando que ningun Español ni Españoles entren á robar ni á otra cosa alguna en las tales casas de los enemigos, hasta ser del todo echados fuera, y haber conseguido el fin de la victoria; sopena de 20 pesos de oro, aplicados en la manera que dicha es.

Yt. Si por escusar y evitar los hurtos encubiertos y fraudes que se hacen en las cosas habidas en la guerra ó fuera de ella, así por lo que toca al quinto que dellas pertenece á su católica Magestad, como porque han de ser repartidas conforme á lo que cada una sirve é merece: por ende mando que todo el oro, plata, perlas, piedras, plumage, ropa, esclavos, y otras cosas qualesquier que se adquieran, hubiesen, ó tomasen en qualquier manera, ansí en las dichas poblaciones, villas, ó ciudades, como en el campo, que la persona ó personas á cuyo poder viniese ó la hallasen ó tomasen, en qualquier forma que sea, lo traigan luego incontinente é manifiesten ante mí ó ante otra persona que fuese sin lo meter ni llevar á su posada ni á otra parte alguna; sopena de muerte é perdimiento de todos sus bienes para la Cámara é fisco de S. M.

É por quanto lo suso dicho é cada una cosa é parte dello se guarde é cumpla segun é de la manera que aquí de suso se contiene, y de ninguna cosa de lo aquí contenida pretendan ignorancia, mando que sea apregonado publicamente, para que venga á noticia de todos: Que fuéron hechas las dichas Ordenanzas en la ciudad y provincia de Taxclateque selado 22 dias del mes de Diciembre, año del nascimiento de nuestro Salvador Jesu Christo de 1520 años.

Pregonáronse las dichas Ordenanzas desuso contenidas en la ciudad é provincia de Taxclatecle, miércoles dia de San Estéban, que fuesen 26 dias del mes de Diciembre, año del nacimiento de nuestro Salvador Jesu Christo de 1520 años; estando presente el magnífico Señor Fernando Cortés, capitan general é Justicia mayor de esta Nueva España del mar Occéano por el Emperador nuestro Señor, por ante mí, Juan de Rivera, escribano é Notario público en todos los Reinos é Señoríos de España por las Autoridades apostólica y Real. Lo qual pregonó en voz alta Anton Garcia pregonero, en el Alarde que la gente de á caballo é de á pie que su merced mandó facer é se fizo el dicho dia. A lo qual fuéron testigos que estaban presentes, Gonzalo de Sandoval, Alguacil mayor, é Alonso de Prado, contador, é Rodrigo Alvarez Chico, veedor por S. M., é otras muchas personas.—Fecho ut supra. —Juan de Rivera.

No. XIV.—See vol. iii. p. 290.

TRANSLATION OF PASSAGES IN THE HONDURAS LETTER OF CORTÉS.

[I have noticed this celebrated Letter, the *Carta Quinta* of Cortés, so particularly in the body of the work, that little remains to be said about it here. I have had these passages translated to show the reader the circumstantial and highly graphic manner of the general's narrative. The latter half of the Letter is occupied with the events which occurred in Mexico in the absence of Cortés and after his return. It may be considered, therefore, as part of the regular series of his historical correspondence, the publication of which

was begun by archbishop Lorenzana. Should another
edition of the Letters of Cortés be given to the world,
this one ought undoubtedly to find a place in it.]

A lake of great width and proportionate depth was the difficulty
which we had to encounter. In vain did we turn to the right and to
the left; the lake was equally wide in every direction. My guides
told me that it was useless to look for a ford in the vicinity, as they
were certain the nearest one was towards the mountains, to reach
which would necessarily be a journey of five or six days. I was extremely puzzled what measure to adopt. To return was certain death;
as, besides being at a loss for provisions, the roads, in consequence of
the rains which had prevailed, were absolutely impassable. Our situation was now perilous in the extreme; on every side was room for
despair, and not a single ray of hope illumined our path. My followers had become sick of their continual labor, and had as yet reaped
no benefit from their toils. It was therefore useless for me to look to
them for advice in our present truly critical position. Besides the
primitive band and the horses, there were upwards of three thousand
five hundred Indians who followed in our train. There was one solitary canoe lying on the beach, in which, doubtless, those whom I had
sent in advance had crossed. At the entrance of the lake, and on the
other side, were deep marshes, which rendered our passage of the
lake considerably more doubtful. One of my companions entered
into the canoe, and found the depth of the lake to be five-and-twenty
feet, and, with some lances tied together, I ascertained that the mud
and slime were twelve feet more, making in all a depth of nearly forty
feet. In this juncture, I resolved that a floating bridge should be
made, and for this purpose requested that the Indians would lend
their assistance in felling the wood, whilst I and my followers would
employ ourselves in preparing the bridge. The undertaking seemed
to be of such magnitude that scarcely any one entertained an idea of
its being completed before our provisions were all exhausted. The
Indians, however, set to work with the most commendable zeal. Not
so with the Spaniards, who already began to comment upon the
labors they had undergone, and the little prospect which appeared of
their termination. They proceeded to communicate their thoughts
one to another, and the spirit of disaffection had now attained such a
height that some had the hardihood to express their disapprobation of
my proceedings to my very face. Touched to the quick with this

show of desertion when I had least expected it, I said to them that I needed not their assistance ; and, turning towards the Indians who accompanied me, exposed to them the necessity we lay under of using the most strenuous exertions to reach the other side, for if this point were not effected we should all perish from hunger. I then pointed in the opposite direction, in which the province of Acalan lay, and cheered their spirits with the prospect of there obtaining provisions in abundance, without taking into consideration the ample supply which would be afforded us by the caravels. I also promised them, in the name of your Majesty, that they should be recompensed to the fullest extent of their wishes, and that not a person who contributed his assistance should go unrewarded. My little oration had the best possible effect with the Indians, who promised, to a man, that their exertions should only terminate with their lives. The Spaniards, ashamed of their previous conduct, surrounded me and requested that I would pardon their late act ; alleging, in extenuation of their offence, the miserable position in which they were placed, obliged to support themselves with the unsavory roots which the earth supplied, and which were scarcely sufficient to keep them alive. They immediately proceeded to work, and, though frequently ready to fall from fatigue, never made another complaint. After four days' incessant labor the bridge was completed, and both horse and man passed without the slightest accident. The bridge was constructed in so solid a manner that it would be impossible to destroy it otherwise than by fire. More than one thousand beams were united for its completion, and every one of them was thicker than a man's body, and sixty feet long.

*   *   *   *   *   *   *   *   *

At two leagues' distance from this place, the mountains commenced. From no words of mine, nor of a more gifted man, can your Majesty form an adequate idea of the asperity and unevenness of the place which we were now ascending. He alone who has experienced the hardships of the route, and who himself has been an eye-witness, can be fully sensible of its difficulty. It will be sufficient for me to say, in order that your Majesty may have some notion of the labor which we had to undergo, that we were twelve days before we got entirely free of it,—a distance altogether of eight leagues ! Sixty-eight horses died on the passage, the greater part having fallen down the precipices which abounded on every side ; and the few that escaped seemed so overcome that we thought not a single one would ever afterwards prove serviceable. More than three months elapsed before they re-

covered from the effects of the journey. It never ceased to rain, day
or night, from the time we entered the mountain until we left it; and
the rock was of such a nature that the water passed away without collecting in any place in sufficient quantity to allow us to drink. Thus,
in addition to the other hardships which we had to encounter, was that
most pressing of all, thirst. Some of the horses suffered considerably
from the want of this truly necessary article, and but for the culinary
and other vessels which we had with us, and which served to receive
some of the rain, neither man nor horse could possibly have escaped.
A nephew of mine had a fall upon a piece of sharp rock, and frac-
tured his leg in three or four places; thus was our labor increased, as
the men had to carry him by turns. We had now but a league to
journey before we could arrive at Tenas, the place which I mentioned as belonging to the chief of Tayco; but here a formidable
obstacle presented itself, in a very wide and very large river, which
was swollen by the continued rains. After searching for some time,
one of the most surprising fords ever heard of was discovered. Some
huge jutting cliffs arrest the progress of the river, in consequence of
which it extends for a considerable space around. Between these cliffs
are narrow channels, through which the water rushes with an impetuosity which baffles description. From one of these rocks to another
we threw large trunks of trees, which had been felled with much labor.
Ropes of bass-weed were affixed to these trunks; and thus, though
at imminent risk of our lives, we crossed the river. If anybody had
become giddy in the transit, he must unavoidably have perished. Of
these passes there were upwards of twenty, and we took two whole
days to get clear, by this extraordinary way.

* * * * * * * * *

It were indeed an arduous task for me to describe to your Majesty
the joy which pervaded every countenance when this truly inspiring
account was received. To be near the termination of a journey so
beset with hardships and labor as ours had been, was an event that
could not but be hailed with rapture. Our last four days' march subjected us to innumerable trials; as, besides being without any certainty
of our proceeding in the right direction, we were ever in the heart of
mountains abounding with precipices on every side. Many horses
dropped on the way; and a cousin of mine, Juan Davilos by name,
fell down a precipice and broke an arm. Had it not been for the suit
of armor which he wore, he would have been infallibly dashed to
pieces. As it was, besides having his arm broken, he was dreadfully

lacerated. His horse, upon which he was mounted, having no protection, was so wounded by the fall that we were obliged to leave him behind. With much difficulty we succeeded in extricating my cousin from his perilous situation. It would be an endless task to relate to your Majesty the many sufferings which we endured; amongst which the chief was from hunger; for, although we had some swine which we had brought from Mexico, upwards of eight days had elapsed without our having tasted bread. The fruit of the palm-tree boiled with hogs' flesh, and without any salt, which we had exhausted some time previous, formed our only sustenance. They were alike destitute of provisions at the place at which we had now arrived, where they lived in constant dread of an attack from the adjoining Spanish settlement. They needed not to fear such an event; as, from the situation in which I found the Spaniards, they were incapable of doing the slightest mischief. So elated were we all with our neighborhood to Nico that all our past troubles were soon forgotten, as are the dangers of the sea by the weather-beaten sailor, who on his arrival in port thinks no more of the perils he has encountered. We still suffered greatly from hunger; for even the unsavory roots were procured with the greatest difficulty; and, after we had been occupied many hours in collecting them, they were devoured with the greatest eagerness, in the shortest space of time imaginable.

No. XV.—See vol. iii. p. 328.

LAST LETTER OF CORTÉS TO THE EMPEROR.

[I give this Letter of Cortés entire, *Ultima y sentidisima Carta*, his "Last and most touching Letter," as it is styled by Vargas Ponçe, who has embraced it in his important collection from the archives of Seville.*

* [It has since been printed in the Col. de Doc. inéd. para la Hist. de España, tom. i., affording an opportunity for correcting the almost innumerable errors which disfigure the transcription of Vargas Ponçe and render it scarcely intelligible.—ED.]

It may be called touching, when we consider the tone of it, as compared with the former correspondence of its author, and the gloomy circumstances under which it was written. Yet we are not to take the complaints contained in it of his poverty too literally; since at his death, but three years after, he left immense estates. But these estates were so much embarrassed by his expensive and disastrous expeditions in the South Sea that his income during the rest of his life seems to have been scarcely sufficient to meet his ordinary expenditure. The last days of Cortés, wasted in ineffectual attempts to obtain redress from the court whom he had so signally served, remind us of the similar fate of Columbus. The history of both may teach us that the most brilliant career too often leads only to sorrow and disappointment, as the clouds gather round the sun at his setting.]

Pensé que haber trabajado en la juventud me aprovechara para que en la vejez tubiera descanso, y así ha quarenta años que me he ocupado en no dormir, mal comer, y á las veces ni bien ni mal, traer las armas á cuestas, poner la persona en peligro, gastar mi hacienda y edad, todo en servicio de Dios, trayendo obejas en su corral muy remotas de nuestro hemisferio, ignotas, y no escriptas en nuestras Escrituras, y acrecentando y dilatando el nombre y patrimonio de mi Rey, ganándole y trayéndole á su yugo y Real cetro muchos y muy grandes reynos y señoríos de muchas bárvaras naciones y gentes, ganados por mi propia persona y espensas, sin ser ayudado de cosa alguna, hantes muy estorvado por muchos émulos y invidiosos, que como sanguijuelas han reventado de artos de mi sangre. De la parte que á Dios cupo de mis trabajos y vigilias asaz estoy pagado, porque seyendo la obra suya, quiso tomarme por medio, y que las gentes me atribuyesen alguna parte, aunque quien conociere de mí lo que yo, beré claro que no sin causa la divina providencia quiso que una hobra tan grande se acavase por el mas flaco é inútil medio que se pudo hallar, porque á solo dios fuese el atributo. De lo que á mi rey quedó, la remuneracion siempre

estuve satisfecho, que ceteris paribus no fuera menor por ser en tiempo
de V. M., que nunca estos reynos de España, donde yo soy natural y
á quien cupo este beneficio, fuéron poseydos de tan grande y Católico
príncipe, magnánimo y poderoso Rey; y así V. M., la primera vez que
vesé las manos y entregué los frutos de mis servicios, mostró recono-
cimiento dellos y comenzó á mostrar voluntad de me hacer gratifica-
cion, honrrando mi persona con palabras y hobras, que pareciéndome
á mí que no se equiparaban á mis méritos, V. M. sabe que rehusé yo
de recibir. V. M. me dijo y mandó que las aceptase, porque pareciese
que me comenzaba á hacer alguna merced, y que no las reciviese por
pago de mis servicios; porque V. M. se queria haber con migo, como
se han los que se muestran á tirar la ballesta, que los primeros tiros
dan fuera del terrero, y enmendando dan en él y en el blanco y fiel;
que la merced que V. M. me hacia hera dar fuera del terrero, y que
iria enmendando hasta dar en el fiel de lo que yo merecia; y pues
que no se me quitava nada de lo que tenia, ni se me había de quitar,
que reciviese lo que me dava; y ansí vesé las manos á V. M. por ello,
y enbolviendo las espaldas quitóseme lo que tenia todo, y no se me
cumplió la merced que V. M. me hizo. Y demas destas palabras que
V. M. me dijo, y obras que me prometió, que, pues tiene tan buena
memoria, no se le habrán olvidado, por cartas de V. M. firmadas de
su real nombre tengo otras muy mayores. Y pues mis servicios hechos
hasta allí son beneméritos de las obras y promesas que V. M. me
hizo, y despues acá no lo han desmerecido; antes nunca he cesado de
servir y acrecentar el Patrimonio de estos reynos, con mil estorvos,
que si no obiera tenido no fuera menos lo acrecentado, despues que la
merced se me hizo, que lo hecho porque la merecí, no sé porque no
se me cumple la promesa de las mercedes ofrecidas, y se me quitan
las hechas. Y si quisieren decir que no se me quitan, pues poseo algo;
cierto es que nada é inútil son una mesma cosa, y lo que tengo es tan
sin fruto, que me fuera arto mejor no tenerlo, porque obiera entendido
en mis grangerías, y no gastado el fruto de ellas por defenderme del
fiscal de V. M., que a sido y es mas dificultoso que ganar la tierra de
los enemigos; así que mi trabajo aprovechó para mi contentamiento
de haber hecho el dever, y no para conseguir el efecto dél, pues no
solo no se me siguió reposo á la vejez, mas trabajo hasta la muerte; y
pluguiese á Dios que no pasase adelante, sino que con la corporal se
acabase, y no se estendiese á la perpetua, porque quien tanto trabajo
tiene en defender el cuerpo no puede dejar de ofender al ánima. Su-
plico á V. M. no permita que á tan notorios servicios haya tan poco mi·

ramiento, y pues es de creer que no es á culpa de V. M. que las gentes
lo sepan ; porque como esta obra que Dios hizo por mi medio es tan
grande y maravillosa, y se ha estendido la fama de ella por todos los
reynos de V. M. y de los otros reyes cristianos y aun por algunos infieles, en estos donde hay noticia del pleito de entre el fiscal y mí, no
se trata de cosa mas ; y unos atribuyen la culpa al fiscal, otros á culpas
mias ; y estas no las hallan tan grandes, que si bastasen para por ellas
negárseme el premio, no bastasen tambien para quitarme la vida,
honrra, y hacienda ; y que pues esto no se hace que no deve ser mia la
culpa. Á V. M. ninguna se atribuye ; porque si V. M. quisiese quitarme
lo que me dió, poder tiene para ejecutarlo, pues al que quiere y puede
nada hay imposible ; decir que se vuscan formas para colorar la obra,
y que no se sienta el intento, ni caven ni pueden caber en los reyes
unjidos por Dios tales medios, porque para con él no hay color que no
sea transparente, para con el mundo no hay para que colorarlo, por
que así lo quiero, así lo mando, es el descargo de lo que los reyes hacen.
Yo supliqué á V. M. en Madrid fuese servido de aclarar la boluntad que
tubo de hacerme merced en pago de mis servicios, y le traje á la memoria algunos de ellos ; díjome V. M. que mandaria á los del su consejo
que me despachasen ; pensé que se les dejava mandado lo que abian
de hacer, porque V. M. me dijo que no queria que trajese pleyto con
el fiscal : cuando quise saberlo, dijéronme que me defendiese de la
demanda del fiscal, porque havia de ir por tela de justicia, y por ella se
habia de sentenciar : sentílo por grave, y escrebí á V. M. á Barcelona,
suplicándole que pues era servido de entrar en juicio de su siervo,
lo fuese en que obiese Juezes sin sospecha y V. M. mandase que
con los del Consejo de las Indias se juntasen algunos de los otros,
pues todos son criados de V. M., y que juntos lo determinasen ; no
fué V. M. servido, que no puedo alcanzar la causa, pues quantos mas
lo viesen mejor alcanzarian lo que se devia hacer. Véome viejo y pobre
y empeñado en este reyno en mas de veinte mil ducados, sin mas de
ciento otros, que he gastado de los que traje é me han enviado, que
algunos de ellos debo tambien que los an tomado prestados para en-
viarme, y todos corren cambios ; y en cinco años poco menos que ha que
salí de mi casa, no es mucho lo que he gastado, pues nunca ha salido de
la Corte, con tres hijos que traygo en ella, con letrados, procuradores,
y solicitadores ; que todo fuera mejor empleado que V. M. se sirviera
de ello y de lo que yo mas hoviera adquirido en este tiempo ; ha
ayudado tambien la ida de Árgel. Pareceme que al cojer del fruto de
is trabajos no devia hecharlo en basijas rotas, y dejarlo en juicio de

pocos, sino tornar á suplicar á V. M. sea servido que todos quantos jueces V. M. tiene en sus Consejos conozcan de esta causa, y conforme á justicia la sentenciase.—Yo he sentido del obispo de Cuenca que desea que obiese para esto otros jueces demas de los que hay ; porque él y el licenciado Salmeron, nuebo Oidor en este Consejo de Indias, son los que me despojáron sin hoyrme de hecho, siendo jueces en la nueva España, como lo tengo provado, y con quien yo traigo pleito sobre el dicho despojo, y les pido cantidad de dineros de los intereses y rentas de lo que me despojáron ; y está claro que no han de sentenciar contra sí. No les he querido recusar en este caso, porque siempre crey que V. M. fuera servido que no llegara á estos términos ; y no seyendo V. M. servido que hayan mas jueces que determinen esta causa, serme ha forzado recusar al Obispo de Cuenca y á Salmeron, y pesar mehía en el ánima porque no podrá ser sin alguna dilacion ; que para mí no puede ser cosa mas dañosa, porque he sesenta años, y anda en cinco que salí de mi casa, y no tengo mas de un hijo Varon que me suceda ; y aunque tengo la muger moza para poder tener mas, mi hedad no sufre esperar mucho ; y si no tubiera otro, y dios dispusiera de este sin dejar sucesion, ¿ que me habria aprovechado lo adquirido ? pues subcediendo hijas se pierde la memoria. Otra y otra vez torno á suplicar á V. M. sea servido que con los Jueces del Consejo de Indias se junten otros jueces de estos otros Consejos ; pues todos son criados de V. M., y les fia la governacion de sus reynos y su real conciencia, no es inconveniente fiarles que determinen sobre una escriptura de merced, que V. M. hizo á un su vasallo de una partecica de un gran todo con que el sirvió á V. M., sin costar trabajo ni peligro en su real persona, ni cuidado de espíritu de proveer como se hiciese, ni costa de dineros para pagar la gente que lo hizo, y que tan limpia y lealmente sirvió, no solo en la tierra que ganó, pero con mucha cantidad de oro y plata y piedra de los despojos que en ella ubo ; y que V. M. mande à los jueces que fuere servido que entiendan en ello, que en un cierto tiempo, que V. M. les señale, lo determinen y sentencien sin que haya esta dilacion ; y esta será para mí muy gran merced ; porque á dilatarse, dejarlo hé perder y volvermehé á mi casa : porque no tengo ya edad para andar por mesones, sino para recogerme á aclarar mi cuenta con Dios, pues la tengo larga, y poca vida para dar los descargos, y será mejor dejar perder la acienda que el ánima. Sacra Magestad : Dios Nuestro Señor guarde la muy Real persona de V. M. con el acrecentamiento de Reynos y estados que V. M. desea. De Valladolid, á tres de Febrero de quinientos quarenta y quatro años. De

V. C. M. muy humilde siervo y vasallo, que sus muy reales pies y manos besa.—El Marques de Valle.

Cuvierta á la S. C. C. M., El Emperador y Rey de las Españas.

Tiene este decreto :—Á su Mag. del Marques del Valle, *3* de Febrero de 44 :—*Nay que responder :* parece letra de Covos.

Original. Archivo de Indias.

No. XVI.—See vol. iii. p. 335.

FUNERAL OBSEQUIES OF CORTÉS.

[The original of this document is in the Hospital of Jesus, at Mexico ; and the following literal translation was made from a copy sent to me from that capital.]

THE INTERMENT OF THE MARQUIS OF THE VALLEY OF OAJACA, HERNAN CORTÉS, AND OF HIS DESCENDANT, DON PEDRO CORTÉS, WHICH TOOK PLACE IN THIS CITY OF MEXICO, FEB. 24, 1629.

The remains of Don Hernan Cortés (the first Marquis of the Valley of Oajaca), which lay in the monastery of St. Francis for more than fifty years since they had been brought from Castilleja de la Cuesta, were carried in funeral procession. It also happened that Don Pedro Cortés, Marquis of the Valley, died at the court of Mexico, Jan. 30, 1629. The Lord Archbishop of Mexico, D. Francisco Manso de Zuñiga, and his Excellency the Viceroy, Marquis of Serralbo, agreed that the two funerals should be conducted together, paying the greatest honor to the ashes of Hernando Cortés. The place of interment was the church of St. Francis in Mexico. The procession set forth from the palace of the Marquis of the Valley. In the advance were carried the banners of the various associations ; then followed the different orders of the religious fraternities, all the tribunals of Mexico, and the members of the Audience. Next came the Archbishop and the Chapter of the cathedral. Then was borne along the corpse of the Marquis Don Pedro Cortés in an open coffin, succeeded by the remains of Don Hernando Cortés, in a coffin covered with black velvet. A banner of pure white, with a crucifix, an image of

U*

the Virgin and of St. John the Evangelist, embroidered in gold, was carried on one side. On the other were the armorial bearings of the King of Spain, also worked in gold. This standard was on the right hand of the body. On the left hand was carried another banner, of black velvet, with the arms of the Marquis of the Valley embroidered upon it in gold. The standard-bearers were armed. Next came the teachers of divinity, the mourners, and a horse with sable trappings, the whole procession being conducted with the greatest order. The members of the University followed. Behind them came the Viceroy with a large escort of cavaliers; then four armed captains with their plumes, and with pikes on their shoulders. These were succeeded by four companies of soldiers with their arquebuses, and some with lances. Behind them banners were trailed upon the ground, and muffled drums were struck at intervals. The coffin enclosing the remains of the Conqueror was borne by the Royal Judges, while the knights of the order of Santiago supported the body of the Marquis Don Pedro Cortés. The crowd was immense, and there were six stations where the coffins were exposed to view, and at each of these the responses were chanted by the members of the religious fraternities.

The bones of Cortés were secretly removed from the church of St. Francis, with the permission of his Excellency the Archbishop, on the 2d of July, 1794, at eight o'clock in the evening, in the carriage of the Governor, the Marques de Sierra Nevada, and were placed in a vault, made for this purpose, in the church of Jesus of Nazareth. The bones were deposited in a wooden coffin enclosed in one of lead, being the same in which they came from Castilleja de la Cuesta, near Seville. This was placed in another of crystal, with its cross-bars and plates of silver; and the remains were shrouded in a winding-sheet of cambric embroidered with gold, with a fringe of black lace four inches deep.

INDEX.

INDEX.

ders of, respecting his bones, 67, *note*, 330. Dejected, 69, 70. Proceedings in Spain in regard to, 73. Conspiracy against, in the camp, 75. His bodyguard, 80. His forces, 83. Makes three divisions, 85, 86, *note*. With his fleet at Iztapalapan, 95. Takes post at Xoloc, 99. His movements on the causeway, 102. Levels buildings, 105, 112, 153, 162. His proffers to Guatemozin, 125, 178, 179, 180, 185. Assaults the city, 129. Reconnoitres Alderete's route, 130. Seized and rescued, 134. Anxiety respecting, 138, 139. Gives the command to Sandoval, 141. His entries into the *tianguez*, 169, 171. Murderous assault by, 182. His last assault, 186. His reception of Guatemozin, 191; permits him to be tortured, 218. Sends detachments to the Pacific Ocean, 221. Rebuilding of Mexico by, 223, 233, 239. His Third Letter, and one from the army, 224, 226. Sends costly presents to Spain, 225, *note*. Complaints against, in Spain, 227. Board appointed respecting, 231. The charges against, and the replies, 232, 291, 313. Commission and powers given to, 234. Founds settlements, 243. Joined by his wife, 245. The ordinances made by, 245, *note*. His scruples about slavery, 247, 250, 330. Suppresses the royal in-

structions annulling *repartimientos*, 248, *note*. His desire of religious teachers, 251. His regulations respecting agriculture, 256. Voyages and expeditions of, 257. His instructions for expeditions, 260. Looks into the resources of the country, 260, 264, 285. His expedition to Honduras, 264, 290, *note*, 396, *note*. His Fifth Letter, 266, *note*, 297, 454. At Truxillo, 284. Further plans of conquest by, 284. Embarks and returns, 287. Sick and despondent, 288. Driven to Cuba, 288. At San Juan de Ulua and Medellin, 288. Triumphal return of, to Mexico, 289. Superseded by a *juez de residencia*, 290. Further faction against, in Spain, 291, 296. Urged to assert his authority, 294. Ordered to leave Mexico, 295. Ordered to Spain, 297. Arrival of, in Spain, 300. Meets Pizarro, 300. At Guadaloupe, 303. His reception, 304. His interview with the emperor, 305. Marquis of Oaxaca, 306. Gift of land to, 306. Not reinstated in government, 308. Captain-General of New Spain, 309. Second marriage of, 309. Embarks for New Spain, 312. An investigation of his conduct by the Royal Audience, 313. Accused of murdering his first wife, 313. To keep ten leagues from Mexico, 316. Welcome to, at Tezcuco, 316. Retires to

for collecting, ii. 106. See *Tribute.*

Ribera, on Indian maps, i. 103, *note.*

Rich, Obadiah, ii. 96.

Rigging saved and used, i. 366, ii. 175, 262, 419, iii. 24.

Rio Gila, remains there, iii. 383.

Rio de Tabasco, i. 225, 274, iii. 267.

Ritter, i. 58, *note.*

River of Banners, i. 225, 290.

River of Canoes, ii. 242, 245, 247.

Robertson, William, i. 39, *note*, 116, *note*, 315, *note*. Inconsistency of, respecting a colony, 327, *note*. Cites a harangue from Solís, 328, *note*. Spelling of proper names by, 341, *note*. On the First Letter of Cortés, 357, *note*. Error of, as to Montezuma's gift, ii. 197, *note*. On Cortés' expedition to Honduras, iii. 290, *note.*

Rock of the Marquis, iii. 95.

•Roman Catholic communion, i. 288, 354.

Romans, on their successes, i. 24, *note.*

Royal Audience of New Spain, iii. 296. Their investigation of Cortés' conduct, and treatment of him, 313, 316. Superseded, 315, 316. Disagreement of Cortés and the, 316. Superseded by a viceroy, 321.

Royal Audience of St. Domingo, ii. 217, 221, 428, iii. 74.

Royal Council of Spain, i. 275.

Ruins, antiquity of American, iii. 394.

S.

Saavedra, ii. 68, *note*, 72, *note*, iii. 134, *note.*

Sacrifices. See *Human sacrifices.*

Sacrificial stone, i. 76, 79, ii. 314, iii. 143.

Sahagun, Bernardino de, i. 67, *note*, 70, *note*. Account of, and of his Universal History, 89–92. Noticed, 122, 125, *note*, 148, *note*, 151, *note*, 152, *note*. On Aztec counsels to a daughter, 153, *note*, iii. 405; to a son, i. 155, *note*. Cited, 319, *note*, ii. 7, *note*, 35, *note*, 268, *note*, 270, *note*, 293, *note*. Says Montezuma and others were strangled, 310. Noticed, 314, *note*, 359 *note*, 383, *note*, 393, *note*, 420, *note*, 450, *note*. On a sacrifice of Spanish captives, iii. 143, *note*. On the devastation at Mexico, 155, *note*. Cited, 163, *note*, 169, *note*, 172, *note*, 178, *note*. Notice of, 214. On the demolition of the temples, 254, *note.*

St. Antonio, Cape, i. 255, 259, 260.

St. Augustine, iii. 358, *note.*

St. Domingo. See *Hispaniola.*

St. Francis, convent of, i. 389, *note*, iii. 289.

St. Hypolito, iii. 185.

St. Jago de Cuba, i. 222, 224, 242.

St. James, appearance of, in battle, i. 283, *note*, ii. 329, 388, *note.*

St. Lucar, i. 363, ii. 210.

St. Peter, patron saint of Cortés, i. 262, 283, *note.*

St. Thomas, identification of Quet-

w*

44*

THE END.